NO RETREAT, NO SURRENDER

NO RETREAT, NO SURRENDER

Labor's War at Hormel

Dave Hage and Paul Klauda

WILLIAM MORROW AND COMPANY, INC.
NEW YORK

Library of Congress Cataloging-in-Publication Data

Hage, Dave.
    No retreat, no surrender: labor's war at Hormel / Dave Hage and Paul Klauda.
       p.   cm.
    ISBN 0-688-07745-5
    1. Geo. A. Hormel & Company Strike, Austin, Minn., 1985–1986.
2. Geo. A. Hormel & Company.   3. United Packinghouse, Food, and Allied workers. Local 9 (Austin, Minn.)   I. Klauda, Paul.
II. Title.
HD5325.P152   1985.A874   1989
331.89′28649′00977617—dc19   89-3089
                                                                                    CIP

Printed in the United States of America

First Edition

1 2 3 4 5 6 7 8 9 10

BOOK DESIGN BY PATRICE FODERO

For Therese and Rita

ACKNOWLEDGMENTS

Between September 1984 and September 1986, we collaborated on so many Hormel stories for the *Star Tribune* that assistant business editor Bob Schafer created a special computer command—code-named "Spam"—to automatically top our dispatches with a *Klauda-Hage* byline and an *Austin, Minnesota,* dateline. So our first word of thanks goes to our editors at the *Star Tribune.* We are especially grateful to Bob, whose guidance and encouragement made all the difference in our ability to cover the story, and who took the time to read our manuscript in its roughest form. We also thank Larry Werner, who let us run with the story long before the strike became national news and helped convince his peers of the story's importance. In addition, we benefited enormously from the insights and companionship of our colleague Neal St. Anthony, properly the third reporter in the Spam brotherhood. Bob Jansen, the paper's chief librarian, also provided crucial last-minute help.

For historical materials, we are deeply indebted to Fred Blum, a pioneering scholar in labor relations at Hormel and its union; to Richard Daugherty, author of a comprehensive Hormel company history called *In Quest of Quality;* to librarians of the Austin Public Library, who led us into all the right piles of clippings; to

Acknowledgments

Martin Duffy and his oral history project at the University of Minnesota; and to the Minnesota Historical Society and archivist Mary Klauda for steering us to detailed narratives of the 1933 strike and union documents from the 1930's through 1950's.

Bob Wiseman, John Guarino, John Fossum, and Mario Bognanno of the University of Minnesota also provided valuable insights, though our conclusions are not necessarily theirs.

We also owe an enormous debt of gratitude to the officers—past and present—of the United Food and Commercial Workers international union and Local 9. Similarly, the executives and managers at Geo. A. Hormel & Co. helped us immensely. Collectively, they put up with hundreds of hours of questions and patiently answered requests that must have seemed endless.

A special word of thanks goes to Jeanne Hanson in Minneapolis, who made this book happen, and to Jane Meara at William Morrow, who made it much better.

Our friends, in and out of the news business, put up with plenty of rambling conversations about roving pickets and low-wage packers. Thanks for listening.

Therese Sexe and Rita Klauda were among our wisest counselors, to say nothing of the time they gave up to cover for our absence as husbands and fathers.

Barbara Klauda was alive when her son started covering this story. She died of cancer before it ended. Her influence as a writer made an unmistakable impression on his work.

Finally, a word of thanks to the people of Austin. Throughout this agonizing period in their history, despite the most intense and repeated scrutiny of outside reporters, they remained friendly, helpful, and kind. We wish them all the very best.

—DAVID HAGE AND PAUL KLAUDA
Minneapolis, February 1989

INTRODUCTION

Outside the day was gray and blustery, a reminder for April visitors that spring comes late to southern Minnesota. But inside the small-town hockey arena, the air was warm and steamy with hundreds of bustling bodies. On the arena floor, row upon row of folding chairs were filling up with union members, who filed in from a spirited march down Main Street. The bleachers rippled with moving bodies and waving banners that read: WORKERS UNITE! and NEW YORK SUPPORTS YOU, P-9! Men wearing flannel shirts and cowboy boots streamed in through doors at the rear, trailing excited children by the hand. At long tables across the back women in blue jeans and softball jackets sold caps and buttons reading P-9 PROUD. Near the entrance a young man with a silver star dangling from one ear debated dialectical materialism with a retired meat-packer.

On a stage at the front of the arena an officer of the Philadelphia United Electrical Workers' union huddled with a longshoreman from Long Beach, California. A young black woman from a Detroit bakery workers' union checked the notes for her speech while a labor editor from Minnesota's Iron Range joked with a civil liberties lawyer from New York City. And when a handsome young man in a cardigan sweater swept in from a rear entrance with a phalanx of beefy bodyguards, the crowd erupted with a chant of "P-9! P-9! P-9!"

For one afternoon in April 1986 Austin, Minnesota, seemed the center of labor's universe, and a meat-packers' strike against Geo. A. Hormel & Company was the new model for labor's militants.

A union officer from Boston told the crowd, "The labor movement abandoned the air traffic controllers in 1981. But we'll never let that happen to a union again. No more PATCOs!" Bob Brown, a vice-president of the United Electrical Workers in Philadelphia, said, "That which is given from above can be taken away without a struggle because it was never fought for. That which is won from the bottom cannot be taken away without a fight." David Soul, a TV actor with an interest in labor issues, told the striking meat-packers, "I'm not here because I'm a celebrity. I'm here because I'm the father of seven boys, and when I teach them about values, I'm going to tell them to look to Austin, Minnesota."

Twenty-four hours later the Reverend Jesse Jackson would arrive in Austin on a peacemaking mission. His message to the strikers: "What Selma, Alabama, was to the civil rights movement in 1964, P-9 is to collective bargaining in 1986." Small-town white Minnesotans who had never met a black person held up their babies for Jackson's kiss.

By that April day, of course, the meat-packers' strike against Hormel was all but lost. Of 1,529 men and women who walked off the job in August 1985, nearly 500 had crossed their own picket line when Hormel reopened the packinghouse five months later. Another 200 had retired or resigned to find other jobs. Hormel had hired some 600 nonunion replacement workers and said the hundred-million-dollar packinghouse was running at full steam. For the 800 P-9 members who remained on strike there was little hope of getting their jobs back. The union, which once dominated the Austin economy, was coming apart at the seams. Members who had bolted across their own picket line were earning the same ten-dollar hourly rate that they had overwhelmingly rejected before the strike began. The "scab" replacements were working for two dollars an hour less, resulting in a two-tier wage system that the union's leaders deplored. A yearlong Corporate Campaign to pit consumers and corporate allies against Hormel had produced a flurry of headlines, but little more than a shrug from company executives, bankers, and customers. The campaign's main targets—Hormel and First Bank System in Minneapolis—posted record sales and profits. A series of crucial contract arbitrations had yielded nothing but defeat for Local P-9.

Not only was the strike lost, but for all the show of support, Local P-9 of the United Food and Commercial Workers (UFCW) was virtually isolated. The union's national meat-packing division was in retreat. The chain of eight Hormel packinghouse unions that had bargained together for years was in disarray. The labor movement was regrouping after five years of Reaganomics. Austin itself was torn in two. Neighbors didn't speak; families fell apart. Tires were slashed; lawns doused with chemical herbicides. Clergy preached peace from the pulpit, only to be spurned by their own parishioners. St. Edwards, a Catholic church that opened its doors to house peace-keeping troops, was renamed "Fort Edwards," and longtime P-9 parishioners stopped attending Sunday mass. A waitress in this once-friendly town remarked, "You don't know who you can talk to anymore."

And yet in April 1986 P-9's fight was just catching on as a national labor cause. Like PATCO five years earlier, P-9 seemed to be a pivotal force, a union the entire labor movement must rally around or else hand its enemies a symbolic victory. For six years unions had granted concessions to corporate America: wage cuts by airline mechanics; pay freezes by autoworkers; longer workweeks by printing pressmen. The wages of American workers, after adjustment for inflation, had fallen in eight of the previous thirteen years and were now lower than in 1970. P-9's struggle appeared to be a chance to draw the line and threaten corporate America with a fight for its concessions. If the one clearly profitable company in a troubled industry could extract wage cuts, then how was organized labor to stop concessions anywhere in the nation's economy?

Emerging at a nadir of union membership and public sympathy for organized labor, P-9 also held out an irresistible model of rank-and-file vigor. Jim Guyette's charismatic leadership and the populist organizing skills of his hired strategist, Ray Rogers, seemed to offer a promise of grass-roots democracy. Their corporate campaign to bring consumer pressure on the financial allies of big employers promised a novel way to recapture public sympathy for the plight of working people. The spunk of these rural Minnesotans offered hope that labor still had the resolve to stand and fight. The leaders of P-9 even had a look of sincerity about them. Business Agent Pete Winkels looked like a graduate student in his crew-necked sweaters and moccasins, a pack of Winstons and a cigarette lighter always clutched in one hand. Guyette, in his cardigan sweaters, Levi's cords, and cowboy boots, even a cowboy hat occasionally, had the look of labor's lone rider. P-9's vice-president, Lynn Huston, came across like a mischievous biker—aviator sunglasses, a Harley-Davidson T-shirt, and a Cheshire-cat grin beneath a drooping mustache. These were labor leaders just a year or two off the packinghouse floor, workers whose calluses hadn't gone soft, who hadn't grown accustomed to board meetings and expense accounts, yet who seemed as savvy and articulate as any of labor's entrenched bosses and who had a clearly articulated moral vision. These were labor activists with priorities built on mortgages and mangled hands, not white papers developed in working conferences, plainspoken earnest leaders unafraid to take labor's message to the public.

At a time when Big Labor seemed remote and bureaucratic, P-9 was unusual in one other respect. For more than a year it had defied the leaders of its parent union, the 1.1-million-member UFCW, the second-biggest union in the AFL-CIO. P-9 wasn't the first union local whose members rebelled over local conditions and strayed from a national strategy built on national trends. But seldom, if ever, has an internal union battle been waged with the publicity and venom of P-9's war with the UFCW. The hiring of Rogers and later the use of roving pickets to shut down other packinghouses, the boycott of Hormel products—all were debated bitterly by labor strategists in union halls from New York City to Long Beach, California. It became an extraordinarily open feud within a labor movement that traditionally keeps its arguments to itself.

If the feud's bitterness was unusual, its sentiment was not. Labor's setbacks in the 1980's had led to all manner of rank-and-file uprisings. In the United Steel Workers one affiliate after another deposed local moderates and elected militants in the wake of concessionary contracts negotiated in the early 1980's. In the United Auto Workers Victor Reuther, the surviving brother of the combative Reuther clan, became the elder statesman of a growing militant wing. In 1983 dissident Teamsters triggered the rejection of a national freight contract supported by Jackie Presser that would have cut wages and benefits for laid-off and newly hired truck drivers. In 1984 twenty-eight hundred UFCW grocery clerks working for the Kroger Company rejected a concessionary contract negotiated by their leaders, prompting the shutdown of forty-five supermarkets. In 1985 seventeen hundred cannery workers in Watsonville, California, defied their leaders and struck Watsonville Canning over concessions. Somehow P-9 became the symbol for all those angry union members who thought their leaders had lost the will to fight.

A coalition of local union officers from around the country, called National Rank and File Against Concessions, had adopted the meat-packers' strike as a "pivotal battle." In a stunning show of grass-roots support, some one million dollars in donations had flowed into the Austin union hall from unions and other sympathizers around the country.

So when Guyette stepped to the microphone that Saturday afternoon, there was something almost messianic about him, a scornful voice that lashed Hormel, a mingling of humility and destiny in his remarks. Not eight hours earlier Mower County authorities had issued a warrant for his arrest in connection with a plant gate demonstration the previous day. All day long Guyette had been in hiding. He appeared only as the rally began, materializing at the back of the arena surrounded by bodyguards in blue satin jackets inscribed NO RETREAT, NO SURRENDER in gold thread across the back. Now a fugitive from justice, he magnetized the crowd even as P-9's cause galvanized the militants of organized labor. In the crowd was an advance woman for Jesse Jackson, briefing reporters on Jackson's itinerary, irrefutable proof that P-9 had seized the nation's attention. All around Guyette were able young union leaders with a vision of class struggle drawn from labor's roots, yet possessed of brains and charm and an almost scholarly understanding of economics and politics. Huddled around the stage was a brain trust of lawyers from Austin, St. Paul, and New York. From the stage of the noisy Austin arena that afternoon, it was possible, even easy, to imagine

13

that this labor dispute would touch off a new working-class uprising.

Labor activists weren't the only people watching Austin, Minnesota. Corporate America, too, had taken a bloody nose from the decline of basic industry. It, too, wanted to see how the showdown in Austin would conclude. Chrysler Motors had gone to the brink of bankruptcy in 1981. Braniff Airlines had gone over the brink. Swift & Company, a meat-packing giant that once overshadowed General Motors, had split in two under competitive pressures and closed one packinghouse after another.

Ironically, Hormel was ill suited to play the heavy in a labor-management showdown. Of the old-line meat-packing companies—Wilson, Swift, Armour, Morrell—Hormel was the last to cut wages as the industry went into a tailspin in the early 1980's. Hormel's products—Spam, bacon, chili, Cure 81 hams, and Dinty Moore beef stew—enjoyed the kind of consumer benevolence associated with children's lunches and Sunday picnics. Hormel was responsible for several innovations in meat-packing labor practices, evidence of the founding family's ability to meet corporate goals and workers' interests simultaneously. Hormel was also the best managed of the old meat processors, a small-town family enterprise that fought its way into the Fortune 500 and survived the takeover struggles that buffeted the meat-packing industry in the 1980's. In fact, it was among the most profitable companies in the industry—a point that only embittered workers when Hormel told its unions in October 1983 that it planned to seek wage cuts like its competitors'.

The fact that Hormel had asked for concessions without pleading distress heightened the interest for management observers as well as labor activists. Countless corporate executives around the country were watching to see if the executives of Geo. A. Hormel & Company could cut labor costs without going to the brink of disaster. The Carnegie-Mellon School of Management eventually gave CEO Richard Knowlton an award for crisis management, and for months after the strike was over, Hormel executives on the speakers' circuit found themselves approached by corporate admirers who congratulated them for whipping the union.

Yet Knowlton and his top chieftains were unaccustomed to

such backslapping. They prided themselves on their quiet ability to get along in Flyover Land, away from Wall Street, away from the storied stockyards of Chicago. This was a hundred miles from Minneapolis in a town of twenty-three thousand where the Hormel stockholders' meeting doubled as a civic ball and the chairman's kids went to school with the meat-packers' kids and the National Barrow Show saluted the area's prizewinning hogs. This was a company where the corporate dining room had Formica tables and vending-machine coffee in cardboard cups, a company that put shoeshine machines in the men's room so the Hormel men could go out in the world giving the very best impression of their company. To Hormel's management, the entire ordeal was a strange nightmare, rooted in an unbelievable set of unpredictable coincidences. A corporate office that never shut down for anything but blizzards found itself under siege by a bunch of radicals from who knew where.

There is another, sadder view of the Hormel strike. Appearing on ABC's *Nightline* program in January 1986, U.S. Labor Secretary William Brock had called the dispute "a tragedy . . . a failure of collective bargaining." It was a fresh, even startling assessment coming at a moment when other employers were privately praising Hormel for standing firm and union militants were hailing P-9 for its uncompromising stance. But it said a great deal about the origins of the Hormel strike. To people who followed Hormel's negotiations with P-9 through the spring and summer of 1985, there was a nagging sense that the company and the union were operating in separate realities. While P-9's leaders took their case to the public in a series of increasingly emotional leaflets and news conferences, Hormel's negotiators clammed up and saved their ammunition for the privacy of the bargaining table. While P-9's leaders predicted that corporate greed would crush the American middle class, Hormel negotiators said P-9 was turning down the best deal in the industry. What seemed a great crusade to P-9 and its supporters seemed a puzzling aberration to Hormel's executives.

What Brock meant was that the Hormel dispute had frustrated a collective bargaining system that is designed to keep two parties on track with each other. The system is designed to leave wage and benefit decisions in the hands of the private sector, where labor and management can butt heads in a test of will, bluff, and economic power until they reach a compromise that is best for both parties and, presumably, the economy as a whole. To compensate for their inexperience or failure to communicate or for simple bad blood, the system builds in layer on layer of safeguards: lawyers; consultants; international union reps; state and federal mediators. But in this case two federal mediators, two state mediators, the governor of Minnesota, a renowned Harvard arbitrator, and even Jesse Jackson could not reconcile the parties in this small-town showdown.

The Hormel strike, in addition to being a tale of industrial decline and trade union militance, is a story of how fifty years of labor peace soured so badly that even these safeguards failed.

In that respect the young man at the microphone that afternoon was not just the union's leader but its symbol as well. The son of a Hormel meat-packer and a meat-packer himself for eighteen years, Guyette knew the good money and the hard work. Like most P-9 members, he had grown up polite, quiet, and friendly in a small-town way. Like many of them, he had dropped out of college and abandoned other, grander plans to sign up for the best paycheck in Mower County. Like them, he knew Hormel as a company so omnipresent that it seemed to reach into every corner of his town. Like them, he had grown up believing that Austin equaled Hormel and Hormel equaled Austin and that going to work for Hormel was as much a part of life for a young man in Austin as playing softball and raising a family. Like them, he had turned on a company that he felt had turned on him.

There was something else about Guyette that embodied the paradox of Austin's meat-packers. Events had not been kind to P-9 that winter and spring—Hormel had successfully reopened the packinghouse, a Democratic governor had sent in National Guard troops to keep it open, Hormel was posting record profits, and P-9 itself would be in trusteeship in a few weeks—yet the meat-packers persisted, to the increasing puzzlement of observers around Minnesota and the country. They rejected concessions accepted by other meat-packers. They declared a new strategy with each new setback. Like his people, Guyette never saw defeat in the headlines. Like them, he was driven by some grievance beyond the comprehension of outsiders.

The showdown at Hormel can be read as tragedy—a failure of collective bargaining, and unemployment for more than a thousand workers. It can be read as economic history—the product of crushing pressure on American industry and the American standard of living. It can be read as a labor-management textbook—a struggle emblematic of the combative 1980's, a union that resorted to militancy and novel tactics, a company that took a rigid and legalistic approach in a time of crisis. Or it can be read as mystery—the puzzle of workers who felt so aggrieved that they martyred themselves in a labor dispute everybody else told them to give up.

Thirty-five years earlier, in a book examining Hormel's model labor relations, sociologist Fred Blum described Hormel's first strike in 1933 and the many innovations wrought in the ensuing years by the company founder's son, Jay C. Hormel, and the fledgling union. Blum spent three years working side by side with union butchers in the old Hormel plant, probing their work, their lives, and the monotonous grind of one of the nation's bloodiest, most dangerous industries. He studied the bond of worker incentives that held union and management together—and apart—in this insulated little packinghouse town. Blum concluded that it would take a strange and puzzling upheaval to put Hormel's meat-packers on strike again.

He was right.

CHAPTER

1

They called it the 9:55 death ride.

A sleek Plymouth GTX barreling down a quiet Austin street, nineteen-year-old Pete Winkels at the wheel, his buddy John Morrison hanging on for his life in the passenger seat, both of them late for ten o'clock class across town at the Austin Junior College.

It was the fall of 1967, and the death ride had become a fixture of the young and independent life that beckoned two pals like Morrison and Winkels in prosperous Austin during the 1960's. Fresh out of high school, testing new waters, they could take some chances and have some fun, secure in the midst of their friends, their families, and the strong unwritten traditions of a small midwestern town. They spent a good deal of time together in Austin's bars, where Pete, with the town's sharpest tongue, had been known to get fights started, and John, with a meat-packer's punch, had been known to finish them.

They made an odd pair, Pete already putting on weight and squinting under thick black hair, John trim and graceful with the wary movement of an athlete; Pete with thick glasses and his Winstons, John with a thick wrestler's neck and big hands that left the impression of a much bigger man; Pete with a quick tongue and a penchant for quoting Churchill and Thoreau, John with quick fists and a tongue tied in knots. They hadn't known each other well in high school. John, an all-state wrestler, was at Austin High. Pete, an all-world comedian, was at Austin Pacelli, the Catholic school. But there was something star-crossed about these two, different as they were. Born a year apart, they were sons of tough-minded meat-packers who didn't mind telling management where to get off. Married a year apart, ushers in each other's weddings, destined, like many young men growing up in Austin in the 1960's, for the big packinghouse on the north edge of town.

The Austin where Pete and John grew up doesn't look like the scene of a great industrial struggle. The streets are clean; the people, polite. The air is fresh—except for the pungent smell of Spam on hot days. The plains, flat as a tabletop and dotted with windbreaks of elm and oak, stretch off in every direction: north a hundred miles to Minneapolis; east ninety miles to the Mississippi River; south twelve miles to the Iowa border. Oakland Avenue, the east-west thoroughfare, runs in from Interstate 90 on the west past a suburban-style strip of motels and stores, past the big athletic field where the Austin High Packers play football on Friday night and their peewee brothers scrimmage the next morning, past block after block of big, neat Victorian and Dutch revival houses, and into the middle of town. There it intersects Main Street, a straight, broad avenue of brick storefronts, cafés, and banks. Main Street runs north half a mile until, just outside downtown, it opens onto a plain next to the Cedar River and a view of the big Hormel packinghouse, sprawled across more than twenty acres like a ship anchored at the edge of town.

One block east of Main Street, Austin's character starts to change. The churches and banks give way to strip joints and bars in a profusion that is rare for rural Minnesota. Ten blocks east of downtown, Fourth Avenue dead-ends at the abandoned Milwaukee Road depot and an intersection that almost seems to hide from the great steeple of St. Augustine's Church back west of Main Street. A tavern called Bobee Jo's anchors one corner with a bright red arrow pointing out the entrance and other bars fill out the block, neon signs for Pabst and Schmidt glowing in their dark windows. It's a corner you would expect in Detroit or Milwaukee, blue-collar cities of the old Midwest, not in the clean Lutheran towns of Minnesota farm country. But the corner signals that this is a blue-collar town, a town with a history of weekly paychecks, wild Friday nights, sweat, and even a picket line or two. A packinghouse town.

In this town it didn't really matter so much if Pete and John were late for class. The two-year college was supposed to be the ticket out of Austin for bright young people like them, an escape from the grinding packinghouse work that consumed their fathers and grandfathers. This was the 1960's, and the world beckoned with more opportunities. Morrison and Winkels were at the head of the baby boom generation, seasoned by Vietnam, civil rights, and television, poised to make their mark on the world outside Austin. Like their friends, they would join the service or go to college or vocational school, maybe get up to the Twin Cities, find a job, get married, and start a family. Hello, world, good-bye, Austin. It seemed so simple.

But in Austin the scent of Hormel money wafted out of the tall smokestack next to the Cedar River along with the aroma of Spam, and it had a sirenlike effect on even the most ambitious kids in town. They knew the work was tough, usually gruesome, often dangerous. They had seen their fathers come home at night exhausted, suffering pain that made it impossible to sleep. But that's why Hormel jobs paid the best paychecks. Baby boomer or not, you could spend four years in college and never come close to landing a job that provided financial security so quickly.

So after a year or two at the junior college, the death rides stopped for Pete and John. Hormel had started a summer jobs program for college students, and one by one their high school pals donned the white smocks and rubber boots of the packinghouse. With every month it seemed more stupid to put off a job that would pay twenty thousand dollars. Pete, who had signed up for the summer work program in June 1967, went into the packinghouse for good the next year. John quit school, too, and in July 1968 signed on as a "miscellaneous boner" in the "extra" gang of workers who floated through the plant filling vacant jobs.

But there was more to working at Hormel than joining a long tradition of Austin men and women who stood in line for the Hormel paycheck. There was a union, one of the oldest and proudest industrial unions in the nation, a union that had made labor history with a big strike in 1933 and had thrown its weight around for decades since. Labor history was a palpable presence in Austin—as real as the low brick union hall on Fourth Avenue and as human as the stories Pete heard in the living room of his uncle John, a veteran of the 1933 strike. John Winkels had helped found the Independent Union of All Workers in 1933, back in the days before the AFL-CIO and George Meany and big union headquarters in Washington, D.C. He'd been alive when they laid the first brick of the Austin Labor Center. He had been arrested in 1938, when union members marched down Main Street to protest the discharge of a clerk at the local Montgomery Ward's, one of many times the meat-packers' union flexed its muscle in a town it had organized wall to wall.

All this history was alive in Austin. It looked down from the pictures on the Labor Center walls, and it echoed in the bars and cafés where old-timers still boasted of the union's glory days. It was true that the grit of the old-timers had softened to apathy during the prosperous years after World War II, and not even door prizes at membership meetings could draw a quorum to the union hall. But when hard times returned in the 1980's, the hall and the union awakened like sleeping giants. Pete and John recalled what seemed like a lifetime of stories they had heard about packinghouse work in the bad old days, the birth of their union, and an era of almost forgotten militance.

When the Great Depression reached southern Minnesota, Hormel was in the hands of the founder's son, forty-year-old Jay Catherwood Hormel, who ran the company from 1929 to 1954. Jay pulled his company through the first years of the Depression, and by 1933 he had as many as thirty-five hundred men and women on the payroll. Jay was a stern and astute businessman, by most accounts, but he also wanted labor harmony and a productive work force. He already had started innovating with wage and job-security protections, practically unheard of in packinghouse work. Any number of his employees could recount personal conversations with Jay on the packinghouse floor. Nonetheless, his employees were hardly the envy of the community, as they would be in the 1960's. Parents loathed the thought of their daughters marrying "packinghouse rats," a nomadic bunch unable to hold steady jobs. Before forming the union in 1933, workers earned a paltry fifteen dollars a week for six days' work, about a dollar less than the national average in manufacturing. Many who held irregular employment, such as farmers who caught on during busy winter months, earned as little as nine dollars a week.

Packinghouse work in the 1930's represented a big improvement over the steaming carnage depicted by Upton Sinclair in *The Jungle*, but it was gruesome and dangerous work nonetheless. Men on the killing floor stood ankle-deep in blood, laboring in sweltering heat in the summer and chilling cold in the winter. They were packed in among each other all day long, swinging razor-sharp knives greased with blood, slicing within inches of their fingers and each other. There was always the risk of a four-hundred-pound hog running amok if the first-kill men didn't do their job right. The pace was dizzying for a rookie, numbing even for a veteran, exhausting for everyone.

Despite Jay Hormel's wage innovations, work in the 1930's was wildly unpredictable. Hopeful young men would travel dozens of miles to show up at the Hormel hiring office, then mill about until a foreman came in off the killing floor, spotted the youngest, biggest, and strongest applicant, and put him on the payroll. Those lucky enough to get hired had no protection from getting fired. Foremen were famous for discharging a worker one day so another foreman could rehire him the next day at a lower wage. The hours, too, varied wildly. It wasn't uncommon for the men to show up Monday morning, work for three hours, and be sent home at ten for lack of work. The work would last a little longer Tuesday as Hormel's hog buyers got busy, longer still Wednesday and Thursday. By Saturday the men would work from dawn until ten o'clock at night.

Whether any particular job was tolerable was almost entirely at the whim of the foremen, who ruled the packinghouse floor with dictatorial vengeance. Foremen promoted and demoted men at will, often on the basis of personal favors or family ties. Complaints were futile. The men were afraid to speak up lest they lose their jobs, knowing that hundreds of unemployed people were waiting outside to replace them.

By 1933 the meat-packers were ripe for organizing, and the perfect organizer had come their way. Frank Ellis was a character straight out of the rough-and-tumble frontier, a packinghouse rat and a nomadic rabble-rouser. Born in 1888 in St. Joseph, Missouri, he walked his first picket line at the age of sixteen, joining his father in a 1904 national meat-packing strike. His father died a year later, apparently of infection after he had broken his leg in a packinghouse. Frank left home the same year to become an itinerant organizer for the Wobblies—the International Workers of the World. The Wobblies were perhaps the nation's most militant labor organization in the early 1900's, a ferocious organizing force throughout the timberlands of the Northwest, the mines of the West, and the farm fields of the Midwest. Ellis traveled from town to town in boxcars, riding with bums, taking one job after another, organizing one packinghouse after another.

By the time he arrived in Austin in the early 1930's, he had organized more than a dozen meat-packing plants. In the process, he recounted later, he had his "ears knocked off" more than a few times by company detectives and delivered his share of black eyes to scabs from Texas to Washington state. He was stocky and coarse-spoken, given to bow ties and greased-back hair, deeply committed to the Wobbly philosophy of populist industrial unionism. But the Wobblies had been widely discredited for their antiwar stance in World War I and by the avowed socialism of some of their leaders. Many of them went underground during the "red scare" of 1919, and within a few years the union was all but dissolved. Ellis feared that the conservative small-town Minnesotans in Austin would balk at the name Wobblies, so he proposed another representing similar principles: the Independent Union of All Workers. Oddly enough, Hormel had promoted Ellis to foremen because he was a skilled sausage-skin maker, and he wasted no time hiring his old Wobbly buddies and spreading them around the plant as informal organizers.

In the winter and spring of 1933 Ellis chatted about unionism with men during cigarette breaks and after work. Ironically, however, it was one of Jay Hormel's paternalistic innovations that provided the spark Ellis needed. Jay dreamed up an old-age insurance program to be financed by a payroll deduction of twenty cents per worker per week. He directed his foreman to "sell" the program on the plant floor, but workers balked at the prospect of a reduction in their take-home pay. On the afternoon of Thursday, July 13, an aggressive foreman forced one meatcutter to sign up against his will. That drew a mob of workers who shut down the kill floor for ten minutes until the foreman returned the man's sign-up card. This collective defiance strengthened the resolve of the men to stand up to the foreman, and that afternoon after work about twenty-five of them gathered in Driesner Park, on the south edge of Austin along the banks of Dobbins Creek, to plan further action. Word of the meeting spread, and when the men reconvened that evening in nearby Sutton Park, hundreds of meat-packers showed up. Somebody sent for Frank Ellis, who, sensing his opportunity, gave a sermon urging collective action and told the men they needed a union. That night six hundred members signed up at a dollar for men and fifty cents for women. The next day Ellis, Harold Harlan, and Soren Cardell met with a local lawyer to draw up the union's charter, and on July 15 one thousand workers signed up at another Sutton Park meeting. From then on, the organizing meetings continued, sometimes in the park, sometimes in a rented room above an Austin shop. On Sunday, July 23, the members met to elect a slate of officers, including Olaf J. Fosso as president and Frank Ellis as business manager.

Two months later the union activists were ready to confront Jay Hormel. At a special meeting on Friday, September 22, they resolved to insist on recognition of their union or stage a strike the next morning. But Jay was not about to be intimidated. Austin merchants organized an emergency meeting with union leaders before dawn the next morning to talk the men out of striking, but Jay threatened to lock out the workers and even take his packinghouse out of Austin. When workers showed up at daybreak, the plant gates were locked and skirmishes broke out with police and plant guards. At the last minute, however, Jay had a change of heart and signed an agreement with Ellis and other leaders recognizing the union, agreeing to bargain collectively and to establish seniority rules and grievance procedures.

But the infant union made virtually no progress in persuading Hormel to improve wages and working conditions. Less than two months later Ellis and Fosso decided to test their new union's power with a demand for a twenty-cent hourly raise and a new grievance procedure. Jay Hormel replied in an open letter to the union that competitive pressures prevented him from raising wages in the absence of productivity improvements. He also refused to submit their wage request to arbitration.

Ellis and Fosso called another union meeting for Friday night, November 10. The plan was simply to take a strike vote—not because they genuinely felt ready to walk out but to send a message to Jay. Ellis's speech was a stem-winder, and the strike vote passed overwhelmingly. Little did Ellis know that some intoxicated enthusiasts at the back of the crowd were so buoyed by the news that they dashed back to the packinghouse and told night shift workers on the sheep kill to clear out and set up picket lines. Soon the other departments followed. When word reached the union hall that the men were walking out, Ellis and Fosso figured it was either discredit their own members or call a strike. By nightfall, for better or worse and largely by accident, Hormel's first strike was under way.

At midnight Jay came down to the plant to address a mob of five hundred strikers who were huddled around bonfires outside the plant gates, trying to keep warm while savoring their revolt. He mounted a makeshift platform and in a quiet voice warned the men that their strike was illegal because they hadn't given him the strike notice required in their September agreement. But he said he wouldn't try to break the strike or resume operation without twenty-four-hour notice to the union. He did ask the strikers to let Hormel's office workers pass through the picket line, and he asked for union volunteers to police the building.

The strike remained friendly through the rest of the night and much of Saturday morning. But near noon a report reached the picket line that nonunion employees were still inside the plant, slaughtering sheep. Enraged at this apparent betrayal, about four hundred pickets stormed the plant with clubs and rocks, shoving guards aside and crashing through doors and windows. They swept through the plant, chasing out workers and foremen. One foreman, who refused to yield his ground, was beaten. Another tried to make off down the Cedar River in a rickety rowboat that quickly sank, much to the amusement of the watching pickets. The mob came upon Jay Hormel meeting with other executives and nearly carried them out as well. But Jay warned them against violence and asked for a few minutes to finish his conference and lock up his office. Accounts of his exit differ. Some old-timers remember Jay's being carried from the plant; other sources say he walked out with an escort of several hundred strikers and a pistol-toting guard who made sure no one laid a hand on him.

This brash display put Jay Hormel on the spot. The New Deal was getting under way, and Franklin Roosevelt's legislative program made it easier for unions to organize. Closer to Austin, militant Teamster leaders were organizing in Minneapolis, and other radical leaders were appealing to thousands of farmers protesting low prices and foreclosures brought on by drought and the Depression. Yet Hormel thought he was doing his part to help workers ride out tough times. He had begun tinkering with a guaranteed wage plan to smooth out seasonal fluctuations in paychecks. When hard times hit the industry in 1929, Hormel had been the last packer to cut wages. Now he was shut out of his own packinghouse, where twenty million pounds of meat were spoiling on the rack. The refrigeration system, which had been shut off, would burst if it weren't turned back on. Hormel considered asking for federal troops on the ground that one million pounds of the meat were the property of the federal government. He was not enthralled with Minnesota Governor Floyd B. Olson, a Farmer-Laborite and former Wobbly, whose election Hormel had vigorously opposed the year before. At one point that day he became so incensed that he called his father in California and threatened to sell the business to Swift & Company and move from Austin. But Mower County Sheriff Ira Syck counseled that it might be possible to get the state militia to disperse the pickets without bringing direct intervention by Governor Olson. At four o'clock Saturday afternoon, Syck, fearing the worst, sent the following telegram to the governor: "Situation here so unruly that deputizing of ununiformed and poorly-armed citizens would precipitate guerrilla warfare with pitiful casualties on both sides. . . . In order to avoid needless bloodshed, I appeal to you to dispatch militia to take situation in hand before nightfall at latest."

Olson was not about to break the strike. Unbeknownst to Jay Hormel, the governor mobilized three hundred national guardsmen in Owatonna thirty miles away, but he told Hormel he wanted an arbitrator to settle the dispute. Ellis, who knew Olson personally, did not want troops in Austin and assured the governor that the strike would remain peaceful. Nonetheless, Ellis arranged the help of the Farm Holiday Association, a group of radical farmers, to police the roads into Austin to keep out scabs.

Saturday night, while the pickets warmed themselves around bonfires, eating sandwiches and drinking coffee, Hormel met at the First National Bank with Frank Starkey, head of Minnesota's State Industrial Commission and Olson's representative. They were joined by Congressman F. H. Shoemaker, a Farmer-Laborite like Olson, who offered his assistance as a mediator. Hormel distrusted the congressman but mentioned his concerns about spoiling meat. Shoemaker headed for the union hall to approach Ellis. Meanwhile, Ellis had been secretly sending maintenance men into the plant to keep the refrigeration system operating. He, too, feared the spoilage of federal meat and wanted to avoid the wrath of the government. As Shoemaker arrived at the union hall, he overheard one of Ellis's maintenance men ask if it wasn't time to adjust the temperature again. The secret was out. When Jay Hormel learned that the meat was not in danger, his resolve hardened, and he refused to meet with union leaders. But he did call Governor Olson again and warned of violence against his property.

Early Sunday afternoon Olson finally traveled to Austin with two aides. He met for three hours with Ellis and Fosso, then drove over to the Fox Hotel to meet with Jay Hormel, then to the home of Hormel's uncle John G. Hormel for a special meeting of the company's board of directors. Olson proposed that they turn the dispute over to the state Industrial Commission, which would set out a code of conduct for both sides and arbitrate the strike's toughest issues, such as wages and a grievance procedure. Olson then took a hastily typed three-page proposal back to the union hall. After two hours of haggling and a pledge by Olson that all the strikers would be rehired, Ellis and Fosso signed it. At four forty-five on Monday morning, Olson returned the agreement to the Hormel home, shook the owner's hand, and told him, "Jay, I think you have a lot of poise."

A half hour later Ellis sent word to the pickets of a mass meeting at ten that morning in the city armory. The building was packed when Olson arrived to address the strikers. He told them that he was a friend of labor but that they had taken over someone else's property illegally. He urged them to accept the settlement and trust the Industrial Commission. "I can't be in the position of defending labor when labor is in an illegal position," he said. "I can't be put on the spot. . . . [I]f I have to choose between my proper duty and my sympathy I will be obliged to choose duty." Ellis spoke next, expressing lukewarm support for the settlement but acknowledging that Olson had been fair to the workers. The settlement was approved overwhelmingly.

By Tuesday morning the plant was back to virtually full operation. The workers eventually were awarded raises of two to four cents an hour, lifting the base wage to about forty-five cents an hour. The agreement also led to the formation of a union-management board to police the new seniority system so that employees had some guarantee of their jobs and the right to promotions.

With the strike settled, however, Ellis and his activists in the Independent Union of All Workers scarcely took a breather. They set about organizing the rest of Austin's workers, from restaurant cooks to shop clerks and even some farmers, a task that took most of the 1930's. When they met resistance, they held mass meetings, rioted in front of stores, and, in 1935, burned a judge in effigy outside the Mower County Courthouse in the middle of Austin. Several skirmishes in the packinghouse led to brief sit-down strikes and Hormel eventually bought tear gas for use in case of a union attack on the plant. At its peak some years later the union represented all but four businesses in Austin. Soon the Austin business community responded with antiunion organizations such as the Secret 500 and the Citizens' Alliance, which elevated tensions further. Undaunted, the union ran a candidate in the city election in 1934 and started its own newspaper, the *Midwest American* (later *The Unionist*), to counter criticism from the only other paper in town, the Austin *Daily Herald.*

By the late 1930's, however, the union had established itself as Austin's second major institution after Geo. A. Hormel & Company. Business leaders recognized that they had to live with the powerful force, and there followed a long period of peaceful co-existence. Hormel and the new union continued to suspect each other's motives and battle each other's demands, but their struggle took the form of a tug-of-war under rules that, though often unwritten, were well understood.

A key reason for the harmony was Jay Hormel himself. Through a series of bold labor innovations, he spawned a work environment in which workers held unusually steady employment, earned regular paychecks, and controlled their pace of work with no risk of being arbitrarily fired. He started with a wage plan utilized by a number of other packinghouses before the Depression. Known as straight time, it guaranteed workers stable year-round paychecks regardless of fluctuations in work caused by volatile hog supplies. He would pay his workers full paychecks every week, no matter how many hours or how few they actually worked. Any hours they worked over the standard workweek, which ranged from thirty-six to forty hours, would go into a bank, and any short weeks would draw down hours from the bank. At the end of the year, if a worker had hours left in the bank, he or she would get a lump-sum paycheck near Christmas. Skeptics in the union challenged the plan as an attempt to disguise work speedups or avoid the effects of a soon-to-be-passed national minimum wage, but it was adopted nonetheless. And it had a huge repercussion: No worker could be laid off without fifty-two weeks' notice. Suddenly bankers and car dealers were willing to lend money to these blue-collar workers now that they were guaranteed a steady stream of paychecks so far in advance.

The second of Jay's innovations was the gain, an incentive scheme that supplemented the butchers' wages when they beat certain production quotas. A packinghouse is full of intricate jobs—heading hogs, trimming fat off hams, boning picnics (the hog's front shoulder)—and the meatcutters got better and faster as they stayed on the job. Soon they discovered any number of shortcuts in the number of knife strokes they made or the way they sharpened their knives. Jay's incentive scheme rewarded these shortcuts and made the Austin plant one of the most productive in the nation. It had the additional bonus of converting workers into their own supervisors; it was to their own advantage to work as efficiently as possible.

In addition, Jay shared profits with workers at the end of year, providing what for many was a holiday bonus amounting to the equivalent of several weekly checks. Even more remarkable,

Hormel unfurled these strategies in an era when most companies chafed at compliance with new federal laws dealing with labor relations. Jay Hormel in fact supported Local 9's drive for CIO affiliation in the late 1930's because he felt it would allow him to pay his workers higher wages and still be competitive. He thought it made good business sense.

In 1940 Hormel and Local 9 negotiated a permanent "working agreement" with no expiration date. It was to govern contract matters between the two sides for the next forty years and give workers in Austin an almost unheard-of degree of economic security. It obligated Hormel to pay prevailing industry wages and virtually eliminated the threat of strikes. It meant that workers' paychecks were steady week after week regardless of work load, and jobs were guaranteed a year in advance. With incentive earnings, profit sharing, and other local sweeteners, the Austin workers quickly rose to the top of the industry pay scale, exceeding the average by as much as 30 percent in the early 1950's.

The working agreement also helped ward off possible work stoppages at least three times in the late 1940's and early 1950's. In one instance, in 1948, Jay Hormel persuaded the union to keep working through a national meat-packing strike by boosting workers' pay and guaranteeing that he would adjust it to the new industry level once the strike was over. After initially voting overwhelmingly to authorize a strike, workers went along, fearing that a walkout could cost them some of their lucrative benefits. To support union members who eventually went on strike at other companies, Austin workers contributed 10 percent of their take-home pay for the duration of the dispute.

Hormel's guaranteed wage plan, regarded as the most advanced in the nation, earned the company a national reputation among sociologists and industrial relations experts. In 1948 Harvard sociologist Fred Blum came to Austin to conduct an in-depth study of the plan and its effects on Austin. For two summers and all of 1950, he worked in the packinghouse, probing the bonds among Hormel, the union, and Austin. He interviewed workers individually, in groups, and in large meetings at city hall. He also quizzed company executives, supervisors, and foremen. In a 1953 book, *Toward a Democratic Work Process*, Blum wrote that the working agreement had radically changed the relationship between workers and the company.

Workers felt they were selling a product, not a service, to Hormel, Blum found. Most were proud to work for Hormel despite the grinding, monotonous work. With the chance to earn incentive pay, they could set their own pace and discipline themselves, earning 60 to 100 percent more than their base pay. If the weather was nice or hunting season had opened, they could leave as soon as they met their quotas. If they needed extra money, they could keep working for bonus pay. The union provided security. The company provided the best paying packinghouse, if not job, in the nation. Even malcontents had to concede it was better than anything else they could find.

Blum found that the nagging boss system that contributed to the 1933 strike had been peacefully neutralized. Workers grew accustomed to viewing foremen as record keepers who ordered supplies and kept an eye on product quality. With workers policing themselves, discipline became rare. When it became necessary, it usually was handled through a brief closed-door meeting in the employment office known as the "bullpen." Line speeds were maintained by the work gangs, which developed elaborate systems of spelling colleagues so they could sit down, smoke cigarettes, or go to the bathroom without a slowdown in production. "Formerly you had to run your ass off to get them guys to work," Blum quoted a foreman as saying. "Now you can just stand around and watch."

Jay Hormel's techniques dumbfounded and infuriated his competitors and even some of his management colleagues in Austin, who thought he had sold out to the union. But his concern for workers, which earned him the nickname of the Red Capitalist, was always linked to the company bottom line, a fact often overlooked later in the nostalgia for his labor practices. If there were no earnings, there was no profit sharing. If earnings fell, so did contributions to employee pensions. The much heralded incentive pay system, in theory, benefited the company as much as workers. Guaranteeing jobs and wages for a year in advance meant little labor turnover through the peaks and valleys of the cyclical commodity business. It also meant that strikes were virtually pointless as long as Hormel matched prevailing industry wage patterns and that Jay Hormel's workers could go on getting more skilled and more efficient at a time when many packing companies saw their workers come and go in a matter of months. Still, Jay's innovations had the effect of insulating his employees from many of the hazards that swept through other meat-packing towns like Chicago, Kansas City, and St. Joseph: seasonal layoffs; erratic paychecks; frequent strikes; the need to take the lead in contract negotiations.

If Jay Hormel was making a name for himself around the country, so was the Independent Union of All Workers. By the late 1930's Frank Ellis had organized packing plants in Albert Lea, South St. Paul, and Faribault, Minnesota; Mason City, Waterloo, and Ottumwa, Iowa; and other towns, bringing them all under the banner of the Austin union. Though the Amalgamated Meat Cutters and Butcher Workmen of North America was the nation's dominant meat-packing union, the Independent Union of All Workers had become a major organizing power across the Upper Midwest.

It was about this time that John L. Lewis, then president of the United Mine Workers, began to press for a new kind of national union. Most of the AFL unions were based on crafts or trades at the time—one union for plumbers; one for machinists; one for meatcutters. Lewis and others began to feel that the new industrial organization created by mass production required a new kind of union, one that would represent a factory wall to wall, be it an auto factory, a steel mill, or a meat-packing plant. The concept did not go over well, however, with the AFL leadership, and in 1936 the federation expelled Lewis and the Mine Workers, who went on to form the rival Committee for Industrial Organization, later the Congress of Industrial Organizations. But the industrial union concept caught on, and the next year the United Auto Workers won recognition from General Motors and the Steel Workers Organizing Committee won recognition from U.S. Steel. Lewis asked for a meeting with Ellis and proposed that Ellis's independent union join with others to form the Packinghouse Workers Organizing Committee under the aegis of the CIO. Even then Austin's meat-packers were an independent-minded lot: They approved the measure on May 22, 1937, by just 396–326. In 1939 the Austin union became the ninth packinghouse union to join the CIO and was chartered as Local 9, PWOC-CIO. Still, the various packinghouse organizers chafed under this informal arrangement, and in 1943 they were granted their own charter as the United Packinghouse Workers of America. The burgeoning union in Austin was chartered as UPWA Local 9.

Though it was now part of a big national machine, the Austin union remained an important cog. In 1940 Ellis was elected president of the Minnesota state CIO. In 1943 he became the new UPWA's vice-presient for organizing and spent the next nine years working out of the union's headquarters in Chicago. A year later another Austin organizer, Joe Ollman, was appointed the UPWA's assistant international director of organizing. Svend Godfredson, who had been Local 9's chief publicist, by that time was already editor of *Packinghouse Worker,* the house organ of the national union. Frank Schultz, elected president of Local 9 in 1945 and destined to become its second seminal leader, also went on to become an international vice-president of the UPWA. In 1946 Ralph Helstein, a Minneapolis lawyer who represented Local 9, was elected president of the UPWA.

Bridging the Austin local and the new national union was Ellis's fierce commitment to industrial unionism, the legacy of the Wobblies. The UPWA was progressive in other respects: It had gone on record in support of wage parity for women at a time when employers commonly and openly established lower wage scales for women. UPWA locals commonly assessed themselves special dues supplements to support organizing efforts so that other workers could come under their umbrella. Pictures taken at UPWA conventions typically showed a number of black faces among the delegates at a time when black Americans held few positions of power. Ellis defended all these principles fiercely. In fact, Ellis had been approached by an organizer from the Amalgamated Meat Cutters and Butcher Workmen of North America shortly after he formed the Austin union. The organizer told Ellis he had a promising future in the labor movement and could have a good job with the AFL if he would turn over his skilled butchers at Hormel to the Amalgamated Meatcutters. In a 1973 interview Ellis recalled his response: "Fuck you. We got a labor union here with all the people together."

So despite Local 9's geographic isolation and despite Hormel's second-tier role in the meat-packing industry, the workers in Austin formed a powerful and influential body. Historically the members of Local 9 could say they had helped create the UPWA. Tactically they had the security of a direct pipeline to international union headquarters in the event of bargaining trouble. That did not, however, make them dependent on the parent organization. The UPWA had been formed out of several autonomous unions with aggressive and highly independent leaders. It continued a strong tradition of local independence, even contempt for the parent body. The union consisted of ten regions, each run by a director elected from within the region. The regional director could not be removed from office by the international, a rarity among unions today. The union's constitution also granted enormous power to the rank and file and a directly elected executive board; local presidents had relatively little power to make appointments or run meetings. Local 9 was independent enough that during Frank Schultz's tenure as an international vice-president, he never moved out of Austin and seldom allowed international representatives into town. He was suspicious of his superiors in the union and jealous of Ellis's almost legendary stature in Austin. He was famous for using his clout to squeeze a little extra out of Hormel's personnel chief, Fayette Sherman. If Sherman balked at a Local 9 proposal, Schultz would threaten to bring in the international. And in fact, international reps never appeared at the Austin bargaining table until Schultz left office.

The combination of this powerful, headstrong union with a company that wanted and could afford labor harmony produced an informal alliance in Austin that kept friction to a minimum. On the packinghouse floor it was a rare dispute that defied settlement between a foreman and a grievance officer. If they couldn't solve it, they might take it to the union's department chairman or the plant manager, but seldom did it go outside the plant to lawyers or arbitrators. Controlling their own pace and production, the men found ways to spell each other and develop coffee breaks that stretched from fifteen to forty-five minutes. In 1950 it wasn't uncommon to walk across the street into the Plant Café at 9:00 A.M. and find the place full of meat-packers taking a breakfast break while their colleagues on the line kept up the pace. The foremen didn't care; they, too, were taking forty-five-minute coffee breaks. In some departments where management had attempted to speed up production, the union won a corresponding increase in the gang size—to the point where half a dozen gang members were perpetually in the locker room playing cards. Again, the foremen didn't mind; that reserve crew in the locker room gave them a ready pool of replacements if someone got injured or fell sick on the line.

When it came to big contractual matters, it was said that Schultz and Sherman could sit down over a schooner of beer or dinner at the Alcove Restaurant, the finest in Austin, and hammer out an agreement. Schultz, the legend has it, would take a verbal summary back to the rank and file, say, "Here it is, boys. It's the best we can get," and it would win ratification. Members of the union's executive board during those years say the process was actually a good deal more complicated; they remember scrutinizing the company's offers sentence by sentence before putting them before the membership. But Sherman and Schultz did know each other's minds, and in more than twenty years of bargaining with each other virtually every one of their agreements was ratified by the rank and file.

In any case, the contract never expired, as most labor agreements do today, but instead perpetually renewed itself. The only tinkering came when one party or the other wanted to change something—a work rule for management, perhaps, or a wage increase demanded by Local 9. Then they simply filed a grievance, haggled it out, and wrote their solution into a memorandum of agreement. No one really kept track of all those memorandums; it was assumed that Sherman and Schultz knew what they had agreed to over the years, and both sides would take their word as final on any dispute. Some of Local 9's old-timers claimed that Schultz would maneuver Sherman into signing two and three contradictory memos of understanding on the same topic, then produce whichever one suited the union's needs at the moment. By 1959, when a young lawyer named Chuck Nyberg started in Hormel's legal department, fifteen years' worth of memorandums of agreements filled a set of ring binder notebooks that covered a bookshelf nine feet long. (A typical labor contract today for a

36

large factory can be reproduced in a pocket-size eighty-page booklet.)

Nobody forgot, however, that this was a tug-of-war over profits, wages, and working conditions. When Nyberg joined Hormel straight out of law school at the University of Minnesota, Sherman told him he'd better get acquainted with Schultz. One afternoon a few days later Schultz turned up in a foul mood. He walked into the anteroom outside Sherman's office, gave the young Nyberg a fleeting glance, and said, "Sherm, I need to talk to you about something." Nyberg recalled the ensuing interview as one of the most extraordinary displays of anger he had ever seen: Schultz shouted, waved his hands, tore the cap off his head and threw it on the ground, hollered some more, stomped up and down on the cap, and stormed out of the room. Nyberg thought he was witnessing a man who had taken leave of his senses, and told Sherman so. "Naw, Chuck," Sherman told the young lawyer. "That was Schultz's way of introducing you to labor relations."

In some respects Local 9 held a decided advantage over Hormel during the period after World War II. Hormel was a big company in a small town that could ill afford to pick a fight with five thousand workers who controlled up to 75 percent of its production. Hormel was Austin, and Austin was Local 9. Wages were so high that some of the meat-packers hid their paychecks from their wives for fear that the town's grapevine would learn just how much they earned. A handful of the men weren't so shy—they would stop in four or five bars on payday to show them off—and union officers had to discourage the practice for fear of igniting jealousy. In 1951 three out of four Austin workers owned their homes, giving the city one of the highest rates of homeownership in the nation. Austin's population peaked with thirty thousand residents in 1960, but its affluence still sets it apart from most of the slumping rural Midwest. As recently as 1984 one out of ten Austin workers took home thirty thousand dollars. Main Street businesses weren't the only beneficiaries of having a Fortune 500 firm for a neighbor. Hormel executives dominated Austin's volunteer, business, and civic organizations, and union members were elected mayor as often as not. The company gave lots of money to the community through the Hormel Foundation, spearheading drives for a YMCA, nature park, hospital, and municipal swimming pool.

But Austin remained a working-class town. During the 1950's virtually every establishment in town was unionized, a legacy of Ellis's wall-to-wall organizing. The strip joints and bars of the east side gave Austin a regional reputation for blue-collar night life, and the Hormel paychecks guaranteed lively weekends. Still, the union was a civic mainstay, sponsoring youth baseball teams and working extensively in local politics. It wasn't uncommon to see rank-and-filers socializing with executives at the Austin Country Club, and children befriended and dated each other without concern about their parents' jobs.

By 1960 Austin was a microcosm of postwar America: comfortable, affluent, a model of the economic dominance that economist Lester Thurow has described as "effortless superiority." The Hormel workers were king of the hill in meat-packing, even as America was king of the hill in the world marketplace. This was the great American accomplishment: Men of simple education and no social privilege could get factory jobs and assure themselves lives of middle-class affluence. Hormel's guaranteed annual wage and profit sharing symbolized the postwar peace pact between American industry and labor: Labor would not challenge the right of capital to a profit as long as capital shared that profit in steadily growing increments. Though the union skirmished often with Hormel management, no one questioned that what was good for Hormel was good for Austin and its people. Pete Winkels described it as the *Leave It to Beaver* era: cozy; unworried; confident.

But Hormel and the Austin leaders could not build a wall around their community. Coming into play were forces as big as the globe itself—forces that Hormel could not ignore, that the union could not forestall. By the time John Morrison and Pete Winkels joined the union in the late 1960's, Local 9's history embraced two strands: one a tradition of give-'em-hell militance; the other an unspoken peace pact between the company and the company town. The next fifteen years would test those strands mightily and pull Morrison and Winkels painfully apart.

CHAPTER
2

If Pete Winkels and John Morrison felt insulated from the pressures of the real world when they first stepped onto the packinghouse floor, their new boss certainly did not. In August 1969 thirty-seven-year-old Dick Knowlton took over as manager of the Austin plant, marking the return of yet another Austin native to the company for which his father had toiled. He had left Austin in 1950, a three-sport jock, yearbook editor, and college recruited football star. He returned a veteran of Hormel's sales ranks, having turned down a chance to play professional football after college because of his loyalty to the packer on the prairie. But now, as chief of operations and sales for the Austin plant, he was charged with tackling a problem that had confounded his predecessors and was steadily eroding Hormel's stairstep earnings. Very simply, the Austin plant was starting to lose money. Renowned as the largest packinghouse of its kind in the world, the venerable flagship was fast becoming the company's Achilles' heel. The causes were no mystery to management, but finding the right solution had befuddled executives in Hormel's corporate office for nearly a generation. Now it was Knowlton's turn to try.

Part of the packinghouse's losses stemmed from its age. The plant was essentially a throwback to the days of Upton Sinclair's Chicago stockyards. Parts of the sprawling complex dated back to the company's founding in 1891 by George Albert Hormel, a tanner's son from Toledo who moved to Austin and remodeled an old creamery. An unsightly patchwork of brick buildings, smokestacks, hog sheds, and rail sidings, it rose to eight stories, and its floor space covered the equivalent of three suburban shopping malls. Inside was a jumble of industrial saws, splitting equipment, steel tables, chutes, and chains that collectively constituted sophisticated disassembly, processing, and canning lines. But the vertical structure meant that thousands of animals slaughtered each day on the main floor had to be transported upstairs via conveyor belts for processing, then hauled back down for storage and shipping. While that setup had worked in the plant's early days, subsequent building additions and the need to push through higher volume were making it uneconomical and more costly.

Jay Hormel had been widely recognized for being the first in the industry to see the problems with vertical packing plants, the standard industry design for decades. Shortly after the end of World War II he even went so far as to have blueprints drawn up for a one-story building on a piece of pastureland just north of the Austin plant. If he and his top executives ever actually discussed the idea of building there, they never took it seriously enough to warrant a cost analysis. After Jay died in 1954, his successors tried to work around the old plant's flaws by rearranging various processing lines and installing more modern equipment. The inefficiency was eliminated in newer Hormel plants that were built to move meat horizontally through a one-story building, but no amount of tinkering by company engineers and designers could reverse the Austin plant's obsolescence.

To hear management tell it, one other aspect of the plant virtually sealed its unprofitability. The incentive system, prized by the union and perhaps the most appealing aspect of showing up for work every morning, had gotten seriously out of whack. The system, also known as the gain, had been implemented by Jay Hormel as a tool to reward extra production with bonus pay. But production standards were low enough that by the mid-1960's workers in the most labor-intensive jobs, such as slaughtering animals, could supplement their base wages by an average "gain" of 87 percent and still take ten-minute breaks every hour. Every time management tried to raise the standards, Local 9, not surprisingly, asked for more workers to do the work. Hormel tried to modernize around the problem with laborsaving machines, but the benefits were only short-term. Each time new equipment was installed, the union negotiated a "mechanical gain," amounting to a 35 percent bonus on top of base wages to compensate workers who lost their gains opportunity to automation. Even janitors and cafeteria workers received wage supplements to compensate them for not earning the production gain.

In theory, Jay's incentive plan was mutually beneficial, rewarding a dollar's worth of extra production with a dollar of extra pay. But as time wore on, there proved to be no scientific method for determining production standards on jobs along ever-modernizing processing lines. Numerous studies were commissioned, but they produced more disagreements than answers on which labor and management could agree. The problem was compounded when Hormel tried to match standards at its competitors' plants, which strove to pay comparable base wages but often didn't have identical processing lines, let alone the same incentive schedules.

The system also was difficult to police. Foremen, who sometimes made less than union members, grew accustomed to giving workers product orders in the morning, then letting them work relatively unsupervised. Workers had a financial incentive to watch themselves, but that invariably led to cheating. Workers padded the hours they spent on jobs with lucrative incentive schedules and shortened the time they spent on those that offered little bonus pay. They also accused foremen of undercounting their production, so that eventually some work teams designated one person to do nothing but count their production all day. The work got done all the same, and those differences caused little problem when wage levels were low during the 1930's and 1940's. But as labor costs steadily rose with expanded employment and overall inflation, the effect on profits became harder to ignore, especially in light of competitive pressures to keep expenses under control.

History offered Knowlton few solutions to the plant's problems because the only serious threats to its survival had occurred before the incentive plan was introduced. Much of the last two generations was an unbridled success story, following on the heels of the 1933 strike through a booming period of expansion after World War II. At the center of that growth was the Austin plant, for years the company's only plant and, even after other facilities were added, by far its largest employer. In fact, each jump in Austin's population, which reached thirty thousand people in 1950, could be directly linked to Hormel's hiring patterns.

But the past did shed light on Hormel's resiliency during hard times, starting with the development of an improved refrigerator car in 1893 that helped big Chicago packers drive out of business hundreds of packers west of the Mississippi River. Hormel, barely two years old, was among a handful to survive. In 1917, after more than two decades of expansion, George Hormel encountered his first labor dispute when one hundred butchers, seeking a pay increase and assurance of steady work, walked off the job. Hormel eventually gave them both. Four years later Hormel nearly went out of business after discovering that an assistant controller named Cy Thomson had embezzled $1.2 million of company funds. It took an emotional plea by George Hormel to persuade his Chicago bankers to carry $3 million in debt while the company tried to recover. Hormel admitted at the next stockholders' meeting in 1922 that the business would have been bankrupt had Thomson taken money for only a few more months. But he also was stung by the insubordination and eventually laid off many top people.

In the wake of those problems, Hormel began forging onto the national food scene in the late 1920's, when Jay Hormel, by now a Princeton dropout, took over for his father and introduced Americans to canned hams. It was a telling move that highlighted the differences between father and son. Jay established himself as a somewhat unpredictable entrepreneur unafraid of a challenge, while his father had always been a cautious stickler for detail and cleanliness, known for picking up scraps of meat that had fallen to the floor and scolding the responsible party. But if the packinghouse was George's baby, Jay nurtured it to adulthood, following his father's lead and gaining hands-on knowledge of its inner workings to cut waste, maintain cleanliness, and improve quality.

In 1929, buoyed by the success of canned ham, Jay Hormel

rolled out canned chicken, which promptly flopped during the belt-tightening years of the Depression. After the strike in 1933, he pressed on with such can stalwarts as Dinty Moore beef stews, Hormel chili, and, in 1937, Spam. In an unprecedented move, Hormel bought full-page four-color ads in national magazines such as the *Saturday Evening Post* and *Ladies' Home Journal* and bought advertising on a national radio program featuring George Burns and Gracie Allen. Sales began to grow, although Hormel, primarily a one-plant company, produced 75 percent of its output in Austin.

The strategy was interrupted during World War II, when the plant was converted to a war facility that produced millions of pounds of meat for the government. After the war Jay Hormel renewed his commitment to workers by rehiring every person called for military duty while keeping wartime replacements on the payroll. With consumer demand surging, he made a standing offer to hire all Austin high school graduates, and plant employment eventually ballooned to more than five thousand people.

Hormel also knew that to keep his workers busy, he had to keep advertising. Foremost among his goals was to make Spam a national product, with such lofty name recognition among luncheon meats that it would define the market the way Kleenex became almost a generic name for facial tissues. Spam earned a dubious wartime reputation, with Russians praising it as "Roosevelt sausage" and comedians ridiculing it as a ham that didn't pass its physical. Actually, it's a mixture of ham and pork shoulder, and Hormel promoted it with a popular dance line known as the Hormel Girls, who made radio and live appearances in big cities around the country. Thanks in part to Spam's smashing success, Austin workers grew accustomed to receiving fat profit-sharing checks every Thanksgiving. Merchants loved it, too, even if they didn't eat it, because those checks, sometimes amounting to twice the price of a new car, could always be counted on to settle year-end overdue accounts and generate big-ticket sales for Christmas.

Buoyed by surging consumer demand after the war, Hormel began to expand outside Austin. The decision sent a tremor down Main Street, whose merchants feared that Hormel was finished expanding in town. But the problem, at least initially, was one of geography. Hormel's livestock buyers bought animals from as far as 150 miles from the plant and sent nearly two million hogs a year through the Austin abattoir. The long, bumpy truck ride to the plant, especially during hot summer months, took its toll on the animals in weight loss and bruises. In 1948 Hormel acquired a small packinghouse in Fremont, Nebraska, and the next year replaced it with the one-story plant that Jay had envisioned. He dispatched one of his top lieutenants, M. B. "Tommy" Thompson, to manage the plant and ordered him to make a fresh start. "I don't want you to make the same mistakes that we made in Austin," Thompson was told.

Jay Hormel never spelled out in detail what those mistakes were, Thompson recalled later, but Jay knew something was amiss with the incentive plan before he died in 1954. To Thompson, who joined Hormel in 1931, the theory was sound, but somehow the proprietary sense that Jay had instilled in Austin workers was growing to unhealthy proportions. A sense of entitlement had settled into the packinghouse because low standards made the incentive gains ridiculously easy to earn, a circumstance that flew in the face of Jay Hormel's insistence that his labor innovations be consistent with enhancing the company's profits.

Fremont was different. When the new plant opened, there was no long civic history of involvement with Hormel, no sense of entitlement, and no UPWA. Fremont workers were represented by the UPWA's less militant rival, the Amalgamated Meatcutters, and Hormel saw it as a chance to start anew with labor. Hormel instituted an incentive system with production standards that more closely matched the industry's. As a result, Fremont workers developed a sense of having earned their gain, Thompson thought, not simply being rewarded by entitlement. The single-story design also made slaughtering and processing more efficient, even to the point of having movable walls that allowed entire departments to be refigured. Coupled with the purchase of slaughterhouses in Mitchell, South Dakota, and Fort Dodge, Iowa, Fremont gave Hormel geographic diversity and increased its livestock-buying market area. Thompson managed the plant for eleven years, helping it become the company's most profitable facility.

Fremont's financial performance became a symbol for the expansion ahead. After 1953 virtually every move to expand outside Austin—sausage plants in Algona and Knoxville, Iowa, expanded processing facilities in Dallas and Houston, a new processing plant in Atlanta—had less to do with geography than with the higher cost of doing the same work in Austin. Hormel eventually went coast to coast with meat-processing and distribution plants from North Carolina to California. It successfully introduced several new products, including Little Sizzlers pork sausage in 1961 and Hormel's top-of-the-line Cure 81 ham in 1963. The company's research and development team also unveiled a resealable package to keep luncheon meats fresh, the first of several packaging breakthroughs that helped Hormel shed its reputation for putting everything in a can.

Those profitable moves were engineered by Austin's "other" Hormel workers, the headquarters staff, based in a single-story brown brick office across the freeway from the plant. Commodity traders were in constant contact with the Chicago Mercantile Exchange, where the company's single biggest expense—the price of livestock—changed every few seconds. Cattle and hog buyers fanned out across the Corn Belt, where Hormel had two other packinghouses and a handful of meat-processing plants that churned out sausage, wieners, hams, bacon, and an assortment of canned products. Sales and marketing teams were on the road, trying to make inroads in grocery stores from California to New York and eventually in foreign lands. Dozens of employees based in Austin reported each day to a large open room in the corporate office, where they sat side by side at desks not separated by makeshift walls or partitions. The offices of the chief executive and the top vice-presidents were intentionally located nearby, a carryover from Jay Hormel's affinity for mingling with his workers. When the lights were turned on every morning, the room became the corporate nerve center, responding to wild swings in livestock prices while trying to put more Hormel products in refrigerators and kitchen cupboards nationwide.

But problems with the incentive gain in Austin remained a nagging source of frustration for four Hormel presidents—Tim Corey, Robert Gray, Thompson, and I. J. "Jim" Holton—who led the company in the twenty-five years after Jay Hormel's death.

On the one hand, they felt a special commitment to their Austin workers, a loyal, skilled bunch of friends and neighbors who had helped carry the company through its lean years. But they also fretted about being beholden to a reward system that had become entrenched in the workers' way of life even though it was increasingly out of sync with the industry.

The executives' consternation also gave rise to a popular belief in Austin that after Jay Hormel died, his successors forgot his concern for workers, that the family feeling was lost to a mind-set that was more business-oriented and focused on the bottom line. Those feelings were especially directed at Thompson, a gruff-talking executive who served as president from 1965 to 1969. When he came back to Austin from Fremont, Thompson vowed that Hormel would "quit giving it away." With the strong union and sense of entitlement among workers, he recalled later, the company would have to fight just to hold the line. Once during a trapshooting outing with friends, Thompson remarked that unless the situation in Austin was straightened out, "we'll all be living in tar paper shacks." The translation that got back to the union, however, was that Thompson wanted to set back workers to the days of living in shacks. Thompson insisted that the remark was taken out of context and that his concern was for the effects on the entire company, management included. But the damage had been done. Thompson's remarks stung workers who had grown up believing Hormel would always take care of them. Now it seemed that the company wanted to crush them. Around the union hall the incident became an infamous, if incorrect, example of the company's new corporate mentality and made union leaders especially defensive whenever Hormel made overtures about concessions. To old-timers who had worked for Jay Hormel, someone they had once drunk beer with at the American Legion hall, it hardly seemed like the same company.

"Jay died too soon," recalled Holton, a gentlemanly Austin lawyer who started with Hormel during the postwar expansion in 1947 and succeeded Thompson as president. He recalled many meetings during the late 1950's and 1960's in which company executives tried to prove the incentive system's problems to the union's executive board. The company produced ledgers for the Austin plant showing page after page of red figures. "It's possible that maybe Jay could have set the thing right, although I'm not too sure about that," Holton said later in an interview.

Eventually the task fell to Knowlton. Tall, sturdy, and ruggedly handsome with close-cut hair and narrow eyes, he was stiffly identified as "R. L. Knowlton" in company publications and protocol. But around Austin, teachers, classmates, and friends remembered him as Dick or Richard. Even before he had graduated from Austin High in 1950, he had logged two summers in the plant, spelling veterans like his father when they took vacations. As a student at the University of Colorado he worked part-time as a Hormel salesman. He was a star guard in college, drawing an offer to turn professional with the Philadelphia Eagles. He was offered a coaching job at Colorado. With degrees in economics and geography, he was asked to join a Denver brokerage and real estate house. But he turned them all down. Thirty years later, in a newspaper interview, he denied that he was ever seriously interested in any of them. He insisted that there was only one thing on his mind: going to work for Geo. A. Hormel & Company.

But unlike his father, his classmates, and the Morrisons and Winkels, Knowlton was not headed for the packinghouse floor. His calling was to take what the workers produced and sell it to consumers. He was married in 1954, spent two years in the Air Force, then started with Hormel as merchandising manager at the Fremont plant. Three years later he was back in Minnesota, where he spent the next ten years in various sales management positions, eventually returning to Austin. His status as a rising star was confirmed in 1969, when, after spending four months working each job along the plant's processing lines, he took over as plant manager. He would be responsible for more than three thousand people, including men who worked with his father, his former high school classmates, and those in the younger generation who were just climbing aboard the Hormel gravy train.

But if workers were to continue to prosper, the plant would have to stop losing money. Knowlton was determined to try a different approach from those of his predecessors. On average, the plant was running at only 80 percent of industry standards and in some departments as low as 60 percent. Since he inherited dual control of operations and sales, he decided to run the plant wide open, hoping increased volume through slaughtering and processing lines would compensate for inefficiencies and labor costs. The move paid off in his first year, when the plant recorded increased sales and its first profit in years. He continued the strategy for the next five years, and the plant outperformed Fremont in profitability in 1971 and 1972 before returning to losses in 1974. The underlying trend was always the same: The canned meat products such as Spam made money, while the more labor-intensive operations—killing and cutting hogs and cattle—showed losses.

The losses were greatest in the beef kill, which had one of the highest-paying incentive schedules in the plant and had been losing an average of more than a million dollars a year since 1966. Knowlton made a special effort to patch it up, but despite Hormel's efforts to modernize and seek wage compromises with the union, he was unable to sustain profitability for long. A key reason was that the beef industry was being revolutionized by low-cost, often nonunion packers, most notably Iowa Beef Packers, later known as IBP, Inc., a ruthlessly efficient subsidiary of cash-rich Occidental Petroleum. Hormel's belt-tightening moves caused deep bitterness in the union. At one point the entire membership was asked to vote on a company demand to cap the incentive pay of beef kill workers. The outcome left many beef workers disgruntled that fellow union members in other departments had taken money away from them. Finally, in 1976, Hormel quit the beef business altogether and delivered layoff notices to 226 people, putting many of the workers in John Morrison and Pete Winkels's generation just a few names from the bottom of the seniority list.

Shortly after Knowlton was named a corporate vice-president and board member in 1974, he headed an engineering study of the Austin plant. He found that it would cost thirty-five million dollars to straighten out the inefficiencies in the Austin plant, modernize it to industry standards, and meet existing federal safety and pollution control requirements. When Knowlton presented the study to the board of directors, he reminded the group that even with the improvements, Austin would still be saddled with an old plant. The board subsequently agreed to discuss building a new plant, and in January 1975 Hormel Chairman Jim Holton announced plans to build a forty-million- to sixty-million-dollar state-of-the-art plant in Austin rather than make improvements to the old packinghouse. But for the union, there was a catch. Management linked the decision to rebuild to negotiation of a new set of work rules that, most notably, would not include an incentive system. A new plant could not operate with a gains plan that no longer bore any relation to reality.

But the union was not about to give it up without a fight. Although its leaders recognized the physical shortcomings of the old plant, the request for such a huge concession drew immediate and loud opposition. Two generations of workers had grown up with the system that helped establish them as the best-paid meat-packers in the country. The two sides began negotiating in October 1975, while the rest of Austin sat back and waited for a quick resolution. But a deadline for the following January passed without an agreement as neither side would budge. They continued to negotiate throughout 1976 and into 1977 until finally, in June, the union agreed to vote on an eight-year proposal that eliminated incentive pay and forbade a strike for the life of the contract. Despite the threat of layoffs if they balked, workers overwhelmingly rejected the pact. Optimism fizzled in Austin as Hormel summarily announced plans to rebuild its Austin gelatin plant in Davenport, Iowa. The company also began looking elsewhere for plant sites, and town leaders feared the worst. Holton, sounding resigned to rebuilding elsewhere, pledged that if the worst came to pass, Hormel would wind down its Austin operations as gradually as possible.

Union leaders dismissed Holton's comments as a bluff. Other members of Local 9 began digging up old speeches by Jay Hormel and other historical documents, trying to prove that Hormel was legally obligated to stay and always act in Austin's best interests. In October, as rumors hinting at Hormel's imminent departure swirled about town, Holton, Knowlton, Local 9 Business Agent Dick Schaefer, and the union's Chicago lawyer, Gene Cotton, appeared for two and a half hours on a live question-and-answer TV show. The effort was designed to clear the air, but it left Holton, a mild-mannered man whom friends dubbed "Gentleman Jim," visibly upset as he ended the show with a pointed jab at the union's obstinance. "If you had sixty million dollars to invest and you heard the discussion tonight," he asked viewers, "would you invest in Austin, Minnesota?"

It was a question that nobody wanted to answer. But Hormel executives, Knowlton included, had sentimental ties to Austin. The employees were classmates, family friends, and neighbors who had helped Hormel achieve the big leagues of meat-packing without leaving for the big city. They also had experience, which was becoming an increasingly rare commodity for meat-packing firms putting plants in new towns. Knowlton knew from experience the devastation left behind by a plant closing. During the mid-1970's he visited Ottumwa, Iowa, where John Morrell & Company closed a meat-packing plant and left thirty-two hundred people out of work. He did not want to see the scene repeated in Austin. Too many good packinghouse towns were shriveling up and dying, and Knowlton didn't want Austin to be one of them.

Yet some board members from outside the company were privately questioning the wisdom of putting such a huge investment in the same small town where Hormel was headquartered. They feared that problems at the plant, including labor disputes involving a large work force, could disrupt management of the company. Hormel was no longer a small company with one plant; it had annual sales of a billion dollars and facilities spanning the country. It could ill afford to be taken hostage by local problems by having its executives too close to the action. But Hormel cherished its small-town ties. It had never donned a flashy metropolitan corporate presence, and its executives relished the way East Coast writers and Wall Street analysts kept rediscovering it like some forgotten beacon of prosperity in the middle of Flyover Land.

As Austin headed into 1978, however, there was little evidence that Hormel planned to rebuild in town. That winter 226 layoffs that had been announced the year before took effect as Hormel discontinued its beef-slaughtering operations. The company also announced that another 325 people would lose their jobs a year later. Minnesota Governor Rudy Perpich visited Austin but was unable to get the parties to budge. Hormel's threats to build elsewhere seemed more real when it secured land options in cities in Minnesota and Iowa and explored a site in Illinois. The idea was to build three 600-employee plants instead of one large facility in Austin. Talks with the union sputtered into the spring before turning serious. Eventually word slipped out that a breakthrough had been reached, but townspeople didn't know for sure because both sides were tight-lipped and kept the press at a distance. Then, on May 26, everything collapsed. Hormel issued a statement saying that it would not build a new plant in Austin. The news, after two and a half years of frustration, had a ring of finality that crushed even the most optimistic spirits in town.

It turned out to be another bluff, designed to bring the talks to a head, and it worked. One month later the union voted, 1,324–502, to accept an agreement that ensured a new plant in Austin. The incentive pay system was scrapped, and workers agreed not to strike until the new plant was open and running for three years. In return, Hormel promised to pay prevailing industry wage rates and agreed to an elaborate system to wean workers off the incentive plan. Union members would defer their cost-of-living increases and other raises until the new plant opened. The money would go into interest-bearing escrow accounts, then be paid back to workers each week after the new plant opened, bringing their take-home pay up to what it had been under the incentive system. The idea was that inflation would bring up base wages so that when the escrow ran out, they would make no less than they had in the old plant. The plant would initially employ 1,025 people, meaning that the union ranks would be trimmed nearly in half. But the plan was to avoid layoffs by luring workers, half of whom were at least fifty years old, with sweetened provisions into early retirement. The agreement drew plenty of opposition before it was ratified, but workers seemed mollified by Hormel's pledge that they would never take home less pay in the new plant.

With the signing of the new-plant agreement, Knowlton's stock reached new heights. In 1979 he was named Hormel's seventh president, replacing Holton, and later added the titles of chairman and chief executive officer. He was forty-eight when he became president, the youngest of three candidates. Holton was impressed with Knowlton's sense of entrepreneurship and recommended him for the job. Hormel had prospered under conservative leadership, but Knowlton brought a willingness to tinker with new products, try new packaging ideas, and take more risks on acquisitions. Knowlton spent the next four years reinvesting company profits by pouring $225 million in capital improvements into the company. He continued a modernization program that included renovating or rebuilding eleven plants in fourteen years. He also pushed his marketing people for new products such as chili-filled wieners and ready-to-serve breakfast sausage to expand Hormel's supermarket presence. Raised in the old pork business, Knowlton was becoming an architect of the new business, demanding more from automation and technology than from labor. He steered away from slaughtering operations, where profit margins were thin to nonexistent, in favor of value-added convenience foods with higher earning potential. Once an old-line meat-packer like Armour and Wilson, Hormel now wanted to count itself among the Pillsburys, Campbell Soups, and other major national food companies.

The new plant seemed tailor-made for that strategy when it officially opened on August 9, 1982, in the same pasture that Jay Hormel had designated back in 1945. It was the most automated meat-packing plant in the world, full of robots, self-guided storage and retrieval vehicles, ham presses that deboned meat with a single knife stroke, new technologies for processing meat, and a computer inventory management system. It eliminated many backbreaking jobs from the old plant. When it ran full speed, it would be capable of slaughtering two million hogs a year and producing two hundred million pounds of meat.

Though high start-up costs caused the new plant to lose money in its first year of operation, Hormel remained profitable while other packers, hit by the 1981 recession, fell victim to the inefficiencies of old plants, high labor costs, corporate spin-offs, and bankruptcy. During Knowlton's first four years at the helm Hormel's earnings were flat, fluctuating from $27 to $32 million, an unspectacular performance considering its sales volume of $1.4 billion. The company's return on investment was about 13 percent, well below the 20 percent rates of its food competitors. But Wall Street analysts were impressed enough to honor Knowlton twice with awards for his stewardship during the industry's unprecedented hard times. With new products coming on line,

Hormel had a kind of corporate momentum, an eagerness in management to work out the new plant's kinks and test its limits.

Knowlton was confident that workers would carry a good attitude into the new plant as well. In the old plant's last few years, supervisors tried to break in employees to new work rules, most notably shorter breaks. Once in the new plant, workers who formerly received incentive gains were paid supplements from the money they had placed in escrow. The supplements amounted to 20 percent on top of their weekly paychecks. Knowlton so liked what he saw that in the plant's first year he quietly hired six hundred new people and added a second shift for the hog kill. Early reitrements had succeeded in trimming the work force in half, but the new hires brought plant employment up to seventeen hundred people. Knowlton had visions of pushing it up to twenty-two hundred.

A month after the official opening, on September 13, thirteen thousand people showed up at a plant open house to kick off a new high-tech chapter in the story of America's meat-packing industry. After speeches by dignitaries and politicians, thousands of curious Hormel workers and retirees took a peek at the hundred-million-dollar marvel that they had heard so much about for the past seven years. It looked all the more remarkable next to the soon-to-be-demolished old plant. Austin celebrated for four days with a host of festivities, including a hog-calling contest and a Hormel-produced 1,050-foot hot dog. Capping it off was a night of fireworks over the Cedar River, with the old and new plants silhouetted in the background. "It is an accomplishment which all of us have worked toward together," a company brochure proudly proclaimed, "and one which will shape the future of our jobs and our Company."

It seemed almost prophetic. The first Austin-born chief executive since Jay Hormel opened a plant in the same pasture that Jay had pondered thirty-seven years earlier. Both men established their corporate personas by showing a little more dash than their predecessors, probing for new products and being willing to spend more advertising money. Faced with industry upheaval, they were poised to carry Hormel out of the throes of national recessions and into the vanguard of the food business. By 1985 parallels would again emerge.

CHAPTER

3

      If Hormel and Local 9 had moved meat-packing out of Upton Sinclair's dark and bloody nineteenth century, Dick Knowlton's spanking new packinghouse brought it into the twenty-first. Except for the meat that moves through it, the plant looks like any modern factory to the untutored eye. Outside, it is low and sleek, a long brick expanse surrounded by acres of asphalt parking lot. Inside, it is all white walls and stainless steel—more institutional than industrial. Overhead conveyor belts clank along under a ceiling three stories high. The floor of textured concrete is damp and puddled from frequent washings. Forklift trucks zip back and forth, carrying pallets of cardboard boxes. Workers wearing white smocks and yellow rubber boots stand at speeding assembly lincs, dropping sausages into prefolded cartons or sliding hams into clear plastic bags. There is little to suggest the steaming carnage of Sinclair's Chicago packinghouses in *The Jungle,* in part because Hormel rarely admits visitors to the actual killing floor.

    What sets this giant plant apart is the air. Damp from water and quantities of raw meat, chilled to a steady forty degrees to prevent spoilage, it penetrates like a knife. The smell changes from one cavernous room to the next: pickling spice where the hams sit in giant vats of brine; hickory smoke where sausages hang in smokehouses as big as garages; garlic where salamis and pepperonis dry by the hundred on great steel racks; blood where the long carcasses rise by overhead chain from the kill floor to the cutting room.

What the packinghouse does represent is perhaps the world's most efficient facility for converting a live hog into ham, bacon, sausage, Spam, and dozens of other products. Sixty-five hundred hogs a day enter from pens at the south end, are hosed down to remove dust and aid the electrocution that awaits them, then are stunned with a six-second jolt of 220-volt electricity administered with a gun behind the ear and on the back. The animals are shackled by the rear legs and hoisted on steel spreaders for a sticker, who slices open two arteries in the hog's throat to kill it. With blood spurting onto the floor, a conveyor chain carries the carcasses to a scalding tank, where the hogs are dipped into 140-degree water to loosen their hair, then through a dehairing machine, where a series of paddles beat the hair off. The remaining hair is shaved off, and a steel bar called a gambrel stick is inserted between the rear hooves to spread the legs and hoist the hogs to the dressing room. The carcasses are sawed open from pelvis to brisket before the guts are "snatched" and placed in a pan for federal inspectors. A man with what looks like a huge set of scissors, actually a power "head dropper," severs the spinal cord at the back of the neck, so that the hog's glands are exposed to more inspectors. Three more men with long, sharp knives all but sever the head from the body with a series of four careful cuts through the jaw and jowls. The hog's head is removed to the head bench, where cutters remove meat from the tongue and cheeks. Lard, meanwhile, is trimmed from the carcass, and the carcass goes to a chilling room for overnight refrigeration.

From the chilling room the carcass will move down another line for disassembly into "primal cuts": loin, butt, belly, ribs, ham, and picnic (front shoulder). An automatic carcass splitter halves the carcass down the spine; then each half is laid flat on a moving belt. The carcass goes under a table saw, which cuts off the hindquarters, which will become hams and pigs' feet. A man with a hand-held rotary saw cuts the side of pork into belly and loin. Another with a big U-shaped knife scrapes the loin, while still another with a fillet knife slices the ribs from the belly. The ribs will be shipped to supermarket butchers and other wholesale meat dealers. The bellies—long slabs of fatty meat—will be smoked, pressed into rectangular slabs in a hydraulic press, and sliced into bacon. The hams and picnics move on to boning tables or boning presses, then to pickling vats and smokehouses to become hams.

It is not an operation that Upton Sinclair would have recognized. A worker who once snipped sausage links apart with ordinary scissors now does hundreds in an hour using hydraulic snips. On the pepperoni line a man stands at a rotating disk fitted with projecting steel tubes; the disk spins every six seconds, a new tube comes up, the man slips a pepperoni casing over it, and the machine squirts spiced meat into the casing. At a hot dog stuffing machine, a man slips perhaps twenty feet of plastic casing over a steel arm, then stands back as the arm twirls lazily, spinning off a string of twenty or thirty hot dogs in less than sixty seconds. Next to the great stainless steel smokehouses sits a separate little shack housing a set of Honeywell computers that monitor the meat's temperature and acidity. Another computer monitors the plant's daily output together with the incoming flow of hogs and calculates the most cost-effective way of slicing up the day's hogs into the desired batch of hams, frozen entrées, or Little Sizzler sausages.

The centerpiece, of course, and the most highly automated operation is the Spam department. Inside a cavernous room lined on three sides by industrial shelving three stories high sits a great rectangular iron boiler, rust red, perhaps forty feet long, eight feet wide, and several stories high. The plant was built around it, including a tall enclosure that juts up from the sprawling roofline. With the boiler and a long, serpentine canning line, just seventeen people can produce more than 500 cans of Spam in sixty seconds, more than 1,000,000 cans of Spam per week. Nearby, racks of shelving tower thirteen levels high, filled and emptied by robot cranes directed by computers, with a capacity of six thousand pallets: 20,736,000 cans of Spam.

When Kathy Buck started at the plant in late 1983, she was thirty-seven years old, a mother of two girls and five boys, owner-manager of two ice cream parlors, and anything but a radical. She didn't know a lot about unions and didn't see much need for them. Though she had lived in Austin since grade school, she didn't come from a "Hormel family," meaning neither of her parents worked in the packinghouse. She had fallen in love with Paul Buck, followed him around the country while he did his military service, and started raising kids. Her experience with Hormel consisted of nine years working in a chemistry lab at its research and development office in the late 1960's and 1970's. She had wanted Local 9's representation for her department in those days—not because she had much faith in unionism but because she thought that coming under the umbrella of the union would get her the union profit sharing and wages on top of the merit raises already paid to nonunion employees. But then she and Paul moved to Colorado with the kids. She spent several years as a waitress, as a bookkeeper, and briefly in a Samsonite factory in Denver.

Back in Austin in 1983, she heard that Hormel was hiring again to staff the new plant. She hadn't lasted long at the Samsonite factory, and friends teased her that she would never survive the grueling work at Hormel's. The company was hiring ten to twelve people a day, but some, rumor had it, never even went back again once they picked up their uniform and saw what the inside of a packinghouse really looked like. She met two other women and three men hired the same day, and together they made a pact to survive at Hormel's. She went to work on the night shift.

Kathy's first job was in the cutting room, trimming meat off neck bones. Three people worked that station, and on her first night Kathy was assigned to watch one for two hours and learn the skill. The next night she was on the line trimming neck bones herself. On the third night she noticed that two new hires were assigned to watch her. On the fourth night they were next to her on the line. She had become the senior member of her gang after four nights.

About a week later Kathy was coming back from a coffee break when she slipped on a greasy spot on a set of stairs. She caught herself by grabbing a handrail with her right hand. But she came down hard on her tailbone, and her right shoulder ached. She went to the medical department, but she was afraid to file a medical claim until her thirty-day probation was up. So she had

Paul wrap the shoulder before she left for work the next day, and she went back to the cutting room.

"This is crazy," she told herself each night as she left the plant at 3:00 or 4:00 A.M. Some nights her fingers cramped so badly from lifting and cutting meat in the forty-degree air that she had trouble unbuttoning her butcher's coat and couldn't get her car keys in the ignition. She noticed similar problems for the people working around her. At another station near the cutting room three men ran machines skinning flesh off hog hides. On most nights two of the machines were operated by novices who were learning the job and working at about half the normal pace. At the third machine was a strapping young man who was working twice as fast so that their gang would keep pace with the line.

"You don't need to do two people's work," she told him during a break one night.

"It doesn't bother me," he replied. "I can take it."

"What's going to happen in a few years, when you can't take it anymore?" she asked.

Kathy knew enough about unions to guess that there were contractual protections against overwork and injury, and she knew that there were supposed to be union shop stewards in every department to enforce the contract or take problems to department or divisional union chairmen. She also knew that a new employee still in her thirty-day probation period could get fired for any reason, and talking to a union steward didn't seem smart.

It was about this same time that Pete Winkels had what was to become a famous outburst. Pete, who was in his mid-thirties at the time, was boning hams, one of the most pressured and skilled jobs. Life was not going well for Pete in November 1983. He had just separated from his wife of thirteen years, and he had the care of their three children. He had managed to find a baby-sitter for them till he got off work at 6:00 P.M., but life was running him ragged. One night, about quitting time, the boning foreman walked by and told the crew that the line would run late that night; they couldn't expect to get off work till 7:30. Pete was already exhausted, and getting to a phone to call the sitter was out of the question. He lost control. He stormed after the foreman, swearing a blue streak and waving his razor-sharp boning knife. People who knew Pete Winkels understood that, while he might think of some imaginative things to tell the foreman, he was not a violent man. Still, this was quite a spectacle to the "new kids" who had come to obey, even fear their foremen. When Pete cooled off and returned to the boning table, they started asking him: "How can you treat a foreman like that? Can't you get fired for something like that?"

Pete spent the next few minutes explaining the contract's disciplinary protections and that such incidents were common in a packinghouse. But he noticed that from then on new workers came to him with questions and problems.

Hormel veterans, too, noticed that this new plant was a demanding place. They got memos forbidding all sorts of behavior that had been tolerated in the old plant: eating snacks on the job; spitting on the floor. Even the locker rooms, home of lunch-hour card games and raucous pranks, were kept up to a new standard of tidiness. Bathrooms were outfitted with red lights that flashed when they were occupied. Remote cameras mounted in the freezer constantly scanned the room, giving workers the feeling they were in prison. There was a new security scanner at the guard shack and magnetic ID cards. For the first time, guards checked the meat-packers' lunch boxes when they left work.

Then too the new plant seemed to be laid out for machinery, not people. Like other new factories, it was horizontal—all on one story and covering one million square feet. It became popular to complain that a fifteen-minute coffee break was consumed in two seven-minute walks to the break room and back. That was an exaggeration, but it could take several minutes out of a break to get off the line to one of the break rooms up above the processing floor. In addition, the new rules forbade going home for lunch, a common practice in the old plant and one of the most prized breaks from the daily grind. What's more, the old plant's cafeteria had been replaced by a handful of small Spartan lunchrooms with vending machines and microwave ovens.

But all that was minor compared with the work. Hormel and Local 9 had conducted a number of time-motion studies in the old plant and had determined that incentive pay notwithstanding, the work pace was 20 percent below industry average. It didn't console the "502 Club," the ones who had voted against the new-plant agreement, that their union had agreed about the work standards; they were stuck working 20 percent faster with no increase in pay. At first foremen told them to take their time adjusting to the faster pace. There was no rush; there was time to ease into things. But only a few weeks went by before the new young foremen, under pressure from upper management or eager to prove their mettle, were insisting that workers meet the higher pace immediately. Hormel responded quickly to safety complaints, but with so many novices learning the difficult knife jobs, cuts and scars were inevitable.

If the technology made many jobs easier—and it clearly did—it was the other jobs that became the subject of coffee break complaints. Where ham boners had assistants to empty their slop buckets in the old plant, they had to do the job themselves in the new plant. In an effort to improve efficiency and reduce distractions for the "knife men," Hormel established special teams of knife sharpeners. But the skilled cutters, who prized their knives and developed personal techniques for keeping them honed to a razor's edge, resented the loss of control over their tools. Some of the most skilled jobs, such as boning out picnics, were being turned over to machines, a step that further depersonalized the plant. On top of that, the new plant was cold. That was a great advantage in preventing spoilage and disease. But many workers found their noses dripping and fingers going numb after six and seven hours in the forty-degree temperatures. And those who had heavy lifting jobs found muscle strains more common in the chilly air.

The people seemed different, too. The Austin plant was like no other in the world, and supervisors and foremen had the unenviable job of getting it to run smoothly as quickly as possible while corporate brass looked on anxiously from across the freeway. Under the direction of plant manager Jim Dinicola, whose rise through the company's sales ranks won him little respect from workers, they went about the costly and time-consuming process of working the kinks out of a $100 million plant. The plant lost $11.4 million in its first three months of operation and showed only one profitable week by the spring of 1983. Veterans looked on quizzically as the hog kill struggled to run at half the pace of the old plant. No one had asked their advice when the plant was designed, and now no one asked when things weren't running right. It was a double slap for many career employees who grew up seeing themselves as integral players in Hormel's prosperity.

What hurt most of all, though, was the loss of that incentive pay. The average worker in the old plant had been adding an average of 66 percent to his base pay. On some production lines the gain was as high as 100 percent. True, Hormel's escrow fund was making up the difference for the six hundred or so who came over from the old plant. But that didn't make things right. The veterans had lost the self-policing dignity of the old plant, the sense of participation that every knife stroke was contributing to their well-being as well as the company's. And the new hires, well, they didn't get escrow money and they had been voted out of a payroll supplement they had heard about all their lives.

Between August 2, 1982, and August 13, 1984, Hormel's massive hiring drive brought 755 new employees into the plant. The "new kids," like Kathy Buck, outnumbered the veterans who had come over from the old plant, and the constant influx of workers made the plant seem unusually chaotic. Industrial engineers were constantly tinkering with the machines and looking over the workers' shoulders. But what proved a key failing for Hormel was this: It was hiring too fast to train the new workers and far too fast to ease them into the rigors of packinghouse work or to introduce them to Hormel as a concerned employer. Instead, they learned the ropes from the plant's embittered veterans, packers who had watched their employer slowly evolve from the paternalistic family firm of their parents' stories into a modern, aggressive, highly competitive corporation. To make matters worse, hundreds of P-9 veterans who had voted for the new-plant agreement in 1976 had since retired under the contract's generous severance provisions. That left behind workers who were highly skeptical of the agreement, feeling they had been left to work under a contract they hadn't liked and hadn't voted for. In the absence of any indoctrination from Hormel management, it was these workers' bitterness that introduced the new employees to Geo. A. Hormel & Company.

So when Hormel came asking for wage cuts in 1983, veterans

and new workers alike took it as a cruel joke. Wasn't theirs the most productive plant in the world? Weren't the veterans already working 20 percent harder than they had in the old plant? Weren't the new kids missing out on incentive gain? They had just climbed on a gravy train they had heard about all their lives, and now the gravy was drying up. Had Hormel forgotten its time-honored promise to take care of Austin and its people?

Pete Winkels wasn't the only veteran who earned a reputation for standing up to management during this period of growing discontent. Throughout the three years that P-9 debated Hormel's new-plant ultimatums, a steady stream of leaflets had issued forth among night shift workers and appeared on union bulletin boards from a group calling itself Committee for a Better P-9. The thrust of these was that Hormel was only bluffing, that Hormel could never leave Austin, and that the company had no right to ask for one concession after another to drive down the workers' living standards. The core of this secretive group was a handful of night shift workers in the loin cooler, a group that gathered in the nightside locker room to debate the company's demands and the posture of P-9's leaders. Their elder statesman was Glenn Howden, and his prize pupil was Jim Guyette.

When Guyette's name first began appearing on the "midnight leaflets" attacking P-9's leadership and Hormel, those who had known him at Austin High were a little puzzled. Guyette was not a kid that anybody would have called a radical when he was growing up in Austin. He was an avid wrestler, a quiet student who clearly was bright but didn't apply himself hard enough to make much impression on teachers. He was a friendly guy who did work hard to make a good impression on the girls and was good for a few laughs with his buddies.

Still, there was something more determined, more self-reliant about Jim Guyette. He grew up a short walk from the old plant in Austin's poorest neighborhood, a collection of tiny white frame houses known as the Crane Addition. Both of Jim's parents were deaf—his dad because of a childhood case of German measles, his mom from a childhood head injury. Jim learned to speak by spending weekends with his grandparents. When insurance sales-men rang the doorbell or the electric company called on the phone, it was Jim who became the family spokesman—or at least a translator of these grown-up issues. Jim was the eldest of five children, and he took the role of older brother seriously. Mary, the next in line, was retarded, and Jim became especially protective of her. Then came three more boys—Jerry, Steve, and Wayne. Jim always looked out for them, too, making sure they had paper routes and were getting along all right at school.

Jim struck out on his own early. Though his dad was making good money—sometimes as much as three hundred dollars a week in the early 1960's, when monthly mortgage payments were seldom over two hundred dollars—Jim insisted on earning his own money. He had his own paper route, then a job pumping gas to buy his own clothes and pay for his own haircuts. He bought his first car at fifteen—getting his dad to sign the papers because Jim wasn't yet old enough for a driver's license. Later he raised hunting dogs; he was an avid hunter who wore a Remington rifle belt buckle. He was no athletic standout, and his paunchy midriff earned him the nickname Guts and, later, Big Guy. He was not the type to pick a fight, as were many of the rough-and-tumble packinghouse kids. But he absolutely refused to back down when he thought he was right. His hunting buddies soon learned just how principled Guyette could be: He withstood tremendous peer pressure and refused to trespass in off-limits corn fields even when it seemed there was no chance of getting caught. Nor could he be deterred when he set his mind on something. As a teenager he floored his friends by swimming halfway across the chilly Cedar River one fall afternoon to fetch a fallen duck.

Like most of the other meat packers' kids in Austin, Jim was familiar with the gripes about hard work for a tough company. His dad, Jack Guyette, wasn't one of the bitter ones. He shackled cattle—one of the toughest jobs—and got along well at the packinghouse, though he was known for a hot temper and occasional pranks. He loved to startle his hearing friends by lighting firecrackers under their chairs while they played cards or by dropping a heavy steel bootpuller on the hard locker-room floor; he couldn't hear the clang any more than he could hear the deafening noise in the beef kill. He stayed out of trouble and bought rounds at the bar with the other guys after work, but with the laughs and the good-natured ribbing also came a certain isolation from co-workers, with whom he communicated by notes or not at all.

Still, Jim wasn't sure he wanted to follow his dad into the packinghouse. The boys at Austin High in the 1960's knew their dads had good jobs, all things considered—good wages, steady paychecks, excellent fringe benefits, and a company that seemed to care about the community—yet they also knew their dads wondered over beer whether after twenty, thirty, forty years cutting open hogs or stuffing sausage casings, they had made the most of their lives. Many resolved to do better than their dads, to attend Mankato State University sixty miles to the west, or at least Austin Junior College, where they could get a two-year degree and a taste of higher education. Jim told his friends he planned to be a schoolteacher; "history" had a nice ring to it. That was a job with some dignity, a job that made a contribution to society. And a job with three months off every summer.

Jim enrolled at the junior college in the fall of 1967 on a general education program. Although Hormel was no longer hiring every high school graduate to fill the plant, it did offer summer work to 350 to 400 college students each year, and a summer job in the packinghouse paid enough to cover a full year's tuition at the school with money left over for room and board and a little "running around." It was irresistible, not just to Jim but to many of his pals. But schoolwork never completely captured his attention, and he couldn't quite escape the allure of Hormel's. The work was familiar, the summer employment often led to a full-time offer, and many of his buddies from high school were already there, taking home the big paychecks. He dropped out of college and, after a four-month stint with the National Guard, went to work in the packinghouse in 1968. "The money was good, it was an honest living," he recalled twenty years later. "It looked like a good company to work for."

They were good times for a whole generation of young men hired by Hormel from 1965 to 1968, perhaps three hundred graduates of Austin High, Austin Pacelli, and other local schools. They earned $240 to $260 a week, which for a single young man was enough to buy a new Pontiac, golf clubs, and a rifle. Guyette teamed up with boyhood buddies Steve Aberg and Danny Leinbeck on hunting trips to Montana and North Dakota and golf outings anywhere they could find a course. Guyette, a fifteen-handicap, kept a spare Arnold Palmer cardigan in his car, always looking sharp and well groomed for nineteenth-hole festivities. When he packed a suitcase, he actually folded his clothes neatly. He lined the ashtray of his car with felt to keep pennies for parking meters. Laid back and almost square, "Big Guy" was the responsible one, the one with the car, the one who stayed most sober at parties, the one who would lend money to cash-strapped friends, the voice of reason and authority who still found a way to have a good time. Like his friends, he enjoyed a good flirt, but he was more of a gentleman who "didn't jump at everything that walked," one of them recalled.

During one of those parties Aberg reintroduced him to Vickie Fossum, one year his junior at Austin High, who was living in Minneapolis at the time. They were married in 1972. Not long after the wedding, friends noticed a more serious side to Jim Guyette. He became a regular churchgoer and began to take Lutheranism more and more seriously. When their first child, Nicole, was born in 1975, Jim and Vickie made it clear that they took child raising seriously, too. The children were not to take rides from strangers, and even close family friends would get a polite no from the Guyette kids.

Friends and relatives also began to notice that Jim Guyette was not one to compromise on an issue he felt seriously about. In the mid-1970's he formed a contracting partnership with his brother Jerry to remodel houses and build speculation homes. The idea was for Jerry, a carpenter, to provide the expertise, and Jim, with his Hormel paycheck, the capital. He joined Jerry on the job on weekends and in the afternoon before heading to his night shift in the packinghouse. If the partnership proved a success, perhaps it would be Jim's ticket out of the packinghouse and into a career in business. (As Hormel shut down its beef operations in the mid-1970's, it had laid off workers to the point where Jim was just four names from the bottom of the seniority list, a sobering lesson about job security in the meat-packing business.) Jim and Jerry did some remodeling jobs and bought a few lots in Austin, then built two speculation houses in Rochester. But it was 1978. Interest rates were creeping up, making it hard for home buyers to get mortgages and costly for the brothers to finance a house they couldn't sell. The partnership came under pressure, and they argued occasionally about money. That winter Jim hired Jerry to make some improvements to a rental house that Jim owned in northeast Austin, then a few months later hired him to build a new house in the Southgate Addition on Austin's southwest side. Jerry understood Jim to say that he planned to move into the house with his family. One day Jerry stopped by the Southgate house and ran into a realtor who told him Jim had sold the house. Jerry called Jim that night and asked to be paid out of the sale proceeds. Jim said the two partners were even because of some help he had given Jerry on a different construction project. Jerry called him again a few days later. Again Jim refused. The next day Jerry got a letter threatening legal action if he didn't leave Jim alone. In May 1980 Jerry finally submitted a written bill to his brother but got no response. Finally, in 1983, Jerry sued Jim for his expenses, and a Mower County judge agreed with him. Jim was ordered to pay his brother $7,887. The two didn't speak to each other for more than two years. Even in 1988 Jim refused to talk about the episode.

About the same time Jim and Vickie started taking a greater interest in civic issues, and they developed a reputation for challenging the power structure that for years had tended to Austin's affairs. They cut their teeth on the kind of small issue that introduces so many taxpayers to the wheels of civic administration. Austin had just two garbage haulers at the time; the town was split down the middle, and each hauler had a monopoly on one half of town. The Guyettes, like a number of other families, thought their fees were too high and the service inadequate. Guyette also complained that the garbageman was going through his trash looking for personal items. They found the city council unresponsive, even after a number of trips by vocal crowds to city council meetings. Eventually they forced the issue to a referendum and opened the city to a third garbage hauler. It was a trivial issue, in retrospect, but it was an early lesson for Guyette in taking on the establishment, organizing an opposition, and finding winning tactics.

In the early 1980's he and Vickie put those skills to use in what was to become the granddaddy of local civic battles: a fight over Austin's participation in an electricity-generating proposal known as the Southern Minnesota Municipal Power Association (SMMPA). Austin had long had its own municipal power plant, a highly efficient and locally controlled utility. When state regulators and civic leaders from several cities suggested that the towns of southern Minnesota go in with Northern States Power, a big privately owned electric utility in Minneapolis, on a regional power-generating scheme, the concept went over well with growth-minded civic planners but aroused skepticism among many environmentalists and Austin taxpayers. It appeared to be the opposite of what environmentalists had been calling for throughout the 1970's—namely, the return to small, environmentally sensitive generating facilities. It also threatened to strip Austin of control over its local electric supply.

To Guyette, who already was suspicious of large utilities and the banks that supported them, it seemed a dangerous, almost sinister proposal. Like the garbage-hauling battle, this one focused on the power structure at Austin City Hall. A vigorous campaign ensued for seats on the Austin Utility Board; a blizzard of letters descended on the Austin *Daily Herald*; city council meetings turned into such heated shouting matches that council members asked for police escorts home. The Guyette faction lost, and Austin joined SMMPA, but not before the city was deeply divided.

Jim and Vickie made names for themselves in Austin as wily and persistent organizers. They became familiar figures at city council meetings—Jim tall and square-shouldered in a cardigan sweater, legal pad in hand as he delivered vehement speeches; Vickie tossing her long light brown hair as she worked the crowd with petitions and phone numbers. They also burned scorch marks between pro-SMMPA and anti-SMMPA politicians that survived more than a decade. And they learned what it takes to build a community organization: how to research large social issues and big corporations; how to write leaflets that would alert their neighbors to alarming developments; how to mobilize phone trees and letter-writing campaigns; how to turn out boisterous crowds for important meetings.

Yet Jim became something of an enigma around Austin during this time. Though he was to become one of the state's leading labor leaders within just a year or two, he was not an ardent trade unionist. During the garbage dispute he came under fire from some P-9 members because the new hauler he brought to town was nonunion. Guyette later dismissed that criticism, saying that unions aren't necessary when an employer treats workers fairly—a view that most trade unionists find highly suspect. He could be charming and playful with friends, teasing them with an unerring instinct for their vanities and foibles. Yet he could also be highly suspicious. When two reporters attended an Austin City Council meeting in 1985, then wound up in a bar with a handful of council members after the meeting, word got back to Guyette that night. The next morning he chided the reporters for violating Minnesota's open-meeting law, a gibe that was only half in jest.

A mediator who got to know him about that time used the word "evangelistic," a word that seemed remarkably apt, considering Guyette's deep religious beliefs. He and Vickie had quarreled with members of their Lutheran church about buying insurance from a fraternal organization that didn't follow their particular creed. Later Guyette said that Hormel's executives "would be judged" by a higher power for their behavior toward their employees. And in an essay published after the strike Guyette said that Hormel executives would be haunted by the hardships, even deaths, they had caused among employees until their policies "reflect the principles taught by one in Nazareth a long time ago."

At any rate the civic battles left Guyette deeply suspicious of authority and soon of his own union. Dick Schaefer, P-9's veteran business agent, had chaired the Austin Utility Board and had crossed Guyette in the SMMPA fight. Now Guyette urged his colleagues in the union to take part in community issues. Everybody had heard stories about the way Local 9 had dominated the civic scene in the 1940's and 1950's, and Guyette reminded his colleagues of the union's active history. Schaefer also had been a lead negotiator for the union during discussions over the new plant, and Guyette was one of many union members who felt Local 9's leaders gave away too much to keep Hormel in Austin.

Then, in 1981, with the meat-packing industry reeling from the nation's recession, the UFCW's national packinghouse director, Lewie Anderson, negotiated a national wage freeze at $10.69 an hour. Guyette, who sat on P-9's executive board at the time, was deeply skeptical. He distributed a leaflet through the plant noting that UFCW officers and Hormel executives weren't taking a three-year wage freeze. Guyette also reminded the P-9 members of the concessions they had made to keep the packinghouse in Austin, implying that they ought to be treated differently when it came time to negotiate wage freezes.

That point touched a raw nerve among the rank and file. Local 9, once a big cog in the UPWA, had lost some of that prominence in 1968, when the UPWA merged with its old counterpart from pre–AFL-CIO days, the Amalgamated Meat Cutters and Butcher Workmen of North America. Local 9's old-timers had always regarded "the Amalgamated" with some suspicion; they felt it lacked the populist militance of the union they had helped create. But by the 1960's the two unions differed little on philosophy, and the merger was just one of many as organized labor solidified into larger bureaucracies during the 1960's. Then, in 1979, the merged union was merged again, this time into the giant retail clerks' union, which represented cashiers and stock clerks at the nation's big grocery chains, together with thousands of other workers in the burgeoning service sector. Suddenly the Austin meat-packers found that their union was just a small division in one of the nation's biggest labor organizations, a mere hundred thousand members out of more than one million. Moreover, their big new parent union, UFCW, wasn't primarily a packinghouse union. Its international president, William Wynn, was a former clerk himself and leader of the retail clerks' union. Local 9 became Local P-9, to signify "packinghouse" in the much larger union. Things were not going the meat-packers' way.

P-9's leadership was undergoing a transition that reflected all these pressures. Since Frank Schultz was defeated in 1969, no president had served P-9 for more than one three-year term. The long feud over the new plant consumed two presidents, including John Hanson, who, along with Business Agent Dick Schaefer, his brother-in-law, was widely credited with negotiating the agreement. But Hanson paid the price in 1980, when he ran for reelection and was soundly defeated by Floyd Lenoch, like him an old-timer but one who was embittered by what he saw in the new Hormel.

In 1982 Guyette decided it was time for an overt challenge to P-9's leadership. He ran for the office of financial secretary, taking on incumbent Audrey Neumann, who had handled union clerical chores of one form or another since 1947. Guyette found fault with P-9's election procedures, taking great pains to obtain membership mailing lists and to have his own poll watchers at the union hall. He lost, but in one of the leaflets from the Committee for a Better P-9, he and Glenn Howden planted a seed that would grow and grow during the next four years. They urged that their fellow members demand that P-9 "examine its relationship to the international union. We should examine what services we receive from the international in exchange for the dues we send them."

These were suspicions that Jim Guyette meditated on back in the loin cooler during the spring and summer of 1983. The meatpackers around him were working harder than ever in a packinghouse that symbolized Hormel's aggressive new emphasis on technology and profits. They had been relegated to one plant among many in the Hormel chain, one union among scores in the big UFCW. They were witnessing the collapse of an American birthright—an ever-rising standard of living—and the breakdown of a local bond—with a paternal company that had cushioned them from the shocks of economic dislocation. The effects of this double blow were driven home every day that they stepped into the chilly packinghouse air, donned the bloody white smocks, and picked up their knives again. Guyette could sense the resentment of the veterans like himself and the frustration of newcomers like Kathy Buck, and he knew what to do about it.

CHAPTER

4

Shortly before the close of business on Friday, April 22, 1983, lawyers for the Wilson Foods Corporation filed papers in the U.S. district court in Oklahoma City, Oklahoma, putting the nation's biggest hog packer into bankruptcy. Reeling from losses that were escalating at $1 million a week, Wilson took aim at one of its biggest expenses and unilaterally cut wages at seven plants by a whopping 40 percent. Bankruptcy was the same technique that TWA, Braniff, and heavily unionized steel companies used to free themselves from onerous contract provisions. With one legal stroke, six thousand of the best-paid meat-packers in the nation became some of the worst paid. When they returned to work on Monday, Wilson had trimmed their base pay from $10.69 an hour to $6.50 and had cut overtime pay, vacations, and holidays as well. It was an unprecedented move by one of the oldest names in meat-packing, the biggest of the "Big Four" packers that for decades put ham, bacon, and hot dogs on American dinner tables and set the living standard for thousands of packinghouse workers across the country.

For Lewie Anderson, the biggest domino had toppled barely a year after he thought he had propped up the entire pork industry. As packinghouse director for the UFCW Anderson had to hold together a national patchwork of labor contracts, built on a forty-year tradition of steadily increasing wages and benefits and improved working conditions for a hundred thousand union workers. The centerpiece was the so-called master agreement, a set of industry working standards that established a national wage rate—Wilson's $10.69 an hour—for 70 percent of UFCW packinghouse members nationwide. For the employers, it took wages out of competition and put everybody on an equal footing. For workers, it provided national bargaining strength in dozens of packing plants around the country.

But the master agreement was being undermined by an unrelenting industry revolution. Dozens of meat-packing plants had shut down since 1979, unable to compete in an increasingly monopolized business. A wave of conglomerate ownership converted many old-line packers into cash cows, bled them of profits and capital, then spun them off again into a reeling independence. Industry overcapacity sapped profits as the inflationary 1970's gave way to the economic contraction of the early 1980's. Upstart packers resisted unions to open plants and pay workers as little as five dollars an hour with scrawny benefits. Unable to compete when hog supplies dwindled, the big packers got out of hog slaughtering, which was labor-intensive and marginally profitable, and into the processing of brand-name consumer products such as sausage and luncheon meats, which was highly automated and highly profitable. It was a familiar scene for Wilson, Hormel, and the others, which had seen many of the same trends force them out of the beef business during the sixties and seventies.

The bargaining environment was deteriorating, too. The 1981 recession forced packers to streamline while soaring unemployment made workers fear for their jobs. As in the auto and steel industries, which also adhered to national-pattern labor agreements, there was pressure for mid-contract concessions. No longer did Wilson, Swift, Cudahy, and Armour set one wage rate for all their plants, thereby establishing a pattern for the entire industry. In the 1980's packers set out to bargain individually, often on a plant-by-plant basis in small towns across the Midwest. If concessions weren't granted, they threatened to close plants, pitting local fears of unemployment against the international's pledge to preserve the national wage rate. Anderson flew from his Washington, D.C., office to hotels and union halls across the Corn Belt, like a chessmaster against a roomful of opponents, urging contract rejection here, granting a concession there, then moving on to the next battle. Bitter strikes erupted in Colorado, Wisconsin, and Iowa. Fifteen plants operated under closing notices in 1981, with major layoffs threatened at three others. From 1980 to 1982 workers at thirty-four plants faced demands for mid-contract concessions and granted them at eight. The remaining plants shut down, in one instance sparking a lawsuit from workers who wanted the UFCW to take a less militant stance and accept concessions that would save jobs.

Anderson was no stranger to such adversity. A high school dropout from Sioux City, Iowa, he had been a packinghouse worker since age sixteen and a union steward since age twenty-four. He had been a leader of the bloody 1969 strike against Iowa Beef in Dakota City, Nebraska, which drew national press coverage after two workers were killed and three others shot during open warfare at the barricades Iowa Beef erected around the plant. In Iowa Beef, Lewie found a truly adversarial employer. Its low-wage, nonunion approach to the beef industry effectively knocked most of the big names out of the business or reduced them to inconsequential players. Even after winning its first contract at Iowa Beef with the 1969 strike, the union had to strike again in 1972 and again in 1977. Lewie went on to take a series of organizing assignments for the Amalgamated Meat Cutters, and then, shortly after its merger with the Retail Clerks International Union, he became the national packinghouse director in 1980. He was just four years older than Guyette, but already his face showed the effects of too many cigarettes, too much coffee, and too many all-night bargaining sessions. His voice was surprisingly soft, his manner polite, but that didn't keep him from slipping into the occasional "ain't" and "bullshit" of the slaughterhouse floor. His mother and his sister still worked on the beef line at Iowa Beef's Dakota City packinghouse.

Faced with a demoralized membership, Anderson set out to restore order with the help of the UFCW's National Packinghouse Committee, a group of twenty-five handpicked union leaders from chains of plants owned by the largest packers. In early 1981 they reopened the master agreement with several major packers, offering to sacrifice short-term wage gains for protection from plant closings and retention of the industry's national wage structure. By the end of the year the Packinghouse Committee had signed three-year agreements with Armour, Wilson, Swift, Hormel, and Oscar Mayer. The pacts called for a wage freeze at $10.69 an hour, suspension of annual cost-of-living adjustments, and no plant closings for eighteen months. They also included provisions to adjust wages, if either side requested, on September 1, 1984, with the unions having the right to strike.

The strategy was a big gamble, but it induced a number of other packers to follow suit. For workers the new deals would provide more job security, Anderson thought. The packers, always complaining about the need to modernize, would have extra capital to pour into their aging packinghouses. So successful were the negotiations in bringing the fragile pork industry together that Anderson declared in a 1982 report to UFCW President William Wynn that "the national pattern has been successfully established and maintained in the pork sector."

But Wilson, despite a commanding 17 percent of the industry's hog-slaughtering capacity, was in sorry shape. It had been spun off from the LTV Corporation, the Texas defense and aerospace conglomerate, in July 1981 with sixty million dollars in long-term debt and several plants in dire need of renovation. The UFCW estimated that from 1972 to 1980 LTV had drained fifty-one million dollars in Wilson profits that could have been reinvested to modernize inefficient plants. More than half its business depended on the cyclical pork market, where profit margins swung wildly with the price of hogs on the Chicago Mercantile Exchange. Even healthy packers earned just a penny of profits per dollar of sales, and Wilson was burdened by a debt-laden balance sheet. Even after the wage freeze in 1981, Wilson lost twenty-six million dollars in the first nine months of fiscal 1983. It was a recipe for failure barring some dramatic action, and even then Wilson would require long-term nursing to become profitable again.

The bankruptcy created an industry-wide scare and shattered Anderson's vision of a secure national wage rate. Wilson's sudden collapse seemed to signal the end of pattern bargaining, echoing the same trend that rippled through America's steel, auto, trucking, and airline industries. The same companies that had agreed to the wage freeze—Armour, Swift, John Morrell, Oscar Mayer, and Hormel—began posturing to free themselves from the master agreement's $10.69 hourly base wage. Under intense economic pressure and facing a rapid downward spiral in wages, the packers couldn't afford to wait two years until their labor contracts expired to strike a new industry deal. With Wilson falling dramatically out of sync, packers that had shrewdly bargained together since World War II were suddenly faced with the prospect of being strangled by their own collective weight.

The tumult hit close to Austin. Just twenty-five miles to the west in Albert Lea, Wilson operated an old brick slaughterhouse on Main Street that employed 1,350 union workers. Like their Austin colleagues, the Wilson workers were covered by the master agreement. Until the wage cut, they helped make Austin and Albert Lea into twin towns, Big 9 Conference archrivals in high school sports that shared the call letters of the local radio and TV stations KAAL and owed their economic prosperity to unglamorous pigstickers. Call them what you want, but packinghouse workers earned good money, bought nice houses and new cars, and owned summer cabins at French Lake near Faribault and on Lake Pepin on the Mississippi River. It was blue-collar work at white-collar pay, which created a social stigma that drew both scorn and admiration from neighbors. But the meatcutters worked hard, they played hard, and they paid their bills on time—an increasingly rare trait among neighboring towns in the Farm Belt.

Their employers were another story, however. The multistory Wilson plant was more than sixty years old and falling apart, a brick patchwork much like the Austin plant ten years earlier. Rumors of its closing circulated every time a union member spotted a company truck fitted with retreads instead of new tires. Business decisions were made a thousand miles away in Oklahoma City by a management team with less than two years of corporate independence. By contrast, the sleek one-story Hormel plant had yet to hit full stride. It was the industry's future, loaded with robotics and cost-saving new technology. There was a sense of local control, too, because executives and common laborers went to the same churches every Sunday in Austin. Hormel still had the feel of a proud little hometown packer, where most stockholders lived within a fifty-mile radius of the rusted basketball hoop outside CEO Dick Knowlton's house.

Those differences help explain why few people in Austin anticipated a repeat of Wilson's troubles at Hormel. Why should anyone worry? Hormel was turning steady, albeit modest, profits compared with other food companies. It paid workers top wages and employed them in renovated modern plants that defied the industry's aged condition. But it did have high labor costs, at least relative to its competition. When board members reviewed earnings reports, they were perplexed by consistent losses in Hormel's slaughtering operations, where hogs were killed and carcasses sliced into primal cuts. This was where the work was most labor-intensive and profit margins were the narrowest—or negative. Even though union wages hadn't budged since 1981, low-cost, frequently nonunion plants were killing hogs for 50 percent less than Hormel. Hormel sold only about 30 percent of its slaughtered pork to other customers, keeping the rest for its own canning and processing lines. But what it sold on the market, it sold at a loss, which had to be made up on the profits from processed meats. And as for the pork it retained for its own processing lines, it could buy the same meat for less from other packers. But that raised quality concerns, and Hormel was proud that it retained full control of meat quality from slaughter to sandwich.

But now the biggest packer in the country was cutting wages, further, destroying any equilibrium established by the 1981 wage freeze. The week after Wilson filed for bankruptcy, Knowlton drafted a letter and distributed it through the Austin plant, reminding workers of the need to cut costs and improve productivity. The letter included no specific mention of wage cuts, but Knowlton admitted at the time that the issue would have to be dealt with soon in Austin, let alone company-wide. The last time Hormel faced low-cost competition had been in the beef business, but rather than fight the growing low-wage presence of IBP, Hormel had simply quit slaughtering cows in 1976. This time would be different. Hormel had closed unprofitable pork-slaughtering plants in Fort Dodge, Iowa, and Mitchell, South Dakota. That left three big slaughtering facilities in Austin, Fremont,

Nebraska, and Ottumwa, Iowa, with another eleven processing plants and fifteen distribution facilities to bring dozens of products to millions of consumers every year. What's more, eleven plants had been refurbished or rebuilt in the past fourteen years, a sign, as sure as the ceramic hog figurines sprinkled about Knowlton's plain office in the corporate headquarters, that Hormel was in the pork business to stay.

Knowlton figured Wilson all but made his case that wage cuts were inevitable. But what he and others in Hormel management didn't fully understand at the time was that a growing faction within Local P-9, symbolized by Jim Guyette, was thinking exactly the opposite. They saw Hormel's healthy earning statements, and to judge by the faster work pace in their new surroundings, the profits seemed to be coming at their expense. They also felt their parent union had betrayed them by giving away too much to get the new plant built in Austin and advocating what they viewed as a wimpy, retrench-until-later approach during the 1981 contract talks. Far from thinking about taking a pay cut, which had never happened in Austin, these disgruntled workers figured it was time to stop giving in and move forward.

If management didn't see it, neither did Lewie Anderson, who had far more pressing matters to worry about. Six thousand Wilson workers, with a 40 percent wage cut shoved down their throats, appeared helpless to fight back. The UFCW filed lawsuits and brought unfair-labor-practice charges before the National Labor Relations Board (NLRB), seeking to force Wilson into restoring the master agreement. But those efforts stalled in court, leading the UFCW to try to negotiate a new wage and benefit package that, because of Wilson's industry dominance, would become the new standard for a national wage rate.

Talks, too, stalled, amid frequent reports of work slowdowns, growing absenteeism, and mounting tension at several Wilson plants. Five weeks after the bankruptcy filing, the UFCW led the workers on strike, the first against Wilson since 1959, in an attempt to force the company to bargain. The rest of the industry anxiously waited while the two sides met off and on for three and one-half weeks. They finally reached an agreement that put the new base wage at eight dollars an hour, a 25 percent rollback from the master agreement. When the new wage was combined with benefit cuts, a total package previously worth seventeen dollars an hour to the average Wilson worker had dropped to about thirteen dollars an hour.

The hit had been taken, and it took just four months for Wilson's biggest competitors to adjust. By September 1983 the $10.69 rate had fallen to $8 at Morrell and to $8.25 at Swift Independent Packing, after both firms threatened to close plants if workers refused the cuts. Armour was sold to ConAgra, which shut down thirteen plants on one Friday afternoon and reopened them the following week with nonunion workers earning $6 an hour. Iowa-based Rath Packing followed Wilson's lead into bankruptcy court. Oscar Mayer, the company most like Hormel in terms of its steady profitability and emphasis on high-margin, brand-name consumer products, initiated talks to cut wages as well.

Hormel should have been the least of Anderson's problems. Historically it followed behind in industry contract talks, always agreeing to abide by terms negotiated by the big packers and the union. Moreover, Hormel didn't fit the international's image of other packers: crumbling; poorly managed; raping workers in attempts to crush unions. Hormel paid top wages, reinvested profits into heavily unionized plants, provided modern places to work, and shared earnings with workers. In fact, some industry circles viewed Hormel as soft on labor, especially in Austin, which always seemed to fare a little better than other Hormel plants, which in turn paid better than the industry average. Whether it was the hometown influence or a carryover from Jay Hormel's legacy, there had to be a reason why there had never been a strike in Austin since 1933.

But Hormel was convinced that it could play follow-the-industry when things turned sour as well as when times were good. After hinting its intentions to P-9 Business Agent Dick Schaefer for several weeks that fall, Hormel told Local P-9 leaders in mid-October 1983 that it planned to cut wages and benefits at the end of the month. The tool was a "me-too" clause in the laboriously negotiated 1978 contract which kept Hormel in Austin. The provision allowed Hormel to set new wage levels if three of five designated packers departed from the master agreement and established a new national pattern for wages and benefits.

Citing Wilson, Morrell, and Swift as having reduced wages to as low as $8 an hour, Hormel told union leaders to expect a wage reduction of up to 25 percent. There was no hint of bankruptcy, layoffs, or a plant shutdown in the air; Hormel reported earnings of $27.9 million that year, which meant another round of profit-sharing checks for workers at Thanksgiving. But Hormel was insistent on lowering wages. "The recent actions by major competitors," a company statement read, "have left the company no choice."

At one anxious meeting earlier in the fall Schaefer warned Hormel negotiators to postpone their demands until after December, when P-9 would elect a new president. Schaefer knew the rank and file were chafing under the pressures of the new plant. By adding more pressure for wage cuts before the election, Schaefer hinted, Hormel would embitter the membership even further and guarantee the election of Jim Guyette, who was aggressively campaigning against more concessions. But Schaefer couldn't seem to get the message across.

Schaefer called Anderson and his assistant, John Mancuso, to a special meeting of P-9's executive board on October 26. They reviewed the 1978 provision and took the position that it was intended to apply only to upward movement of wages and benefits. The board voted to submit the issue to arbitration if Hormel would defer making immediate cuts. That evening Anderson called Robert Gill, Hormel vice-president for labor relations, who agreed that the company would back off any wage and benefit reductions until an arbitrator ruled on the meaning of the me-too contract language.

While they differed sharply over Hormel's right to cut wages, company and union officials who negotiated the provision five years earlier agreed on this much: Nobody envisioned that it would come into play under a falling-wage scenario. Hormel and Local P-9 had always followed the national wage pattern, which, until the Wilson bankruptcy, meant bumping wages and benefits upward or abiding by industry-wide freezes. The me-too provision had emerged during negotiations over the new plant because Hormel wanted a guarantee of no strikes for three years following the opening of the plant. In return, P-9 wanted assurance that wages, riding double-digit inflation at the time, would remain commensurate with the master rate at other packers. The clause was crucial to rank-and-file approval because it gave rise to a widely held belief among workers that even though they couldn't strike, they would never have to take a pay cut.

The timing of Hormel's push for concessions, from Guyette's standpoint, couldn't have been better. That fall he announced his candidacy for P-9 president on a platform of no concessions. His disdain for Hormel and the international was no secret to those who knew him, and his stubborn stance appealed to others who were generally offended that a profitable company was sounding the alarm for concessions. Guyette had served an earlier stint on the executive board, but lost a bid for vice-president to John Anker, a moderate of Guyette's generation, in December 1982. But this time he had a hot issue playing to his strength and the endorsement of incumbent Floyd Lenoch, who thought that P-9 needed a president who would take on Hormel. Lewie Anderson knew vaguely that Guyette was running for the office. Had this been another union—one more tightly structured or facing fewer crises—he might have helped the moderates campaign against him. But Anderson was busy with other locals in real crisis—he was on the road eight out of twelve months in 1983— and he thought Guyette was just one of many young union members angry about wage cuts. Guyette beat Anker by a vote of 351 to 312.

Guyette was still getting acclimated to his new job when a Madison, Wisconsin, arbitrator named George Fleischli ruled on February 8, 1984, that the me-too provision applied to downward wage movement, thus giving Hormel the contractual right to reduce wages and benefits. But the company would have to wait because the new national wage pattern would not be established until adjustments were made at two Oscar Mayer plants. The ruling also gave Hormel the rare authority to recoup wages and benefits already paid to workers. It was an awkward position for the company to be in, Hormel personnel chief Bob Gill admitted at the time. Yet it symbolized Hormel's overpowering bargaining leverage as it headed into one of the most crucial negotiating years in its five decades of dealing with unions. Not only were P-9's seventeen hundred members in trouble, but since they represented one third of Hormel's union workers, their unusual wage battle had the potential to set a wage and benefit pattern for all Hormel workers at other company plants. And in the absence of efforts to negotiate for a better settlement in Austin, the Fleischli decision put P-9's fate and, implicitly, that of union workers company-wide, in the hands of Oscar Mayer workers in Davenport, Iowa, and Madison, Wisconsin, who were fighting concessions at the same time.

Fleischli's decision provided a reprieve for P-9, but little else. On Sunday, March 11, 1984, at a packed four-hour membership meeting at the Austin High School auditorium, UFCW attorney Robert Nichols from Chicago told workers that P-9's bargaining strength would only decline as Oscar Mayer moved closer to a settlement. Pure and simple, he said, the one uncertainty left for P-9 was when and how Hormel would adjust wages. Either wait for Oscar Mayer to settle and take what you get, Nichols advised the crowd, or negotiate a better deal with Hormel, keying on its above-average industry performance.

Anderson was hungry for the latter. He saw Hormel as a rare chance to start ratcheting wages upward after four brutal years of cutbacks. He figured the national wage rollback stopped between $8 and $8.50 an hour. With Hormel, which Anderson admitted was one of the best meat-packers in the business, the packing-house division had a good chance to cut a better deal and pull up workers at other companies as well. But it wouldn't be easy because of the arbitration ruling hanging over Austin. The big plant was Hormel's flagship, controlling 40 percent of its output and capable of slaughtering 1.5 million hogs a year. If wage rates suggested by Fleischli's decision were implemented in Austin, it would likely establish a wage ceiling for other locals in the Hormel chain, which were approaching a wage reopener in their contract on September 1. At a mid-March meeting of the Hormel chain in Chicago, Anderson implored Guyette to push hard for a better settlement.

By that time, however, Guyette and Anderson were staunch ideological opponents, and the rift in their philosophies about unionism edged closer to an open feud. Guyette, who spent his entire meat-packing career in Austin, had been critical of the international because of its willingness to grant concessions during the talks to build the new plant. Anderson had battle scars from

IBP, but when he took over as packinghouse director, concession bargaining was rampant. He first tangled with Guyette in 1980, while pushing a plan to merge P-9 with the Hormel local in Fort Dodge. A tentative agreement by union officers was rejected in a surprise vote by the rank and file, and Guyette's outspoken opposition was an important reason. Anderson told Guyette that he would live to regret that it had failed. As a P-9 board member in 1981 Guyette blasted Anderson's national retrenchment program for granting concessions before employers demanded them.

As president Guyette remained in the minority on his nine-member executive board, but it didn't stop him from showing flashes of defiance. He told the March 11 membership meeting that when the Hormel chain of union locals voted to hold exploratory talks with the company, he had voted against the move. He wrote letters pestering Anderson and Wynn about keeping the Hormel chain intact, particularly with UFCW Local 431, which represented about 820 workers at the Hormel slaughter plant in Ottumwa. With the international's approval, Local 431 had agreed to meet with company officials to discuss mid-contract concessions. Guyette claimed that the move violated the international constitution, and he feared that a settlement would erode the rest of the chain's bargaining position.

But Local 431 was under severe pressure to act fast. Hormel had just laid off 444 Ottumwa workers and shut down its rarely profitable slaughtering operations. Hormel Vice-President William Hunter said it had become more economical to buy slaughtered hogs from outside operators "with operating costs considerably less than ours." As much as Local 431 wanted to be part of the chain, its contract expired in the spring of 1984, seventeen months before the other locals' contracts. Guyette wanted Ottumwa to hold out so it could negotiate with seven other chain locals that faced wage reopeners on September 1. He envisioned common expiration dates in their contracts that would give the chain tremendous bargaining leverage and perhaps the ability to shut down Hormel with a strike.

Anderson viewed Ottumwa with mixed emotions. He was under strong pressure from rank-and-filers to cut a deal to get people back to work. But he also sensed that Hormel, having pushed for cuts in Austin, was probing for soft spots and now putting on the heat in Ottumwa. He knew he had a little time to work, since laid-off Ottumwa workers were getting unemployment benefits that eased the financial burden of losing jobs. However, he still had to move reasonably quickly before the layoffs worsened. Guyette's position of holding off until fall, he thought, was tantamount to letting the plant close. In early May Ottumwa workers rejected a company proposal of wage and benefit cuts. Hormel announced another 114 layoffs. Talks restarted, and by the end of the month workers had ratified a contract that trimmed wages by 21 percent, to $8.50, in exchange for the return of all laid-off workers. But the two-year agreement kept Ottumwa contractually out of sync with the rest of the chain because it expired on April 1, 1986. It was an international-style settlement—concessions for jobs—and Guyette saw it as a sellout.

With such a cutthroat bargaining environment shaping up, Anderson began positioning the Hormel chain for summer negotiations, recognizing that cutbacks were likely but confident that it could take advantage of the company's profitability to do better than at other packers. Guyette had his mind on other things. In the spring of 1984 he suggested to board members that P-9 make financial preparations for a strike and hire a public relations firm to tell P-9's side of the wage-cut issue. By mid-July, after getting no assistance from the international on his PR request, he discussed bringing in a New York labor consultant whom he had read about in *Business Week*, an organizer named Ray Rogers. However, P-9's executive board was skeptical of such a move without the international's support. Guyette wrote to Anderson, who steered the issue to Wynn, who said he would consider it if the Hormel chain gave its approval.

The chain consisted of eight local unions representing workers at nine Hormel plants: Charlotte, North Carolina; Atlanta, Georgia; Dallas, Texas; Beloit, Wisconsin; Fremont, Nebraska; Algona, Iowa; Knoxville and Ottumwa, Iowa (represented by the same local); and Austin. It had grown out of efforts by union workers in the late 1940's to keep each other informed as Hormel began expanding to other cities. During contract negotiations the chain sought to bargain collectively for common interests such as wages, vacations, and holidays and offer its clout in resolving particularly troublesome issues affecting isolated locals.

The heart of the chain was Austin, the biggest and most influential Hormel local and one of the strongest meat-packing unions in the country. The chain chairman in 1984 was P-9 Business Agent Dick Schaefer, an ally of Anderson's, who had been working for several years to negotiate common expiration dates and truly unite the chain's contracts. He knew it wouldn't happen this year because Ottumwa already had settled. And with the industry unraveling, it would be enough of a battle just to keep Austin in line, especially with the arbitration ruling threatening to undermine negotiations for everybody.

Chain negotiations intensified in August as the September 1 wage reopener approached, but both sides kept a close watch on talks at Oscar Mayer plants in Davenport and Madison. If those plants settled, Hormel could implement sharp cuts in Austin, and the chain would be in big trouble trying to negotiate something better. Just as important, no one knew whether P-9 could legally go on strike if the chain sought to shut down the company for added bargaining pressure. Guyette, who had seemed anxious to discuss a strike earlier in the year, had told chain members at a meeting in July that he couldn't say whether Austin could strike with them. The wage reopener in the 1981 contract gave the locals the right to strike on September 1. But another provision in Austin's new-plant agreement of 1978—the multiyear guarantee of labor peace—indicated that P-9 was obligated to keep working until 1985. Without a shutdown in Austin, which was capable of producing almost every food item Hormel sold, most notably Spam, a strike by the rest of the chain locals would lack much needed clout and solidarity. Anderson knew Austin's right to strike fell into a gray area, but Guyette had portrayed himself as a militant concession fighter. At a chain meeting in August, Lewie asked Guyette if he was willing to take the contractual risk and strengthen the chain. Hormel was now dangling a seven-dollar-an-hour wage proposal before the chain, and Lewie demanded a commitment from Guyette to strengthen the chain's hand in confronting Hormel. There was an element of risk in Anderson's strategy, but he thought it was worth a try. If it worked, he thought, the UFCW had Hormel cornered. But Guyette wasn't interested.

The August chain meeting, at a Ramada Inn in Omaha, Nebraska, featured one other surprising development that threatened to derail the chain's bargaining power even further. Guyette and P-9 board member Floyd Lenoch told the chain that they would rather have P-9 take its chances on the Fleischli arbitration ruling than negotiate a settlement granting wage cuts to Hormel. The announcement fitted Guyette's election promise of never granting concessions, but it stunned other chain members, who felt confident that they could negotiate a much better deal than the arbitrator would give them—if they had P-9's support. Without P-9, they faced the strong possibility that Hormel would try to force those arbitration terms on their members. Despite the disagreement, the chain agreed to keep P-9 in the chain negotiations, with a provision that an Austin vote on any tentative agreement would be tallied separately from the rest of the chain, which voted as a block.

The strategies became clear in late August, during three days of chain meetings at the Airport Hilton in Des Moines, Iowa. With locals in Ottumwa and Houston (not a member of the chain) already settled, the seven chain locals voted to negotiate not only on wages but on benefits as well. Guyette voted against the move in a minority dissent. Hormel, after making an initial offer of $6.50 an hour when the talks focused on wages alone, proposed a base hourly wage of $8.75, with reductions in premiums paid for night shift work and the elimination of two paid holidays. In addition, Hormel told P-9 negotiators that if the proposal failed in Austin, the company would implement cuts under the arbitration ruling. The Oscar Mayer plants in Davenport and Madison had reached tentative settlements, and it appeared likely that because of those agreements, the wage rate in Austin could fall as low as $8.25 an hour. Under that cloud, on Saturday, August 25, leaders of each of the chain locals solemnly reported to the UFCW that they would "reluctantly present the proposal for ratification to the people," according to minutes of the meeting.

Guyette seemed unfazed by the gloomy prospects. Shortly before the locals announced their intentions, he proposed that Rogers address a chain meeting in October to present his ideas on corporate campaigns. The motion was defeated, but it marked a curious trait about Guyette that would surface throughout his stint as P-9's charismatic president. His agenda—no wage cuts, no compromise—often seemed detached from the reality of events around him. The rank and file did not send him to meetings to bring back concessions. And as long as Hormel was making money, he wasn't about to do that. What his boyhood friends remembered as an unusually wide stubborn streak in such a quiet kid had become the passion of a labor leader who would let nothing diminish his principles.

The following Monday night the P-9 executive board reviewed Hormel's wage and benefit proposal at its regular meeting and voted, 6–2, to recommend it for approval by the rank and file. Voting in favor were Schaefer, Vice-President Anker, Financial Secretary Audrey Neumann, and board members Keith Judd, Kenny Kneeskern, and Ward Halvorson. They did so because they felt it was the best they could negotiate against the very real possibility of a much worse fate under the arbitration ruling. Opposed were former P-9 President Lenoch and board member Jim Retterath. Like Guyette, who as president did not vote, they couldn't see the logic of concessions from hardworking employees when Hormel wasn't really hurting.

Two days later Guyette presented the proposal in a membership meeting as rank-and-filers pored over their own copies, along with a comparison sheet that had appeared in *The Unionist* and a summary of how the company could implement the Fleischli decision. By all accounts, Guyette tore into the proposal, casting it in negative terms and castigating Hormel for its ruthless attack on workers. His supporters in the crowd hooted and cheered as board members who had endorsed the proposal squirmed uncomfortably in their seats. In a board meeting three weeks later they sharply rebuked Guyette for "not giving accurate and sufficient information" about the proposal. Guyette defended his actions, saying he felt both sides had been presented. Had they criticized their president in front of the membership, the score might have been different, but probably not the outcome. On Friday, August 31, 1984, in a turnout that drew 85 percent of P-9's seventeen hundred members, the contract proposal was rejected by a 9–1 margin.

The rest of the chain rejected the proposal as well. Guyette seized on the defeat as a sign of rank-and-file opposition to the international's retrenchment program. But the other six locals had more leverage than Austin. They could strike, a prospect that

was not lost on Knowlton, who quickly ordered his labor negotiators to fashion a significantly better offer to avoid a massive
walkout. In Austin, Hormel announced that it would implement
new contract terms as soon as Oscar Mayer settled. Those settlements had been delayed because workers in Madison and Davenport had rejected the tentative contract and resumed negotiating.
Anderson laid out that scenario at a September 7 chain meeting
at the Holiday Inn O'Hare in Chicago, which turned into one of
the most pivotal and controversial episodes of the entire three-
year dispute.

During the meeting Guyette and Lenoch reiterated their earlier position that they would rather wait for Hormel to implement new wages and benefits than attempt a strike. Guyette said
a union attorney advised him that P-9 might not have the right to
strike over a wage reopener because of confusion caused by
overlapping contracts governing the new plant. Guyette and Anker said that P-9 wanted to be part of the chain but would not
interfere as the chain members tried to settle their contracts. Anderson concurred, adding that "Austin's problems are more complex than can be handled at this time," according to meeting
minutes. In short, P-9 and the rest of the chain parted ways. The
episode fractured forty years of chain bargaining and ignited the
most bitter intraunion feud in recent history. A November 1,
1984, letter authorized by chain members and drafted by Anderson pinned most of the blame for the split on Guyette. The letter
said that Guyette "informed the Chain that Local 9 was withdrawing" from the chain negotiations, citing its sticky problems with
the arbitration decision and its right to strike. But Guyette, in a
later court deposition, claimed that Anderson asked P-9 to step
aside because of its equivocation over the right to strike and that
he publicly congratulated the union for doing so.

Everyone still argues bitterly about who was to blame, but the
incident came back to haunt them all. In early October the six
remaining chain locals, after authorizing strikes, won an agreement with Hormel that paid workers nine dollars an hour as of
September 1, 1984, and ten dollars an hour on September 1,
1985. Anderson praised it as the best settlement in the industry
and promised to use it as a battering ram to move up wages
across the country. Indeed, it seemed that he was poised to get

the industry moving again, this time in favor of workers. Schaefer insisted that the same offer, including a common expiration date in September 1986, was available to P-9. Hormel's negotiators hinted broadly during the talks that P-9, too, could have the nine- and ten-dollar offer, and Knowlton told reporters that he never intended that the workers in Austin would earn less than their counterparts elsewhere. But the offer never was made formally because P-9 leaders made it clear to Hormel's chief labor negotiator, Dave Larson, that they wouldn't consider taking concessions while the company was making money.

Perplexed by P-9's intransigence, Hormel made good on its promise to implement wage cuts in Austin. On October 8, it reduced the hourly base pay to $8.25, amounting to a 23 percent pay cut from the $10.69 rate, which had survived longer in Austin than at any other slaughtering plant in the nation. Company officials did so almost reluctantly, still holding out hope that workers would realize there was a better offer out there. It wouldn't be the last time that Hormel found itself in the awkward position of taking more dramatic action against the union than clearly seemed warranted.

But P-9 was in turmoil. Guyette protested Hormel's move to implement the cuts. The union made plans for more arbitration. Vice-President John Anker submitted his resignation from the executive board in despair. With Guyette's supporters assuming control of the rank and file, Anker did not want to fight a minority battle from the board. He preferred to do it on the membership floor. His resignation was followed by that of Business Agent Schaefer, whose thirteen years of service failed to warrant even a retirement party. Pete Winkels, who got to know Guyette during the new-plant debate and whose sharp tongue was earning him his own reputation, ran for business agent in a special election and won. Lynn Huston, a 1982 hire who had campaigned for Guyette and helped with Guyette's petition drives, won the vice-presidency. Within a year, of the six board members who recommended Hormel's $8.75 offer, only Keith Judd remained on the board.

Sensing their time had come, Guyette supporters sent two petitions flying through the plant, one asking for a special meeting to hear from Ray Rogers, another to take a strike vote. The board refused to sanction Rogers's appearance but acknowledged Guyette's authority as president to push it through. The board also warned against taking a strike vote unless a walkout could be legally called. However, it had become clear that if Guyette couldn't get the support he wanted from the board, he could get what he wanted by turning to his aggressive rank-and-file supporters. Like Guyette, they had been waiting a long time to have their say.

On Sunday, October 7, just a month after Guyette had expressed uncertainty to chain members about joining a company-wide walk-out, P-9 members voted overwhelmingly to tell Hormel to remove perishables from the plant in preparation for a strike. Workers would report to work on a day-to-day basis. The executive board had the authority to call a strike, which could start by the end of the week. That drew a quick response from Hormel Vice-President Dave Larson, who labeled a strike illegal because of the union's three-year no-strike pledge in the new plant. Anderson had previously warned other chain members that UFCW attorneys also viewed such a strike as illegal and that workers would not honor a P-9 picket line unless it was sanctioned by the international.

Hamstrung by legalities, frustrated by the big wage cut, and unsure of how to respond, an understandably edgy P-9 membership filed into the Austin High School auditorium the following Sunday evening to get the pep talk of its life.

CHAPTER
5

The Austin High School auditorium is a great elegant barn, built in the mock-Gothic style of the 1920's with a soaring ceiling, row upon row of movie house seats, and a broad, deep balcony. On Sunday, October 14, 1984, it saw one of its greatest productions. Scores of P-9 wives paraded outside with placards reading WELCOME CORPORATE CAMPAIGN, while hundreds of meat-packers and their spouses poured inside, packing the auditorium to the walls.

About five-thirty a muscular man in blue jeans and with a clipped black mustache sprang to the lectern with a confident swagger. "I'm going to tell you some things this afternoon that you will not believe," he said in a gravelly Boston drawl. "You will not believe how far the tentacles of the Hormel Company reach. You will not believe the kind of corporate power structure that is lined up against you."

For the next two and a half hours Ray Rogers exhorted the crowd and showed slides describing what he called the corporate-financial power structure that governs American business. Big corporations can't operate without money, he told the curious listeners, and for money they turn to big banks and insurance companies. The arrangement gives corporations a secure source of funding to buy raw materials, build inventories, install new equipment, and erect new factories; it gives the banks a stream of interest income. Often the bank will have one of its executives sit on the board of directors of the client company to give advice and make sure the bank's money is well spent. If the client is particularly important and prestigious, one of its executives may sit on the bank's board of directors to give advice about other loans, the economic climate, and other operational decisions. Sometimes the bank even holds stock in the client company as the trustee of a pension fund. These companies and their banks develop long, historical relationships, sometimes covering several decades of mutual influence.

The secret to taking on your employer, Rogers said, is to find out who holds its purse strings. Tie a knot in the purse strings, he told the crowd, and your employer is powerless. Isolate its executives from their corporate counterparts, and they will run for cover. Expose the company's greed to its buying public, and the company will come to terms. This was the corporate campaign strategy: Wage proxy fights; launch boycotts; embarrass executives at their annual shareholder meetings; pressure their corporate allies; encourage negative publicity about the company's community image; withdraw savings accounts; hold giant rallies to mobilize the community behind you. Rogers showed a slide of a giant circle that represented Hormel. Around the circle were twenty-six arrows pointing at the circle. Each arrow represented some kind of pressure that P-9 could bring to bear: a local bank that might get nervous about handling payroll checks; a regional bank that might reconsider loans to Hormel; a foundation that owned Hormel stock and would be alarmed at the company's impact on the community. Rogers said he could develop a twenty-six-point program, a battle plan from A to Z, that would inexorably build pressure on Hormel's executives, step by step and month by month, until it brought them to their knees. The last step, if needed, was "total annihilation" of the company.

"Do you think these big finance and insurance companies are our friends?" he shouted.

"No!" the meat-packers shouted back.

"What was that?" Rogers yelled, a hand cupped to one ear and a smile spreading across his face.

"*No!*"

"I'm not sure if I heard everybody," he countered with a grin.

"NO!" they roared.

The meat-packers poured out of Austin High School that fall evening as if Austin had won the state high school basketball tournament. If Rogers had told them to rampage down Main Street smashing windows, one recalled later, they might have done it.

Privately, however, P-9 members had a variety of reactions. R. J. Bergstrom, an Austin native and Vietnam veteran whose older brother had worked in the packinghouse for years, had finally gotten a job there in September 1982. Now, just two years later, Hormel was trying to cut the good wages he'd expected to earn. A carpenter by trade, he had never worked in a factory before. But the other guys on his work gang were bitter, and he figured they must be right. The day after Hormel announced its intention to cut wages, his foreman in shipping had lectured the gang: Just because you're getting a wage cut doesn't mean you can slow down on the job. The next day R.J. staged a little protest: He showed up for work carrying a shotgun case. When the guards at the plant entrance made him open it, they found it full of submarine sandwiches and cans of soda pop. This was his lunch box, he explained. They told him to get another lunch box. A few days later R.J. showed up in the lunchroom in a new pair of coveralls plastered with bumper stickers reading HORMEL UNFAIR. If these little protests weren't getting the message across, R.J. figured, Ray Rogers seemed like the kind of guy who could. Rogers's fee for the campaign, $340,000, was a lot of money, but it worked out to just $200 for each P-9 member. Driving home to his house out west of town, R.J. figured that Hormel's proposed wage cut was going to cost him nearly $100 a week. If Rogers's campaign worked, it was paid for in just two weeks.

Larry Jensen listened to Rogers that afternoon and came away ambivalent. He was forty-four years old and had sixteen loyal years with Hormel. But he knew something had snapped in the move to the new plant. Instead of being treated as individuals worthy of respect, Jensen felt, workers were overlooked or ignored. The loss of incentive pay, coupled with the increase in line speeds, made veterans from the old plant feel they were working harder and for less money. The escrow bonus every payday made up for it financially, but not psychologically. In the old plant you could police yourself because of the bonus system, but now the company called all the shots. Like a teakettle warming on the stove, he said, pretty soon the plant was destined to boil over. Whether a labor consultant from New York could make the workers' lives any better, Jensen thought, who knows? He didn't pay much attention to Rogers. At least not right away. Like seventeen hundred other people, Jensen had to go to work Monday morning at a job that offered little time to sit back and unravel the interlocking financial structure of corporate America.

Union members weren't the only ones in Austin wondering about Rogers. Executives at Hormel's corporate office north of the interstate began pondering what Rogers's arrival meant and how to react. Chuck Nyberg, Hormel's vice-president for legal affairs, had never heard of Rogers, but he figured it was about time. The day P-9 announced Rogers's plans to come to Austin, Nyberg went into the legal department's research room, switched the computer terminal from LEXIS, the legal research system, to NEXIS, the general news research service. He typed "Ray Rogers," hit EXECUTE and watched as page after page of news stories from *The New York Times, Wall Street Journal, Business Week,* and a variety of other periodicals began dropping out of the machine. It made interesting reading.

The son of a machinist, Rogers had grown up in the blue-collar town of Beverly, Massachusetts. He was a conscientious objector in the mid-1960's and a sociology major at the University of Massachusetts. On graduating, he joined VISTA and worked as a community organizer among the poor in Appalachia. But he chafed under the bureaucracy of a federal agency; an energetic organizer with a headful of novel ideas about community mobilization and social change, he left to join the Amalgamated Clothing Workers of America.

It was with the clothing workers that Rogers would lay his claim to fame. The union represented thousands of workers in textile mills and men's apparel factories across North Carolina, South Carolina, Georgia, and Alabama. The work was dangerous—cotton dust is thought to cause various lung disorders—and low-paying—textile workers in the late 1970's were earning about five dollars an hour, or one third less than the average U.S. manufacturing employee. Still, organizing them was difficult.

Many were illiterate and couldn't read union leaflets. The mills were built in small towns, so if employees were fired, they had few other opportunities for work. And most of the southern states were so-called right-to-work states, which meant that even if a majority of workers in a plant voted for union representation, those who did not were under no obligation to join. Rogers had organized a successful boycott of the Farrah jean company by threatening area department stores with picketing and demonstrations, then playing one store against the other. It was a classic case of divide and conquer, and Rogers felt he was ready for bigger game. A giant among the textile firms—and one of the least unionized—was J. P. Stevens, maker of sheets, pillowcases, towels, and other household goods. J. P. Stevens had been a chief organizing target of the clothing workers since 1963, yet the company had never signed a union contract.

Staging a walkout against J. P. Stevens would be difficult because the company was far-flung, with roughly ninety plants in many states. The union decided on a campaign of financial pressure: boycotting the company but supplementing that traditional tactic by embarrassing it with its own financial practices and isolating it from its corporate allies. The union hired Rogers as a researcher out of its New York office. A little digging into Stevens's financial documents revealed that the company was a heavy borrower. Among its chief lenders were Manufacturers Hanover Trust of New York and the Metropolitan Life Insurance Company of New York. The union organized a series of demonstrations aimed at Manufacturers Hanover, including a showdown at the company's annual stockholders' meeting. In 1978 J. P. Stevens Chairman James D. Finley resigned from the Manufacturers Hanover board of directors, as did David W. Mitchell, chairman of Avon Products and a member of the Stevens board of directors.

The union didn't let up. It decided to go after Metropolitan Life, which held $111 million in loans to the textile manufacturer. The union hit upon a little-known feature of New York State law: Mutual insurance companies such as Metropolitan, whose policyholders are shareholders, must allow every policyholder to vote in elections for the board of directors. The union put up two of its own candidates for the Metropolitan board, forcing what would have been $9 million in expenses associated with a mail ballot. The three companies never acknowledged pressuring each other, but in 1980 J. P. Stevens finally signed its first labor contract with the union covering thirty-five hundred workers at twelve mills.

Rogers and a friend, Ed Allen, left the union and in 1981 set up their own consulting firm, Corporate Campaign, Inc., in New York City. The J. P. Stevens victory had generated national media coverage and sent ripples through the labor movement. It was a triumph on behalf of workers who needed help and a victory over a company that had successfully fought off unions for years. Rogers's name was featured prominently in several stories about the campaign, and business soon came to his door. That summer the Air Line Pilots Association hired him to draft a campaign against the Texas Air Corporation, the parent company of Texas International Airlines. With airline deregulation starting to open the nation's airways to newcomers, Texas Air had formed a new nonunion airline called New York Air, which the pilots claimed was an illegal runaway from their union contract. Rogers promptly launched a campaign to embarrass New York Air, Texas Air, and their owner, Frank Lorenzo. In 1982 a unit of the Oil, Chemical and Atomic Workers representing four thousand refinery workers in Port Arthur, Texas, hired him to launch a fight against Texaco in a pension dispute. That summer a local of the International Association of Machinists in Providence, Rhode Island, hired Rogers to try to put some punch into a long, bitter strike against Brown & Sharpe, a large machine tool manufacturer. And in December the Texas Building and Construction Trades Council hired Corporate Campaign to draft an organizing drive against Brown & Root, Inc., a giant Houston-based building contractor. Rogers would later work for the United Paperworkers' union in a dispute against the International Paper Company, for the International Typographical Union in Milwaukee, Wisconsin, for the Farm Labor Organizing Committee (FLOC), a union for migrant farm workers in Ohio, and for several other unions.

In many of the campaigns Rogers's "multidimensional" tactics seemed to work. Against International Paper, a giant landholder and user of natural resources, Rogers drafted a strategy that challenged the company's environmental practices. He stacked International Paper's annual meeting in April 1983 with demonstrators and dissident stockholders. In June International Paper signed a peace accord with the United Paperworkers that called for the company chairman, Edwin A. Gee, to meet twice a year with the union president, Wayne E. Glenn, and hash out labor-management problems. It also called for International Paper to renovate two old unionized mills instead of shutting them down. The company never disclosed the terms of the agreement and denied that Rogers's campaign had any effect. But the union's president insisted that Rogers's involvement was pivotal. (Rogers went to work for the paperworkers again in 1987, after a dispute over holiday pay led to strikes and lockouts at International Paper plants in four states. His boisterous tactics were popular with the strikers, but the strikers were still out of work more than a year later.)

Another happy ending came in Ohio, where FLOC had been trying since the mid-1970's to organize migrant farm workers and force truck farmers to provide fringe benefits and pay higher wages. The goal was to duplicate Cesar Chavez's accomplishments with the United Farm Workers in the grape and lettuce fields of California. FLOC already had hit on a novel pressure tactic: It went after the New Jersey-based Campbell Soup Company, which was the largest single customer of the cucumber and tomato farmers. FLOC had been trying since 1978 to get Campbell Soup and the growers to sign a three-way deal in which Campbell would agree to buy vegetables only from growers that had signed labor agreements improving conditions for FLOC's members. For several years the campaign seemed futile. Campbell Soup said the growers' labor policies were up to them. Even the AFL-CIO refused to support a Campbell Soup boycott because the company employed thousands of union members in canning factories. But by the early 1980's FLOC had begun to draw more support. Chavez helped it print handbills. Other unions began to help it raise money, even though the AFL-CIO officially opposed the effort. Rogers, too, lent his support, working for a token dollar a year. Corporate Campaign produced leaflets urging a boycott and pressuring two members of the Campbell board of directors. One was the chairman of the Prudential Insurance Company of New Jersey; the other, a director of the Equitable Life Assurance Society of New York. Rogers also organized busloads of farm workers to protest at the Campbell Soup annual meeting in New Jersey in November 1984. In February 1986 Campbell Soup and its subsidiary, Vlasic Foods, Inc., signed a three-way labor contract with twenty-four major vegetable growers and FLOC. It granted the farm workers wage increases, health insurance, and a forty-eight-hour grievance procedure, and it established committees to study pesticide use and other health issues. It's probably impossible to say how much Corporate Campaign contributed to the victory, but FLOC's leaders credited Rogers with opening their eyes to Campbell Soup's reach and for devising tactics against it.

But there also were cases where Rogers's strategies seemed impotent. Texaco refinery workers in Port Arthur, Texas, hired Rogers in the spring of 1982, three months into a strike over the company's proposal to change pension benefits. Rogers discovered that Texaco Chairman John K. McKinley sat on the board of directors of Manufacturers Hanover Trust. In April Rogers and the union took about two hundred demonstrators to the Manufacturers Hanover annual meeting in New York. The dissident shareholders stretched out the meeting for three hours with repeated questions about McKinley's fitness to sit on the bank's board. But Manufacturers Chairman John F. McGillicuddy came to his defense, and McKinley was easily reelected to the board. Rogers was undaunted, but in June the Oil, Chemical and Atomic Workers' union fired him, saying the campaign cost too much money.

The Air Line Pilots Association (ALPA), too, had second thoughts about Rogers. During the summer of 1981 he brought the union considerable press attention and generated considerable outrage in the labor movement toward Texas Air and New York Air. But in August 11,500 members of the Professional Air Traffic Controllers Organization (PATCO) went on strike and were fired by President Reagan. ALPA's more conservative members feared that the public would confuse them with PATCO; others felt that Rogers's tactics were needlessly confrontational and that they weren't seeing results. ALPA canceled Rogers's contract late that summer; New York Air was still nonunion. "Did he give us a lot of good exposure? Yes," ALPA spokesman John Mazor said at the time. "Did he make New York Air roll over? No."

One of the decade's classic labor showdowns began in October 1981 in North Kingstown, Rhode Island, when sixteen hundred machinists struck the Brown & Sharpe Manufacturing Company, the nation's largest and oldest machine tool maker. The union had won two earlier strikes, but this time Brown & Sharpe was proposing changes in the seniority system to make the plant more flexible and compete with the Japanese. And Brown & Sharpe was prepared. Its business was down, so it could afford to lose some production. It operated with supervisors and a few union members who crossed the picket line. Then it started hiring replacements. By June 1982, the plant was operating with nonunion help, the union's outlook was bleak, and local officers turned to Rogers. He held rallies to build the strikers' morale and issued a series of leaflets attacking Brown & Sharpe executives. He learned that Brown & Sharpe President Donald A. Roach sat on the board of directors of Rhode Island Hospital Trust National Bank, which held 17.5 percent of Brown & Sharpe stock. He pressured other bank officers to remove Roach from the board. He also went after U.S. Senator John H. Chafee, a Rhode Island Republican and a second cousin of the company chairman, Henry D. Sharpe. Meanwhile, Rhode Island unions and pension boards pulled more than $30 million in deposits or pension funds from the bank. But Rogers never quite won the confidence of top officers of the parent union, the International Association of Machinists (IAM). On August 18, the day Rogers planned to announce a wider front against business associates of Brown & Sharpe, the IAM announced that it was terminating his contract. The IAM said that it had paid Rogers more than $112,000 for two months' work and that after eight weeks his campaign was running out of steam. Local IAM officers had high praise for Rogers, but they, too, recognized that victory was not imminent.

"Like anything else, money talks," said Robert Thayer, a district officer of the IAM in Rhode Island. "But the working people in Rhode Island aren't all that affluent; you don't have all that much money in the bank. After a while a campaign like this begins to lose momentum."

Back in Austin, Minnesota, Jim Guyette had read about Rogers in *Business Week* magazine in the spring of 1984, a few months after becoming president of P-9. He was looking for public relations help to counter Hormel's proposed wage cut. He shopped around Austin, checking for ideas with schools, the local radio station, and others in town. A plea to the UFCW went nowhere, leaving Guyette convinced that his parent union would not give him the kind of support he wanted. Guyette called Rogers in New York and explained how angry his members were and what an injustice was being done. Rogers said he wanted to make three things clear. One, he didn't run publicity campaigns. He conducted multifaceted campaigns to bring all kinds of pressure on an employer. Two, he didn't eat meat. Did that disqualify him to represent meat-packers? Three, he wanted a pledge from Guyette's members that they would never allow cruelty to the hogs entering the Austin abattoir. Guyette said thanks, he'd think it over.

Rogers hung up and told his partner, Ed Allen: "We'll never hear from that guy again."

Rogers couldn't have been more wrong. Guyette liked what he heard and was ready to hire Corporate Campaign, Inc., almost immediately. But at that point he lacked a majority of votes on P-9's executive board. Business Agent Dick Schaefer was highly skeptical of Guyette's independent ways. Other members, such as John Anker, Keith Judd, and Ward Halvorson, were hardly about to proceed with any strategy without the international's support. So Guyette went straight to the membership. He enlisted Lynn Huston, one of the "new kids" and by now a Guyette confidant, to circulate a petition through the plant to bring the question up at a membership meeting. The members approved an invitation that led to the October rally.

Lewie Anderson and the rest of the leadership at UFCW headquarters in Washington were no strangers to Rogers's record. And they were as suspicious of him as he was contemptuous of them. Large international unions engender the kind of organizational loyalty among their officers and staff that large corporations build among ambitious executives. As democratic and highly political organizations, unions probably brook more dissent than the corporations, with their autocratic structures. But for reasons of solidarity, organizational self-defense, and perhaps career advancement, staff officers typically sign on with the direction established by the leadership. They don't blow their own horns to outsiders, and they give credit to their superiors. Rogers didn't work that way. He was openly critical of organizing strategies of large unions. He made a specialty of attracting the news media, writing compelling press releases, staging dramatic rallies, and giving companies and unions tongue-lashings tailor-made for a reporter's notebook or a ten-second television news bite. Anderson had other reasons to be skeptical. Rogers had never negotiated a packinghouse contract or even seen the inside of a packing plant. When the old packinghouses were being boarded up in Iowa, Nebraska, and South Dakota, Rogers was in Massachusetts or Virginia or New York. Rogers had never sat across the bargaining table from Dave Larson, Hormel's vice-president for industrial relations. He didn't know the pride and earnestness of Hormel's management, which was accustomed to the kind of midwestern small-town reverence that made image bashing almost tantamount to swearing in church.

Anderson also knew that Rogers already was attracting tremendous attention from the press. Television stations in Minneapolis and St. Paul had covered his October rally in Austin. Twin Cities newspapers were starting to write long Sunday features about trouble shaping up in southern Minnesota. William Serrin, *The New York Times'* respected labor reporter, had been to Austin and written about the unusual showdown shaping up on the prairie. Barbara Kopple, a well-known filmmaker who won an Oscar in 1976 for *Harlan County, U.S.A.,* a documentary about coal miners, was making a new film about meat-packing and spending enormous amounts of time in Austin. The UFCW leaders didn't waste much time in putting out the word on Rogers. They alerted reporters to the disastrous outcome at Brown & Sharpe and to the bitterness left there among IAM officers. They pointed out that five years after the clothing workers' victory at J. P. Stevens, some of those plants were going nonunion again. By the time Rogers returned to Austin for a second rally on December 9 to lay out his Hormel strategy, Guyette's opponents in Austin were calling the New Yorker "a high-priced cheerleader."

Rogers had a more sympathetic ear in the UFCW's executive vice-president, a Harvard Law graduate named Jay Foreman. In the fall of 1981, after hearing of Rogers's successes with other unions, Foreman met with him and pledged fifty thousand dollars of UFCW money to help develop a battle against the New York insurance industry's support of nonunion employers. Foreman met again with Rogers in mid-October 1984, when he came to the UFCW's Washington office to discuss the P-9 situation with Guyette, Huston, and other international officials, including Bill Wynn. With Foreman's help, they succeeded in arranging meetings for Rogers to present his plan to the UFCW's National Packinghouse Committee, a group of select union local chiefs from around the country.

On December 20 the twenty-five-member committee met in Chicago to hear from Guyette and Rogers on the proposed campaign. They were unimpressed. "They're picking the wrong target at the wrong time," Anderson told reporters after he emerged from the meeting. Rogers and Guyette insisted that the UFCW had given them only a cursory hearing, and they were right. The committee was handpicked by Anderson, and it used the occasion not only to debunk Rogers's plan but also to announce a campaign of its own against ConAgra, which operated several Armour plants without unions. While the committee purported to have approved the Armour plan that day, Anderson's staff had already printed up anti-Armour signs, which were displayed at a press conference just minutes after the meeting. The signs tainted the committee's action on P-9's plan and served to erode further the UFCW's credibility in Austin. Asked why the UFCW couldn't support simultaneous campaigns against Hormel and ConAgra, Anderson replied that it couldn't confuse the public with a two-front war. True enough, but in light of his national strategy of helping low-paid workers, it was unlikely that any amount of persuasion in Chicago would have brought the UFCW behind the campaign at Hormel.

What Anderson and the others didn't understand was that they were all but doing Ray Rogers a favor. In *Rules for Radicals,* a 1971 book that has served as an organizer's bible and a volume familiar to Rogers, Saul Alinsky wrote that the organizer can win the trust and energy of a discouraged underdog by making sure that he is personally attacked by large establishment organizations. Alinsky described one incident when he was invited to organize poor black residents of Rochester, New York, after a race riot in 1964. He criticized white churches and the liberal community before he arrived, producing outraged editorials in the major newspapers—and guaranteeing support among blacks. "The job of the organizer is to maneuver and bait the establishment so that it will publicly attack him as a 'dangerous enemy.' The word 'enemy' is sufficient to put the organizer on the side of the people," Alinsky wrote.

In fact, back in Austin Rogers was already well on the way into the hearts of P-9. True, his fees raised a lot of eyebrows among midwesterners, who had a hundred years of skepticism about sending their money off to distant institutions on the East Coast. He already had received $40,000 for a feasibility study on the Hormel campaign. Now he wanted $20,000 a month for six months of campaign work, plus a $180,000 war chest for campaign expenses. In addition, his proposal called for a $200,000 bonus if the campaign succeeded in reversing Hormel's wage cut. The bonus provision (which Rogers never collected) drew howls from the corporate office and the UFCW, which seized on it as evidence that only Rogers would emerge victorious from a fight in Austin.

But for their money, the meat-packers were getting both a coach and a cheerleader. Rogers had important contacts: He knew reporters at *The New York Times* and the television networks. He had valuable skills: culling information from corporate financial statements and documents filed with the Securities and Exchange Commission; writing irresistible press releases; organizing phone banks; and staging crack demonstrations. Behind him in Corporate Campaign's headquarters in Manhattan was a staff of ten.

Yet for all his credentials, Rogers was just a regular guy. To anyone who saw him wearing the same old blue jeans and velour sweat shirts day after day, sleeping in union members' spare bedrooms, and driving a rented Chevrolet, it was clear that this man didn't seek material gain. His pert smile, black mustache, and friendly swagger became familiar around the Austin Labor Center. He was something of a curiosity—a vegetarian who struggled to find something to eat on the meaty menus of Austin restaurants; a confirmed East Coast native who shuddered at the prospect of a Minnesota winter. But those quirks, along with his naive questions about the customs of the Midwest, appealed to the neighborly instincts of union members who were intrigued by their charming visitor. He told marvelous stories about tweaking the establishment, like the time he applied for conscientious objector status and appeared before the draft board wearing his uniform from a part-time job as a security guard. Somebody on the draft board wanted to know how a nonviolent young man could carry a gun. "Bang," Rogers said, pulling the cap gun from its holster. He talked with anybody, sympathized with everybody, and gave off an extraordinary confidence that he knew secrets to make Hormel and its supporters tremble. He wasn't afraid to rankle the establishment. It was as if someone had sent a savior—an unpretentious man of the people who nonetheless had mysterious powers that could topple Hormel.

He wasn't afraid to take on big odds. As a boy, he told reporters, he used to get picked on by the big kid on the block. So he went home and started lifting weights until he could whip the bigger boy. "The one who wins is the one who takes on the bully," Rogers would say. Lifting weights was a habit that stayed with Rogers into adulthood, and so was taking on big guys. "We're going to kick the living hell out of this company," Rogers told his new clients in Austin. "Those poor guys won't know what hit them."

103

CHAPTER
6

The bank clock-thermometer jutting out over Main Street in downtown Austin blinked "−32" as Ray Rogers drove past on his way to the Austin Labor Center. Rogers blinked back to make sure he wasn't seeing things. It was Saturday morning, January 19, 1985, the official kickoff for corporate campaign, the day for P-9 members to launch their publicity battle against Hormel with a door-to-door leafleting effort to each of Austin's ninety-one hundred households. A bitter wind whipped off the fields around Austin and down Main Street. The sidewalks were crusted with snow and ice. Rogers thought it was the coldest day he had ever experienced. "Ed, we're dead," the usually upbeat Rogers told his bearded partner, Ed Allen, as they neared the hall. Forget the fired-up crowds and enthusiasm they had witnessed at the high school rallies in October and December. Nobody's crazy enough to go outside in this kind of weather, he thought. Rogers himself was outfitted for something more like a spring track meet, sporting sweat pants and a fleece-lined denim jacket. He would consider it a victory if he made it a few yards from his parked car to the Fourth Avenue door of the union hall without winding up in an emergency room with a case of frostbite. And he was asking small-town midwestern people whom he had barely met to spend several hours running all over town.

Much to their surprise, when Rogers and Allen stepped into

the lobby of the hall, there were ninety to a hundred men and women waiting for them, bundled up in parkas, snowmobile suits, wool caps, scarves, and gloves. Rogers smiled approvingly. The union members, eyeing their thinly clad guests, smiled back. They quickly outfitted them with long underwear and heavy boots and got to work.

For all its hype as labor's can't-miss weapon of the 1980's, however, the campaign began more like a cancer fund raiser. Taking stacks of leaflets and copies of a special issue of *The Unionist* prepared at Rogers's direction, the men and women took off in cars and fanned out across town. House to house they went across the snowy neighborhoods, stuffing storm doors and mailboxes with the story of a meanspirited 23 percent wage cut imposed by the town sugar daddy on seventeen hundred workers. With the weather and the turnout, they hurried through and finished within a few hours. It was that simple. The P-9 corporate campaign was in business.

Campaign headquarters was the union hall, a low brick building with a big blue sign reading AUSTIN LABOR CENTER. It sat four blocks east of Main Street, neighbors on Fourth Avenue with a music shop, a dormant Art Deco movie theater, and the Tender Maid Hamburger counter. It sat midway between downtown and the site of the old packinghouse a few hundred yards north across the Cedar River. Before Jim Guyette took office, the hall was a pretty quiet place. The president and the business agent had two plain offices there, and Audrey Neumann, the financial secretary, kept the books and presided behind a blond-pine counter at the front. Two other smaller unions in town were also officed there. Workers might drop in to chat briefly about a problem in the plant with Business Agent Dick Schaefer, and there always seemed to be problems. But apathy far outweighed involvement, a sign of the good times that the union had enjoyed after World War II. It was rare that monthly membership meetings drew a quorum of fifty people. Without a hot issue—a contract proposal, for example—the Austin Labor Center was just another building front in town that went about its business from eight to four-thirty during the week and closed up for the weekends.

Since Rogers's arrival, however, the hall had been transformed into a beehive of activity. A visitor could usually find P-9 members or their wives milling about in the front lobby, sipping coffee and trading gossip. A few steps to the right was a long hall running toward the back of the building. Down its right side a series of doors led to offices for Local P-9's executives, the titles written in black lettering on the light pinewood, doors that were constantly opening and shutting as union officers and volunteers popped in and out for meetings and informal conferences. A door on the left side of this hallway opened into a large conference room that Rogers had dubbed the War Room, which served as the campaign's nerve center in those early days. Inside, its walls were papered with signs and maps targeting Hormel and First Bank locations. Here were long phone lists, an archive for leaflets, and big caricatures of Hormel Chairman Richard Knowlton. Neat rows of folding tables were covered with telephones, mailing lists, stacks of leaflets, and envelopes.

The offices across the hall were occupied by P-9's three top leaders: President Guyette, Vice-President Lynn Huston, and Business Agent Pete Winkels. Seldom were all three there at the same time, and as the campaign wore on, it was common to see almost anyone, from executive board members to volunteers, popping in and out of the offices, picking up ringing phones, holding mini-meetings, reviewing copy for leaflets, and chartering buses for leafleting in other cities. If they weren't giving interviews, reading the paper, or mulling over mail from the company, there was always a rumor or two to shoot the breeze about.

Historically the president and business agent were the union's most powerful duo; both were granted leaves from the plant to work full time on union business. Huston still worked as a mechanic in the plant, while Neumann, who began as a union secretary in 1947, handled mostly financial and bookkeeping tasks and took minutes at meetings. Until the new plant was built, the trust between Hormel and Local 9 was such that Neumann took minutes for both sides during meetings on grievances and seniority issues. Guyette usually could be found behind an old gunmetal gray steel desk in his office, a simple room with a couple of file cabinets, a few chairs, and a reproduction of an engraving of an Indian chief, with the inscription "To Give Dignity to a Man Is Above All Things." When Guyette was in, as he usually was in the early days of the campaign, there were always one or two rank-and-file members leaning against the doorjamb, waiting for a moment with him. Winkels's office, like Pete himself, was an unpredictable jumble, often crowded with half a dozen executive board members, volunteers, wives, retirees, the air thick with cigarette smoke and strategy. The desk itself might be occupied by almost anyone from a rank-and-file volunteer to Pete's son Jeremy.

The left half of the Labor Center was divided primarily into two areas. One was a large square room to the left of the front lobby, a sort of arsenal stacked with freshly painted picket signs and smelling of spray paint from the banners strung out to dry on folding chairs: CRAM YOUR SPAM; YOU SAY GIVE BACK, WE SAY FIGHT BACK. A few steps toward the rear of the building was a double door leading into the union hall's meeting room, a miniature auditorium with a low stage at the front. Signs, banners, and union slogans were draped on the walls alongside an American flag. A small podium stood before rows of folding chairs. When the room was full, it could accommodate perhaps five hundred to six hundred people. Usually that was more than enough to handle union business meetings. Once the campaign began, however, the room often overflowed.

In the beginning the campaign's most visible forces were the earnest P-9 supporters, a hard core of two hundred to three hundred members who became known as blue caps because they could be counted on to wear blue "P-9 Proud" hats. Though many were like Guyette, with fifteen to twenty years in the union, they also included grizzled veterans who had started under Jay Hormel and brand-new hires who'd never known the old plant. They were united by a series of 8½-by-11-inch leaflets featuring caricatures that expressed the main theme of the P-9 battle. The first leaflets to hit the street took aim at Knowlton and DeWalt H. Ankeny, Jr., president of First Bank System in Minneapolis. Side by side they appeared in ridiculous caricature, cast as ruthless power brokers determined to crush the working class in their never-ending drive to fill the corporate coffers. In clear, forceful prose the leaflets portrayed Hormel and First Bank as twin powers of evil, connected by bank ownership of Hormel stock, a long-term lending relationship, and interlocking directorships; Knowlton sat on First Bank's board, while Ankeny was a member of Hormel's. Put the pressure on First Bank and Hormel will drop to its knees, the logic went. There was absolutely no reason for wage cuts, they argued, because Hormel was making millions of dollars a year and workers in the highly productive Austin plant could take the credit. They pointed out that Knowlton's salary of $339,000, presumably the largest in Austin, did not include a 23 percent cut. If the cuts were permitted to stand, all of Austin would suffer because P-9ers would have less money to spend on groceries, clothes, and cars. Main Street businesses would have to cut back, by either laying off employees or dropping their wages substantially. At the bottom of each leaflet was a coupon asking for "support" of P-9 workers in their fight to restore their wages. There was no explicit mention of money, no dollar amounts to fill in, but the implication seemed as clear as the attached envelope.

Going door to door, working the phones, stuffing envelopes—it was grunt work, but that's what laying the foundation was all about, Rogers told the troops. Nobody said it would be easy, and considering how deeply Hormel's tentacles reached, he warned, P-9 would have to dig in and fight like never before. This was step one, the first D day of his three-part plan to win back the $10.69 wage rate. In dozens of cities in Minnesota, Iowa, Nebraska, and South Dakota, wherever Hormel had plants or First Bank had banks, P-9ers would pass out leaflets to rally worker and community support. They would demonstrate outside Hormel's annual meeting later in the month, while those owning stock challenged management on its labor relations policies. Around Austin they would tack up wanted posters bearing caricatures of Knowlton and Ankeny. Workers would circulate copies of *The Unionist,* which decried the "cold cuts" caused by Knowlton and Ankeny and the Hormel-First Bank connection.

Step two would begin in late March, when union members would start picketing at First Bank outlets, handing out bumper stickers and leaflets. Rogers stopped short, or so it seemed, of calling for a boycott of First Bank, which could be interpreted by the National Labor Relations Board as an illegal secondary boycott. Rogers simply boasted that the campaign would give First Bank enormous amounts of "free publicity" that would help people understand that every dime they deposited in the bank was being used to undermine the labor movement.

The third and final step was planned for late April, when workers were hoping an arbitrator would award them the right to strike and make hundreds of workers available to heat up the campaign against the bank. Each union member was encouraged to buy a share of First Bank stock, then drive in a several-hundred-car caravan to the bank holding company's annual meeting on April 24 in St. Paul. It was there, Rogers said in a widely published story in the Des Moines *Register,* that workers would "kick the living hell" out of the bank.

On the whole, it was an appealing program, and for many workers it was kind of fun, certainly worth the effort if it could bring about a change in attitudes inside the packinghouse. But first the meat-packers had to convince their own neighbors. The battle for Austin's loyalties had been brewing since Rogers's arrival in October and gave a subtle preview of what was to come in the months ahead. With little fanfare, hand-lettered signs proclaiming WE SUPPORT P-9 began popping up in storefronts on Main Street. They were the work of about three hundred wives of Hormel workers, who had banded together informally to ask merchants to display signs as part of a morale-building campaign. While their work seemed innocuous at first, the wives and the subsequent involvement of Hormel retirees were to assume tremendous importance in perpetuating the campaign by drawing entire families into the fight. Every Thursday, which was payday, a handful of wives picketed outside the plant's north gates, sporting pig noses and signs proclaiming AUSTIN CAN'T SURVIVE $8.25; STUFF YOUR FRANKS, CRAM THE SPAM; and FIRST BANK + HORMEL = CORPORATE GREED. In rain or freezing cold they cheered and waved to workers as they streamed into the parking lot in the morning. Since the gates were a stone's throw off the downtown freeway exit to Austin, there also was plenty of city traffic passing by during the day, and it didn't take long for word to spread through town that the P-9 wives were up to something different. Unlike their mothers, who seldom even saw a paycheck because their husbands feared they would tell the whole town how much money they made, these women were eager strategists who wanted to fight back, sometimes with more spunk than their husbands.

The campaign also called for enlisting outside support from other unions and community groups, and within days of the January kickoff, P-9ers were taking their leaflets a short drive down the freeway to the gates of the Farmstead plant (formerly owned by Wilson Foods) in Albert Lea. They also called on union supporters from the Twin Cities, where they quickly found allies among a diverse handful of young union activists who had banded together during a packinghouse strike in South St. Paul the year before. The campaign also called on steelworkers nearly three hundred miles to the north in Duluth and the economically depressed and heavily unionized Iron Range in northeastern Minnesota. The whole idea was to spread the word that workers were under attack in Austin and that unlike the rest of the industry, P-9 was going to fight back.

But Ray Rogers wasn't the only one plotting strategy in Austin in late 1984 and early 1985. Ever since the October day when he first heard Rogers was coming to town, Chuck Nyberg knew that Hormel had to take the organizer seriously. Nyberg, a lawyer with a fatherly face and grandfatherly voice, had spent his whole career at the Hormel office in Austin. He had grown up in a small Minnesota town near the North Dakota border, attended the University of Minnesota Law School, and gone to work for Hormel in 1959. But he was no provincial and no hick. As Hormel's top labor lawyer he had butted heads with the gruffest negotiators in a gruff union. As an activist in the Minnesota Association of Commerce and Industry, the state's leading business lobby, he had grown deft at political matters as well and knew his way around at the State Capitol in St. Paul.

As he studied all those articles about Corporate Campaign, Nyberg became convinced that Rogers could be beaten at his own game. True, Manufacturers Hanover Trust had yielded to Rogers's pressure in the J. P. Stevens campaign. But then Manufacturers Hanover made money managing huge union pension funds. The Metropolitan Life Insurance Company of New York had yielded because of an unusual state law regulating mutual insurance companies. But Seamen's Bank of New York, another J. P. Stevens lender, had simply said no to the clothing workers' union and waited out the storm. And that was a fight where all of organized labor was behind Rogers. Where the international unions lost faith, as with the airline pilots, or where they downright opposed him, as with the machinists at Brown & Sharpe, Rogers's track record was much weaker.

Moreover, there was a mixed track record in several other corporate-type campaigns to which Rogers had not been a party. (Rogers had no monopoly on corporate campaigns, although he had filed that fall for a trademark on the phrase. A Washington, D.C., public relations firm that had many union clients, the Kamber Group, challenged Rogers's application, and the suit was eventually settled out of court.) Since roughly 1980 several of the nation's biggest unions had applied similar tactics against several of the nation's biggest corporations. In January 1983, for example, the UFCW and the Service Employees International Union, which represented eight hundred thousand health care and maintenance workers, launched a simultaneous organizing drive and corporate campaign against California-based Beverly Enterprises, the nation's largest nursing home operator. The unions released a detailed study of Beverly's health care record and promised to work for tighter state and federal regulations on the nursing home industry. It asked Beverly to sign a "neutrality agreement" pledging not to fight the unions' efforts to organize employees, which led to a reduced level of friction between the company and the unions for the next several years. Litton Industries, a California-based conglomerate specializing in defense contracts and consumer appliances, became the target of a campaign by the United Electrical Workers' union in 1981, after company and union negotiators were unable to sign a contract covering workers at a microwave oven factory in Sioux Falls, South Dakota. The UE branded Litton as the nation's number one labor law violator, with considerable evidence from the National Labor Relations Board, and three years later the two parties reached an accord.

It became clear to Nyberg that there was a pattern developing. Even where a union had the backing of the nation's labor movement, including the considerable resources of the AFL-CIO, three or four years of campaigning might pass before an employer came to the bargaining table at one plant or to sign a vague neutrality agreement. And these were campaigns aimed at

111

companies with serious image problems. Hormel by contrast was a model employer: one of the nation's first industrial companies to recognize a union; a company with unions at twenty-five of its slaughtering and processing plants; not one major strike since 1933; the highest wage and benefit package in the industry. Nor was Hormel as vulnerable to other social action groups. True, the meat industry was not popular among health groups. But Hormel was not a defense contractor and limited its overseas operations primarily to sales. It did not do business in South Africa, although it had discussed a technical services contract with one South African food company. Like any packer, it was not the best-smelling employer to have in town, but the jobs and tax base helped it override municipal concerns about pollution. It could legitimately claim that its premium products—bacon, ham, and sausages—were among the finest on a supermarket shelf. And though many a GI had come home from World War II vowing never to eat another bite of Spam (Hormel insisted that government specifications on its ingredients were to blame), the luncheon meat had earned a special spot for loving ridicule.

It also became clear to Nyberg that Rogers was not the original that the press made him out to be. The lawyer got himself a copy of *Rules for Radicals.* In it Nyberg read what might have been a blueprint for the campaign that Rogers was beginning against Hormel. It said that the organizer should collect stock in companies that are connected to the target company and try to isolate it from its allies. It said that the organizer should ridicule the company in its own community, especially a company used to being taken seriously. It said the organizer should personalize the attack by focusing on the chief executive and making personal attacks on his or her scruples. It said the organizer must give his clients a stake in the campaign, turning them into new celebrities so they get to like their notoriety and stick with the campaign. It said the organizer must fan what discontent there is and invent new issues constantly because interest will flag in any one issue. And all these things came to pass in Austin. (Rogers's analysis of an employer's financial pressure points also had plenty of precedent. During the Flint, Michigan, sit-down strikes of the 1930's, the United Auto Workers turned off the heat in the factories they occupied, guessing correctly that General Motors' insurance company would express alarm when the buildings' fire hoses froze. On a more theoretical plane, economist J. A. Hobson had argued as early as 1905 that in a capital-intensive industrial economy, large banks would control their clients by controlling the flow of capital, an argument revived by none other than V. I. Lenin in 1917.)

Nyberg, Knowlton, and Hormel's other top executives sat down that fall and mapped out a strategy to respond to each tactic. Nyberg would become the company's chief spokesman, to deflect the attack and blunt the assault on Knowlton. He also knew the legal complexities of the dispute and could explain them flawlessly. Nyberg, who had also handled public relations duties in the 1970's, and the new plant manager, Deryl Arnold, an Austin native, would attend classes on handling themselves in press conferences and TV interviews. If they couldn't match Rogers's tongue and Guyette's terse persuasiveness for the cameras, at least they would be equipped to knock them off stride. Though Hormel's exccutives were fiercely loyal to the company and dead earnest about its contribution to the Austin community, they resolved not to respond to ridicule. They would avoid criticizing union leaders by name and try to cool down the personal venom in a small town where even the smallest feuds were magnified overnight. They would watch for new issues—safety, for example, or dignity—to surface and be ready to tell the company's side in a factual, noninflammatory way. They would take periodic opinion polls to see if the corporate campaign was damaging consumer loyalty.

Though soundly conceived, Nyberg's countercampaign hardly got off to a flying start. The company was, after all, up against Ray Rogers, and his publicity efforts left many Minnesotans wondering why a company that was more profitable than its competitors needed the same wage cuts that they did. It was a time of deep concern about the middle-class standard of living, and everyone who had ever read *The Jungle* felt he or she could sympathize with a packinghouse worker. If Nyberg and Knowlton were counting on the storm to blow over, they would be sadly disappointed.

In the meantime, Knowlton, Nyberg, and the other Hormel executives found Rogers's presence highly frustrating. What they considered a patient and generous response to the plunging wages of their competitors was being cast in town as a dastardly deed. It was the first in a string of attacks that took what management viewed as strengths and twisted them against the company. Another was a year-old published remark by a Minneapolis securities analyst, citing the new plant's high productivity, that had been turned on its head. The analyst, George Dahlman from Piper, Jaffray & Hopwood, had marveled at the new plant's automation, noting that Hormel was getting more production from 1,450 workers than it had from 2,250 employees in the old plant. Guyette seized on that as proof that P-9's highly productive workers were responsible for the new plant's high output and, by association, Hormel's industry-leading profits. In fact, the plant lost money in its most labor-intensive operations—hog slaughtering and butchering—making it up only through its more automated, higher-margin processing lines. While the 23 percent cut to $8.25 an hour became a fixture in daily news accounts, Hormel claimed it was still much better than what most of the 850 new plant hires had made before joining the company. Moreover, the 600 veterans from the old plant were receiving a special bonus, averaging $100 to $120 a week, to offset the loss of incentive pay they had earned in the old plant. In most cases the bonus more than offset the wage cut. But P-9 members viewed it as payback of loans that each of them had made to help build the new plant. And the wage cut still amounted to a rollback in the workers' standard of living.

Once the WE SUPPORT P-9 signs began showing up downtown, Hormel executives quietly tried to explain their position to shop owners and emphasize the company's need to stay competitive with other packers. But Hormel was mum about Rogers. It was typical of the conservative image that it nurtured from Main Street to Wall Street. Initially skeptical of Rogers's support in Austin, executives feared that to acknowledge his presence publicly would overstate his credibility to the rank and file. Management also sidestepped specifics about the tactics and impact of the curious campaign, dismissing it as a ruse inspired by a few Guyette supporters that would fade as a majority of workers lost interest. The company instead plotted for the next arbitration decision, which would fine-tune the wage and benefit package already in place. At the same time Knowlton dropped hints that the company was prepared to make a better offer, essentially the same deal that had been accepted by workers at the other Hormel plants in October.

But the day after Christmas 1984 Hormel made an announcement that shocked the town and gave many residents a sense that even if the company wasn't talking, there was anxiety in the corporate office. For the first time in Hormel's history, the annual stockholders' meeting was going to be held outside Austin. The January 29 meeting was slated for Atlanta, Georgia, where Hormel owned a meat-processing plant. The official company explanation said the move had long been under consideration, following the lead of monthly board meetings that were held in satellite locations to give outside directors a chance to see other parts of the company. Management felt stockholders and employees in those cities deserved to hear from the top brass as well. But the clincher for moving it this time was the fear of disruption by P-9 members if the meeting was held in Austin. For years the company had been giving every union member a few shares of stock, a fringe benefit that had not been negotiated with the union but was intended to help workers share in Hormel's success. Now, ironically, management was afraid that many would use their ownership to turn the meeting into a circus, with Rogers in the center ring, harping about a wage cut that was imposed largely because P-9 leaders refused to consider a better deal. Annual meetings were show time for big companies, and Hormel wasn't about to turn its shindig into a regionally televised shouting match in which Rogers would be the biggest winner.

For most billion-dollar companies, moving an annual meeting would cause little stir. They are usually dull, painfully scripted affairs, staged in theaters, auditoriums, and hotel ballrooms selected not for emotional reasons but mainly because they offer enough room. But in Austin the move was a shock, depriving residents of what for years had become a civic celebration that nothing could disrupt, not even three grueling years of company-union battles in the 1970's over building the new plant. It was a fixture of pride that none of Austin's neighboring cities could match, not even nearby and much bigger Rochester with its world-famous Mayo Clinic. Every year the meeting drew a thousand people, who filled up the storied Austin High School auditorium, where many of those in management and union ranks alike had attended school. Many were retired, some were farmers, while others were still employed. All were stockholders, who, along with local civic and business leaders, got all dressed up and brought their spouses to what the *Wall Street Journal* in 1980 dubbed the "social event of the year" in Austin. While the description rankled many in Austin, it offered as good an explanation as any for such a massive turnout. All they would do was say aye to a couple of ho-hum resolutions and listen quietly to a speech from the chairman. Their reward was getting to take home a bag of new Hormel products. Mostly it was a time to chat and say hi to old friends in a family atmosphere. More than any other event in the life of Austin, the Hormel annual meeting reaffirmed the unique bond between an amazingly successful Fortune 500 company and a town that would be nothing without it.

But this year there would be no celebration. Instead, there was a curious debate occurring right on their doorstep, an appeal to their judgment about power and greed. Five days after townspeople found the leaflets in their doors, they turned on their televisions to watch a company-sponsored call-in TV show to answer questions from a broad swath of viewers across southern Minnesota and northern Iowa. The TV show was unusual, too, but it wasn't quite as surprising as moving the meeting. Hormel had used the medium in 1977, when negotiations to build the new plant bogged down and rumors were running rampant about the company's precarious future in Austin. Back then there was a debate involving Hormel Chairman Jim Holton, P-9 Business Agent Dick Schaefer, and Austin Mayor Bob Enright, himself a P-9 member. But not this time. This would be all Hormel, a calculated way for the big company to clear the air in a town where it signed 25 percent of the paychecks and was indirectly responsible for most of the rest. For two thousand dollars, a prime-time hour of TV was money well spent, company spokesman Allan Krejci said at the time. Not only would it reach union members who, according to the company line, were not getting the full scoop from their leaders, but the show would also touch a large cross section of the non-Hormel families in Austin who were being asked by P-9 to take the union's side. What's more, there would be no opportunity for Guyette or Rogers to respond during the show and twist answers in their favor, giving Hormel a rare chance to make its case unfettered. Providing the answers would be Chuck Nyberg, senior vice-president, general counsel, and the company's contract law expert, and Dave Larson, vice-president of human resources and chief labor negotiator.

A blinding snowstorm that night made travel virtually impossible in Austin, but nobody in town would have left home anyway. The rumors were heating up, even more than usual in a town where secrets didn't stay secret for long. How vulnerable was Hormel to the campaign? Could First Bank tell the company what to do? What might the company do in response? Would there be layoffs at the plant? Would the bank force the company to capitulate to P-9? Rogers and the union had a three-month head start in the battle for public opinion, and their unusual tactics had piqued the town's curiosity. More than 150 people submitted questions in writing before the show, and nearly 300 more called in during the evening.

Despite the blowing snow, Nyberg and Larson managed to drive from their homes to station KAAL-TV, located next to a truck stop along Interstate 90. If Nyberg was steeled for this ordeal, Dave Larson was not. As he drove in from his house in the country, he wished that he could have stayed home, or driven up to Minneapolis for a Gopher basketball game with his buddy Krejci, or gone almost anywhere but a television studio to sit under hot lights with pancake makeup on his face. Larson was pushing fifty and was a veteran of the old school of labor relations—the gruff-and-bluff school. He was certainly gruff enough. He had the body of a football tackle—though his preferred game was now H-O-R-S-E at a basketball hoop over his driveway—topped by a full head of white hair neatly combed into a Brylcreem wave. His face broke easily into a smile, but the smile broke just as easily into an "Aw, Christ" expression of disbelief when one of the many young whippersnappers in his life tried to bring him into the twentieth century. A Frank Sinatra fan, Larson had little patience for music made after 1960; a martini drinker, he would snort with scorn at reporters from the big city, "I suppose you're one of these guys who drink white wine." But years of collective bargaining had given him a keen sense of bluff, too, and it wasn't always easy to tell when gruff gave way to kidding. One Saturday morning before the strike a reporter was chatting with Nyberg in a packinghouse conference room when a stocky fellow in spattered work pants and a painter's cap poked his head in the door and asked, "Where did you want those supplies, Mr. Nyberg?" It was Larson, of course, tweaking both the visitor, who knew him only by name, and Nyberg's Saturday morning suit and tie. He might have been one of the top five executives at a Fortune 500 food company, but Larson's idea of a good time was going fishing and drinking beer with his sons. He had grown up in South St. Paul, a meat-packing town, the son of a meat-packer himself. He knew what both sides wanted from a labor contract, and he spoke his mind about it. All these qualities had earned Larson a measured respect from most of the union negotiators who squared off against him. They might tire of his style at the bargaining table—lecturing endlessly and working himself into a lather over the union's demands—but they knew there was always a thread of logic behind his tirades.

Over the years Larson also had made a habit of studying his opponents and even cultivating them as sources. This was especially true of Dick Schaefer, P-9's veteran business agent until 1984, whom Larson respected even when they were too mad to speak to each other. But outside the bargaining room Larson chafed at dealing with the press, which irked him with its fixation on the 23 percent cut and its inability to grasp the contractual complexities of the dispute. Still, he was Hormel's top labor negotiator, having replaced Bob Gill when he retired as vice-president of human resources. Larson knew the issues as well as Nyberg, but he would have gladly skipped the chance to talk about them on television. As they sat down in the studio, both men had a fair idea of the kinds of questions they would face. They had been prepared beforehand, and they were well acquainted with the rumors on the community grapevine.

For the next sixty minutes they made it very clear that Hormel would not be fazed by the campaign and that the First Bank connection had no influence whatsoever on the wage dispute. In matter-of-fact fashion Larson explained that the cutbacks were solely a response to labor cost cutting in the industry, which was threatening to destroy the company's ability to compete. The $8.25 wage rate was implemented only because P-9's leaders refused to consider a better offer that was approved by six other Hormel plants. Why didn't management take a 23 percent cut? Nyberg said it was difficult to recruit top executives to a small town, much less keep other companies from hiring away your own, without competitive salaries. What about Knowlton's plump $339,000 salary? Nyberg said the chief executive twice refused the board's attempt to give him a raise and ranked among the lowest-paid chief executives in the food industry. What about workers having to raise their hand to go to the bathroom? Larson replied that it was a common practice in assembly-line plants that needed to maintain order when trying to ensure smooth production.

On and on the questions went, but the one that lingered on everybody's mind was about jobs. Would there be layoffs in the plant? Of the twenty-five or so questions that were addressed during the program, it was the only question that moderator John O'Rourke posed twice. Larson responded that no layoffs would be considered as long as the present labor package—with its base wage rate of $8.25 an hour—was intact. But if those rates became uncompetitive—for instance, with a return to the $10.69 promised by Rogers—layoffs "are certainly viable options." Although Larson's words didn't say it, the implication was clear: Corporate campaign was a suicide mission.

As print and TV reporters filed their stories that night, Guyette, Rogers, and the P-9 leadership entourage were nowhere to be found to offer their reaction. The snowstorm had stranded them forty-five miles away in Rochester, where they watched the program on TV. Earlier in the day they had accused Hormel of preparing the questions and answers in advance, but the charge seemed hollow considering that Larson and Nyberg could be expected to have studied the issues. As a result, 10:00 P.M. newscasts and next-morning papers published stories that reported Hormel's side without a glib comeback from Guyette or Rogers. In a public opinion battle that increasingly hinged on who got the final word each night, this was a major media victory for Hormel.

The opposing forces collided the following Tuesday, when a busload of thirty weary P-9 members and supporters completed a twenty-nine-hour ride from Austin to the posh Waverly Hotel on the north side of Atlanta. They had taken great delight in Hormel's decision to move the annual meeting, calling it an early victory for the campaign because it showed that Hormel was afraid to face the issues in Austin. It even inspired a new leaflet that featured Knowlton and other executives fleeing the snow and running away from Hormel's problems. Campaign supporters vowed to attend the meeting wherever it was held, and Guyette boasted that it would be one that Knowlton would never forget.

In the parking lot outside the hotel, Rogers gathered the troops and led supporters through brief picketing as unconcerned hotel guests wandered by. The P-9 contingent also passed out leaflets to those heading into the annual meeting, some shareholders taking them out of curiosity, others brushing them aside. And as always, Rogers talked with reporters, telling them of P-9's fight, spirit, and determination to win over the stockholders. Before the P-9ers were allowed in the meeting, company officials verified their credentials as stockholders. Once inside, they dispersed in ones and twos throughout the corporate crowd of 250 people, remaining easily identifiable in their casual slacks, sweaters, jeans, and sweat shirts. A few women sported sweat shirts with the words "Cram your Spam" embroidered on the front. But they were polite and orderly, having been schooled by Rogers on how to conduct themselves in the decorum of a business meeting.

It didn't take long for Guyette to make his presence known. A few minutes after Knowlton had gaveled the meeting to order, Guyette, seated near the front of the audience, stood up during the normally mundane procedure of nominating board members for reelection. He asked Knowlton how those board members could increase their retainer fees while the company was cutting the wages of its workers. Knowlton, addressing Guyette by name, replied that the question would be addressed later in the meeting, during a question-and-answer session. Guyette persisted and demanded an answer immediately, but Knowlton refused to back down and continued the nominating process.

The meeting remained uneventful as it progressed through board elections, approval of auditors, speeches by Knowlton and top executives, and commercials for new products such as Frank

'N Stuff hot dogs. It grew more lively when Knowlton opened the question-and-answer period. The first query came from Guyette, who asked why Hormel did not seem interested in establishing a partnership with its workers by agreeing to a union proposal to tie wages to company profits. Knowlton responded with a rambling ten-minute answer that summarized Hormel's position that it never intended Austin workers to earn any less than those at other company plants. Then Pete Winkels, always bucking convention, stepped up and led a round of applause for Knowlton, his management team, and all Hormel workers for the company's financial performance. After the ovation and kudos from Knowlton, he delved into the control of Hormel stock wielded by the nonprofit Hormel Foundation. Then Lynn Huston tackled safety problems in the Austin plant.

As the session wore on, union members took turns with the Atlanta shareholders, peppering Knowlton with questions, politely applauding each one in a show of support. The queries ranged from the need for wage cuts to Knowlton's $339,000 salary and why executive pay was increasing while workers took reductions. Guyette's wife, Vickie, wanted to know how many executives had their expenses paid to Atlanta, and how much it cost to hold the meeting in such a posh place. P-9 worker Gene Meyer wanted to know whether Hormel was importing Canadian hogs. Knowlton, who knew some of the P-9ers from their days together at Austin High, politely answered each question, never losing his cool or patience, sometimes providing long explanations that overlapped his answers to other questions. To explain Knowlton's salary, board member Clarence Adamy produced a study by Arthur Andersen & Company showing that Knowlton earned only 67 percent of the comparable salaries paid to chief executives of similarly sized companies. That was causing compression on other management salaries, he said, and making it difficult to recruit and hold top executives. Hormel's group vice-presidents earned 73 percent of the salaries paid to their counterparts, while other corporate officers earned 81 percent. "This is not a healthy situation for a company like ours," he said. Shareholders from Atlanta sat quietly and listened and, judged by the business and finance questions they asked, seemed only vaguely interested in P-9's presence.

Only once did the campaign seem to touch a nerve, and it started with Rogers. Showing considerable more polish at the microphone than his new clients, he stood up and said all the fat executive compensation made him think that maybe workers weren't asking for enough. Citing rising retainer fees paid to board members and increased dividends paid to shareholders, he accused management of "trying to steal from the workers to compensate themselves." Before anyone from management could respond, an Atlanta shareholder, sitting near Rogers, interrupted and asked Rogers what he was being paid.

Without missing a beat, Rogers dutifully replied that he and his partner, Ed Allen, earned $425 a week, plus health insurance and per diem expense payments. Added Rogers: "Could I maybe compare my salary to yours?"

"That's none of your business," the shareholder snapped.

Knowlton cut off the questions after seventy-five minutes, drawing a smattering of boos from the union group, and the big confrontation was over. No fireworks. No emotional outbursts. No fistfights. No capitulation by management, no threats of lawsuits. Nobody was thrown out. Guyette contended later that Knowlton left several union questions unanswered, but most of the major issues drew long responses. In the back of the room Hormel public relations officials beamed with pleasure at the amazingly uneventful meeting. The folks in Atlanta got a look at the management and the board, and the P-9 ruckus had been averted.

If the meeting was memorable, the reason had nothing to do with P-9's presence. The biggest news came in two announcements by the Hormel board that recast the battle landscape back in Austin. First, the company said it was beginning a study of the possibility of moving its corporate headquarters out of Minnesota. The study, which had long been sought by the company's outside board members, stemmed from a "negative atmosphere" in Austin fostered by P-9. In addition, the outside directors felt that a Fortune 500 food corporation should be based in a big city where it could draw on a bigger pool of executive talent. Hormel also announced that day that it planned to form a marketing agreement with a big Iowa-based meat-packer, FDL Foods, Inc., and possibly buy the firm. The move would boost Hormel's hog-slaughtering capacity from fifth to second largest in the nation. But more important, it gave Hormel a rich supply of fresh pork, slaughtered at wages well below those paid in Austin, Fremont, or Ottumwa. From a business standpoint, it was a growth-minded move that offered a cheap means of boosting volume. It was timed perfectly: The industry's financial woes allowed Hormel to pick up the FDL slaughtering capacity on very attractive terms. And if P-9 gave Hormel any trouble in Austin, through a strike, for instance, FDL would be more than able to pick up the loss in the procurement and processing of raw materials.

When the P-9 bus rolled into Austin later in the week, supporters proclaimed victory, claiming to have spread the word of their fight. Guyette said the union achieved its goal of raising questions and making stockholders aware of its presence. Vice-President Lynn Huston told how the questions had been greeted with boisterous applause, implying that the P-9 struggle had won over the hearts of those at the meeting.

Nyberg was incredulous. He wondered if P-9 had been at the same meeting. The victory chant grew so loud that Hormel decided to buy some more local TV time and broadcast a videotape of the meeting. But it wouldn't be the last time that Hormel and P-9 leaders, interpreting the exact same set of events, would walk away telling stories full of contradictions.

So much for the public relations aspect of the campaign. There were still economic battles to fight on two fronts. Rogers was right about Hormel in some respects: Many corporations have close ties to their banks—interlocking directorships, for example, or revolving credit arrangements to buy raw materials. Hormel had a long history with First Bank, dating back to 1926, when Jay Hormel organized Austin businessmen to bail out a failing bank that was the predecessor of the First Bank branch in Austin. Since Hormel first sold stock to the public in 1928, a bank officer had sat on the Hormel board, one of the few directorships held by outsiders until the 1970's, while the Hormel chairman sat on the First Bank Minneapolis board.

But this was a case where Rogers's "corporate web of power" seemed more apparent than real. By the 1980's the First Bank relationship meant less to Hormel's balance sheet than in earlier years because Hormel relied far less on its bank than most of its competitors did on theirs. From 1976 to 1985 Hormel had borrowed bank funds twelve times. But when Rogers began calling First Bank a major Hormel lender in late 1984, bank funds accounted for less than one half of 1 percent of Hormel's short-term borrowing. Hormel had no long-term debt with First Bank whatsoever. Hormel's ratio of long-term debt to total capital, a major accounting measure, was just 20 percent—conservative by industry standards and low enough to earn favorable debt ratings from Moody's and Standard & Poor's, the investors' bibles. Hormel had more than fifty million dollars in cash and cash equivalents, an amount that nearly equaled its long-term debt. While the First Bank branch in Austin did business with Hormel, it was primarily processing checks. It was true that First Bank Minneapolis held about 14 percent of Hormel's outstanding stock. But First Bank did not own the stock; the stock was owned by employee pension and profit-sharing funds which First Bank had been hired to manage. As manager of the pension funds First Bank was required by federal pension laws to vote that stock for the benefit of retirees, not for current economic or business reasons. Moreover, 8 percent of the stock was in pension funds for which First Bank did not control the proxies to vote at shareholder meetings.

DeWalt H. Ankeny, the First Bank president who sat on Hormel's board, also seemed to have little chance of influencing the twelve-member board of directors. Seven members were so-called inside directors, top Hormel executives with families, homes, and careers rooted deeply in Austin. This unusual majority relegated the outside directors to a position of providing fresh thinking to a historically conservative company. But the outsiders were in no position to run the business. Of the remaining outside directors, Clarence Adamy and Ray Rose were food industry consultants. Sherwood Berg was an agricultural specialist. Geri Joseph was a former journalist and U.S. ambassador to the Netherlands during the Carter administration, recruited by Hormel during the 1970's, when it became fashionable for corporations to have women on their boards of directors. If there was a liberal and perhaps sympathetic soul in the group, it was Joseph, a Democrat and onetime social crusader. But her experiences in world trade had taught her the brutal lessons of controlling costs if companies wanted to compete. She also was a big fan of Knowlton, whom she credited with transforming an insulated midwestern meat-packer into a wide-awake major-league food company with tremendous marketing poise during one of the roughest economic downswings in the meat industry.

Even if the executives at First Bank System decided to pressure Hormel, other banks would eagerly line up for its business. But it was far from clear that First Bank itself would ever feel any pressure. The bank was even then launching a major advertising campaign to attract business clients and wealthy investors— hardly candidates to boycott a bank on behalf of a labor union. Even to the nickel-and-dime customers who might sympathize with P-9, First Bank meant little more than a checkbook, a bunch of civic contributions, and an annual tennis tournament played on the plaza of its downtown Minneapolis headquarters. True, many bank customers in the 1980's had grown up in the 1960's and 1970's, learning to be suspicious of establishment and corporate power. But getting across the message of interlocking directorships and proxy votes was a tall order among customers to whom the bank was just a place to cash checks—as Rogers and P-9 learned later that spring.

Hormel's executives were pained by Rogers's attacks, but they reasoned that First Bank System was a big, professionally managed bank holding company—the nation's sixteenth-largest—and could be relied on to fend for its own public image. A month before its annual meeting, First Bank issued a position paper refuting corporate campaign claims that the bank could pressure Hormel. Ankeny told reporters that the notion was ridiculous, adding, "We are very frustrated and feel victimized that we are dragged into this debate." Another bank official said the campaign tactics bore characteristics similar to an illegal secondary boycott and hinted that the bank might seek legal action through the NLRB.

Rogers didn't care in the slightest. On April 24 he led about a hundred union supporters from Austin to the posh new Ordway Theater in St. Paul, where First Bank was holding its annual meeting. The meeting was originally billed in campaign plans as a climactic showdown, when Rogers promised that hundreds of angry workers would "kick the living hell" out of the bank.

But the plan was downgraded when an arbitrator ruled that P-9 could not strike Hormel until later, thus depleting the union's ability to flood the annual meeting. Nonetheless, outside the theater a downtown sidewalk was packed with picket signs and meat-packers and their wives and children in blue caps, visors, and jackets. Chanting their now-familiar "They say give back, we say fight back!," they reveled in the attention as they passed out union newspapers to passersby. Inside the meeting P-9ers who had bought shares of First Bank stock were joined by their newly organized Twin Cities supporters. In the past month Rogers had stepped up the campaign, urging unions and other organizations with pension funds, savings, and checking accounts at First Bank to write letters demanding that the bank explain its ties to Hormel. Rogers stopped short of calling for a First Bank boycott, although several union locals in the Twin Cities did pull checking accounts or savings certificates from the bank.

About 150 union supporters were among the 500 people in the spacious theater, hoping to grill First Bank Chairman George Dixon in the same manner in which they had gone after Knowlton in Atlanta. But the bank seemed equal to the challenge. When Dixon opened the meeting for questions, he gave a brief statement laying out the bank's criticisms of the campaign. "It is impossible for us to grasp why the union is spending its energy and its members' money—and taking some risk of being hauled into court on a charge of engaging in an illegal secondary boycott—when, honest and true, this strategy simply won't succeed."

The discussion was more lively than in Atlanta, but no more effective in producing new converts. Boos and catcalls greeted Dixon as he gave what was quickly becoming the bank's pat response—"You give us credit for having power that we simply do not have"—but the normally placid pinstripe crowd erupted in applause. During the hourlong question session Rogers stood up and tried to refute Dixon's claim by announcing that a seventy-million-dollar fund had been withdrawn from one of the bank's affiliates in recent months. Dixon said if it was true, it was news to him, but that it was difficult to know why accounts were opened and closed. In an interview after the meeting Rogers admitted that fifty million dollars had been withdrawn not because of P-9 but because the fund managers wanted a better return on their investment. He claimed that the remaining twenty million dollars were withdrawn after the bank's ties to Hormel had become "prominent," but he refused to name the customer or furnish any other details about the transaction.

Rogers also took aim at Ankeny, telling shareholders that he "brings all of the economic power of this bank into Hormel." Ankeny didn't flinch. "I don't think we heard anything new," the banker said after the meeting. "Our position hasn't changed."

Rogers and Guyette vowed to escalate the battle even further among unions and community activists, but Hormel's contractual position was growing stronger and stronger. In the week between Christmas 1984 and New Year's Day 1985, arbitrator George Fleischli ruled for the second time that Hormel had the right to cut wages and benefits under the me-too clause of the new-plant agreement. Fleischli said Hormel could continue paying workers the $8.25 base wage it had imposed in October but said company and union negotiators should sit down again to work out a compromise on the wage and fringe benefit cuts. He gave them seven days. In an almost predictable turn of events they were unable to agree on a new package, and the matter went back to Fleischli in early January.

He made his third ruling in March, and for the third time he sided chiefly with Hormel. Because of a change in the group of packing companies Fleischli used to calculate the new labor package in Austin, he told Hormel to lift its base wage to $8.75. But for the first time since October, Fleischli gave Hormel the right to cut fringe benefits. The whole ruling was retroactive to the previous October. That meant that Hormel owed its workers about $435,000, or $300 apiece, in back wages. But it also meant that hundreds of the workers owed Hormel money for health insurance, vacation, retirement payments, and other fringe benefits used up between October and March because Hormel hadn't cut the fringe benefits back. In total, most workers owed the company much more than the company owed them. For some who had taken long winter vacations, had babies, or started collecting pension checks in the interim, the liability to Hormel ran into thousands of dollars.

Sensing a chance to forge a new contract compromise, Larson

and Austin plant manager Deryl Arnold agreed to set the new wage at $8.75 and drop the fringe benefit liabilities, which amounted to about $680,000, if P-9 would forgo the fifty-cent retroactive pay increase. On April 4 Guyette rejected the deal. Larson couldn't believe it. By his calculations, Guyette had just cost his members nearly $250,000. The deal was so sweet for the union that Larson caught heat from some Hormel executives for offering it. Had the union gone along, workers would have given up about $300 in wages. As it was, some workers would be paying back Hormel more than $100 from every paycheck from March until August. "That could have been the end of it," Larson said with a sigh.

Instead, Deryl Arnold sent a letter to plant employees the following day, saying that payroll deductions to recoup the retroactive benefits would begin immediately. "I had hoped that our offer would signal the start of the process of building a better relationship between the parties," Arnold wrote. "Instead, your leadership has made it clear once again to the company that it favors a continuation of its campaign of harassment and publicity. . . . Under these circumstances we cannot and will not move forward at the Austin plant."

In reality, the third Fleischli decision was a crushing economic blow to P-9's members. It fulfilled the prediction of UFCW attorney Bob Nichols a year earlier: that Hormel held the cards contractually and that forgoing compromise in the summer of 1984 to adjudicate the me-too clause was suicidal. It left P-9 not only isolated from the other Hormel chain plants but also earning less money. In just five months the other chain plants would get raises from nine to ten dollars an hour, while Austin would still be stuck right around nine dollars. To make matters worse, P-9 learned a few weeks later that another arbitrator had ruled that it could not legally strike Hormel until August, dashing plans for an April walkout. But neither arbitration would affect the much larger fight with Hormel, Winkels said, except perhaps to strengthen the union's resolve.

By this point, however, P-9's public unity was beginning to show some cracks. In the weeks before the Fleischli decision, another war of words had broken out between Guyette and Anderson, this time over a planned appearance by Anderson before

P-9's rank and file. Both men agreed that Anderson should come to Austin to explain the UFCW's opposition to the corporate campaign and just where it stood in support of P-9. But Anderson wanted a members-and-spouses-only session, without Rogers and Allen in the room. He feared another Rogers-inspired rally would break out, with his supporters and their blue P-9 baseball caps turning the meeting into a circus. He didn't want the international sponsoring a meeting that would draw more press to the campaign. But Guyette insisted that Rogers and Allen be present to defend Corporate Campaign in case Anderson attacked them, and he refused to put conditions on the meeting.

Even as Anderson warred publicly with Guyette, he was convinced, like Hormel, that the blue caps did not represent the majority of P-9 members. Except Anderson was doing something about it. Early that spring he started a series of secret weekend meetings in Bloomington, Minnesota, at the Thunderbird Motel near the Twin Cities airport. There he met with P-9 members who disagreed with Guyette and Rogers. Their ranks included John Morrison, who had been a college buddy of Winkels; former Vice-President John Anker, who lost to Guyette in late 1983; and Chad Young, whose father had been a union officer at Wilson in Albert Lea during the 1950's. They pored over P-9 membership lists, ticking off members name by name and guessing their allegiance: Guyette, Anderson, or undecided. They evaluated the company's bargaining position and tried to assess how there might be movement. And they discussed how best to counter the Rogers publicity machine.

Anderson also kept in frequent contact with Dick Schaefer, the former P-9 business agent who had extensive contacts with the more moderate elements of the union and its executive board. From his small home in southeast Austin, a few blocks from Sutton Park, where Frank Ellis had formed the Austin union thirty-two years earlier, Schaefer presided over kitchen-table powwows with Morrison and the others, providing grandfatherly advice on how to deal with Guyette. Schaefer sat in that kitchen like a spider in the middle of a web, scarcely twenty minutes passing without a phone call from Fremont or Ottumwa or Sioux Falls or Washington, every tremor on the nation's meat-packing grapevine coming to his attention. Schaefer had grown up on a hardscrabble farm a few miles from Austin and still wore the plaid shirts and rumpled trousers of a country laborer. But he had apprenticed at the side of Jesse Prosten, a gifted and aggressive negotiator for the UPWA and had quietly become remarkably expert in contract language and bargaining strategy. "We were sleeping with the same whore," he would quote Prosten's description of fruitless contract talks, "but we were having different dreams." He could see that Guyette and Knowlton had different visions for the future of Hormel. He could also see that P-9 had little economic clout over Hormel and that what leverage P-9 had was slipping fast. He was convinced that the last thing Knowlton would ever do would be to hand a victory to Guyette and Rogers. He could see that every passing month of the campaign was driving Knowlton and Nyberg to harsher measures, and he could see no way out if the union's moderates didn't turn P-9 around. Mild-mannered and something of a pack rat, Schaefer had spent years building up P-9 contracts into the most lucrative in the industry. And while he rarely showed it, he was furious that someone as naive as Guyette was on the brink of losing it all.

Finally, in early March 1985, the dissidents decided it was time to move. Morrison, Anker, Young, and about twenty others began circulating a petition inside the plant that called for Anderson to address the membership. One fourth of P-9's members signed it, hoping that a meeting would clear the air about the international's position on the wage dispute and why it opposed the campaign. As a precaution, veteran P-9ers Douglas Saaranen and Donald T. Nelson wrote to International President William Wynn asking him to order such a meeting if Guyette and his board refused to accept the petition.

About the same time Anker went public by reading a letter at a union meeting urging the board to abandon the campaign and seek a negotiated settlement with Hormel before jobs were lost in Austin. He noted that Hormel had made recent acquisitions to position itself for a strike in Austin and suffer minimal financial impact. He urged that members be allowed to hear Anderson and make their own decisions "without being told what Ray Rogers thinks is best for them." It was Anker's most public criticism of Guyette since losing the election. After he resigned as vice-president in the fall, he had kept a low profile. He had hoped that the fourteen months that had passed since his defeat would minimize the appearance of sour grapes. Any chance of that vanished when Guyette printed a stinging attack by Lynn Huston alongside Anker's letter in *The Unionist*. "Any union official worth his salt would have the guts to at least finish his elected term instead of turning his back on the rank and file," Huston wrote.

Anker blamed his loss on a poor showing at the polls by moderate P-9 old-timers who supported him but didn't vote because they planned to retire soon. Though he could have retained his board seat as vice-president, Anker didn't want to be in a position of writing minority dissents that meant little, much as Guyette did when he sat on the board in 1981. Instead, Anker relented to personal considerations and a desire to spend more time with his family. If he were going to criticize the leadership, he would do it like anybody else, from within the ranks, on the floor of the union hall instead of on the stage.

His well-publicized letter and the petition marked the formation of a rump group of dissidents, perhaps thirty strong at first, that came to be known as P-10ers. At first even they admitted that Guyette spoke for a majority of the membership. But they worried that without the international's support, P-9 was cutting itself off from the rest of the industry and key labor organizations such as the AFL-CIO. They disliked the new $8.25 wage rate as much as the most ardent Guyette supporters, but they thought it was foolishness not to seek the $9 wage that Hormel had offered the other chain plants. They also refused to believe that a campaign of slogans and rallies, a campaign that ignored P-9's crippled bargaining position, would do anything but make matters worse. They were extremely suspicious of Rogers and Guyette, claiming they were overstating the levels of support for P-9's fight from Corporate Campaign sojourns to plants and unions around the Midwest.

The splintering of the ranks seemed inconsequential to Guyette. Every democratic organization has its dissidents, he said. He traced the opposition to defeated candidates for union office and reiterated his accusation that the international and Anderson were do-nothings who would only malign the campaign. Rogers was even more resolute. "Do I care if an [AFL-CIO] central body cannot officially endorse this campaign? Show me any labor movement that's more of a moving force than we've got going up here."

CHAPTER

7

Sometime early in 1985 the words "P-9 Proud," painted in large white letters, mysteriously appeared on an abandoned grain silo six miles north of Austin on Highway 218. The message greeted travelers along the most popular route from the Twin Cities and fired the first shot in what was to be a long battle for the loyalties of visitors making their way to Austin. A few months passed before the opposing forces grabbed a paintbrush, crossed out the union message, and wrote "Proud of Austin" on the adjacent barn. Some months later, after P-9 went on strike and Hormel began hiring replacement workers, the words "Scab City" replaced the civic slogan. Back and forth the rustic billboard went until finally, late in 1986, the simple message "P-9 Proud" returned.

The war of the paintbrushes revealed two things about P-9's new tactics against Hormel. First, P-9's partisans were not above using the energetic pranks of a teenager to spread their message. Second, and far more significant, they had finally provoked the people of Austin to take sides in a labor dispute at Hormel.

For years the people of Austin had done their utmost to keep out of fights between Hormel and P-9, and for years they had succeeded. With a Fortune 500 headquarters in their backyard they certainly had good reason to wish for peace. If Austin had a problem with engineering, taxes, business development, or transportation, the most knowledgeable business minds south of the Twin Cities could be reached with a phone call and a cup of coffee. Moreover, the Hormel Foundation poured thousands of dollars into civic projects and scholarships every year. The union, too, was a powerful force. It sponsored softball teams and scholarships and donated money to charity. Rare was the Austin resident who didn't have an acquaintance in the corporate office and a friend or relative who carried a P-9 union card. Gary Nemitz, a onetime council member who ran a newsstand and gift shop on Main Street, spoke for many when he told a reporter early in the corporate campaign, "I can't take sides in this thing. I've got friends on both sides."

To be sure, the pervasive influence of Hormel and P-9 bred resentment. In 1982 the company volunteered the use of its computers to help tally votes in the November election and drew cries of foul because one of its executives was running for mayor. Whenever the city failed to recruit a new business, someone was sure to conclude that Hormel's high wages scared off other employers or that no entrepreneur wanted to set up shop in a packinghouse town. When development officials did score a success, the new jobs could be easily wiped out by the ripple effects of Hormel layoffs triggered by a slump in the livestock market. Even though there hadn't been a strike since 1933, the presence of such large adversaries permeating every social circle was enough to put the town on edge when a fight broke out.

Hormel's corporate presence also contributed to Austin's class tensions. In the early years, when George and Jay still ran the company, there was something almost baronial about the family. When Jay came home from World War I with a French bride, all of Austin felt a tremor of the exotic. For all of the national attention he brought to Austin, however, he was enough of an average guy to leave his stone-walled country estate occasionally and join workers for a beer at the American Legion Club. And when his son, George II, married a twenty-year-old Paris actress named Leslie Caron in 1952, the whole town took note as if she were one of their own.

In the years after World War II class lines took a more modern turn. Main Street came to delineate a certain east-west social order: To the east were the packinghouse, the Milwaukee Road

134

depot, and the Terp Ballroom, while to the west were the hospital, college, and YMCA. Lefty's was the bare-linoleum union bar on the east side; Tolly's, the carpeted white-collar watering hole and dinner spot on the west. Robert Richardson, a high school classmate of Dick Knowlton, charted the split on maps he kept in his boyhood home on the south end of Main Street. The east side was rougher, had more juvenile arrests; mothers frequently joined their husbands slicing bacon in the packinghouse. In high school, hard-nosed east siders filled out the football team while lanky west siders played basketball.

But the affluence created by Hormel did a great deal to erase these barriers, and the distinction became less clear after packinghouse families spilled west across Main Street during the big postwar years. By the late 1960's a two-income union family brought home a staggering forty thousand dollars a year with full medical coverage, spent weekends at a lake cabin near Faribault, drove new cars, and played golf at the country club. While many people in Austin felt class distinctions—the necktie crowd wielded the power; their wives played tennis instead of softball— the distinctions weren't ironclad because almost anybody in management had a brother or a cousin or an in-law in the union. Deryl Arnold, manager of the Austin plant and a man regarded as a humorless taskmaster by many P-9 members, was the son of a forty-six-year union meat-packer and the brother of a former P-9 president. Knowlton himself was the son of a packinghouse worker.

If Austin's noncombatants had learned to wish for labor-management peace, they also had learned not to meddle. Labor relations had always been in the capable hands of Fayette Sherman, Hormel's longtime employment manager, and Frank Schultz, the union president from shortly after World War II until 1969. Each time a contract came up during the 1960's, residents could count on reading the usual charges and countercharges in the Austin *Daily Herald.* But they could remain observers. Schultz would find a way to have dinner with Sherman at the nicest place in town, and they would quietly cut a deal. Usually within a few months life in Austin would return to normal.

Politics operated along the same continuum. Democrats— often union members—usually won the mayoral race. But the seven-member city council divided most of the power, a reflection of the don't-mess-with-success conservatism inspired by the company's benevolent shadow. On one occasion in 1964 Frank Schultz actually recommended Sherman, his bargaining adversary, for the mayor's job. To balance the slate, he asked a congenial union member named Bob Enright to run for alderman-at-large. Both men won, and when Sherman stepped down three years later, Enright took over and served ten years as mayor. Like a pair of thousand-pound gorillas, Enright liked to say, Hormel and P-9 could sleep anywhere they wanted to in Austin. But they knew how to get along.

Ironically, it was Enright who instigated one of the few episodes when city officials did intervene in a Hormel–P-9 dispute. The occasion was the epic battle over a new packinghouse during the mid-1970's. Sherman had retired, Schultz had finally lost a union election, and for three agonizing years it appeared that for once Hormel and P-9 would not settle their differences. After workers rejected a proposed settlement in June 1977, the civic panic was almost palpable. Enright, himself a P-9 member, engineered nearly two dozen meetings between the two sides. Some days they found nothing to talk about but the weather, but Enright kept them at the table. Though the sessions didn't produce a settlement, at least they kept the two sides talking. The following spring, with a series of grudging compromises and elaborate guarantees that came back to haunt both sides, the negotiators hammered out an agreement for Hormel to rebuild in its hometown.

The outcome confirmed what Terry Dilley, a sociologist at Austin Community College, had advanced as theory: No matter how serious their differences, the union and the company eventually worked things out because they needed each other. While the community suffered plenty of anguish, it was never asked to take sides. It was OK to fret over breakfast at the Oak Leaf or express an opinion at half time of a Packer football game. But the unspoken rule seemed to say: "Stay out of it; it's not your fight." Even in the rare instance when Enright stepped in, the hard work was done beyond the glare of TV lights and without press releases. It was accomplished among family, among people who were neighbors and whose children played and went to school together.

Now, barely six years later, all the rules had changed. Dissenters from the new-plant debate were wresting control of the union away from moderates who were retiring. Rogers's October rally at the high school had drawn TV cameras all the way from Minneapolis and Rochester. Wives of Hormel workers picketed every week outside the plant, asking motorists to support their husbands. Earnest P-9 members asked their neighbors if they hadn't seen enough of Hormel's arrogance. Coffee shops and restaurants buzzed with stories about this Ray Rogers from New York and his newfangled corporate campaign.

Austin still did its utmost to remain neutral, but Rogers was not about to let that happen. There were no clandestine bargaining sessions this time, no friendly private phone calls. Rogers had seen company towns before, and he knew the kind of complacency that set in when civic leaders could get away with staying on the sidelines. At meeting after meeting, in interview after interview, he insisted that this fight belonged to the people of Austin. A pay cut for the meat-packers meant a pay cut for the grocer, the schoolteacher, and the car dealer, Rogers declared. Whether or not Austin residents agreed with Rogers, they found him hard to ignore. Congenial with the undecided, feisty with the skeptical, he could engage anybody in a lively sidewalk discussion, and he left few doubters unchallenged. Even Austin's most confirmed skeptics couldn't help speculating about Rogers over coffee out at Oak Park Mall. P-9's rallying cry—"Whose side are you on?"—implicitly demanded that Austin residents take sides and turned the whole town into a battleground where spectators would be forced into a game of power versus power.

Finally, almost reluctantly, the people of Austin stepped into the fight. In the fall of 1984 signs popped up in a few storefronts and restaurant windows saying WE SUPPORT P-9. They disappeared before long, but the events of October—the 23 percent wage cut and the hiring of Rogers—eventually gave a townful of opinionated people a chance to debate things that had been bothering them for years. Most of the opposition toward Hormel stemmed from its threat-and-bluff approach to building the new plant, for holding Austin hostage until it got its way. The new circumstances—imposing wage cuts while turning profits—convinced the critics that Hormel was conning Austin again. The case for such deep wage cuts seemed coldly contrived considering that workers hadn't seen a pay hike since 1981. Hormel always seemed to prevail in city matters, whether it was a road improvement, a rezoning, or subsidies for a new business. Finally, these union sympathizers reasoned, it was refreshing that somebody was willing to put the company in its place.

There was an equal undercurrent of resentment toward the workers, a feeling that after fifty years they had finally got their comeuppance. Most people in Austin had never known the luxury of company-paid medical coverage for an entire family or a lake cabin with a speedboat. Non-Hormel housewives remembered year after year of watching grocery prices rise every time P-9 members got a raise. Non-Hormel workers remembered a handful of loudmouths from the packinghouse who would drift through the bars to make sure the maximum number of neighbors saw the size of their paychecks. Sure the meat-packers worked hard—nobody disputed that—but half the able-bodied adults in Austin had applied for those jobs nonetheless. Even when they were laid off, P-9ers received another ten years of health insurance. Their refusal to consider an even better deal than the one the company had imposed smacked of selfishness. While 23 percent was a sobering wage cut, $8.25 an hour was still more than most jobs in Austin paid, and the campaign generated little sympathy when area farmers and casualties of the recession were scrambling to find minimum-wage work.

Other critics focused on Jim and Vickie Guyette, remembering the boycott tactics their group used during the SMMPA utility fight in 1982. The Guyettes were earning a reputation for rocking the boat in a town that had done pretty well by leaving the boat alone. Austin's population was among the oldest in Minnesota, largely because nearly two thousand Hormel retirees lived in the area. They owned their homes free and clear, with sizable pension benefits to live on. The company had treated them well, and the last thing many of them wanted to see was a bunch of people protesting next to their favorite stores on Main Street. Even if they were sympathetic to the union's position, they had been brought up believing that you resolved your problems privately, not in front of a TV camera. A few long-range thinkers even sensed that Hormel management was trying to nip a problem before it got serious. Twenty-five miles to the west, Albert Lea nearly lost thirteen hundred jobs when its run-down Wilson plant was slated for closing. The meat-packing industry was in a tailspin, these citizens reasoned, and if Dick Knowlton's executives weren't careful, they could squander the company's future—and Austin's.

All this conflict was brewing in a town where residents found it hard to get away from their enemies. Jim Guyette could drive his camper truck down Main Street on a Saturday morning and see Chuck and Mary Nyberg stopping into the Oak Leaf for coffee. Lynn Huston could drive in from his place in the country to buy a part for his son's Jeep and run into Dick Knowlton picking up a new set of tires. Dave Larson could head out to the Austin Country Club for a round of golf and find himself teeing off in a foursome behind John "Skinny" Weis, a member of P-9's executive board. Dick Schaefer, now an exile from the Austin Labor Center, could drive his distinctive blue Jeep wagon past the union hall, and be spotted immediately, and be made the butt of jokes over his spying mission.

It wasn't possible to get away from enemies, but they didn't have to drink or eat with each other. Before long, P-9ers and management alike had drawn invisible boundaries throughout Austin, marking their turfs like teenage gangs and resurrecting the east-west borders of their parents' generation. The Oak Leaf, a spacious coffee shop and restaurant near the south end of Main Street, became a pro-Hormel hangout. In the orange-carpeted foyer, along with paintings of ducks and toddlers by local artists, hung a plaque that read, "The Oak Leaf proudly serves and features Hormel products." Young business leaders could meet there for breakfast to plan Spam Days festivities, emerging with Spam T-shirts over their neckties. Straight west a mile on Oakland Avenue, Tolly's Timeout had become almost exclusively a management hangout, where young Hormel executives would show up in brightly colored golf shirts and sporty slacks for a good steak and a highball after nine holes at the country club. The rank-and-filers receded more and more to the east side, much as their fathers and grandfathers had. Pete Winkels, Kathy Buck, and others held court in Lefty's at a table near the popcorn machine and a glass case full of bowling and softball trophies. And if they weren't in Lefty's, they might be next door at Harry's, having coffee and a hot beef sandwich.

These schisms were not lost on Austin's establishment—what establishment there was apart from Hormel and P-9. The dilemma for political leaders and civic activists was this: how to be helpful yet remain neutral. A natural focus for such efforts was Austin's mayor, Tom Kough. Kough (whose name rhymes with "cue") was an engineer in the plant and a P-9 member. He seemed to carry the credentials of someone who could command respect on both sides. He and Knowlton had played football together on Austin High's undefeated Big 9 Conference Champion team. They had graduated six names apart the following June. Kough had worked for Hormel more than twenty years—first as a salesman, then in the beef and hog kill, finally as an operating engineer. In 1982 Kough's antimonopoly stance with the Guyettes during the SMMPA fight helped him beat a company man in the fall race for mayor. But as the town's three-hundred-dollar-a-month mayor, Kough quickly developed a reputation for indecisiveness. Everyone who knew him said his heart was in the right place, but critics said he had a hard time choosing a stand when lobbyists were pulling him in opposite directions on some municipal issue. Kough's pat response was that he was simply trying to do what was right for Austin. And he garnered enough support to get reelected in the fall of 1984. Shortly after that election Kough tried to get Knowlton and Guyette to sit down together to work out their differences at a private Saturday morning meeting. They agreed, but the session disintegrated when Guyette showed up with a string of executive board members and TV cameras trailing after him. Knowlton stormed out, fuming that he had been set up. As the dispute wore on, Kough's support came almost exclusively from those who supported P-9, while his critics took to calling him Low-I (for low IQ).

Austin's council members, however, were determined to take some action. A month after Rogers gave his rousing talk at the high school, the city council unanimously passed a resolution urging both sides to sit down with a federal mediator. The resolution, introduced by council member and P-9 member Gerald Henricks, read, "It is not the intention of the council to interfere with the collective bargaining process," but the council clearly feared for that process in Austin. Henricks, a P-9 moderate who had private doubts about the corporate campaign, felt it would be to the community's advantage to push for an early solution. The city offered to find a mediator, even though mediators traditionally waited for requests to come from labor or management. The effort proved fruitless. Hormel and P-9 already were tied up in arbitration over the wage cut. Guyette told reporters that he thought the council meant well but that this was union business that the union would settle on its own.

Three months later, and barely two weeks after the corporate campaign began, Minnesota Governor Rudy Perpich made a personal peacemaking effort at the urging of State Senator Tom Nelson. Nelson, a Democrat who represented the Austin area, had observed the tension and the saber rattling and thought it was time for a little outside help. He also warned Perpich that voters might feel the governor was ignoring a spat in southern Minnesota that he would have followed closely had it occurred in his native Iron Range. Perpich, seeking to improve his standing among business leaders, also was concerned about Hormel's announcement a week earlier that it planned to study moving its headquarters from Austin. The plan was for Perpich to visit union and company officials separately and then extricate himself by setting up a three-person commission to meet with both sides and help look for solutions.

On the morning of February 4, 1985, the governor's entourage met at the corporate office with Knowlton, Nyberg, Larson, and Public Relations Director Allan Krejci. After hearing a description of the dispute that stressed industry events and intransigent union leadership, they proceeded to the union hall to meet with Guyette and his executive board. Toward the end of this meeting Perpich motioned to his state mediator, Paul Goldberg, to meet him in the hallway. Once outside, Perpich expressed shock. It was as if Hormel and P-9 were talking about two completely different situations, he said. Guyette had raised the conflict to a higher emotional plane, casting the issues in terms of impersonal and insensitive management, unsafe working conditions in the plant, and an assault by corporate America on the middle-class standard of living. Perpich could not believe the contrast. Nonetheless, he went ahead with the plan and appointed a task force consisting of Goldberg, Nelson, and former Mayor Enright to assist in whatever way they could to find a solution. Nyberg and Guyette both promised to cooperate, but Guyette stressed that any talks were not to be construed as negotiations. His board also expressed reservations about having two local politicians step into the fight.

The next Sunday Austin area ministers made their own effort at conciliation by placing cards saying "We Care" in church pews. After delivering sermons that stressed brotherhood and mutual concern, they asked churchgoers to sign the cards and put them in church collection plates for delivery to P-9 and Hormel leaders. It seemed sincere and well meaning; union members and foremen sat in the same pews, and the sight of Austin residents passing cards through their hands in churches across town underscored the community's concern. But the gesture already had been tainted. P-9 leaders had been cautioning their members to resist such efforts, hinting that the company was behind them. Three days before the sermons Business Agent Pete Winkels criticized the clergy for links to business owners who were members of the Austin Chamber of Commerce. Winkels denounced the effort as corporate blackmail to make P-9 abandon its campaign. "We should not let ourselves be misguided, misinformed or our judgment impaired by these efforts," he warned in a bulletin to P-9 members. "This is yet another means with which to pressure you, the Rank & File, into making rash, hurried, unwise decisions."

The failure of the church effort frustrated Larry Maier, a psychologist who had come to Austin from northern Minnesota in 1972 to become director of the city's mental health center. He had followed the anxious months of the new-plant battle in the mid-1970's, but like sociologist Terry Dilley, he had remained on the sidelines. Though still an outsider after twelve years in Austin, he thought he understood the rules. This time, however, he had a sense of foreboding and felt a need to do something about it. It had little to do with his association with either side. He saw the management crowd at Rotary meetings but didn't socialize with them, and his closest friend in the corporate office was an accountant with whom he played poker once a month. On the union side he occasionally golfed or fished with a few guys, but considered his life independent of theirs. What started to push him toward getting involved was Rogers's very first speech and the emphasis on fighting power with power. Maier sensed right away that the idea was out of place in a town like Austin. Then, as he studied the positions staked out by both sides, he concluded that Hormel had all the power. If Rogers and Guyette wanted to fight the kind of battle that would take them to First Bank and the Hormel Foundation, Maier simply could not understand where they would find any leverage.

Maier's foreboding increased in the spring of 1985. He began to feel that the conflict was getting beyond anyone's control and that no one in Austin seemed willing to speak out about it. So he organized a group of twenty Austin citizens—business people, an educator, a few politicians, and some concerned residents—to see what they could do. This group, called the Committee for Positive Action, met and kicked around ideas but kept coming up against the community's reluctance to intervene. The group itself was a good example. Half of the committee members didn't even come to meetings, preferring instead to donate money behind the scenes. With this reluctance in mind, the committee bought a full-page ad in the March 19 *Mower County Shopper,* calling P-9's demands unattainable and urging area residents to take a stand. "Since our community is being held hostage, we feel P-9 leaders are morally obligated to respond favorably to a strong statement from the community," the ad said. Included was a clip-and-return coupon urging P-9 to accept the so-called chain offer negotiated at other Hormel plants. In the days that followed, more than thirteen hundred coupons poured in to the committee. It wasn't as many as Maier had hoped, but it was five times greater than the normal response to coupon ads in the *Shopper.*

Buoyed by the sentiment, Maier called a press conference for the morning of April 2 to announce the results, hoping for a "little headline grabber" that might kick the community off center. Instead, when he showed up in the basement council chambers at Austin City Hall, he got his first taste of P-9's wrath. Guyette was there with a crowd of hat- and button-clad P-9 PROUD supporters. Maier opened the conference by reading a prepared statement, which he finished uninterrupted. But when he started to answer questions, the P-9ers became vocal. His do-gooders had never worked in a packinghouse, they said. They had never taken a pay cut, and they couldn't understand the frustration of P-9. Guyette was more direct. "We don't represent people who sent in coupons," he said. He also linked Maier's stance to Hormel money that went to build the hospital, which owned the mental health center. As the questions wore on, Maier grew frightened by the sneering intimidation, more frightened than he had ever been in his life. When he went home, his phone starting ringing, and the harassment continued. The anonymous callers didn't change his mind, and he certainly didn't change theirs. But he gradually came to sense that speaking out had made him something of a pariah in Austin. Whenever he was around, nobody wanted to talk about Hormel.

But Austin was slowly turning against P-9's leaders and Rogers, while still trying to maintain neutrality with its members. In the days preceding a new rank-and-file vote on whether to fund the corporate campaign, a flurry of anticampaign advertising appeared in the weekly *Shopper* and Austin *Daily Herald.* The dissident P-10 faction ran ads urging the union to return to the bargaining table and seek the chain contract that Hormel had signed with its other plants. A group of Hormel office workers criticized P-9 leaders for employing a "nearsighted, all or nothing smear campaign" that could result in Hormel's leaving Austin altogether. Hormel employed about six hundred nonunion people between its plant and corporate office. "We all have close friends and relatives working in the plant," the office workers wrote in one of the ads. "We just want it understood that we feel their union's executive board is not acting in their membership's best interests. Concessions have to be made on both sides."

Then, in the first week of May, the city council intervened again. By a 7–0 vote, the council urged Guyette to end the union's contract with Rogers and drop the campaign. The resolution came from council member Brad Swenson, a social worker and a neighbor of Guyette's who generally considered himself a liberal and a supporter of the working class. Still in his early thirties, Swenson was the council's junior member, a former Austin radio reporter who quit in 1984 and landed a counseling job in a local crime victims' center. Before moving to Austin in 1979, he and his wife had lived on the equally union-conscious Iron Range in northeastern Minnesota. But as the campaign gained notoriety, people whom Swenson had never met before were stopping him on the street, pleading with him to do something about it. Not only was pressure building within the community, but Swenson sensed it within himself. He feared all the publicity was giving Austin a bad image and that it had to stop before it got worse. He tossed around a number of ideas with other people about what to do before settling on a resolution. After checking with other council members, including P-9 members Bob Dahlback and Gerald Henricks, Swenson went ahead. "Because of the failing economic conditions in Austin, it is no longer in the city's best interest to maintain neutrality," the resolution said. "Thousands of livelihoods are at stake. We are all affected by the outcome." Mayor Kough thought the action was a little premature. He said he thought P-9's members should decide for themselves whether to retain Ray Rogers. But despite pressure from P-9, he took no steps to veto the measure.

If Swenson's resolution had any impact on P-9, it was to confirm the suspicions of Guyette's supporters. Swenson was part of Maier's Committee for Positive Action, and his resolution only proved to P-9ers that Austin was a company town, captive to Hormel and unwilling to tamper with a relationship that channeled thousands of dollars of grant money into the hospital, YMCA, and other civic projects. Guyette brushed aside the council's vote as an attempt to turn the victims of wage cuts into villains. A week later he joined Winkels, Huston, and a host of P-9 supporters at the city council meeting to criticize the resolution and give Swenson a taste of what his friend Maier had gone through. Swenson knew it was coming, and before the meeting, he tried to build an emotional shield around himself. He remembered from his days as a reporter being shocked at the verbal abuse showered on council members during the acrimonious utility dispute. Council members had demanded police escorts back then, and he wondered how bad it would get this time. Many of the same people were back with a new issue, lining up at microphone, and this time Swenson was on the receiving end.

When it came time to answer the stream of questions, he sat in his high-back chair and said nothing. He wasn't sure if he didn't want to respond, if he didn't know how, or if he felt it wouldn't do any good if he tried. But the more they grilled him, the more he sensed that they wanted nothing more than to intimidate him with their numbers. On that score, it got to be a kind of challenge. Swenson started to smile back. There really wasn't any need to be afraid, he thought.

But neither Swenson's resolution nor his demeanor could disarm P-9 or ease the tensions in Austin. In early June a petition backed by the P-10ers directing the executive board to negotiate for the chain offer was rejected by union members by a four-to-one margin. Later that month members also voted to resume funding the corporate campaign with weekly three-dollar assessments. With the international showing no sign of intervening, and Hormel positioning itself for more trouble, the pressure in Austin continued to build. In a town where waitresses served coffee on a first-name basis, where manager and laborer shared the same church pew, where Guyette might run into Knowlton on a Saturday morning shopping trip, there was no release for the pressure. Austin residents did care, as the church cards said, but only a few months later the gesture was beginning to look terribly naive and foolish. The rifts between Hormel and P-9 seemed to grow wider with every attempt to heal them. "You don't know who you can talk to," a waitress at the Pepper Mill lamented that spring, implying that in a town like Austin the grapevine would carry any ill-considered comment back to the executives at Hormel or the officers of P-9. For a town that had grown up with all the prosperity and happiness of the *Leave It to Beaver* community that Pete Winkels remembered, Austin was becoming a dangerous place to crack a smile.

CHAPTER

8

Lewie Anderson had made plenty of trips to Austin before, but never with a police escort. On Sunday, April 14, 1985, having finally agreed with Guyette on terms for a meeting, Anderson and his entourage flew to Minneapolis and drove to Austin. Anderson had also addressed plenty of angry rank-and-file meetings before; but seldom had he received death threats from his own members, and Austin police and UFCW officials decided to take no chances. Police met the UFCW entourage at the edge of town and escorted it to a back entrance of Austin High School. Anderson was a little nervous, but he hadn't quite given up hope that he could explain the UFCW's position on the P-9 dispute and bring the feisty local back into the fold. For officers of the parent union and for the people of Austin, his visit was the trump card, the best shot at reaching the rank and file directly and cutting through the suspicion that Guyette had created out of months of fruitless correspondence. For the rank and file, however, it was a very different opportunity. A handful of sympathizers was hoping Anderson would make his case and prevail. But a much bigger group, including critics and those with mixed feelings, expected an accounting, an explanation of why the international wasn't supporting its most steadfast local. And a third group, the Guyette loyalists, were ready to give Anderson hell.

Once more the great old Austin High auditorium was packed

wall to wall with union members. Outside, women and children paraded on the sidewalk with signs reading LEWIE, YOU'VE BEEN A LONG TIME COMING and WHY SHOULD WE GIVE 23 PERCENT FOR AN-OTHER V.P.? But this time the rally was not designed for TV cam-eras and reporters. Anderson had insisted that this be a true membership meeting, closed to family members, the media, and Ray Rogers. A sergeant at arms stood at each entrance, checking union cards, and the doors closed when the meeting began. Rogers, however, was not to be denied his chance for more pub-licity. Waiting until the last minute, when all the UFCW officers were in place onstage, he herded a dozen reporters into a small office just off the wings, where the proceedings would be piped in over a speaker. For the next five hours the reporters huddled in chairs and on the floor with notebooks and tape recorders, taking down every word of the meeting, ferrying in and out covertly for trips to toilets or the telephone lest they be spotted by international officials.

After opening remarks from Guyette, Wendell Olson, the UFCW's regional director in Bloomington, Minnesota, introduced Jay Foreman and an assistant to Bill Wynn. Foreman tried to be-gin on a conciliatory note. He told a few jokes, but the meat-packers were not amused. He moved on to a somewhat fatherly lecture about the error of P-9's ways. He told them that Lewie Anderson wasn't a villain, that Anderson represented the views of the top UFCW leadership. "This is a family dispute," he said. Though Foreman had been sympathetic toward Rogers before the campaign began, he was even more concerned now that the Austin members had spurned the UFCW's advice and launched an expensive and ineffective campaign. "Straying local unions can do so much harm to sister unions," Foreman said. "Each time one local union breaks off from the pack, we are weaker and they are weaker." Hoots and catcalls filled the air.

Now it was Anderson's turn. He began by denying the charge that he was soft on employers. If P-9's members thought he was so concession-prone, he said, they should talk to the meat-packers at Oscar Mayer's packinghouse in Perry, Iowa. There rank-and-file members had been ready to give the company a pay cut to six dollars an hour in late 1982, when Anderson had in-sisted they reject the contract. The local members went ahead and ratified the contract, and the UFCW put them under trusteeship and threw out the contract. Or they could talk to workers in Estherville, Iowa, where the UFCW opposed a 28 percent wage cut by John Morrell & Company and local clergy actually prayed in the street that the UFCW would OK the concession to save jobs. In 1982 the UFCW dusted off Article 23 of its constitution, a little-used provision that required a local union to get the international's permission before ratifying any local agreements. That year the UFCW invoked Article 23 more than eighty times in an effort to hold ranks among frightened locals that were bolting from the pattern contracts and granting concessions. Between 1980 and 1984, Anderson said, some sixty major packinghouses had shut down, many because the UFCW refused to approve wage concessions by local unions. "We're the ones who took the position that closed plants, for crying out loud," Anderson said. "Now tens of thousands of packinghouse workers have lost their jobs in this industry, and even if you achieved ten dollars and sixty-nine cents in Austin again, it's the ten-dollar-and-sixty-nine-cent jobs that will be the first to go."

The members of P-9 were not buying. One after another, they moved to floor microphones, demanding to know why the international union wasn't behind its most militant local, why Anderson applied his wage strategy at the bottom instead of holding the line at the top, why the international was lining up other meat-packing locals against P-9. "The real reason you're against us," one worker shouted, "is that once we get our ten dollars and sixty-nine cents back, the others will see they don't need you anymore."

Guyette presided calmly at the lectern, maintaining order and keeping the questioners in line. But he was also biding his time. This was a long-awaited opportunity to confront Anderson personally for what Guyette regarded as a long history of betrayal, including a key bargaining development now four years old. When most of the speakers on the floor had had their say, Guyette harked back to 1981 and the last set of contract talks between Hormel and its nine chain plants, during which Anderson had led the union negotiating team. Those talks had produced a contract summary, Guyette said, which explicitly promised that there would be "no increase or reduction in rates"

over the contract's lifetime. When negotiators brought that summary back to Austin for ratification, union members understood
it to be a guarantee against wage cuts, Guyette said. But when
Hormel came asking for wage cuts in 1983, and when P-9's negotiators turned to their contract, the clause was missing. Guyette
had generated quite a stir over the so-called missing language in
the weeks before Anderson's visit. He even demanded that the
international bring up Anderson on charges of deceiving the
membership. Now he pursued the question doggedly.

Anderson spent more than an hour trying to defuse it. In the
first place, he said, the missing language referred to the contract's
cost-of-living mechanism, not base wages. The paragraph that
Guyette cited was plainly under the heading "Cost of Living Adjustment," and it meant that Hormel could freeze the workers'
COLA increments; it didn't refer to base wages, he said. He noted
that Guyette and Floyd Lenoch had been part of Austin's bargaining committee in 1981 and knew full well what was being negotiated. If Guyette hadn't liked it, why hadn't he brought it up then?
It had been packinghouse practice for decades to take a summary
to the membership for ratification while lawyers were dotting the
i's and crossing the *t*'s. If the final contract didn't say "no increase
or reduction in rates," that was because it spelled out in legal
terms that the COLA provision was frozen. That didn't mean
there were substantive differences between the contract and the
summary. Finally, he said, the 1981 contract was irrelevant to the
Austin wage cut. Hormel was relying on its 1978 contract with
P-9 alone, the special arrangement to assure that a new plant
would be built in Austin. It was the 1978 contract that contained
the me-too clause that allowed Hormel to cut wages. Arbitrator
George Fleischli had ruled that on the wage adjustment issue the
1978 contract superseded Hormel's 1981 chain contract, and a
UFCW lawyer had warned P-9 about it in the spring of 1984.

For all of Anderson's labored explanations, he sounded highly
suspicious to an auditorium full of frustrated union members, and
the questions went on and on. The meeting dragged on past four
o'clock, then five o'clock, and the meat-packers' fury showed no
sign of letting up. Finally Anderson told the crowd he'd had
enough and the questions were getting redundant.

"You'll stay here as long as we want!" came a shout from the crowd.

"That's what you think," Foreman replied, and he and Anderson made a beeline for the door and headed to their car, parked across the street. They had plenty of company from reporters and hostile P-9ers as they made the short, brisk walk. Anderson told reporters to meet him at the Holiday Inn in Albert Lea for a press conference to explain everything. When a small caravan of reporters and P-9ers arrived at the motel, Anderson and Foreman were in the bar, collecting their wits over beer and cigarettes before going in front of the lions again. But if Anderson was shaken by the five-hour confrontation, he didn't show it. By the time he got into the press conference room, it was packed with P-9 members, and the press conference, too, deteriorated into a rank-and-file interrogation.

With the bitter failure of Anderson's visit, a new pessimism began to sink in around Austin and at Hormel corporate headquarters. Dave Larson had never quite expected the rank and file to bolt on Guyette, but that didn't keep him from hoping. He knew P-9 members were bitter—hell, he thought, nobody liked the prospect of wage cuts. Still, as he watched the TV news reports of Rogers's rallies, he sometimes wondered if these were the same people he had been working with and living with for years. He hoped that as the campaign dragged on, the rank and file would recognize that they weren't doing the company much damage and that 90 percent of other meat-packers already had taken wage cuts like the ones Hormel sought. Now it was clear that the UFCW had no magic spell to call off the corporate campaign, that Lewie Anderson couldn't ride into town, dethrone Jim Guyette and change fifteen hundred minds.

With P-9's members clearly behind Guyette and beyond the UFCW's reach, Nyberg and Larson began positioning themselves for war at the bargaining table. On May 31 Hormel announced its intention to terminate the labor agreement with P-9 on its expiration date in August. Though the step appeared procedural and moot, it gave Hormel several important advantages. The old contract automatically renewed itself for one year unless one side canceled it. Terminating the contract freed Hormel from one of the most restrictive provisions of the annual-wage feature: fifty-two weeks' notice before any layoffs. With the contract's expiration in August, Hormel would be free to lay off workers at will. The old contract contained another remarkable provision: Laid-off workers had first preference for any new openings for ten years, with the company picking up their health insurance premiums for the entire period. Terminating the contract freed Hormel from that provision as well. Finally, terminating the contract would free Hormel, if the parties bargained to an impasse, to impose brand-new wages and working conditions in the Austin plant when the old contract expired. Under federal labor law, that would leave P-9 only two choices: Work under the new terms or go on strike. In years past imposing a settlement was a power seldom exercised by employers because it risked provoking a strike. But it had become more common in the 1980's, when unions were reluctant to strike and high unemployment gave employers a ready pool of strikebreakers.

In case anyone missed the point of its contractual maneuvering, Hormel sent a more obvious signal that it was preparing for the worst: In May it bought eighty thousand dollars' worth of barbed wire to string atop the storm fence encircling the Austin packinghouse. Hormel spokesman Allan Krejci said the barbed wire would provide better security year-round but added, "In the event of a strike, this might be needed."

In the last week of June P-9 and Hormel negotiators finally sat down at the bargaining table to begin work on a new contract. What transpired at the bargaining table was remarkably symbolic of the entire dispute. At an informal prenegotiations meeting in the basement of the Oak Leaf restaurant, Dave Larson, Hormel's chief negotiator, announced that he would turn the talks over to Bill Swanson, personnel manager in the Austin plant, and a team of assistants. There was a logic to this—Larson was in charge of labor relations for all of Hormel's plants, and the negotiations about to commence concerned Austin alone—but the decision also reflected Larson's utter frustration over negotiations that had taken place so far. One morning the previous December his team had driven over to the Austin Labor Center for a session to resolve the issues from Fleischli's arbitration decision. They talked from about ten-thirty in the morning until noon, then broke for lunch, unable to agree even on what the other companies' contracts said about vacations. When they resumed at one-thirty the management team drove back to the union hall and took their places and the P-9 team filed in. No Guyette. Larson asked where he was and was told that he had locked himself in his office at the start of the lunch break and had not emerged. Five minutes later Guyette walked into the bargaining room with a legal pad in hand and read a prepared statement denouncing the company's demands for concessions. End of session.

The Hormel negotiating team in June included Bill Swanson; Dave Gardner, who was Larson's assistant in labor relations; Jim Cavanaugh, who was an assistant to Nyberg in the legal department; Jim Alexander, Hormel's benefits manager; and a few assistants. P-9's team consisted of the eight-member executive board plus Guyette and Joe Hansen, the new UFCW regional director from the Twin Cities. The board consisted of Keith Judd, Skinny Weis, Floyd Lenoch, Kenny Hagen, Jim Retterath, Lynn Huston, Pete Winkels, and Audrey Neumann, who was playing a less active role because of health problems. Of P-9's three top officers, only Guyette had ever been through contract talks before, and he had been a dissenter in 1981 and 1984. Of the other six board members, four were veterans with varying lengths of service. But contract talks in the past had always meant sitting in a Chicago hotel playing cards or watching TV while Jesse Prosten or Lewie Anderson and Dick Schaefer did most of the negotiating. In addition, the board was working without the benefit of a Chicago law firm, Cotton, Watt, Jones, King & Bowlus, the UFCW's meat-packing lawyers who had led most of the Hormel contract talks for years. Guyette was suspicious of the firm's close relationship with the international and its involvement in the earlier contracts that had caused so much confusion in Austin. P-9 eventually brought in Ron Rollins, a young but seasoned Minneapolis labor lawyer whose client list included such unusual unions as the Minnesota Orchestra Musicians' Association and the Twin Cities Newspaper Guild. He was rare in that he had solid bargaining experience but wasn't afraid to take on a client that was becoming a pariah in mainstream labor circles. He knew P-9 was bucking the current, but he also respected Guyette as someone fiercely committed to a cause. Still, his white-collar clients made some board members uneasy about his ability to represent a gruff working-class bunch that slaughtered hogs all day long.

For his part, Guyette fumed that the executives who really made decisions at Hormel weren't at the table. Since he was the head of P-9, he argued, Hormel should come to the table with its top man, Dick Knowlton. Others on Guyette's team took the whole business less seriously. P-9's vice-president, Lynn Huston, thought nothing of showing up at negotiations in a Harley-Davidson T-shirt and aviator sunglasses, grinning under a handlebar mustache and combing back his long, curly hair with styling mousse. Huston, who had once been a supervisor at an Austin building products store, knew a little about management psychology and never missed an opportunity to tease the corporate executives across the table from him. He would compliment them effusively on their suntans or their expensive pens, then watch as they squirmed in confusion. Before one meeting Huston arrived early and arranged the Hormel team's chairs so that three were widely spaced along the table and four were bunched together at one end. He anticipated that the junior members of the committee would confine themselves to the cramped chairs, deferring to their superiors to take the others. That was exactly what happened, and Huston spent a good deal of the meeting chuckling over their discomfort. Lenoch, P-9's former president, took the role of embittered elder statesman. Winkels surrounded himself with stacks of books and legal pads and an ever-present bottle of orange juice. He developed a talent for shooting holes in the company's logic and called himself "Guyette's designated asshole."

Larson and his team had never encountered anything quite like this cocky hostility. They were used to negotiators, labor or management, who cussed and hollered and pounded the table and stormed out of bargaining sessions. They were used to hearing union leaders bad-mouth the company. That was fair game. In fact, it was part of the ritual, proof that you were doing your best for your side. Larson knew the rituals well. He had been in talks that could have been settled hours, even days before a strike deadline. But time and again both sides held out to the last minute, staying up for marathon twenty-four-hour bargaining sessions and finally reaching a compromise at the stroke of midnight. If you didn't operate that way, they reasoned, how were the union members or the top executives going to believe that you fought for the very best deal? But Larson also knew that behind the hollering and posturing, successful talks required two ingredients: a willingness to compromise and some degree of trust, even if it lay between only one member of management and one member of the union bargaining committee. Larson knew that contracts were not settled between two big groups facing off at a big mahogany table. They were settled on the phone after the committees had retired for the night, over a quiet cup of coffee, or in a small room with just him, a mediator, and one or two union representatives.

What they were not prepared for was utter contempt, even sarcasm at the bargaining table. Guyette, Winkels, and Huston had a pretty good idea that negotiating involved certain rituals; they just found the rituals suspect and refused to take them seriously. The difference between them and the company negotiators, Winkels later remarked, was that Larson's team appeared to go through the motions seriously but regarded it as just a job, while P-9's teams regarded the dispute as a personal crusade but refused to take the process seriously. Winkels later wondered if it was a mistake to show their contempt so abundantly.

For all appearances that month, P-9 remained more active on the sidewalk and in the courtroom than at the bargaining table. At the end of May P-9 had filed suit in the U.S. district court in Minneapolis asking a judge to order Hormel to clarify its implementation of Fleischli's arbitration ruling. P-9 said in the suit that it hoped to submit the issue to Fleischli still another time. In other words, even after three well-argued decisions had gone against them, Guyette and the executive board refused to acknowledge that they had lost and that Hormel had the legal right to cut wages.

On the corporate campaign front, every week seemed to bring new tactics. P-9 issued a special edition of *The Unionist* citing the Austin packinghouse for one of the highest injury rates in the nation. In vivid detail and grotesque pictures it told stories about the anguish of P-9 men and women whose wrists, hands, shoulders, and backs were mangled in the new plant's rush to profitability. It was one of many times when P-9 and Hormel seemed to operate off completely different sets of facts. Guyette said repeatedly that in 1984 the Austin plant had 202 injuries per 100 workers. He said the information came from a Hormel memo. In fact, it came from a nurse's log in the packinghouse, and it included every visit to the nurse's office, whether it be for an aspirin, a Band-Aid, or a major injury. Hormel issued a detailed response, including a brochure on safety in the plant. Statistics from the Occupational Safety and Health Administration (OSHA) showed that each side had a point. Hormel as a whole had fewer serious injuries than the meat-packing industry in general during 1983, 1984, and 1985. (The standard industry measure is a "lost workday injury"—an injury serious enough that a worker has to go home and can't return for his or her next normal shift. Hormel's average for the period ranged from 11.6 to 14.9 lost workday injuries per 100 workers per year. The industry average in those years ranged from 15.1 to 16.2.) But OSHA statistics for the same years also showed that the Austin packinghouse had more lost workday injuries than the rest of Hormel's plants and more than the industry average. Hormel blamed the influx of inexperienced workers and said that Minnesota's system of compensating injured workers, which pays a relatively high percentage of lost wages, encourages workers to stay home. (In 1986 Hormel's lost workday injury rate fell to half the industry average, and the rate in Austin fell to one fourth the industry rate.) Still, everybody knew that the injury rate in Austin had been high as the stream of new workers came into the plant and learned the difficult jobs, and the members of Local 9 showed off their own scars from knife slashes and carpal-tunnel surgery to prove the point.

P-9 also continued to spread its message in the Twin Cities, making speakers available for union meetings and sending delegates to evening gatherings of the new Metro Area Support Group, a group of sympathetic union activists. On June 25 P-9 sent a caravan of workers to Iowa, for a solidarity rally with workers at UFCW Local 431 at Hormel's packinghouse in Ottumwa. Guyette and Winkels knew that Ottumwa was crucial if it came to a strike. Ottumwa was one of three big Hormel plants that slaughtered hogs, providing the raw material that anchored the company's operations across the Midwest. Austin was the biggest, with Ottumwa and Fremont, Nebraska, providing strategic diversity. Equally important, it was the only other Hormel plant where workers were not prohibited from staging a sympathy strike if Austin walked out.

Though few, if any, of the P-9ers realized it at the time, they were retracing the steps of their forebears: Frank Ellis had taken his organizing bandwagon to Ottumwa in the mid-1930's, and packinghouse workers at the big Morrell packinghouse there had signed on with the Independent Union of All Workers in 1937. The turnout for P-9 in 1985 was small, in part because the Ottumwa local's officers sided with Lewie Anderson, not Guyette. But the P-9ers were undaunted; they knew that many in the rank and file were still deeply bitter toward Hormel, going back to the layoffs of 1984. They were looking for a chance to fight back, and P-9 was more than willing to fuel their anger with their own stories about Hormel's misdeeds in Austin.

In June P-9 opened a whole new front in the campaign by attacking the Hormel Foundation, a charitable trust established by George Hormel and his son, Jay, in 1941. The foundation was one of the many features that set Hormel apart from other corporations. It poured millions of dollars into Austin charities and civic organizations over the years, but it had a second purpose: assuring local control of the company they had founded. George and Jay feared that after they died, outsiders might gain control of the company, leaving the town that had been so good to them with nothing. They bequeathed the foundation nearly half of the company's common stock and wrote articles of incorporation establishing a foundation board of five to fifteen members, all of whom had to be Mower County residents whose chief financial interests were in Austin. This turned out to be a prescient move because, during the corporate takeover wave of the 1970's and 1980's, it kept control of the stock out of reach of Wall Street arbitrageurs and safely in the hands of local business and civic leaders.

By 1985 the foundation controlled 45.6 percent of Hormel stock either through stock it owned or its ability to vote stock in family trusts—virtually insuperable control of the company. Its board consisted of Knowlton; three retired Hormel executives; the retired chairman of First Bank Austin; six executives of local nonprofit organizations, such as the YMCA and the United Way, that received foundation grants; one active businessman; and two Austin attorneys. For better or worse, the foundation kept Hormel virtually impregnable to outside ownership or management.

In its founding documents Hormel executives insisted that the foundation's chief purpose was not to benefit the family or restrict control of the company but to ensure that whoever controlled the Hormel company had the best interests of Austin in mind. Skinny Weis had done a lot of research into the foundation even before P-9 hired Ray Rogers, and now Rogers and Guyette began to hammer away at the theme of local interests, resurrecting concerns that had last surfaced during the stormy debate to build the new plant. In a special issue of *The Unionist,* they documented Hormel's gradual expansion outside Austin and asked how a 23 percent wage cut for Austin workers could be considered in the best interest of Austin. Eventually they asked retired federal Judge Miles Lord, a controversial judicial activist in Minneapolis, to investigate the foundation and called on Minnesota Attorney General Hubert Humphrey III to explore whether the foundation's incestuous nature violated state law. Neither investigation produced results, but that didn't stop P-9's amateur legal researchers from insisting that they had irrefutable proof that the foundation could revoke the wage cut with a simple phone call to top management.

Chuck Nyberg watched these developments with a mixture of amusement and alarm. It was true that the foundation was an unconventional arrangement that restricted stockholder control of the company and was vulnerable to government scrutiny. On the other hand, he was confident that Hormel could defend its position: A healthy company was vital to a healthy Austin, and wage cuts were vital to Hormel's health. Knowlton and the Hormel directors were determined not to go to the brink of bankruptcy like Chrysler or Braniff to find out if wage cuts were essential to its health. As for P-9's earnest efforts to gain support in Ottumwa and the Twin Cities, Nyberg knew the die already was cast: P-9 would not get a better wage offer than its counterparts at the other Hormel plants. On that Knowlton was firm. It had been risky enough, Knowlton liked to say, to commit to ten dollars an hour at the other plants when Hormel had to compete with plants that paid five dollars an hour. Knowlton, Nyberg, and Larson knew that to give in to P-9 at this stage was to hand Guyette and Rogers an enormous victory that would haunt Hormel for years.

On July 2, with only six weeks to go on their current contract, P-9's negotiators gave Hormel their contract proposal. Larson and his team were stunned. The document was the most extraordinary wish list they had ever seen. It proposed raising wages from $9.25 to $12.50 an hour and restoring the old plant's incentive system. It asked for reinstatement of cost-of-living raises, with adjustments twice a year. It proposed "well pay" bonuses of 10 percent per week for every employee who showed up for work every day. It allowed any worker from Austin to transfer at will to any Hormel plant anywhere in the country—and work there under the terms of the Austin contract. It called for Hormel nearly to double its Austin work force to twenty-two hundred workers and, for every product that could be produced in Austin, to pull that production line out of Hormel's other plants and return it to Austin. It asked for paid clothes-changing time of one hour a day. It reduced work loads to the level of 1978, 20 percent below those in effect in the new plant. It called for an end to the guaranteed annual wage and proposed that Hormel pay overtime as it was worked, but it retained the fifty-two-week layoff notice. It also granted union members the right to strike over any safety issue or any grievance at any time—a right that is rare in today's labor contracts. The document revealed such a yawning gulf between P-9 and Hormel that Larson knew that day that a strike was all but inevitable. Bill Swanson, the plant's personnel manager, glanced through the proposal and told P-9's team, "Why don't I just hand you the keys to the plant?"

It was, in short, a breathtakingly ambitious contract, an attempt to rewrite forty-five years of bargaining history in one stroke. Hormel negotiators weren't the only ones who were stunned. Dick Schaefer had helped fashion many of P-9's contract provisions during his thirteen years as business agent. He learned of P-9's new proposal through his network of sources within the union and was aghast. In his experience, and the experience of most seasoned negotiators, it was unheard of to put a whole new document on the table. Guyette and the other executive board members said they were responding to rank-and-file frustration over operating under multiple contracts: the new-plant agreement; the transition agreement from the old plant; the 1981 UFCW wage freeze agreement. They wanted to clean the slate. But the maneuver ran enormous tactical risks. For starters, most labor contracts represent an accumulation of benefits, compromises, and arcane practices built up over a period of years. It's much easier to work off a familiar document and propose changes here and there. For another, existing language has been tested by practice and each side knows how the other side will apply it—or exploit it. But most important, all the desirable features of a contract remain intact unless the parties agree to change them or one side gives them up. To present a complete new contract implicitly gives up the old one and opens the door for the other side to scrap provisions that took years of bargaining to achieve. That is exactly what Hormel did.

Like Larson, Joe Hansen was thrown a little off-balance by these unconventional developments. Ostensibly he was sitting with P-9 as an observer and adviser in case the local negotiators needed outside expertise. And he was not without hope. Earlier that spring he and Wendell Olson, who was about to retire as the UFCW's regional director, met with Guyette and Floyd Lenoch in the UFCW's Bloomington office. Hansen, still a little unsure of the ground in Austin, let the veteran Olson take the lead. Olson warned Guyette and Lenoch that despite the corporate campaign, Hormel would never give Austin more than the other plants had. Austin's historical privileges were gone, he warned, and Hormel simply was not going to reward a group of militant leaders. Lenoch acknowledged as much, and the session left Hansen with a certain confidence that the P-9 board knew the reality of the situation. Later that spring, at a packinghouse convention, Guyette had approached Hansen and asked him to be the international's representative at talks in Austin. Hansen knew that there was bad blood between Guyette and Anderson, who normally would have represented the UFCW in packinghouse talks. He had no trouble arranging it with Anderson. Hansen felt some confidence that there still could be a bridge between the international union and P-9, and he knew he was probably the only bridge left.

Besides, Hansen had considerable sympathy for P-9: He had worked in a packinghouse, had the credentials of a dissident, and himself had bucked the UFCW more than once. Hansen had grown up in Chicago and Milwaukee and spent an abortive semester at both the University of Wisconsin and Marquette University, then gone to work in a packinghouse to support his wife and the baby on the way. He wasn't particularly interested in unions until he went to work in the meat department of a National Foods supermarket in Milwaukee and fell in with a group of older butchers who became good friends and began dragging him along to union meetings. Before long Hansen was a regular at union meetings, then a candidate for union office, and eventually one of the local's most promising leaders. But he was young and had a mind of his own. In 1968 he worked for Robert Kennedy's presidential campaign, even though the AFL-CIO was behind Hubert Humphrey. In 1972 he threw himself into the George McGovern campaign, even though George Meany kept the AFL-CIO neutral, fuming over McGovern's reforms of the Democratic party. Much like Guyette, one day, Hansen even got himself thrown out of a state AFL-CIO convention in 1972 for distributing McGovern leaflets.

Still, Hansen was intensely loyal to his union, then the Amalgamated Meatcutters and Butcher Workmen. When Wendell Olson, his regional director, visited Milwaukee one day to recruit a new staff member, somebody in Hansen's local recommended the young activist. He took the job, moved to Bloomington, and became one of its most effective organizers. He was eventually promoted to Olson's chief assistant and in the spring of 1985 succeeded him as regional director for the Upper Midwest.

Once talks began in Austin, however, Hansen's confidence began slipping. With his experience negotiating dozens of supermarket and packinghouse contracts he was pretty sure that he could get movement out of Swanson and Gardner, at least on noneconomic issues such as seniority and safety. But he also knew that P-9 would have to start paring down its list of demands. Seasoned negotiators know that a bargaining committee must do as much horse trading internally as with the other side, balancing one issue against another, drawing up priorities and casting off minor demands to focus on the crucial ones that are worth pursuing at the table. After meeting with Hormel's team, the P-9 team would caucus alone and Hansen would urge them to trim their list of demands or at least to draw up a list of priorities. They reviewed their proposal for hours at a time, trying to find items they could do without. But each time Hansen suggested something was unnecessary—a day off for country dwellers to vote in township elections, perhaps, or a demand that Hormel share vending-machine profits with P-9—someone on the committee defended it, and nobody on the committee seemed to have the will to boil down the list. If their inexperience showed anywhere during negotiations, it was here. Maintaining such a large list of demands implied that P-9 had bargaining leverage to achieve them. Guyette was convinced that the campaign was bringing pressure on Hormel, but the signs were less than convincing. With the UFCW at odds with the local's strategy, there was good reason to question how much support it would provide if talks collapsed into a strike. If the leverage was there, P-9 had a chance to make great strides. If not, the big list could become a liability when the time came to start horse trading because the union would have to give away a lot to get a little.

For its part, Hormel wasn't racing toward compromise either. Swanson delivered the company's first proposal on July 17, just a month before P-9 could legally strike. It was P-9's turn to be stunned. Larson and Swanson felt Hormel was entitled to the drastic cuts awarded by the arbitrator Fleischli, and they modeled their proposal on Fleischli's decision. The proposal cut night shift premium pay from twenty-one cents an hour to ten cents. It reduced the number of holidays from ten to eight. It cut the maximum amount of vacation from six weeks to four. It reduced the duration of sick leaves and the amount of pay workers receive while sick. It also abolished all "past practices"—informal traditions usually favorable to the union that had crept into the plant's operation over the years and had attained virtually the power of contract language. It drastically restricted the plant's grievance and arbitration system. (Traditionally, when a worker is disciplined and files a grievance, an outside arbitrator can rule on two issues: whether the employee broke the contract and what the punishment should be. Even when he finds the employee guilty, the arbitrator typically reduces the punishment from discharge to some lesser discipline. Under Hormel's proposal, the arbitrator would have the power only to determine whether the employee had broken the contract, not to soften the discipline.) It also contained a curious paragraph that came to be known as the Ray Rogers clause, which banned union leafleting and boycotts. Finally, the proposal radically rewrote the plant's seniority procedures, giving supervisors more power to transfer workers from one job to another.

What scared attorney Ron Rollins most about the company's approach, however, was its rigidity at the bargaining table. He tested its flexibility on a few innocuous issues and found almost no movement. By late July he noticed that Hormel's negotiators kept using the word "impasse" and implying that contract talks had reached a stalemate. He began to fear that Hormel was using a tactic that was becoming common among aggressive employers: Present harsh contract proposals; present them late in negotiations; then engage in "surface" bargaining so that there would be little chance for settlement. If the union struck when the contract expired, the employer was free under federal law to impose its final offer and dare the workers to return under its terms—or hire replacements.

It didn't comfort Rollins and P-9's officers that Hormel was getting legal advice from Thomas Krukowski, a Milwaukee labor lawyer with a growing reputation for aggressive tactics against unions. Krukowski had represented an employer group called the Milwaukee Independent Meatpackers Association during a notorious and violent strike by a thousand packinghouse workers in 1974 and 1975. The employers filed a number of lawsuits and unfair-labor-practice charges against the meat-packers' union, and by the beginning of 1975 the workers had decertified their union and the strike was broken. The firm where Krukowski started also had represented management in bitter strikes against Harley-Davidson and Master Lock in Milwaukee. Krukowski himself subsequently published a handbook for employers on handling unions, and by the early 1980's he had made the AFL-CIO's national "rub sheet" of lawyers considered union busters. (Two years later, in a case involving another Milwaukee meat-packing firm, the NLRB accused one of Krukowski's staff lawyers of doing just what Rollins feared at Hormel: counseling an obstructionist bargaining strategy in the hope of provoking a strike. An administrative law judge for the NLRB subsequently found that correspondence between Krukowski's assistant and the client also suggested they never intended to bargain in good faith. Krukowski denied that his firm had done such a thing and said the judge misread the correspondence with the client.)

At Hormel Krukowski took a less active role. He was hired in 1983 to handle the Fleischli arbitration hearings—not because he was a union buster but because he was hardworking and familiar with the meat-packing industry, according to Nyberg. Krukowski never sat at the bargaining table for Hormel and never drafted actual proposals, but he did advise Hormel on the legal aspects of the strike, including how to restrict picketing, how to reopen a struck plant, and how legally to implement a final contract offer. Rollins subsequently filed an unfair-labor-practice charge that Hormel had bargained in bad faith during these summer months, but the NLRB found that Hormel had bargained in good faith. Still, Hormel's switch from the big, genteel Minneapolis firm of Dorsey, Whitney to Krukowski's scrappy Milwaukee firm sent an aggressive signal to P-9's negotiators.

Hormel's negotiators weren't talking publicly about their strategy, but they had little reason to start making compromises with P-9. Nyberg and Larson had been suspicious of Guyette since the day he was elected, and the hostility expressed in the corporate campaign gave them no more faith in him. They felt they were in a position of strength, considering the company's diversification in recent years and P-9's lack of support from the UFCW, and they saw no reason to start offering compromises until P-9 did.

On July 26, after eleven fruitless bargaining sessions, Hormel sent its loudest possible signal to the P-9 rank and file that it would not be fazed by a walkout. It announced completion of a marketing agreement with FDL Foods, Inc., a hog-processing company based in Dubuque, Iowa, that allowed Hormel to sell FDL products under the Hormel label. Actually the term "marketing agreement" was a little disingenuous. In fact, the deal turned over all of FDL's pork production directly to Hormel and vastly increased Hormel's outside sources of raw meat. Though little known as a supermarket brand name, FDL had an enormous hog-slaughtering capacity—roughly two thirds of Hormel's own slaughtering capacity and easily enough to replace the slaughtering done at the Austin packinghouse. Joining forces with FDL gave Hormel roughly 10 percent of the nation's hog-slaughtering capacity, making it number two in the nation. It also gave Hormel a ready source of pork, bacon, and sausage in case P-9 went on strike. Moreover, the meat-packers at FDL, though represented by the UFCW, were making only eight dollars an hour. That meant that Hormel could weather a strike in Austin, replace the lost capacity, and actually save money on wages. Knowlton publicly hinted that it would even allow Hormel to grow, a stunning accomplishment considering that its flagship plant might be mothballed.

Guyette dismissed the agreement as "an effort to pit FDL workers against workers in Austin." In effect, he was right, but his proclamation did not diminish Hormel's bargaining leverage. Hansen and Rollins could see that after a month the union negotiators weren't getting anywhere, and P-9 decided it was time to ask for outside help. The same day that Hormel announced the agreement with FDL, Hormel and Guyette agreed to ask for help of a federal mediator.

The two sides sat down with mediator Hank Bell on Saturday morning, August 3, in the basement of St. Edwards Catholic Church. Bell, a former electrician who had joined the Federal Mediation Service and built a reputation as a gruff but resourceful mediator, indicated at once that the prospects were bleak. The two negotiating teams were doing little but bashing heads when they sat down together, with the very real prospect that they were making matters worse instead of better. Bell decided it was time to put the teams in separate rooms, a common mediation tactic, while he shuttled back and forth, testing their positions and prodding them for movement. Bell also suggested a change of scenery. The church basement was cramped and offered little room for subcaucusing. Rollins once called a subcaucus with Guyette and Cavanaugh and they ended up in a little room where the Reverend Donald Zenk changed clothes before mass. But

Guyette didn't want to stray far from Austin; it seemed that every time the executive board left town, Hormel or the UFCW dropped some new bombshell, trying to rattle his rank and file. Both sides eventually agreed to adjourn to a Holiday Inn in Albert Lea, twenty-five miles to the west on Interstate 90.

Bell knew that time was short and that he had to keep the pressure up. He called the parties together for seven straight days of grueling negotiations. Often he left the P-9 team alone for hours to search for compromises, with obvious comments like "I think I'll take a walk and see you in three or four hours." Slowly P-9's executive board started paring down its list of demands. On August 7 they dropped the wage proposal from $12.50 an hour to $11.25 and gave ground on holidays, vacations, job bidding, and several other issues. In addition, P-9 offered to tie wages to profits: If Hormel didn't match its 1984 profit of $29.5 million, P-9 would take wage cuts to $10 an hour. Larson laughed when he saw that proposal. He had been the original author of a scheme tying wages to profits more than a year earlier, in contract talks with the Ottumwa local. Except under Larson's proposal, Hormel would cut wages first and raise them later if profits materialized. The way he calculated P-9's scheme, Hormel would forgo millions of dollars in profits over several quarters before wages would ratchet down to $10 an hour. Besides, a profit of $29.5 million wasn't much of a target for a company that, with the FDL acquisition, was almost 50 percent bigger than it had been in 1984.

It wasn't until August 9 that Hormel put its wage proposal on the table. P-9 was shocked again. Hormel proposed a base wage of ten dollars an hour, but with a very big catch: New employees would be hired at eight dollars an hour and never rise to more than nine dollars an hour. This was the kind of two-tier wage system that had crept into labor agreements all over the country. Even though two-tier systems protected the wages of current employees, they had the potential to divide new workers from veterans and gave companies an incentive to discharge older employees and replace them with new ones. Hormel also presented another appendix, this one dealing with insurance and retirement. Hormel wanted to cut its pension contributions to bring them in line with Fleischli's award, and it wanted to establish deductibles and copayments for the workers' health insurance. Finally, the agreement abolished the workers' traditional fifty-two-week layoff protection on the argument that P-9 wanted to get rid of the guaranteed annual wage. (The two had always been linked so that an employee who worked too many long weeks or too many short weeks under the annual wage would have a full fifty-two weeks to make up the hours or use up excess hours. If workers were going to be compensated every week for their overtime, Hormel saw no reason to guarantee fifty-two weeks of employment.)

That night, with the contract due to expire at midnight, Hank Bell tried a new tack: He asked each side to select a small team to meet face-to-face in another motel room. P-9 was represented by Guyette, Winkels, Rollins, and Hansen. Sitting in for Hormel were Swanson, Gardner, and Cavanaugh. By most accounts, the very fact that they were meeting face-to-face seemed to give the sub-committees a fresh momentum. Hansen suggested that because they were so far apart on so many issues, they try to pare down their lists to the key issues. He and Swanson started going down the respective proposals. Swanson and Gardner acknowledged there might be some room for movement on the issues of seniority and management's right to deploy workers in the plant. Swanson said P-9 would have to compromise on its demand for the right to strike over any safety hazard. Guyette responded that he didn't know how P-9 could compromise when its members were getting hurt in the plant. Hansen got back on track, and they resumed going down the list, but Guyette interrupted again. Finally, Cavanaugh broke in and asked: "What is P-9's bottom line?" Rollins responded by asking for the company's bottom line. Swanson lost his patience. In a low, steady voice he began lecturing Guyette. He insisted that Guyette didn't really want a settlement. He said he didn't believe Guyette was interested in peace between P-9 and Hormel. Finally he accused Guyette of being out to destroy Hormel and Austin. Guyette didn't say a word. Bell didn't say a word. Silence fell on the room. Then Winkels erupted into a torrent of invectives at Swanson. The talks broke off in a mood of bitterness and frustration. On Saturday morning, with their old contract officially expired, the two teams met once more. Swanson told P-9's negotiators that the August 9 proposal was Hormel's final offer and said that if they wanted to keep talking about an enormous range of issues, there was no point in meeting any longer. Talks broke off after an hour.

In many respects, the company's final offer matched the contract offered to the rest of the Hormel plants a year earlier—including the ten-dollar hourly wage effective on September 1. Practically, that meant a raise of seventy-five cents an hour for the Austin workers. But it had huge drawbacks. It was a three-year deal, which meant that Austin would remain out of sync with the other chain plants, whose contracts expired in August 1986. It eliminated the guaranteed annual wage and the fifty-two-week notice of layoffs. Its two-tier wage structure topped out at nine dollars an hour for new employees. Perhaps worst of all, its changes in the seniority system would give management more power over job assignments and the worker's right to bid from one job to another. Outside of wages, few contract provisions matter to packinghouse workers as much as seniority. In a meat-packing plant, where some jobs are strenuous and dangerous while others are comparatively easy, job assignments can seem grossly unfair unless there is some impartial system to determine who gets what job. Bidding on jobs by seniority established a sense of fairness and gave the union members much valued power to control their own fate and improve their lot over time. It also eliminated managerial favoritism as an influence on job assignments. Few things threatened peace and fairness in the plant as much as tinkering with the seniority system. Larson insisted that the proposal was a competitive offer, a fair one based on Fleischli's recommendations. But to a cynical observer—and there were plenty in the rank and file—it seemed that Hormel knew P-9 was in a mood to reject whatever the company put on the table, so it put something on the table that would leave its negotiators room to move later.

The next afternoon the membership was back at Austin High School for another meeting to hear Guyette present the company proposal. The meat-packers were restless, and with the scent of a strike in the air, the meeting dragged on for three hours. To some, the ten-dollar wage was beginning to look a lot better than it had twelve months earlier, before P-9 had lost two more arbitration decisions and before Hormel had started preparing for a strike. But when Guyette stood before them and recapped the seniority, wage, and layoff provisions, he got thunderous boos. From Keith Judd, the veteran moderate, to Lynn Huston, the young radical, the executive board unanimously recommended its rejection. Even Guyette's nemesis John Anker, climbing on his bicycle to ride home after the meeting, said he could not vote for it. The meat-packers were ready for a showdown, and Hormel's offer only made them angrier. A formal secret ballot vote was scheduled at the union hall for Wednesday.

On Tuesday Austin was buzzing with rumors about that afternoon's edition of the Austin *Daily Herald.* When the paper came off the presses, it contained a full-page ad by Hormel defending the contract offer that Guyette had denounced so vigorously. It described conditions in the nation's meat-packing industry and laid out the wages paid by other packing companies—almost all lower than Hormel. It laid out the offer in simple and appealing language: ten dollars an hour; four weeks' vacation; full medical insurance. It pointedly asked, "If you worked for this company, would you reject this offer and go on strike?"

A look at the demographics and the history of P-9's membership provides clues to that question, if not the answer. Of the 1,529 members of record in early August, nearly everybody could find a reason to go on strike. They fell into three well-defined camps. First were the old-timers, more than 300 strong with thirty to forty years of service to a company that had treated them very well financially. Hired from 1941 to 1952, many were veterans of World War II and Korea, with high school educations, paid-off mortgages, and children grown and out of the house. They had the seniority, the good jobs, and control of the union, at least until Guyette was elected. While many lacked his bitterness toward Hormel, they could remember rather proudly a time when P-9 pushed Hormel around, not vice versa. In addition, members of this generation had the least to lose in a strike. Many had accumulated five-figure nest eggs of Hormel stock through years of purchases through payroll deductions and subsequent splits. In any case, they generally had smaller living expenses than workers with young children and would have the least trouble weathering a strike financially.

Next were the baby boomers, the 260 people hired in 1967

and 1968, the first big hiring push after 1952. Together with a smattering of hires from 1965 to 1975, they rivaled the older group in size and were battling among themselves for control of the union, as evidenced by the Guyette-Anker elections. They were almost exclusively men in their mid-thirties to mid-forties, who came of age during Vietnam and got at least a taste of college, if not a four-year degree. Many started as summer help in the old plant, trying to make as much as they could by tackling the hardest jobs that paid the best. The prudent ones owned stock, too, while others spent heavily on boats and beer. Regardless, many yearned for the good life that they had grown up hearing about from their fathers. But the longer they worked for Hormel, the more cutbacks they faced. Some thought jobs in the new plant were safer and easier, even if the rules were a little more rigid. Others couldn't stand the place. Guyette's election suggested that most were tired of concessions, and the 1984 wage cut pushed them closer to a fight. Many were in the prime years of supporting wives and children, and locked into packing-house careers—just as Hormel began to show a new, less generous face.

The last group—850 new-plant hires—represented a majority of the membership, but had a mere one to three years of experience in the packinghouse. About 370 people—or roughly the same number that elected Guyette president—had been on the payroll less than a year when the cuts were imposed and Rogers made his first fight-back speech. As many were under twenty-five as over thirty-five, reflecting diversity not found in the other two groups. Their ranks included 140 women, nearly three times the number in the old plant. Few in this group had ever seen the inside of the old plant, so the loss of work rules and incentive pay should have meant little to them. But most had known no other P-9 president than Guyette, and their introduction to Hormel was filled with praise for the old Hormel and spite for the new one. Their ages suggested that unlike the sixties hires, who had marched from college into the packinghouse, many of the new bunch had started careers and held jobs before getting hired by Hormel. Hormel wasn't their first job, and some didn't care if it wasn't their last. While they were most vulnerable to the financial hardships of a strike, their allegiance to Hormel was short and untested.

On Wednesday morning the meat-packers began filing into the Austin Labor Center to cast their ballots. All afternoon long they filed in and out, usually in groups of three and four. Outside, TV cameramen and reporters patrolled the sidewalk and parking lot, grilling union members about their votes and their assessments of the offer. The mood was festive: Supporters drove past the union hall honking their horns; P-9 members waved from the parking lot; several walked the sidewalk carrying P-9 PROUD signs, chatting and drinking coffee. Inside Guyette met with Winkels and other executive board members, preparing for a press conference that evening. About 6:00 P.M. a rumor swept the union hall: Austin's Channel 6 had reported that the UFCW suspected irregularities in the voting and would throw out the election. Guyette, after some hurried phone calls to Washington and his lawyers, dismissed the report. The polls closed at 8:00 P.M., and P-9's election committee disappeared behind a locked door with the ballot boxes. At 10:00 P.M. Guyette emerged with his familiar yellow legal pad and a sheet of paper. Reporters assembled at the stage of the Labor Center's meeting hall, surrounded by some 200 meat-packers standing two and three deep along the back wall. A chorus of boos and jeers came down on the reporter from Channel 6, but Guyette quieted the group. Beaming with pride, he announced that the rank and file had rejected the offer by a margin of 1,261 to 96. The executive board would prepare a forty-eight-hour strike notice for Hormel immediately. Cheers and hooting rose from the back of the hall. The showdown was on.

News of the vote provoked a variety of reactions around Austin that night. At the home of Barb and Frank Collette, the news crackled over the radio about ten-thirty. When Frank had hired on at Hormel in 1982, it seemed like the beginning of their adult dreams come true. They had married early—she seventeen, he eighteen—and left Austin after she graduated from Austin High in 1962 while he traveled with the Air Force for nearly fifteen years. They moved back to Austin in time for their son, Steve, to attend Austin High for his senior year and play football just like his dad.

With Frank's Hormel paycheck, his military pension, and Barb's paycheck from selling cosmetics at Younker's department store, they could live comfortably for the first time in their lives. They bought their first house, a two-story colonial with a double garage near the Oak Leaf restaurant, and their first new car, a Chevy Citation, and even had enough for Frank to buy a little Chevy Luv pickup truck. Barb got her real estate license, and life got even better. For the first time in her life she had a dress-up job where she wore nylons and makeup to work every day.

Then one day Frank came home and said the union was talking about a strike. By this time they had started to see aspects of Austin they'd never noticed as teenagers when they left. For example, there were cliques in Steve's high school class—some kids whose parents worked at the corporate office; others whose parents were meat-packers. Frank had been a master sergeant in the Air Force and always considered himself a management guy. But he didn't think much of management at Hormel. Then there was the sneering way the other real estate brokers talked about the meat-packers. They made the best money in town, her colleagues said, what were they complaining about? Still, Barb tried to talk Frank out of striking. "You can't be that stupid," she would tell Frank after the kids went to bed.

The night of the strike vote Barb had been afraid to ask Frank how he voted. Finally, after the news came across, she worked up the courage to ask him. He said he had voted for the strike. "How can you be so stupid?" she cried. "Don't you know what this means?" She ran upstairs, slammed the bathroom door, and sobbed for half an hour.

Most people in Austin reacted less emotionally since the months of feuding had created a sense of inevitability. But the news of the vote still made the town catch its collective breath. At the Austin *Daily Herald* reporters and editors huddled to plan strike coverage. At Oak Park Mall on Interstate 90, merchants compared notes on inventories and consumer spending. Police Chief Don Hoffman redrew the week's work schedules to make sure he had plenty of squad cars to patrol the plant. Earlier that spring Hoffman had attended a police seminar on civil disobedience. The speaker was Bob Lutz, then deputy police chief in Minneapolis, who had handled numerous peace demonstrations at the headquarters of Honeywell, Inc., a Minneapolis electronics and munitions manufacturer. Hoffman was impressed and had one of his captains give the same training to each of his officers: how to avoid violence; which laws to enforce on the spot and which to ignore. He had talked extensively with Rogers and Guyette, and he was confident that union members he had known since grade school were not going to get out of hand. Now he reviewed these preparations and studied quirks of labor law with Mower County Judge William Nierengarten.

At UFCW headquarters in Washington Jay Foreman reacted philosophically. He thought P-9's decision was wrongheaded, but he also felt Hormel had really rubbed it in by making a plainly inadequate final contract offer. He still had hope that the UFCW and P-9 could patch things up. Lewie Anderson was less optimistic. He recognized that Hormel had been preparing for nearly a year, had been stockpiling product and arranging new sources of pork, and he told Foreman he thought P-9 was being led to slaughter. On Thursday P-9's executive board received a last-minute plea from the UFCW and union leaders at eight other Hormel plants. They urged P-9 to settle for the same contract offer accepted by those plants the year before. P-9's executive board rejected the request. On Friday Anderson responded with a position paper saying that P-9 was creating an "easy opportunity" for Hormel to move jobs out of Austin and whipsaw one Hormel plant against another. Nonetheless, the UFCW granted strike sanction to P-9, the parent union's endorsement that entitled union members to earn strike benefits of $65 per week. But in a telex to Guyette, UFCW President William Wynn warned: "Local 9, contrary to the counsel of the international union, the Hormel chain, and the national packinghouse committee, has broken with the chain and pursued an independent and isolated course. These decisions were made by the local union, presumably with the knowledge that in breaching solidarity they could not expect it."

Later that day Minnesota Auditor Arne Carlson, the only Republican in top office in the state's government, urged Governor Perpich to convene an emergency meeting of the state's executive council to ask Hormel and P-9 to observe a cooling-off period and submit their dispute to arbitration. But Paul Goldberg, director of the state's mediation bureau and Perpich's chief adviser on labor relations, convinced Perpich that it was too late to intervene.

Friday, August 16, at 11:00 P.M. the Austin Labor Center was unusually quiet. Guyette sat in his office talking with a newspaper reporter, Huston was in Winkels's office next door, chatting with a couple of rank and file members. A handful of others were in the War Room or milling about in the hall outside Guyette's office, but there was none of the usual bustle. At 11:30 Huston climbed behind the wheel of his big old maroon Chrysler Imperial, Guyette climbed into the passenger seat, and they glided through the dark night to the packinghouse. Guyette delivered to plant manager Deryl Arnold a letter officially informing him that P-9 was about to go on strike. From the plant's front office they wheeled around to the plant's west gate, where the streets were lined with hundreds of wives, children, retirees, and other supporters, singing, chanting, and waving placards under the streetlamps and glaring television lights. A few minutes later Guyette reemerged from the packinghouse, leading a procession of night shift workers. They marched back out to the gate, chanting and cheering under the glare of television cameras. Demonstrators counted down the clock as if they were revelers in Times Square on New Year's Eve. When the clock struck midnight, for the first time in fifty-two years P-9 was on strike.

CHAPTER
9

Austin woke up Saturday morning and began moving about with the uncertain bustle of a community treading strange ground. Cars and trucks trolled past the Labor Center on Fourth Avenue, their occupants honking, waving, or just peering curiously at the union hall. On Main Street business was brisk, but merchants and patrons weren't quite sure what to say after remarking, "Well, they did it." At the Law Enforcement Center Chief Hoffman held his usual Saturday morning briefing for local reporters—and one or two from out of town—and said all appeared quiet at the plant, the corporate office, and the union hall. Along Oakland Avenue near Driesner Park, where out-of-town traffic comes into Austin from the freeway, a group of wives from the United Support Group waved picket signs and chanted to passing motorists. At the corporate office north of the freeway, Chuck Nyberg, Dave Larson, and a handful of other executives met to consider the next step in contract talks and prepare a statement for the news media. Out at the packinghouse P-9's picket teams probably were the only people in Austin that morning who knew exactly what to do. Clustered at the three main gates in groups of four and five, they ate sandwiches and cookies, drank from thermoses of coffee, and waved triumphantly at the stream of supporters who motored past throughout the day.

About two o'clock in the afternoon Guyette was sitting behind his desk, taking phone calls and conferring with strikers, who trailed out into the hallway and milled about from the front door to the War Room. Suddenly there was a mild commotion. Outside the front door one of Hormel's ubiquitous white security sedans had pulled up to the curb. Two guards got out and approached the union hall, looking as if they were walking into a lions' den. Among the strikers inside there was also a sense of anxiety, as though they should prepare a rough reception for emissaries of the company. But then no one knew exactly what to do. The guards asked for Guyette and quickly turned over a letter from Bill Swanson, the plant's personnel manager. Back in his office Guyette opened the envelope and perused the contents. It was an invitation to resume contract talks, but it said that "marathon bargaining sessions would be fruitless" unless P-9 substantially changed its position. In it Swanson also said he could not reconcile Guyette's conciliatory attitude in public with his militant stance at the bargaining table. Guyette read the letter, then flipped it to a reporter sitting across his desk and asked, "What exactly does 'reconcile' mean?"

The truth was that nobody in Austin that day could reconcile himself to the circumstances. They all had prepared themselves for the worst, but that didn't make it any easier to believe that they were witnessing the first walkout at Hormel in fifty-two years.

Dave Larson was in his office, a somewhat impersonal room decorated with wildlife prints, a miniature Hormel truck on the desk, and big windows overlooking the corporate parking lot and the woods beyond. Larson had prepared himself intellectually for a strike. He took a somewhat paternalistic view of labor relations, and he viewed the strike as something that P-9's members had to get out of their system. If the strike reminded him of a safety valve, it also reminded him of a harebrained project dreamed up by one of his three boys. You knew it would flop, but you couldn't tell the strikers that. You might as well let them go ahead find out for themselves. If they didn't strike, he told himself, they would tell themselves for years that they had cheated themselves, that they had missed a chance to humble the company. But he never doubted that the strike would fail. If Larson was intensely loyal to Hormel, he was also intensely confident of his bargaining position. He knew that Hormel would never willingly grant $10.69 an hour, much less the $11.25 P-9 had last asked for, and he didn't see how P-9 could bring enough pressure on the company to force the wage increase. Hormel was willing to maneuver on other issues—seniority, the two-tier wage system, safety—but P-9 would not get back to $10.69 an hour. Hormel had won wage cuts from two thousand union meat-packers at its other plants, and there was no way it would give the Austin employees any more. The last thing Hormel executives wanted was to reward the tactics of Ray Rogers and Jim Guyette.

What really rankled Larson was that the strike's activists seemed to be having so much fun, while the Hormel executives were so miserable. The corporate headquarters employed six hundred people, and many were working long days. Executives on the front line, including himself, Nyberg, Arnold, and Knowlton, were lying awake nights, picking their way through the minefield of reporters' questions and generally squirming under a strange new spotlight. The irony killed him: Hormel was in a position of strength, operating most of its plants and making money, while P-9 was locked in a desperate fight. The white-collar employees drove out of the corporate office with paychecks, while their counterparts ten blocks away were picking up trifling strike benefits.

But that didn't erase the sense among the corporate employees that their company was under siege and that things in Austin were terribly out of kilter. Knowlton had grown genuinely frantic over the threatening phone calls to his family. A few days after the strike began, someone tampered with the brakes on a car usually driven by his wife, Nancy. Had the problem not been discovered at a slow speed, the outcome could have been fatal. A daughter attending college in St. Paul had been threatened, and another living in Iowa had her car windows smashed. The incidents particularly unnerved Knowlton, who expected to take abuse himself but grew livid when it was directed at his family. Every time he had to be out of town, Nancy left, too, sometimes to stay with her family in Colorado. His house, located in a well-to-do neighborhood near downtown, was protected by guards twenty-four hours a day. Windows in his office were shielded with bulletproof glass, but that didn't stop vandals from spray-painting them. Knowlton brought security guards with him everywhere, even to Minnesota Gopher football games in Minneapolis and the governor's mansion in St. Paul. Other executives had Hormel security officers patrolling their homes as well. Nyberg put an answering machine on his telephone at home so that he and Mary could screen out the threatening calls, and his eyes were ringed with red from strain and lack of sleep.

Guyette and Rogers, however, had completely disavowed violence. P-9's activities, apart from the gang of glowering meatpackers who usually accompanied Guyette, gave the impression of some Sunday social event. Though Larson knew that plenty of P-9's members were highly distressed, the public face of the strike was all enthusiasm and high energy. Rogers always wore a smile and walked the picket line with a jaunty gait. Huston and Winkels joked their way through news interviews. Even the cynical old-timers, Floyd Lenoch and Skinny Weis, were buoyant. Guyette was confident, and the blue caps—the most ardent activists in their button-festooned P-9 hats and jackets—seemed elated with a new sense of adventure and self-importance. While many union members used their new leisure to squeeze in more golf or fishing, the blue caps quickly came to the realization that they could devote full time to the cause.

So in the early days of the strike Larson busied himself with a bargaining strategy that would get things back to normal. Publicly Hormel refused to divulge plans for reopening the plant. Nyberg would say only that the company could not let a hundred-million-dollar packinghouse sit idle indefinitely. Privately Hormel executives were trying to get more specific. When Larson briefed the board of directors a few days into the strike, he counseled patience. He personally gave the strikers six weeks: two to get the excitement out of their system, two more to feel the strictures of life on sixty-five dollars a week in strike benefits, and two more to get good and restless for a settlement. Larson urged the board to let the plant sit a few weeks. He figured the negotiators could get back to the bargaining table and have something hammered out by the end of the company's fiscal year on October 31. That all could change if the international took a more aggressive stance against the local; but Hormel executives waited all summer for that to happen, and it never did. Like the

UFCW chieftains in Washington, they were slowly coming to the realization that Guyette's power base ran much broader and deeper than they had ever expected. Larson personally hoped that P-9's members would turn against Guyette, but by this time he didn't see any reason to expect it.

Like Larson, Kathy Buck considered the strike inevitable. But that was about all she and Larson had in common. In her mind Hormel had forced the showdown by demanding unnecessary wage cuts, and P-9 had a duty to shut down the packinghouse to defend its members. Certainly the gravity of being on strike worried her and Paul. They had seven kids, the eldest a daughter preparing for college. But they didn't have to live on the strike benefits—forty dollars a week with occasional twenty-five-dollar supplements from Joe Hansen's regional office—because she was off work on an injury and was collecting workers' compensation when the strike started. In addition, she and Paul had the two ice cream parlors that had supported them for eight years. Her biggest financial worry was that Hormel would terminate her workers' compensation on the ground that she was healthy enough to work for P-9. She was injured, "but that doesn't disable my mouth," she told her pals on the campaign trail.

Kathy Buck spent a good deal of time at the Austin Labor Center those first few days of the strike. As she lingered over coffee after strategy meetings, she and the other strikers reminded each other of the company's profits, of the work pace in the new plant, of Hormel's historic domination of Austin. The more they talked it over, the angrier they got. Hormel was making a good profit. Knowlton and the other executives hadn't cut their salaries. Stockholders hadn't taken a cut in their dividends. If the most profitable company could demand wage cuts, what was going to happen to workers at the less profitable companies? Through all the good years under Hormel, Austin people had never needed to worry much about events in the outside world. Now that outside events were working against them, Buck and her pals at the Labor Center found these forces all the more suspicious and sinister. Against those odds, Buck figured, the members of P-9 had to sustain their struggle and concentrate on the positive.

In fact, Rogers and the volunteer committees of P-9 were generating a great deal of activity, and Kathy Buck found the strike's first weeks rather invigorating. She had been active in the corporate campaign throughout the spring and summer; as a laid-up worker she had the time to attend daytime meetings of the Support Group as well as evening rank-and-file meetings. She was a member of P-9's Communications Committee, which dispatched her frequently to Minneapolis and St. Paul for speeches to unions, peace organizations, and clergy groups. Now that the strike was under way, the committee widened its focus. Buck and other volunteers traveled to Duluth, St. Cloud, and other small cities in the region, occasionally making three or four speeches in a day. They made phone calls and sent leaflets to other union locals around the country, using a mailing list from the National Rank and File Against Concessions, a grass-roots coalition of unions led by militant local officers. They felt the news media were portraying their fight as one over sixty-nine cents an hour—the difference between Hormel's offer of $10 an hour and the familiar $10.69 rate they were striving to restore. That theme didn't play well with farmers or social activists who were making only $4 or $5 an hour. But when they expanded on issues such as safety and dignity, they found themselves warmly received, and all the travel became rewarding.

The Communications Committee's work underscored why P-9 became such a potent force even though the formal labor establishment remained cool toward it. It was headed by Charles Peterson, a 1966 Austin High graduate who had used the GI Bill to put himself through Mankato State University even as he worked nights in the old plant. Armed with degrees in business and sociology, he was one of five loin pullers in his gang with four years of college. Shortly before the strike began, Peterson joined Rogers on a speaking engagement in Chicago. When they came back, the union tapped him to lay the groundwork for providing financial help for P-9 families during the strike. He assembled a team of ten to twelve strikers, well educated like himself, to anchor the committee. They became his workhorses, and he teamed them with three to four others in a car and sent them out on the road four to five days a week throughout the fall. They traveled extensively through Minnesota, Wisconsin, and Iowa, each time telling the union's story and delivering a simple message: P-9's families needed help. Their pleas routinely drew warm reactions from unions that had benefited from P-9 donations during their own times of need. As a result, despite admonitions by Wynn that the union donations should be channeled through the UFCW office in Bloomington, Peterson's crews brought back hundreds of thousands of dollars, which were channeled into the Support Group, the hardship fund, and a special program by which unions "adopted" a P-9 family.

As one of the workhorses Buck found herself developing new friendships with veteran P-9ers, and she found a whole new gratification from spreading P-9's story and hearing the complaints of other workers. In August P-9 sent a caravan of three hundred members on a weeklong swing through Illinois, Iowa, and Nebraska, camping out in meat-packing towns and visiting other unions, spreading word of their fight. It got to be like a big family, with the men getting up early to start a campfire and make coffee for the women. For Buck, the strike activities were slowly building a new kind of solidarity.

In early October the executive board recognized her efforts and chose her to accompany Guyette on a West Coast tour to spread P-9's message among California unions. She felt honored by the choice and a little intimidated to be traveling with a labor leader who by now was gaining a national reputation. She found Guyette very serious, very businesslike, but also very polite. As her intimidation eased, she found herself teasing him and chiding him for being so straitlaced. Time and again her jokes would puzzle the stern Guyette, but she would simply explain, "It's a joke, Jim." After about four days in California, with local union activists proudly showing off California's cultural diversity to their new midwestern friends and making the rounds of Mexican, Greek, and Chinese restaurants, Buck couldn't help laughing when Guyette meekly complained, "Doesn't anybody out here serve meat and potatoes?"

For John Morrison the strike seemed neither inevitable nor invigorating. He had known for weeks that it was going to happen. It was clear to him that neither Hormel nor P-9's executive board would back down. But to Morrison the strike resulted from specific choices by specific people, choices that could have gone otherwise if the union had had different leadership. Now he wondered how long it would take for those decisions to change. In his long efforts to dissuade the rank and file from the corporate campaign he had taken a lot of informal opinion polls. Now the majority of his fellow union members seemed to think the strike would last two or three weeks. After that, they assumed, the negotiators would get back to the table and both sides would find some room for compromise. But Morrie, as his friends called him, was a good deal less optimistic. He had listened skeptically when Rogers laid out the array of weapons still available to P-9 as the campaign escalated: a boycott of Hormel products; pressure on Hormel's customers in the grocery and fast-food industries; roving pickets to shut down other Hormel plants. Now they were on strike, and it was clear to him that Rogers and Guyette were not prepared to launch an all-out assault on Hormel. At best, they seemed prepared to continue Rogers's strategy of unleashing new weapons one at a time, with much fanfare and much warning to the company. Morrison woke up the morning of August 17 telling himself: "I may now have taken the final step to losing my job."

The job meant a great deal to Morrison. It was security; it was the foundation underneath life with his wife, Mary, and their sons, Jeff and Jamie. It was his link to his parents and to good buddies like Ron Bergstrom, R. J.'s brother, who had started at the packinghouse one day before John and had worked by his side for years. It was the mortgage payment on their small, immaculate bungalow on one of Austin's countless quiet streets west of downtown. It made the payments on his Suburban wagon and set money aside for Jeff, who was in high school, and Jamie, still a preschooler, to go to college. Now all that was in jeopardy: the job; the house he and Mary had worked so hard to remodel; the stable life with friends and family. He had some money put aside—enough to keep up car and mortgage payments for a few months. But that was money that could have gone toward tuition or an addition on the house. Now it would be shot, spent on a cause he thought was pointless and engineered by leaders he didn't trust.

Morrison tried to keep busy, but it was a struggle. He was a pariah at the union hall because of his opposition to Rogers and Guyette, so union activities were definitely off limits. He and

Bergstrom worked on a few projects around the house, then worked construction for a few days to pick up some extra cash. That fizzled after they were told they would have to join the trade union—for a $300 membership fee—with no guarantee of continued work. He lay low for a few weeks until October, when he turned to his winter ace in the hole, refereeing hockey games. An accomplished skater and no-nonsense athlete, Morrison had been officiating for several years and could pick up $150 to $200 a week between B-league professional hockey and youth hockey at Riverside Arena in town and sometimes up in the Twin Cities.

Still, Morrison hadn't given up on the rank and file. He calculated that after a few more weeks of watching fruitless tactics on the corporate campaign trail, and no progress at the bargaining table, the membership would grow restless and turn up the heat under Guyette, Rogers, and the executive board. That outlook mirrored the advice he was getting from Lewie Anderson, who also hoped that after eight or nine weeks the rank and file would lose patience with Rogers and lose faith in the strike. In the meantime, however, Rogers's critics had no formal plan to counteract the strike activities. Anderson and Hansen worried that any overt intervention would seem heavy-handed, having the effect of quashing local autonomy and alienating more P-9 members than it would persuade. In addition, Anderson was embroiled in negotiations at Wilson Foods, Farmstead Foods, and John Morrell. His credibility at an all-time low within P-9, he purposely kept his distance from Austin throughout most of the fall.

As much as Anderson and international officials hoped for a palace revolt, however, it became increasingly clear that they had underestimated Ray Rogers. When he launched the corporate campaign, Rogers warned that if P-9 walked out, he would transform the Hormel work force into a strike force. Five days into the strike, on August 22, twelve charter buses left Austin in a pouring rainstorm bound for the Twin Cities to demonstrate outside First Bank System headquarters in downtown Minneapolis. By the time they arrived, fears of a washout were replaced by high-noon sunshine. Some three hundred P-9ers ringed the block, waving placards, handing out leaflets, and singing songs. Along South Sixth Street, a one-way thoroughfare past the bank's entrance, the meat-packers lined both sides of the street, forming a gauntlet on either side of the lunch-hour traffic. Chanting, "You say give back, we say fight back," they waved at the passing motorists and handed leaflets through the windows of cars stalled in traffic. The mood was festive—a sort of holiday for the small-town residents in the heart of the big city. Their reception was friendly, too. Though most of the pedestrians and motorists reacted with puzzlement to this link between a packinghouse in Austin and a bank holding company in Minneapolis, they were curious and seemingly charmed by one of the most unusual demonstrations ever held in downtown Minneapolis.

Rogers and Guyette were riding high that sunny day. Guyette, wearing a cowboy hat and carrying his ever-present briefcase, stood against the First Bank building, giving one interview after another to local reporters. Rogers patrolled the picket line, giving pep talks and warning the demonstrators to obey the police. It was a buoyant time for P-9 and its leaders. Thousands of leaflets were going out; thousands of dollars were pouring back in, with Hormel and First Bank clearly discomfited by all the ruckus.

In a quiet office tower suite high above the sidewalk, First Bank's Jim Ulland was preparing a response. A former state legislator from Duluth, Ulland was a newly hired senior vice-president, whose tasks included monitoring the campaign's impact on the bank holding company. Shortly before the strike began, it didn't seem like much. In seven months of antibank canvassing, the bank had documented about fifteen accounts that were closed, mostly at First Bank Austin, as a result of its involvement with Hormel. While the tally was likely higher than that when undocumented cases were included, it still represented minuscule influence on a bank holding company with eight hundred thousand accounts system-wide in several midwestern states. Nor was Ulland very impressed with Ray Rogers's ability to analyze a bank balance sheet. In June, with reporters pressing for evidence that consumers were pulling money from First Bank, Rogers cited figures that assets at First Bank Austin had fallen from $152 million in December 1984 to $137 million in March 1985. But on a bank balance sheet, of course, assets represent loans, not deposits. An analysis of savings accounts and savings certificates at First Bank Austin showed that balances had risen every month since Rogers arrived in the fall of 1984. On Wall Street, First Bank System's stock rode the bull market from $27 per share in January to nearly $40 per share in August, showing no effects whatsoever from the campaign. It became a running joke among Guyette's opponents that if you wanted to raise your company's stock price, you should hire Ray Rogers.

But Hormel was beginning to tire of the bank bashings. During the Minneapolis demonstration the company's Milwaukee lawyer, Thomas Krukowski, hired private investigators to pose as graduate students with video cameras to film P-9 members, hoping to find strikers urging passersby to boycott or pull their money out of the bank. Nyberg was increasingly convinced that the union was committing an illegal secondary boycott and saw the demonstration as a prime opportunity to gather evidence. A week later the company, armed with the new footage to bolster its case, filed an unfair-labor-practice charge with the NLRB and called on the federal government to bring the First Bank campaign to a halt. Rogers seized on Hormel's charge as evidence that the campaign was hurting the company and its banker, though there was never substantive evidence to that effect.

That same week P-9 launched a "solidarity caravan" of three hundred strikers on a driving tour of meat-packing towns in Illinois, Iowa, and Nebraska. Driving by day, camping by night, they leafleted packinghouses and held outdoor friendship rallies in campgrounds. The itinerary was built around plants that could become crucial in cutting off Hormel's production capacity: packinghouses operated by FDL Foods in Dubuque, Iowa, and Rochelle, Illinois; Hormel plants in Ottumwa, Iowa, and Fremont, Nebraska; and even a John Morrell & Company plant in Sioux City, Iowa.

In most of the towns the local union establishment was hostile because of P-9's feud with the UFCW, but that didn't stop Rogers and Huston from organizing evening campfire rallies where local union members could hear P-9's story. Generally it followed three themes. One was an attack on Hormel's profit seeking. The second was a stinging rebuke of UFCW leaders for failing to rally behind P-9. And finally, Guyette planted a seed of unrest by telling workers that their contracts with Hormel might not be valid because they had never been signed. If the contracts were no good, the reasoning went, workers at other Hormel plants shouldn't feel restricted by provisions preventing them from honoring a P-9 picket line at their plant. The point didn't mean much in the weeks shortly after the strike began, but it would gain tremendous significance as P-9 developed plans to dispatch roving pickets, who would set up picket lines at other plants and try to shut down the entire company.

The chautauqua got a mixed reception just about everywhere. In Ottumwa about 150 out of 900 union members showed up for a boisterous rally with the visiting P-9ers. The union's chief steward, Arkey Bride, said that his members sympathized with P-9's plight but that he couldn't say where the majority stood. In Fremont, where local officers were openly hostile to P-9, about 75 of the plant's 850 workers greeted the P-9ers at their union hall, but local officers were conspicuously absent. Following a potluck supper, Guyette talked up the fight and got workers so furious at Anderson that one of them volunteered to ride his motorcycle hundreds of miles to Austin that night to fetch a videotape of Anderson's now-famous five-hour grilling on April 14. In Dubuque, where union workers were earning only eight dollars an hour to slaughter hogs that ended up as Hormel products, the local union officers denounced the corporate campaign, but a number of their members turned out to hear P-9's message. Still, the caravan was a tremendous morale booster for the P-9ers. Most of them had traveled rather little, and even though the meat-packing towns of Iowa and Nebraska were hardly vacation paradises, this was a radical break from the grinding routine of life in Austin. Many of them had been on camping trips before, but not one like this. The sense of mission from traveling together and carrying a message was intense, and communicating directly with other meat-packers in other towns was quite outside their experience.

On September 18 a caravan of 160 P-9ers drove to Sioux Falls, South Dakota, where 2,500 meat-packers were on strike against the giant John Morrell & Company packinghouse. They planned to join Morrell workers on the picket line, shake a few hands, and distribute leaflets. The Morrell workers, however, were earning only $8.75 an hour when they struck, fighting a company proposal to cut wages another seventy-five cents. The local union's business agent, Tom Gross, warned P-9 to stay out of Sioux Falls. "Our people are on the street for the same thing they've been offered," he told reporters as the P-9 caravan arrived. "I think they're on a sinking ship and they're trying to get people on board with them." When told of the warning, Guyette responded, "You'd think we had leprosy."

P-9 drew the same mixed reaction in their own state. In September it sent a delegation to St. Paul for the annual convention of the Minnesota AFL-CIO, spotting a chance to get thousands of leaflets in the hands of loyal unionists. But federation President Danny Gustafson, a seasoned labor leader who had fought his way up from the ranks of plasterers through Byzantine organizational politics, knew that P-9 was breaking all the rules. Like the presidents of other state "central bodies" around the country, he had received a letter from AFL-CIO President Lane Kirkland warning that the corporate campaign did not have the support of the UFCW and that the federation therefore could not support it either. In addition, Gustafson already had met with Guyette that summer and warned him that the state federation could not support the campaign. The action against First Bank looked to Gustafson like a secondary boycott, an effort to drag a third party into a labor dispute and a violation of federal labor law. Back in his days with the building trades, Gustafson had skirmished with the courts over a boycott at a construction site, and his unions were still paying fines months after the strike ended. Gustafson was not about to get the Minnesota AFL-CIO embroiled in lawsuits. He also had told Guyette that the AFL-CIO would raise money to support the strikers—it eventually contributed more than fifty thousand dollars—but that he was going to send it through Joe Hansen's UFCW office, not directly to P-9's Austin Support Group, which wasn't accountable to outside regulators. Like Hansen and Anderson, he wanted to make sure the money went to help strikers, not one of Rogers's projects. After a heated exchange with the leafleters Sunday morning, Gustafson banned the leaflets from his convention and told Guyette to keep his internal feud with the UFCW out of the AFL-CIO. The convention eventually passed a compromise resolution "supporting all strikes in Minnesota," but it did not single out the biggest and most obvious strike in Austin. At the time it seemed like internal union politics, but the lack of support from Danny Gustafson, perhaps Minnesota's most influential labor leader at the time, came to have big implications in the months ahead.

Meanwhile, Hormel was starting to fight back. On August 29 the company imposed the wages and working conditions it had presented to P-9 before the strike began. With nobody actually working in the Austin packinghouse, the step appeared to be an empty legal technicality. But it had important implications. If Hormel reopened the plant and started hiring workers, they would go to work on the company's terms: the two-tier wage system; the more restrictive seniority rules; no annual wage; and no extra layoff notice. The step attracted some puzzlement and little attention at the time but promised to cause enormous complications if the stalemate was not resolved.

On September 9 Hormel scored a legal victory when the NLRB agreed with its complaint that the corporate campaign constituted an illegal secondary boycott against First Bank. Federal law allows a striking union to boycott the products of its employer, such as Cure 81 hams. But it does not allow unions to boycott a third party such as a grocery store that sells Cure 81 hams. Ronald Sharp, the NLRB's regional director in Minneapolis, ruled that First Bank System was a third party to the strike and that the corporate campaign was, in effect, calling for a boycott of First Bank. Rogers insisted that he was not asking consumers to pull money from the bank. He said that customers could simply make their dissatisfaction known to bank officers and that the bank's executives could make their dissatisfaction known to Dick Knowlton. But Sharp was having none of it. The board ruled that despite Rogers's careful avoidance of the word "boycott," the campaign's use of phrases such as "break the Hormel–First Bank connection" implied a boycott against the bank.

P-9's lawyers struck an agreement with Sharp and the board's staff attorneys calling for the union to curtail its picketing and leafleting of the bank if the NLRB dropped the charges. Undaunted, on September 12, P-9 staged a second demonstration, this one at the downtown headquarters of First Bank St. Paul, ten miles east and across the Mississippi River from downtown Minneapolis. It was another festive day, with chanting and singing and visiting with curious St. Paul residents. By some coincidence, the University of Minnesota pep band was playing across the street at a rally for the Gopher football team. Happy to oblige, as strains of the "Minnesota Rouser" filled the air, P-9's demonstrators briefly switched their chant to "Go, Gophers, Go!" Within several days an angered Sharp went to federal court in St. Paul and persuaded U.S. District Judge Edward Devitt to issue an injunction barring P-9 from picketing and handbilling at First Bank banks. At the time it seemed another small, procedural defeat. But it legally tied Rogers's hands in one of his most visible publicity tactics. Even the injunction, however, did not stop Rogers.

On October 7 Rogers and Huston led a contingent of seventy-five to one hundred union members to demonstrate outside a First Bank subsidiary in La Crosse, Wisconsin. Hoping to sidestep Devitt's order, the demonstrators set up their signs across the street from the bank while three people without signs passed out leaflets at the door. The scene thoroughly annoyed Hormel, which thought its problems with bank picketing were over. Before the entourage had returned to Austin, the company filed yet another unfair-labor-practice charge, seeking once again to penalize P-9 for staging an illegal secondary boycott. This time the bank protests ceased.

Hormel was moving on other fronts as well. On October 1 plant manager Deryl Arnold announced that the Austin plant would resume limited production with supervisors running the processing lines. Although the two hundred supervisors seemed a ludicrously small work force in a plant that could handle ten times as many, they actually accomplished a lot. The giant Spam line, for example, required only fifteen to twenty people to produce thousands of cans of Spam a day. By concentrating the staff on the plant's most automated operations, Hormel managed to produce modest quantities of Spam and processed meats, while operating parts of the plant that were the most efficient and least costly. Hormel had quietly hinted that it would move production out of Austin if the plant were struck, and slowly made good on the threat. A new line of popular and highly profitable Frank 'N Stuff chili hot dogs that was destined for the Austin plant was set up in Houston instead. Hormel also began moving unspecified meat-processing machinery to its other plants. Meanwhile, Hormel made up for its loss of slaughtering by buying pork from

IBP, the nation's biggest meat-packing company; FDL; and small meat-processing plants all over the Midwest. With the industry suffering from excess capacity, Hormel had little difficulty finding more than thirty companies eager to supply it with pork, beef, and other products.

In the third week of October P-9 responded with its first actual threat to shut down other Hormel plants. Rogers dispatched leafleting teams from the Austin Labor Center to Hormel and FDL plants in Iowa, Illinois, and Texas. They greeted workers at the plants and handed out leaflets reading, "Your labor is being used against us." Within two to three weeks, Guyette said, teams of strikers would set up picket lines at those plants and ask the other workers to stay off the job. He also said he was ready to ask UFCW President Bill Wynn for official sanction of the roving pickets. Hormel promptly posted notices in the Ottumwa and Fremont plants, warning that any sympathy strikers would be permanently replaced. Wynn said he wanted to examine the labor contracts at other plants to see if the workers could stage sympathy strikes without losing their jobs.

While the P-9ers were on the campaign trail, leaders of the P-10ers were spending Sunday afternoons in the Minneapolis suburb of Bloomington meeting with Joe Hansen and Lewie Anderson at the Thunderbird Hotel. By now it was impossible for Anderson to communicate with the Austin rank and file with any credibility. If the membership was to be persuaded, it had to happen from within. He told the P-10ers he was sympathetic but said it was up to them to get their own union back. He urged them to lobby more of their fellow members and to hold Guyette accountable for bargaining progress at membership meetings. Morrison and Anker were now joined by Chad Young, a stocky young meat-packer's son from Albert Lea, and Doug Saaranen, a 250-pound, no-nonsense packinghouse veteran who lived on a farm south of Austin. Together, they spent hours poring over membership lists, checking off names according to who was firmly on board with the campaign, who was riding the fence, and who had lost patience with Rogers and Guyette. In early October they came forward to urge the rank and file to call a membership meeting "to discuss the union's problems, not Ray Rogers's problems." They knew they could count on every meeting being packed with two hundred to three hundred of the most loyal Guyette supporters and an unpredictable number of fence-sitters. That meeting disintegrated into a chaotic shouting match as the blue caps refused to listen to the heresy of the P-10ers.

Utterly frustrated by internal channels, the P-10ers tried one last stab. They bought a full-page ad in the Austin *Daily Herald* denouncing the corporate campaign as a "miserable failure" that had divided the UFCW, alienated Austin, and made Hormel more hostile. It was signed by 137 P-9 members, including Morrison, Young, and Saaranen. It called for the executive board to go back to the table and ask Hormel for the same offer that the rest of the chain had accepted a year earlier. It was the first time they had gone on record in a public forum challenging their union's direction, and they called in reporters for small sessions to announce their plans and frustrations. Young said they believed the majority of P-9ers were sitting on the fence, and Morrison said that the P-10ers could not get their message across at union meetings.

The P-10ers also issued a four-and-half-page position paper outlining their critique of the corporate campaign and P-9's isolation from the other meat-packing locals. They took the risky step of openly admitting they had been in consultation with the international union and urged a return to the UFCW strategy. "We need to recognize a strategy when it has failed and shift to a new strategy instead of riding a dying horse to the bone yard," the group wrote. They said they would launch their own newsletter to reach the membership and would run candidates in December elections for four open seats on the P-9 executive board. Guyette noted pointedly that Anker and Morrison had lost in previous bids for union office and said theirs was a philosophy rejected by the rank and file.

If the fence-sitters felt any compulsion to join the P-10ers, the verbal abuse that they took at meetings like the one in October made them think again. Guyette's supporters were vocal, well organized, and downright hostile in their attacks, and in the whipped-up emotion of a union meeting, it seemed smarter to keep your head down than stick your neck out. In a town like Austin, hard feelings and animosity quickly became coffee shop gossip, and labels of "crybaby" and "whiner" were hard to shake. If only a handful of the P-10ers had the guts to speak out, it was easy to see why those in the middle stayed in the middle. Besides, Guyette and the blue caps had a good point: In a union, democracy rules, and the continual opposition of P-10 leaders Anker and Morrison could not be divorced from election sour grapes. Unlike Guyette, they were not smooth operators. Anker was usually quiet and reserved, more thoughtful than outspoken, and hardly a firebrand at the podium. Morrison, also a failed candidate, was better known for his fists than his mouth, and people often found him too abrasive for their liking. Moreover, their links with the international poisoned their chances among a broad segment of workers who simply didn't trust Washington bureaucrats who were thousands of miles from Austin's problems.

Meanwhile, Guyette strove to get Bill Wynn's approval for roving pickets. At a membership meeting on October 19 P-9 voted to stand behind union members at any other local who lost their jobs honoring a P-9 picket line. It was a peculiar pledge considering that P-9 didn't seem to have the clout to win even its own demands at the time. Much of the executive board felt that if they could get past Anderson and Jay Foreman, Wynn would give them a fair hearing. In October Guyette, Rogers, and Ed Allen traveled to the AFL-CIO's annual convention in California to confront Wynn and federation president Lane Kirkland about labor's support for their fight. The Austin contingent was beginning to feel the effects of isolation from the mainstream of labor and wondered if a reconciliation was possible. At a cocktail reception Rogers approached Wynn and asked if they couldn't let bygones be bygones. He extended his hand. Wynn, whom Rogers once called "a slimy labor leader," refused. Later that night Hansen, Wynn, and a few other UFCW officers were having a drink at the hotel bar when they noticed Rogers, Guyette, and Allen with some friends at another table. There was an icy silence across the room. But when Hansen ran into Allen during a trip to the men's room, Allen repeated that Guyette wanted a chance to talk with Wynn. OK, Hansen said, lunch tomorrow—Wynn, Guyette, and me.

When they met the next day Guyette pressed Wynn to sanction the roving pickets. He laid out his analysis of Hormel's profitability and mistreatment of P-9. And he insisted that with roving pickets, they really could hurt the company. Wynn was skeptical, but he listened. Finally he told Guyette: The key is to know when you're winning and when you're not. Sure, a union has to give any fight its best shot, but it also has to know when it's time to settle. He reminded Guyette of an old labor axiom: The mark of a leader is not being able to take your people out on strike. It's being able to take them back to work. Before they parted, Wynn agreed to call a meeting of the Hormel chain to discuss the request.

On November 5 Bill Wynn called the P-9 executive board to Chicago, together with officers from the rest of the Hormel chain. Most of the chain locals—Fremont, Ottumwa, Beloit, and the others—sent their two or three top officers. P-9 brought most of its executive board, plus about forty blue caps who wanted to rally behind the board. One of the other chain officers bridled at Guyette, remarking, "They don't intimidate me. I could bring forty guys along, too." Ordinarily the supporters would not have been allowed in an officers-only meeting, but Wynn agreed to let the whole Austin contingent sit in on the discussion.

The meeting opened with Anderson and Guyette, each laying out his analysis of P-9's strategy. The mood was polite but cool. When they finished, several of the chain representatives took shots at Guyette: P-9 wouldn't go along with the chain offer in the summer of 1984, when the chain needed its support. Why should P-9 expect the chain's support now? Why had P-9's emissaries been coming around bad-mouthing the other chain leaders in front of their own members? A handful of the Ottumwa contingent stood up for P-9, arguing that it was time to teach Hormel a lesson. Gradually the discussion turned to the effectiveness of roving pickets. A few of the officers said they weren't sure they could get their members to honor a picket line sent from Austin, but Wynn squelched that discussion. If the UFCW sanctioned roving pickets, he said, the UFCW would expect its members to honor them. Then Wynn asked Guyette the question of the day: "What's your bottom line? What would it take for P-9 to go back to work?" Guyette refused to be pinned down. Then he asked Wynn: "Are you committing me to the same ten-dollar rate before you'll sanction roving pickets?" Wynn knew that Hormel had in the past sometimes thrown in sweeteners for Austin that other plants didn't get. He said no, but that P-9 had to get closer to common ground with Hormel. He said he had taken thousands of workers out on strike and never let any of them crawl back yet. He urged P-9 to give Hormel one more chance at the bargaining table. Then, in a bombshell that caught the other chain officers off guard, Wynn told Guyette that he would sanction roving pickets if P-9 knuckled down to serious bargaining—and if Hormel refused to budge.

When they emerged from the closed-door session, they read the following joint statement to waiting reporters:

> The International Union reaffirms its support of Local P-9 and the 1,500 workers on strike in Austin in their efforts to achieve an honorable and fair contract. Along with Local P-9, the International Union will seek to meet with the Hormel Company to resume good faith negotiations. The Local Union and the International are deeply concerned with the issues of health, safety, and effective grievance procedure, common contract expiration dates and worker dignity as well as economic matters. Local P-9 has pledged to negotiate in good faith and, in response to employer modifications in its final offer, is prepared to modify its proposals. If Hormel fails to or delays in bargaining in good faith, the International Union will sanction extension of P-9's picket lines to other Hormel operations.

Guyette and the others were jubilant. They read the statement to mean that P-9 all but had sanction for roving pickets and that the UFCW would stand behind its battle against Hormel. Kenny Hagen and several of the blue caps pumped Joe Hansen's hand in the hallway outside; finally the UFCW was behind P-9 again. Back in Austin the P-10ers were devastated. It appeared that their special relationship with the UFCW was dissolved and that Wynn had betrayed their loyal opposition and signed on with Guyette. It was an incomparable setback to their campaign. Just about everyone else, including Knowlton, was slightly stunned.

But the carefully worded statement was loaded with hidden

meanings. It pointedly required Guyette to compromise with the company, something he had yet to do, and it handed extra power to Hansen to oversee P-9's behavior at the bargaining table. In fact, Wynn really did hope for good-faith negotiations by both sides. An astute negotiator himself, he calculated that if this pledge enabled P-9 to narrow the dispute to one or two key items, perhaps he could sit down personally with Knowlton and hammer out the final ingredients. As it turned out, he had no idea that the two sides were still miles apart on dozens of issues.

Within ten days Wynn found it necessary to issue a clarification. In a telegram sent to Guyette and released to the news media, Wynn said:

> Reporters have informed us that you are predicting no good faith bargaining by Hormel and threatening an immediate extension of picketing to plants outside Austin. This may be sheer rhetoric and posturing, for I am confident that you understand our position. However, we feel obligated to apprise the reporters that no sanction has been granted to extend picket lines, that we are hopeful that the company will bargain in good faith, and that we will evaluate reports by our representatives as to the good faith evinced by both the company and the Local and the prospects for an honorable settlement before making any decision to sanction an extension and involve other Hormel members in Local 9's strike. Unless and until we sanction an extension, our members outside of Austin would be taking serious risks and the Local Unions could be faced with costly and risky litigation if they respected extended picketing. Local 9's so-called guarantees are no protection against these risks.

Guyette was undaunted. He was convinced that Hormel wouldn't move far enough to satisfy any reasonable union leader that it was bargaining in good faith. "Now is the time Hormel is hurting," he told reporters.

On November 25, four weeks after the end of its fiscal year, Hormel released its financial results for 1985, the first concrete measure of the strike's impact. For the entire year sales rose 3.3

percent to $1.5 billion, and profits were up almost one third, to $38.6 million. For the three months that ended October 26, total sales grew by nearly 7 percent, even though the giant Austin plant had been shut down for all but three weeks of the quarter. The quarter's profits were up 83 percent from the final quarter of the previous year. If one subtracts out the effect of the FDL acquisition, Hormel's sales were probably down slightly from the previous year, but even so, its profits were up substantially. Guyette called the profits "obscene" and noted that they contradicted Hormel's argument that it couldn't make money without wage cuts. But the figures also demonstrated that Hormel had come through round two of the labor struggle with scarcely a bruise. As Knowlton had quietly predicted during the summer, Hormel was capable of growing even with its star plant shut down.

CHAPTER

10

Since the strike's first day, one question echoed across Austin and through the Hormel corporate office: How long can they hold out? Family budgets built on four hundred dollars a week were desperately pinched by life on forty to sixty-five dollars a week in strike benefits. While three hundred of the strikers were in their fifties or early sixties, their homes paid off and a little Hormel stock in their safety-deposit boxes, nearly half the membership was under thirty-five—many of them with new mortgages, new cars, and new babies. Few had expected the strike to last beyond October, and few had saved up personal nest eggs. Most had relatives to rely on for temporary loans, or working spouses to bring in a hundred to two hundred dollars a week. But for many, the hardship was extreme. R. J. Bergstrom, for one, had three children and a wife who did not work. One day that fall he put the family car and pickup truck on a trailer, drove them to a nearby junkyard, and sold them for a few hundred dollars' cash. That left the family ten miles outside of Austin with only a motorcycle for transportation. Mower County's unemployment rate was just 4.8 percent that fall, but most of the available jobs paid only four to five dollars an hour. There were seasonal jobs in September and October—loading turkeys, painting houses, harvesting soybeans—but by November those jobs were winding down. Some of the strikers left town in search of work. When confronted with premiums of about two hundred dollars a month, roughly two thirds dropped their health insurance and gambled that their families would enjoy good health.

Yet as the weeks went by, the strikers' resolve seemed to stiffen rather than wither. Their indignation deepened, their volunteerism accelerated, and their support from outside militants grew stronger. Within the friendly, upbeat confines of the Austin Labor Center, the question was not so much how could they continue, but what could stop them.

If the union hall had been a popular gathering place since Ray Rogers came to town, it now became an absolute beehive. With nothing but time on their hands, scores of P-9 members found it the best place for coffee, gossip, and moral support. And the Rogers organization took full advantage of their time and interest. Volunteers came and went in a steady stream down the hall corridor outside the offices of Guyette, Winkels, and Rogers. Across the hall, the War Room bustled with campaign activity. Strikers, spouses, and retirees sat at long tables, stuffing envelopes and folding leaflets, while members of the Communications Committee plotted speaking tours on the big maps pinned to the walls. There were committee meetings everywhere: Communications Committee; Welfare Committee; Roving Picket Committee. An informal gift shop became the source of new strike paraphernalia almost every week: buttons; caps; jackets; bumper stickers.

This volunteer organization was run largely by the United Support Group, an organization founded by P-9 wives before the strike started. Once the strike was under way, it expanded to include retirees and other supporters from the community, and it evolved into a highly efficient machine for raising funds from outside Austin and converting the money into valuable services for the strikers. It also produced a number of committed and talented leaders of its own: Guyette's wife, Vickie; Support Group chair Jan Butts; Carole Apold; Cindy Rud; and Barb Collette, who had finally decided that her husband and his union were right to take on Hormel.

With Rogers's assistance, the women and retirees turned the union hall into much more than a nerve center for a strike. It became a full-fledged social service agency capable of providing almost anything but major surgery, one striker joked. Down a flight of stairs off the front lobby was a large basement divided into several rooms. The first door on the right led to the food shelf, a room stacked floor to ceiling with canned goods, cereal, bread, noodles, produce donated by local farmers, and sometimes eggs, milk, and cheese. A second room was packed with shelves of secondhand clothes. A third door led to a kitchen outfitted to feed hundreds of people, with a six-burner restaurant stove, a Vulcan oven, a deli-style meat slicer, a Coke cooler, and big commercial stainless steel sinks. The rest of the basement served as a community soup kitchen, and at mealtime on most days the basement filled up with dozens of strikers and their families, seated on folding chairs and card tables, sharing lunch and gossip.

Another room held Santa's Workshop, where a handful of P-9's hobbyists with jigsaws and sandpaper made wooden airplanes and teddy bears for the children's upcoming Christmas. Car trouble? P-9 would send out a mechanic; after all, it represented the machine shop men who kept Hormel's physical plant running. Leaky pipes? Well, the membership included Hormel maintenance men who could fix your plumbing as well as Hormel's boiler. Marital problems because money was getting tight? P-9's Tool Box knew how to fix anything with a referral to Mower County Social Services. At a loss for company in the middle of a weekday? Stop in at the soup kitchen for soup and a sandwich. The union hall also was headquarters for perhaps the most sophisticated speakers' bureau ever organized by a striking union. As many as seventy-five well-versed strikers, most of them with college educations, were ready to crisscross the country on short notice to tell the P-9 story.

Rogers, the master organizer, knew that such a well-oiled organization accomplished two goals at once. It helped 1,422 families stave off poverty during a siege without paychecks. But it also kept them busy, together, and in high spirits. Rogers knew that few things are as demoralizing as sitting at home alone all week doing nothing, especially for a group of rural Minnesotans with a hard-earned work ethic. By putting countless skills to work—carpentry, cooking, organizing, plumbing—he and his partner, Ed Allen, kept the membership busy making meaningful contributions to the union's common good.

In doing so, Rogers was fulfilling every commitment he had made to P-9 members nearly a year earlier, when he first stepped up to the podium in the Austin High auditorium. After analyzing Hormel's power structure, he had fashioned a campaign to exploit it. From that first sub-zero Saturday morning in January, he had enlisted hundreds of union members as volunteers, involving them in every rally, leafleting, bank protest, and caravan to other plants. As he promised before the walkout began, he had created a strike force that had accelerated the campaign's attacks on Hormel and First Bank. He kept the media constantly focused on the workers' struggle, championing their cause with fiery speeches in union halls across the Midwest. He tapped into his vast network of labor sympathizers and started a flow of thousands of dollars into the Austin Labor Center. Under his savvy direction, P-9 was snowballing into a national cause, with momentum that was sweeping small-town Minnesotans into a battle that seemed to supersede their own lives.

But as Rogers's campaign devoured the energies of P-9 members, it was equally powerful in stiffening Hormel's resolve. What Rogers viewed as key steps to victory, Hormel denounced as obstacles to serious negotiations, much less a settlement. Nyberg and Arnold were fond of accusing Rogers and P-9 of using "harassment, intimidation and threats" in place of traditional collective bargaining. Each time it seemed that negotiators made progress, there was another bank protest, another call to boycott Hormel customers. Hormel refused to be bullied, especially by someone it viewed as a paid agitator with little to lose in Austin. As much as Rogers predicted a P-9 victory, Hormel was equally determined that it wouldn't happen on his terms.

Through it all something of a siege mentality was developing inside the Austin Labor Center. Support from the people of Austin was almost nil. At best the townspeople made it clear they wanted a settlement; at worst they implied that the P-9ers were selfish and overpaid. The UFCW, though it was paying strike benefits every week, repeatedly expressed its lack of confidence in Rogers and Guyette. As for legal skirmishes, P-9 had lost three times before an outside arbitrator, twice before the National Labor Relations Board, and once before a federal judge. Newspapers and television stations were beginning to suggest that the strike was ineffectual. Even mainstream unionists in Minnesota were turning a cold shoulder; at one Teamsters luncheon in St. Paul, a speaker from P-9 was told that if he wanted an audience for bad-mouthing his own union, he should go back to Austin.

But there was also a lifeline from the outside world, one that was growing stronger each month. Rogers's leaflets had reached hundreds of union halls around the nation, and gradually his grass-roots approach began to flourish. P-9 found financial and moral support in pockets of the labor movement in the Twin Cities, where there was an informal network of militant union officers; on the Iron Range, which had a history of independent-minded labor leaders; and in other union halls from coast to coast. Rallies in Austin during March and June 1985 attracted hundreds of union supporters, from steelworkers in Pittsburgh to musicians in Los Angeles. As the support widened by word of mouth, Austin became something of a pilgrimage site for the nation's labor militants, who traveled to southern Minnesota by the carload and came away in awe of this rank-and-file machine. Money flowed in, too. Rogers had been worrying all fall about supporting all those families without paychecks. Then a novel idea occurred to him. On November 25, P-9 sent out a fifty-thousand-piece mailing to sympathizers around the country, asking them to enroll in Adopt-a-Family, a Rogers innovation that allowed supporters or union locals outside Austin to subscribe for the maintenance of a P-9 family with monthly contributions. At its peak Adopt-a-Family was paying up to two hundred dollars a month to more than a thousand of the strikers' families.

It's easy to see what attracted the nation's labor militants to P-9. Socialists who despaired about the complacency of American workers saw in P-9 a group of workers alienated from capital. Activists for union democracy who bemoaned the apathy of union members saw a rank and file who were genuinely involved and conversant in the issues of their fight. Even labor militants with no particular ideological leaning were heartened by such an enthusiastic and engaged rank and file.

Four of the most active and influential supporters came from Minnesota: two college professors, an autoworkers' union president, and a grievance chairman at a small St. Paul steel mill. The chairman of the Metro Area Support Group in the Twin Cities was Peter Rachleff, a transplanted East Coast native who taught history at Macalester College, a prestigious liberal arts college in St. Paul. He was a veteran of the antiwar movement, a labor historian, and a self-described independent socialist who had cultivated friendships with a number of Twin Cities union activists. He traveled to Austin in the fall of 1984 for one of Rogers's first rallies. When he drove up to the big neo-Gothic high school, he saw a picket line of hooting men and women, hollering children, dozens of homemade placards, and wicked caricatures of Richard Knowlton. It was, in his words, "what I had waited my whole life as a labor historian to see." He and his friends later joked about the "Austin virus": Anyone who traveled to Austin for a rally or a day at the Labor Center came away infected with the enthusiasm and the unshakable faith that these strikers would beat Hormel. To Rachleff, P-9 represented a remarkable example of authentic working-class solidarity, real life duplicating the militancy he had studied from the 1930's.

A friend of Rachleff and another organizer of Twin Cities supporters was Tom Laney, then president of a two-thousand-member local of the United Auto Workers at a Ford assembly plant in St. Paul. Laney, a combative but perceptive leader whose nose had been broken more than once in fistfights and football games, believed that unions needed to resist their employers whenever possible. They might lose their share of the fights during tough economic and political times, he reckoned, but they would show the companies their resolve. Having battled endlessly with conservatives in his own union and upper officers of the UAW, Laney saw in P-9 everything he wanted in his own local: a rank and file that cared about and took part in union affairs, a union capable of hiring its own experts to fight the company's hired guns, and leaders willing to challenge the complacency of their parent union. His own battles had taught him the value of courage and personal loyalty. He quickly befriended Guyette and became one of his fiercest defenders, calling him a once-in-a-decade leader.

Laney's involvement attracted Paul Wellstone, a political science professor at Carleton College, Minnesota's "Princeton on the Prairie." Wellstone was no stranger to underdog causes. He was an activist in the state's Democratic-Farmer-Labor (DFL) party, and he was known for delivering fiery populist speeches that made him an instant hit at rallies protesting farm foreclosures. A champion of 1930's-style parity pricing of farm commodities, he had political clout to advance his ideas through his membership on the DFL's State Central Committee. He also had spent time working in Governor Perpich's Energy Department and been an unsuccessful candidate for state auditor. Laney brought Wellstone to Austin on a Sunday afternoon in March to speak at a meeting of P-9 supporters. Wellstone took the podium and described the P-9 fight as a major struggle about justice. Union members were lighting a candle for the bottom half of the nation's population by displaying the courage to fight back, he said. It was a stirring speech that combined from-the-gut inspiration with an animated style at the microphone. Among those listening to him that day was Rogers, who immediately recognized his speaking talent and sought to have him keynote future rallies. To Wellstone, the P-9 battle was an avocation, a movement he had long been looking for to provoke the hopes of forgotten people across the country.

Dave Foster, a friend of Laney's and the grievance chairman for a United Steel Workers local at a small steel mill near St. Paul, saw P-9's struggle as a pivotal fight in the battle against wage concessions in U.S. industry. Foster was part of an informal network of young, militant officers in steelworkers' locals around the country. He had watched unions debate the best way to fight concessions since the early 1980's. Only with P-9 did the debate spill outside the confines of unions and into the arena where he thought it belonged: against the companies. Foster, however, was not a fringe militant. He was active in the St. Paul Trades and Labor Assembly, the city's official labor federation, and had been a State Central Committee member in Minnesota's DFL party. Foster was less comfortable than Rachleff or Laney with P-9's attacks on the UFCW. He thought the labor movement's top leaders were, by and large, on the right side and that unionists should save their ammunition for employers. Foster spent time in Austin and talked frequently with Guyette on the phone. He recognized P-9 as a force that could galvanize the nation's militants into an organization capable of fighting wage concessions. To Foster, P-9 represented a group of workers who recognized that their interests did not coincide with those of management or the stockholders and cared enough to do something about it.

Starting in the spring of 1985, Rachleff and Laney organized a vigorous support group that met weekly at Laney's union hall across from the Ford truck plant in St. Paul. It attracted a wide range of militants, from active union rank-and-filers to doctrinaire socialists. At first the group was chiefly a forum for reports from Austin and discussion of tactics to fight concessions. But once the strike started, it became more active. One of the group's members was Jake Cooper, a former truck driver and veteran of a famous Teamsters strike in Minneapolis in 1934, who now owned a suburban supermarket. With Cooper's semitrailer and access to wholesale grocery purchasing, the group recognized that it could make enormous contributions to the P-9 food shelf. During the Labor Day weekend the committee organized a 125-car caravan that delivered two hundred tons of food to Austin, enough for more than two hundred pounds of food for each striking family. That was the biggest of the food caravans; but it set off a wave of similar efforts, and food poured into the Austin Labor Center. Later Rachleff organized a dance and fund raiser at the electricians' union hall in St. Paul, which gave dozens of P-9ers a chance to socialize with Twin Cities supporters and raise money while blowing off steam from the tension in Austin.

The support group also set up speaking engagements for strikers across the state and the Upper Midwest, which had two effects in propelling the strike along. First, the Austin evangelists spread P-9's version of the strike so effectively that Hormel became an almost mythic villain in the labor grapevine. Second, the neophyte speakers returned home from meeting after meeting ablaze with the enthusiasm of their friendly audiences. For all the response P-9 was getting in sympathetic union halls, it was easy to believe that organized labor really stood behind the strikers.

Meanwhile, Foster recognized that P-9 was becoming a banner for labor militants who otherwise had little contact across union jurisdictional borders. Militant steelworkers from St. Paul, for example, kept in touch with steelworkers two hundred miles away on the Iron Range but knew little about like-minded auto-workers across town. In general, the nation's labor movement is organized vertically; it encourages union members who need help to get it within their own union at regional or national head-quarters, but not to go outside to another union. Even the AFL-CIO, the nation's federation of unions, yields authority to its constituent unions and, apart from city and state central bodies, builds few bridges across union jurisdictional lines. A union member who wants to reach out to other unions through the federation must obtain approval from the top officers of his or her own union first before the federation will lend its support. That's one reason why there were so few precedents for a rogue local like P-9. The international unions retain enormous power over their local affiliates—money for political contributions, lawyers to help with grievances and lawsuits, campaign assistance in local union contests—and it's easy for them to crush dissident local officers. Now, however, there was a parallel labor movement forming, one that sociologist Stanley Aronowitz has described as a horizontal labor movement, in contrast with the vertical structure of the AFL-CIO. Like-minded activists were reaching across jurisdictional lines and "taking their own counsel," as Aronowitz put it.

In June Foster, Laney, Guyette, and Bob Bratulich, head of a large steelworkers' local on Minnesota's Iron Range, sent a letter to fifteen friends and acquaintances around the country, inviting them to a rally in St. Paul and a picnic in Austin later that month. Nearly seventy showed up, many from as far away as Los Angeles, Pittsburgh, and Boston. Foster recognized that P-9 was a cause that could unite the dozens of loosely organized activists he had encountered over the years. In August he sent another letter to a similar group of one hundred people, inviting them to the founding meeting of the National Rank and File Against Concessions in Gary, Indiana, in August. Nearly 170 showed up, and NRFAC was born. Four months later five hundred union activists attended the first national convention of NRFAC. At both meetings P-9 was the headline event. Clearly Austin had caught the attention of the nation's labor movement and was drawing strong support from the militant fringe. Whether or not a victory in Austin could actually help other unions fight concessions, it was regarded as a crucial symbolic struggle.

Gradually P-9 began to attract other activists farther to the left. By revealing frustration with the nation's economic and political system, P-9's struggle created a natural opportunity for left-wing organizations looking for chances to share their analysis of the world and attract new members. In addition, P-9 was a born-again symbol to leftists who had a keen sense of American labor history. It was the vestige of the UPWA, one of the nation's most militant and populist unions, yet it had been swallowed up into one of the nation's biggest and most bureaucratic labor organizations. Now, with a spontaneous outburst from its rank and file, it had launched a struggle against both corporate profiteering and bureaucratic unionism. The Socialist Workers party (SWP), one of the nation's biggest and best-organized left-wing parties, had a full-time organizer in Austin for months. SWP reporters wrote frequently about P-9 in the party's paper, *The Militant,* and the SWP eventually published a short history of the strike and opened a bookstore in Austin. The Progressive Labor party, a radical Communist group that calls for revolution rather than reform, sent organizers from Minneapolis almost weekly and from Chicago occasionally. The strike also drew organizers from the Communist party of Minnesota and the Dakotas, the Central Committee of the Marxist-Leninist party of the USA, and the Workers League. Soon it became common to find Trotskyite or Stalinist organizers patrolling the sidewalk in front of the union hall, handing out leaflets and newspapers. A Socialist Workers party leaflet read, "U.S. Hands Off Nicaragua—No Contra Aid! No to Union Busting—Support P-9! Break All U.S. Ties With Apartheid! Stop Farm Foreclosures!" The *Workers' Advocate* announced: "Support the Defiant Hormel Strikers!" One headline in the Progressive Labor party newspaper, *Challenge-Desafío,* read, SMASH SCABS! RED SOLDIERS SUPPORT HORMEL STRIKERS—BOSSES SHAKE.

The presence of avowed Communists and socialists in Austin caused considerable distress in the business community and at the police department. Hormel executives made sure that visiting reporters knew about the presence of the outsiders, as if to suggest that Commies had filled the void left by mainstream labor.

They also worried that despite P-9's nonviolent exterior, outsiders were more likely to cause trouble in their quiet town. In October Police Chief Don Hoffman, normally an unexcitable administrator, asked Guyette to require police passes to the union hall for visiting reporters because he feared that outside agitators were masquerading as journalists. Soon the grapevine had it that Communists were running the strike and that Rogers had recruited Guyette into a left-wing organization.

In fact, Guyette was somewhat cool to the leftists. A lukewarm Democrat who had sampled a variety of teachings (and even once attended a John Birch Society meeting), Guyette was not about to sign on with anybody else's ideology. He certainly was no fan of the Soviet Union or any other Communist nation he knew of. He forbade the outsiders from handing out leaflets or newspapers inside the Labor Center and objected when sympathizers tried to hand out their own leaflets as if they were P-9 literature. Of the sectarian squabbles that raged among the various socialist and Communist parties, Guyette said, "I'm not really into, you know, who shot Trotsky. He's dead, and he isn't going to come back to life."

Guyette did, however, defend the leftists' freedom to distribute leaflets and spread their views. He would tell critics, "I don't care if somebody's a Buddhist or a Baptist, a socialist or a Republican. If they're not eating Hormel products, we can certainly agree with that." He also knew that they could help P-9 in countless ways, and he didn't want to offend them. They provided important moral support by telling the strikers they were on the right path, and they took P-9 leaflets and financial solicitations home with them when they left Austin. Later P-9 would get crucial support from the husband-wife team of Margaret Winter and Steve Wattenmaker, who had moved to Minnesota from New York about two years earlier. Wattenmaker, a pipe fitter by trade and a former member of the Socialist Workers party, was a gifted writer of fund-raising appeals, and he briefly became a volunteer assistant to Rogers in the spring of 1986. Winter, a civil liberties attorney who had represented the SWP and other progressive groups, spent several months in Austin during the winter and spring of 1986 defending P-9 and its members in several court actions.

Still, Guyette didn't pay much attention to the political analysis offered by P-9's new supporters. He regarded P-9's struggle as a battle against Hormel, an economic rather than a political fight. He recognized that larger forces came into play—decisions against P-9 by the NLRB and federal judges, for example. And he recognized a sympathy of interests with other causes, such as the civil rights movement and family farmers. He even came to believe in a permanent struggle between workers and bosses. "There's always going to be a boss, and there's always going to be somebody who works," he said later. "And between them there's always going to be conflict." But his chief target remained Hormel. Already Guyette was getting more advice than he needed from all quarters, and he was not about to follow orders from somebody who arrived one weekend to sell newspapers outside his union hall.

Pete Winkels, too, kept an open mind toward the leftists. He enjoyed the intellectual stimulation of an argument with the new hangers-on, but he was far from naive—either about economic history or about the recruitment efforts of left-wing organizations. Winkels lacked Guyette's suspicious nature, but he kept the leftists at bay with humor. He immediately nicknamed the SWP Sex Without Partners, a gibe at its lack of personality, and taunted two other organizers, "One of you guys is with the FBI, and the other is with the CIA, and you're both jealous of each other."

If Guyette and Winkels were savvy enough to take the outsiders with a certain panache, their rank and file were reacting somewhat more emotionally. Hormel had threatened their standard of living. Rogers had stimulated them with a new sense of empowerment. The outside militants showered them with fresh ideas about government and society. All these forces combined to radicalize scores of P-9 members who had never worked a phone tree, never been in a march. Like many middle-class Americans, they believed that they lived in a fundamentally just world: The law was fair; corporations and workers could share the profits of a successful enterprise; the government was there to serve them; citizens who worked hard got ahead. Gross and persistent injustice simply was not part of their experience. The strike was a rude awakening: Unanticipated forces cut their paychecks; government bureaucrats repeatedly sided with Hormel; the courts tied their hands. Once they found themselves in what they saw as a grossly unfair situation, they began to see injustice all around them.

So when supporters of the antiapartheid movement, or Women Against Military Madness, or critics of capitalism described other injustices in the world, the P-9ers listened with a new sympathy. Gradually they discovered what sociologists call "expressive social movements," that being on strike meant doing more than walking a picket line or sitting at home. It meant pitching in with colleagues at a sympathetic union hall. It meant traveling and getting on TV. It meant contributing to a higher cause that produced a kind of moral satisfaction that many had never experienced before. One after another, people who had never even written their senators were turning into political activists skeptical of large corporations. They explored the links between government and business, examined the tenets of capitalism, and immersed themselves in economic analysis and political activism.

When Barb Collette first got involved in the United Support Group in the fall of 1985, she had never been arrested. She had never had a speeding ticket or a warning. She had never even owned a pair of blue jeans. But she now found herself on a collision course with civil disobedience. During the spring and summer of 1985 Collette found herself decidedly ambivalent about what was happening to her husband's union. At the real estate office where she was a broker, co-workers kept asking her if those crazy meat-packers were really going to strike and if Frank was going with them. Barb said she didn't think so, and she even hoped privately that they wouldn't go on strike. But the day after the strike vote her colleagues were full of disdain for the meat-packers and especially Guyette. "Let's just not take sides," she told them, "because if it comes to that, I'll stand by my husband." Within a matter of weeks, however, it was clear that they weren't on the same wavelength, and she quit. It wasn't long before she was down at the Labor Center pitching in with the other husbands and wives and retirees. By November Barb Collette, who had cried for half an hour the night P-9 voted to strike, found herself in the thick of the Support Group.

When she saw her first copy of *The Bulletin,* a tabloid published by the Workers League, it scared her. She had never seen words like "fascist" applied to her own government and had never heard anyone seriously call for a class war. Even after she got to know some of the socialists, she continued to feel a certain distance. "It's not quite like being a Republican," she joked with her friends. Later, when one group unfurled a Communist flag at a P-9 rally, Frank Collette flew into a rage. Many of the men in Austin had fought for America in Korea and Vietnam, and they were not about to stand by while some outsiders promoted communism. A fistfight broke out, and the flag disappeared.

Like Guyette, Barb Collette regarded P-9's fight as economic rather than political, and she resented the socialists' efforts to put their own ideological brands on it. Whenever organizers would start in on the virtues of socialism or communism, Collette would challenge them to name a socialist or Communist country that worked better than America. In her judgment they never could. She knew they gravitated to situations like P-9's strike and banked on people's discontent. Later she came to feel that they were trying to use P-9 for their own ends. She felt that they abandoned P-9 one by one as the union no longer followed their format for revolution or social change.

Still, the experience changed the way she thought about institutions and people who challenged them. She read the tabloids with an open mind and often felt that they told the truth about P-9's struggle in a way that mainstream newspapers and TV stations did not. Increasingly it looked to her as though the nation's big institutions—news media, government, courts—were aligned on the side of business, against workers.

If Collette didn't embrace any of the various ideologies, she culled from them a greater skepticism and vigilance toward corporations, the courts, and the nation's law enforcement agencies. She was astonished that policemen would take her picture at demonstrations or write down her license plate number. She was outraged a few months later that she was sent to jail for thirty hours on a misdemeanor charge after being arrested in a demonstration at the Hormel corporate office, when most people would get off with a ticket and a fine. "I don't think we have the freedom we think we have," she told reporters who came to Austin. "Five years ago or so I felt my responsibility stopped at the voting booth. Now I'm aware that my responsibility goes beyond that. Complacency breeds ugliness; that's when other powers chip away at what you had."

Her view of corporate America also grew more skeptical. Frank's father, uncle, and grandfather all had worked happily for Hormel. Her father had sold cars to Hormel workers for years. Until the strike she never hosted a family Thanksgiving or Christmas without a Hormel ham. She genuinely believed that what was good for Hormel was good for Austin. As November's brisk days gave way to the white chill of December, Barb Collette began to feel that Hormel treated its workers like so many worms and that only a naive person could believe that the rest of corporate America was any different. She began to feel that the workers' interests did not necessarily coincide with those of the corporations. And she wasn't so sure that political institutions like her own city council or governor would stand behind the workers if it came to a showdown.

Like many of her colleagues in P-9, she didn't quite buy the various lines she heard from the many outside supporters. But they reinforced her sentiment that P-9 was fighting the good fight. And they deepened her determination that P-9 had no choice but to fight on.

Larry Jensen saw injustice, too, but he didn't see social revolution as a way to correct it. A lean man whose silver-rimmed glasses matched his neatly combed hair, he had lived within twelve miles of Austin for his entire law-abiding life. His wife even worked in Hormel's corporate office. Like many pragmatic P-9ers, he wanted nothing to do with getting in trouble now. He and Charles Peterson, his fellow Communications Committee coordinator, got into a loud argument with Rogers one morning when the topic of civil disobedience first came up. Rogers said P-9 members could close the plant by lying down in the street and getting arrested. An incredulous Jensen asked how he could expect to get another job if he had an arrest record. Rogers told him that it shouldn't bother him. Replied Jensen, "You don't have to write your résumé," referring to

Rogers's own business. According to Jensen, they nearly came to blows as the tiff ended.

Jensen remained determined to continue the strike, even though he was growing skeptical of Rogers and all the fringe groups latching onto the cause. He respected everyone's right to express himself; but it seemed to him that the left-wingers were hanging around the union hall too much, and he didn't really know why. Some, he discovered, misrepresented where they were from, pretending to be from the University of Minnesota when they actually were based in Detroit. One P-9 member dispatched to drum up support in Florida came back pertrified after spending a night with a P-9 sympathizer whose home was draped with Communist flags. Jensen had grown up without a father because of World War II, and when he spotted the red and black hammer and sickle flag on the auditorium stage where his three daughters had attended high school, he exploded. Seated with some friends near the stage, he jumped over three people and confronted a man standing near the flag. "I'll give you ten seconds to get that flag off my stage or I'll kill you!" Several union members interceded and told Jensen to settle down. They confronted the man and, by Jensen's count, argued for fifteen minutes before the flag was taken away. Jensen was floored that it took that long to get it removed.

Still, he was not about to rock the union boat. He was a life-long unionist, having worked as a retail butcher in Rochester until he joined Hormel in 1968. Most of his time was in the hog cut department, where carcasses were carved into hams, bellies, and loins. In his last three years, after the move into the new plant, he worked in smoked meats. When the strike began, his job was to organize speakers and travel across the state as a P-9 ambassador. With his soft-spoken demeanor, Jensen spread the story of P-9's contract battle to labor groups, service clubs, business associations, anyone who would listen. He was no cheerleader, no complainer, no cussing lunatic full of conspiracy theories. Even businessmen who opposed what they saw happening in Austin came up to him after his talks to compliment him. After listening to Jensen, they knew why he was fighting, and they respected him for it.

He carried the message fifty-four times from Austin to the

Twin Cities, a two-hundred-mile round trip, during the strike. He crisscrossed the state from Duluth to St. Cloud and Rochester, usually accompanied by three or four people from his committee. Even though his job was part of the well-oiled Rogers machinery, Jensen took little interest in the campaign itself. Like most union members, he had attended the first meetings at which Rogers spoke but then kept his distance and left the leafleting, bank protests, and traveling to Guyette's most fervent supporters. Once the strike started, however, and he had more free time, he became a loyal, eager volunteer.

About two months into the strike Jensen began to sense that the contract battle that he was telling people about—for better pay and a little more respect on the shop floor—was reaching a turning point. Federal mediator Hank Bell had called the two sides together to meet on October 14 in Rochester for the first time since talks broke off before the strike. But shortly before the meeting, Rogers had organized his bank demonstration in La Crosse, Wisconsin, apparently disobeying a federal judge and thoroughly annoying Hormel.

The Wisconsin trip, on the eve of resumed talks, got Jensen to thinking. Many rank-and-filers he knew, people who were solidly behind the fight, were getting restless. They were not P-10ers who sided with Lewie Anderson. They were not devout blue caps in Guyette's corner. They weren't even organized. But they probably came closest to representing the union's silent, faithful majority. They simply felt that the time had come to resume bargaining, to bring the dispute to an end and get everybody back to work. Eight weeks was a long time without a job. Savings had been tapped, unpaid bills were stretching out, and the holidays were coming up. They wanted to get things moving.

But the bank picketing had resumed, even when it seemed to flout the law directly. Reports out of the Rochester talks were not promising. The company was showing a new brand of toughness and hinted that it was through playing games with P-9. At the union hall there was cheery talk about Santa's Workshop and all the homemade toys for P-9 kids at Christmas. While it was a laudable effort, it got people in Jensen's circles really wondering when this thing was going to end. Was the point to negotiate a contract or make children's toys? Jensen privately began to reflect on what the strike was really about. As P-9's contract issues began to share the limelight with the rhetoric of socialists, Communists, and labor militants who were ecstatic about P-9's fight, a nagging question creeped into his mind: Just whom was this strike supposed to benefit? He'd known the answer back in August, but now he wasn't so sure.

November 1933: Members of the fledgling Independent Union of All Workers
block a road to the Hormel packinghouse. Workers shut down the plant for three
days before Minnesota Governor Floyd B. Olson intervened and negotiated a
settlement.

Star Tribune (Minneapolis/St. Paul)

November 1933: Pickets warm themselves outside the packinghouse gates. Fifty-two years later, the scene would be repeated on virtually the same spot.

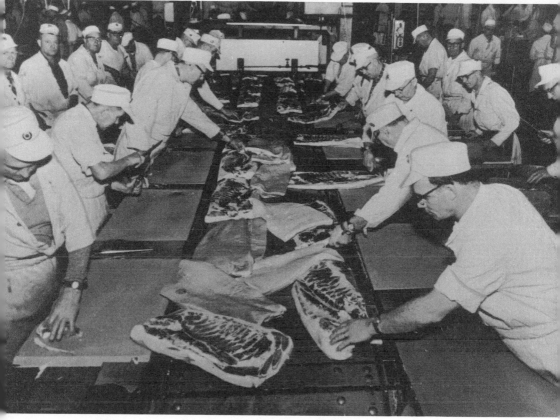

January 1965: A meat-trimming line in the old Austin packinghouse.

October 1984: Jim Guyette, ten months after taking office as local P-9 president, explains the tactics of a "corporate campaign" to fight Hormel's 23-percent wage cut on 1,700 union members.

March 1985: Lewie Anderson meets with reporters in the Twin Cities to explain why the UFCW opposes local P-9's corporate campaign.

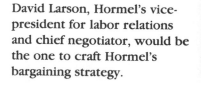

Willis Woyke/Austin *Daily Herald*

David Larson, Hormel's vice-president for labor relations and chief negotiator, would be the one to craft Hormel's bargaining strategy.

Geo. Hormel & Co.

Willis Woyke/Austin *Daily Herald*

May 1985: Local P-9 President Jim Guyette, Vice-President Lynn Huston, and Business Agent Pete Winkels show their displeasure at an Austin City Council meeting after the council voted 7–0 to urge the union to drop its corporate campaign.

Larry Salzman

December 1985: An uneasy Joe Hansen tells reporters and P-9 members that the UFCW can't endorse Hormel's final contract offer, but thinks "it's the best we're going to get."

Star Tribune (Minneapolis/St. Paul)

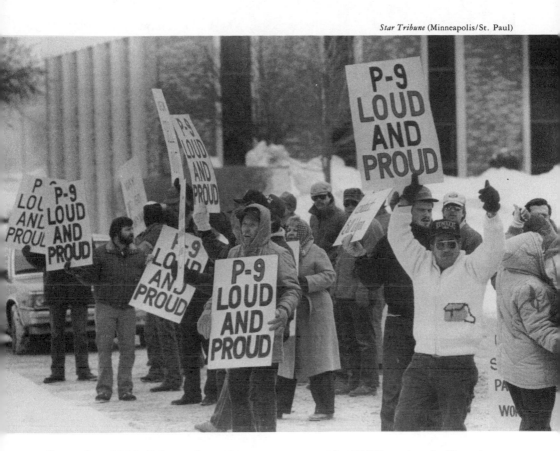

December 1985: P-9 members demonstrate outside UFCW regional offices in Bloomington, Minn., after the international union hints that P-9 should accept Hormel's final offer and end the strike.

December 1985: P-9 Vice-President Lynn Huston at a press conference called by local officers to denounce the UFCW and criticize Hormel's final offer.

Larry Salzman

Larry Salzman

January 1986: Local P-9 President Jim Guyette and Hormel's Chuck Nyberg shake hands on the set of "Almanac," a Twin Cities television show, three days before Hormel is to reopen the strike-bound packinghouse. After debating vigorously, the two agree to a last-minute bargaining session the next morning. It collapses after an hour.

Star Tribune (Minneapolis/St. Paul)

January 1986: P-9 supporters jeer replacement workers who show up at the packinghouse to fill out job applications after Hormel announced that it would reopen the plant with or without P-9.

January 1986: At the United Auto Workers' hall in St. Paul, Guyette addresses more than 500 supporters, telling them P-9 will need their support on the picket line when Hormel starts hiring nonunion replacements the next day.

Larry Salzman

Star Tribune (Minneapolis/St. Paul)

January 1986: National Guardsmen line up at dawn to keep pickets at bay after Minnesota Governor Rudy Perpich decides that law and order is threatened in Austin.

Star Tribune (Minneapolis/St. Paul)

January 1986: Using a police loudspeaker, Ray Rogers claims victory as he tells P-9 supporters that Hormel will not reopen the packinghouse on January 21, the National Guard's first full day in Austin.

February 1986: Ray Rogers is handcuffed in a police van after his arrest on the P-9 picket line.

Larry Salzman

Star Tribune (Minneapolis/St. Paul)

February 1986: An estimated 2,000 union supporters from across the country march through Austin to a boisterous rally at the high school auditorium. Even as chances appeared slim that P-9 could win the strike, its nationwide appeal was escalating among labor militants.

Star Tribune (Minneapolis/St. Paul)

April 1986: Austin police carry off a demonstrator during a dawn demonstration in which 300 strikers and out-of-town supporters block access to the plant's north gate. Though the strike is all but lost, the demonstration kicks off a three-day weekend of anti-Hormel protests by thousands of supporters who travel to Austin.

April 1986: Tear gas billows into the crowd of demonstrators after police try unsuccessfully to remove them by force. Seventeen demonstrators are arrested and police issue arrest warrants for Jim Guyette and Ray Rogers on felony riot charges.

Willis Woyke/Austin *Daily Herald*

May 1986: Kathy Buck, a latecomer to the P-9 board, at a press conference with Guyette. Buck remained a stalwart supporter of the corporate campaign long after Hormel had declared the strike over.

July 1987: Pete Winkels, removed as P-9's business agent, addresses a crowd of union sympathizers in Austin during a counter-demonstration to the city's celebration of the 50th anniversary of Spam. Ray Rogers looks on in the background.

Larry Salzman

July 1987: Once high school classmates, Hormel Chairman Richard Knowlton and P-9 member Dave King talk during the Austin celebration of the fiftieth anniversary of Spam. An embittered King made an emotional plea before Knowlton to settle the dispute at the Hormel annual meeting in January 1986. He retired rather than return to work.

December 1988: John Anker brought a more moderate philosophy of unionism to the president's office at the Austin Labor Center. He had been defeated by Jim Guyette for the presidency of local P-9 in December 1983, then elected after Guyette was ousted and the trusteeship was lifted in 1987.

CHAPTER

11

On Friday, November 15, federal mediator Hank Bell called negotiators for P-9 and Hormel back to the bargaining table, this time at the Kahler Hotel in Rochester, thirty-five miles northeast of Austin. The Kahler occupies an entire block in downtown Rochester and is crisscrossed with corridors, coffee shops, gift counters, and all the conveniences for the thousands of patients who flock to Rochester each year for treatment at the renowned Mayo Clinic. Bell hoped that a new setting might shelter the negotiators from reporters—and produce some progress.

Guyette came to the table with a new pledge of support from the UFCW: Hormel must bargain in good faith or Wynn would sanction roving pickets. Whether or not he believed Hormel's earnings statement for the fourth quarter, Guyette had to know that P-9 could not win while the other packinghouses operated. The new talks were his chance to show Wynn that Hormel was out to bust P-9. Dave Larson came to the table with the understanding that seasoned professionals from the UFCW would watch over Guyette's shoulder and scrutinize the talks. Wynn and his public relations chief, Al Zack, were careful to avoid saying publicly that the UFCW had put P-9 on a leash. But they sent a Washington-based international rep, Al Vincent, to sit in on the talks and instructed Guyette that Joe Hansen would be reporting back to Wynn on progress at the table. Larson felt that for the first time P-9 would have to pay heed to its parent union. Bell and Hansen, who desperately wanted a settlement, came to the table with the knowledge that Christmas was drawing close, fourteen hundred families were scraping by on meager strike pay and donated food, and pressure was building on both sides to settle the strike.

The omens, however, were not promising. One day before talks resumed, Guyette and Rogers called a press conference in St. Paul to announce that P-9 was extending the corporate campaign to two prominent Hormel customers. They planned to leaflet Burger King outlets, which bought 90 percent of their bacon for bacon cheeseburgers from Hormel, and Hy-Vee supermarkets, a popular grocery chain in the small towns of Iowa and southern Minnesota. The leaflets carefully avoided the word "boycott," but they encouraged customers to "make your dissatisfaction known" to Hy-Vee and Burger King. Knowlton and Nyberg were livid. The normally mild-mannered Nyberg told reporters: "This is typical. They make a gesture at collective bargaining while their true efforts are directed toward harassment of the company, intimidation of its customers, and threats toward companies with whom we do business." Of the impending contract talks, Nyberg added, "It dims any cause for optimism." Guyette was not about to be chastened. "If I were a dog, I might worry that I have to roll over for the master," he told a reporter. "But we don't consider ourselves dogs."

The campaign's new tactic hardly made Hormel any more conciliatory. In addition to resisting proposals that would put Austin significantly ahead of their other plants, Hormel's executives were growing more determined with each new phase of the strike. The meat-packing industry had enormous excess capacity, and pork producers all over the Midwest were more than happy to have Hormel as a customer rather than a competitor. Hormel was paying a lot of money to move machinery around and ship pork from suppliers to its processing plants, but it was also saving big money on labor costs in Austin. Its fourth-quarter earnings had proved it could weather the strike, at least temporarily.

In addition, if talks proved fruitless and Hormel decided to reopen the plant without a settlement, plant manager Deryl Arnold would have a dream contract in place. The implemented agreement called for wages of eight dollars an hour for new hires (lower than at some of Hormel's competitors), enormous flexibility to deploy workers as the flow of work required, competitive fringe benefits, and an arbitration clause that gave the company considerable leeway in disciplining workers. Larson and Knowlton were willing to continue negotiating on some features, such as the two-tier wage system and reduced seniority, which they knew the union despised. But they were no less confident of their overwhelming bargaining leverage. By this time even the normally circumspect Nyberg, with all his lawyerly restraint, had come to refer to P-9's proposals as "off the wall." He and Larson simply did not believe that Wynn would hold Hormel's feet to the fire over such demands.

Still, Larson wanted to be certain of his ground. He was somewhat puzzled by the various accounts of P-9's meeting with Wynn in Chicago, so he called Hansen to ask exactly what Wynn meant when he said that Hormel must bargain in good faith. Hansen said that Wynn insisted on three things: Number one, Hormel must show genuine willingness to move in response to movement by P-9. Number two, P-9 must do the same. Number three, Hormel had to come off the two-tier wage system. Hansen said the UFCW's priorities included serious discussion of safety, wages, and seniority.

Larson repeated what was to become an article of faith for the company's negotiators: The company had a contract in place that it could legally enforce, and Hormel was not changing it. But company officials were willing to meet with union negotiators and consider what they had to say.

Larson had decided by this time that he should return to the table in person. There was still something of the stern father in him, and even though company protocol didn't require his presence, he wondered if in his own gruff way he could drive home the severity of their mutual plight. He opened the first session at the Kahler with a long lecture, telling Guyette and the others that the strike had dragged on long enough, that Hormel's wage proposal would put them in the top 10 percent of the nation's meatpackers, and that they had an obligation to their rank and file to draft a new proposal that could realistically lead to a settlement. Hansen listened quietly, impressed with Larson's presentation, how it hammered home what the whole dispute was about. It was blunt and full of exasperation, like Larson himself. But when he looked up from his notes, Larson saw Guyette staring at the ceiling and Huston chuckling quietly. Larson erupted. There was something about the young mechanic's cocky demeanor that always irritated Larson, and some in the room thought Larson was actually going to reach across the table and throttle him. Instead, he turned to Bell and muttered, "We will not stay at the table under these conditions. Mr. Mediator, I turn it over to you."

Larson told Bell that the law required him to keep negotiating but that nothing could make him stay at the table across from these upstarts. From that day on Bell "wore out a lot of shoe leather," as Guyette later described it, in the arduous process of shuttle mediation—sliding back and forth from one caucus room to another, probing and testing each side for common ground that might bring them together.

Six days later a strike settlement at the Morrell packinghouse in Sioux Falls, South Dakota, two hundred miles west of Austin, shed light on just how deeply Hormel and P-9 were divided. Like their UFCW brothers and sisters in Austin, about twenty-five hundred Morrell meat-packers once earned the $10.69 wage rate. But the threat of massive layoffs in 1983 had brought it down to $8.75. When contract talks stalled in 1985, Morrell workers went on strike shortly after P-9. Now, with Anderson assisting in negotiations, they got a contract calling for an immediate twenty-five-cent raise to $9 an hour, with eventual raises to $9.75 by 1988. UFCW spokesman Al Zack in Washington said the agreement would put pressure on Hormel because it put a major geographic competitor back in operation. Hormel spokesman Allan Krejci said the pact demonstrated that P-9 was being unrealistic: A tough and militant group of meat-packers at one of the top five pork companies had settled for a dollar an hour less than what Hormel had on the table. Guyette's reaction was scorn: The UFCW had again settled for a contract that would leave wages lower in 1988 than they had been ten years earlier.

With such divergent views of something so straightforward, it wasn't surprising that Bell had P-9 and Hormel negotiators huddled in separate rooms. He was not about to risk another face-to-face insult session. For a week he shuttled back and forth, this time with the assistance of a second mediator, Donald Eaton. They pressed each side hard to boil its case down to the three or four most vital issues. They leaned on Larson with all their might: Wasn't there some way to redraft the company's position and give P-9 a chance to save face and hold another vote? They leaned on P-9, too, and they didn't mince words: Why did they keep beating on this thing? Didn't they see the company held the cards? Couldn't P-9 give more ground and come up with something the company would at least consider seriously? What they got in return was another recitation of P-9's long list of complaints.

In the P-9 subcaucus Hansen also began to lean on board members. He told them they were being unrealistic on the wage demand of $11.25 and that they were going to have to jettison many other issues to get close to the company's position. Guyette was still holding out for the guaranteed annual wage and the old seniority system, demands which Bell said Hormel rejected. By this time the board's moderates were starting to have doubts. Keith Judd, one of four holdovers from the pre-Guyette regime, in particular felt it was time to compromise. Judd, who had worked for Hormel for nearly forty years, had held various offices in the local and believed deeply in the power of the international union. He had opposed the corporate campaign from the start and believed it was bad unionism to flout the UFCW. He held his peace in public, but he kept his channels open with P-9ers and retirees who opposed Guyette. Occasionally he quietly lobbied with Floyd Lenoch and Jim Retterath, who had also joined the board before Guyette and worried now and then that P-9 was not winning this war. Judd and Lenoch, who preceded Guyette as president, had been friends for years and often drove home together from the bargaining sessions, each reviewing his doubts and convictions. One night as Judd pulled up at Lenoch's house, Floyd turned to him and said, "These kids are going to wake one morning and find themselves in a trusteeship."

But Lenoch, the board's self-styled father figure, also was deeply bitter toward Hormel and had campaigned for Guyette, his chosen successor, in 1983. Skinny Weis, too, was convinced that this was no longer the paternalistic Hormel he had started working for in 1948. Back in the caucus room, Guyette formed an unshakable trio with Winkels and Huston, and they had little trouble convincing Lenoch and Weis to persevere. In a gesture of compromise, however, P-9's negotiators agreed to give Hormel a new proposal. On November 23 the committee drafted an offer that fell back to the language of the expired contract on seniority, work standards, holidays, grievance, and arbitration and other noneconomic issues. Then, after much internal haggling over the appropriate wage level, they dropped their wage demand to $10.69.

Meanwhile, back in Austin, the three militants had gained a confirmed new ally on the executive board. P-9's longtime financial secretary, Audrey Neumann, had retired in September, after being hospitalized in May with a heart condition brought on by work-related stress. On November 23 P-9 held a special election for her post. Kathy Buck decided to run. She felt ready to make a bigger contribution to the union. She figured there ought to be a woman on the executive board, and she felt that it needed more than one person, Huston, representing new workers in the plant. In a test of strength against more moderate elements in the union, she defeated a P-10 sympathizer, Ward Halvorson, 318–232, with three other candidates splitting another 473 votes. Her election put three of P-9's eight board members solidly behind Guyette. Though Lenoch, Weis, Kenny Hagen, and Jim Retterath had occasional doubts about the strike's success, none was ready to compromise.

Talks recessed during the first week of December because Guyette and Huston were needed in Minneapolis for an NLRB administrative trial on Hormel's secondary-boycott charge against the corporate campaign. P-9 also was in the middle of local elections for vice-president, the job held by Huston, and two seats on the executive board, held by Judd and Retterath. Huston and Judd were running again, but Retterath announced plans to step down, saying that negotiations were getting a little too crazy for him and it was time to give somebody else a shot at leading P-9. The election was a long-awaited opportunity for Morrison, Anker, and the other P-10ers to assert themselves and get a voice on the board. But it slipped through their fingers. Their candidate to oppose Huston, a moderate named Dave Ring, withdrew from the race when another moderate, Darwin Sellers, announced unexpectedly. Sellers, however, ran a quiet campaign and refused to criticize P-9's direction or challenge the corporate campaign. Chad Young, a staunch opponent of Rogers and Guyette, ran for a board seat in the field of eleven candidates that included three vigorous Guyette supporters. Several of the other candidates quietly expressed reservations about the strike's direction, but none openly associated themselves with the P-10 movement. When the ballots were counted, Huston defeated Sellers, 654–435, for vice-president, Judd was reelected, and the other board seat went to Carl Pontius, a hard-line Guyette supporter. In the executive board balloting Judd led the field with 420 votes, his experience and familiarity overcoming any liability caused by his moderate stance, while Pontius finished a clear second with 295. Young finished fifth, with 204 votes, behind Larry Jensen and Merrill Evans, one of Guyette's most active and visible supporters. With the rank and file's new endorsements, the board returned to the bargaining table confirmed in its militancy.

When talks resumed, however, Hormel negotiators showed little movement. The bargaining strategy carefully mapped out by Nyberg and Larson left the company in an enviable position. Hormel had implemented its August contract even though no one was working, and in the absence of a settlement, federal labor law gave Hormel the power to enforce that contract on anybody who came to work in the plant. But management would lose that authority if in subsequent negotiations it moved off that position. Hormel was walking a fine legal line, obligated to bargain in good faith but unwilling to tinker with its August contract. In the days since November 15, Larson had told Bell that Hormel was willing to hire an ergonomics expert to study dangerous jobs and an industrial engineer to study job loads. But he insisted that P-9's economic proposals were out of the question. Clearly P-9 would have to make drastic changes in its position to lure Hormel off the implemented contract, and Bell told the union negotiators as much.

Bell, however, had been a mediator long enough to have a pretty big bag of tricks. As Christmas approached, he became increasingly eager to develop a proposal that could give the rank and file a chance to vote on an end to the strike. He approached Larson and said that he and Eaton thought they could find some common ground on the two-tier wage system, seniority, and safety. Would it be acceptable to draft a compromise and present it as Hormel's offer? Larson said no, Hormel was not making a new offer. All right, Bell replied, what if the mediators drew up a proposal, called it their own, and got P-9 to agree to take it to the rank and file? That would give the union a chance to vote on an improved offer. Yet it would protect Hormel's implemented contract in case the union said no. Larson assented.

On December 13 Bell and Eaton walked into the P-9 suite at the Kahler with a few sheets of paper in their hands and a brief lecture. They said they had what they were calling the "mediator's proposal." It was their work, they said, representing a few points of compromise by the company, and Larson had agreed to sign off on it if P-9 did. They asked the board to consider it, and consider it carefully. They said they believed it was a better deal than workers at other meat-packing companies were getting and they believed it was the best P-9 would get. It was the end of the road. They handed out outlines of the proposal and left. The room fell silent as the board members, Hansen, and Rollins pored over the proposal. There was a sense of gravity in the room. P-9's leaders might disagree over whether this really was Hormel's final offer, but they all knew that P-9 would have to make a decision: Accept it or raise the stakes considerably.

The proposal was built on Hormel's final offer in August, but Bell and Eaton persuaded Larson to move on several key issues. The proposal abandoned Hormel's demand for a two-tier wage structure—that is, permanently lower wages for new employees. It reiterated a base wage of ten dollars an hour for all production employees, bringing them into parity with the rest of the Hormel chain. It did not restore the guaranteed annual wage or the fifty-two-week layoff notice, but it required the company to pay overtime as it was worked. It called for Hormel to hire an ergonomics expert to study P-9's safety complaints and make recommendations, although it didn't commit the company to follow the suggestions. The company also would bring in an industrial engineer to study the jobs that P-9 said were overloaded. In place of the onerous seniority language of August, which gave management enormous discretion in assigning workers, it substituted seniority language lifted directly from the union contract in Ottumwa. It also conceded to the union's request for expedited arbitration of outstanding grievances, compromised on consideration of "past practices" in the plant as guidelines for future rules, reduced the length of probation for new employees, dropped a company demand for virtually unlimited use of temporary employees, and promised a six-month written notice of a plant closing. In a handwritten letter on a page and a half of legal paper, Larson told Bell and Eaton that Hormel would accept the changes if P-9 would hold a ratification vote and come back to work by January 3.

But most of P-9's executive board believed that this was not the end of the line. In fact, they questioned whether it wasn't really a Hormel proposal in disguise. It didn't seem possible that Bell and Eaton could have had the time to put it all together. And if it was a mediator's deal, why didn't P-9 get any say in it? Regardless of who put it together, the proposal fell so far short of their demands—on safety, on seniority, on wages—that they could scarcely embrace it or recommend it to the membership. Board member Kenny Hagen felt sick. If this is all we've achieved after all these months of struggle, he thought, people at home aren't going to take it.

The executive board was ready to reject it out of hand, and they felt confident that Bill Wynn, too, would reject it and finally authorize an escalation of their battle by sanctioning roving pickets. Their hopes didn't last long. As he prepared to leave the Kahler that afternoon, Joe Hansen called UFCW headquarters in Washington to talk to Jay Foreman, Wynn's top assistant. Foreman didn't even want to hear whether Hansen could recommend the offer or not. Just tell me what it says on the key issues, he told Hansen: safety; seniority; the two-tier wage system. When he heard that Bell had gotten Hormel to budge on all three, he told Hansen to bring P-9's officers to Washington to meet with Wynn.

They met the following Monday, December 16, in a reception room outside Wynn's eleventh-floor office at UFCW headquarters on K Street. The meeting was brief and to the point. Wynn told Guyette and the others that the proposal wasn't everything that he desired, but that in his view it represented genuine compromise by Hormel. He asked for their opinion. Guyette said it was unacceptable, that a company as profitable as Hormel could afford to pay more than ten dollars an hour, that the Ottumwa seniority rules were inferior to those P-9 had always enjoyed, and that his members didn't trust Hormel to implement any of the safety or work load recommendations of outside experts. Wynn asked Guyette for his alternative. Guyette replied that P-9 would strike another seventeen weeks if it had to, according to those who attended the meeting. The next day Wynn's office announced that while the UFCW could not make a recommendation on the proposal, it wanted P-9's membership to vote on it. Spokesman Al Zack said the UFCW would conduct a secret mail ballot starting later that week, an unusual step that reflected the UFCW's concerns about peer pressure on anyone who had to vote at the Austin Labor Center.

Back in Austin, the mediator's proposal and the UFCW's announcement touched off a bitter reaction, as if any hint of compromise was a threat to P-9's crusade. Unable to block a vote on an offer that fell far short of their pledged goals, P-9 leaders were not about to let it convert their rank and file. Meanwhile, another Twin Cities food caravan had arrived on Sunday, December 15, with more than twenty tons of food. Rogers cited it as evidence that the meat-packers could hold out forever. On Wednesday Lynn Huston went on Austin's KAUS radio and listed a number of objections that many P-9 members found deeply frightening. He said the proposal gave Hormel unlimited rights to transfer workers from one department to another. He said Hormel was offering fringe benefits even worse than arbitrator George Fleischli had ordered. He said senior employees could be laid off if the company eliminated their jobs and they were unable to perform the jobs of less senior employees. He was wrong on each count. Huston also said that the contract's wage language contained a loophole allowing Hormel to pay $9.35 an hour, not $10. He noted correctly that new employees would start at a lower, probationary wage but said it appeared that a new employee who missed a day of work would go back to the start of the probationary period. He was wrong about that latter point as well. In subsequent interviews Huston and Guyette expressed suspicion of the proposal because P-9's executive board had had no input into it and surmised publicly that it was a company offer dressed up as a mediator's proposal. As suspicious of Wynn and Anderson as the UFCW was of P-9, Huston announced on Wednesday afternoon that P-9 would conduct its own vote on the proposal.

The next morning before dawn, scores of P-9ers turned up at the packinghouse, drove in circles around it, honking to protest the offer, and finally blocked the main gates just as supervisors were due to report for work. Milling in the crowd and supervising the demonstration, Rogers met a reporter from KAUS and launched a string of invective at the UFCW. He said the demonstration had been arranged at a rank-and-file meeting the previous night to express spontaneous outrage. He called the mediator's proposal "ridiculous," accused the UFCW of collaborating with Hormel to "jam it down our throat," and predicted that the UFCW would rig the mail ballot and never count the votes. The demonstrators cleared off when police arrived about 8:00 A.M., but the warning shot had been fired: P-9 had tactics to shut the plant and was willing to use them. The next day Hormel's lawyers went to the Mower County Courthouse and asked for a temporary restraining order that would limit P-9 to three pickets at each gate and forbid blocking access to the plant. That afternoon plant manager Deryl Arnold fired off a telegram to Guyette accusing him of misrepresenting the mediator's proposal and demanding that P-9's leadership describe it accurately.

The mediator's proposal put Joe Hansen in an awkward position. He knew it fell well short of what the executive board and Rogers had led the membership to believe they could get. Yet it offered compromises on the key issues of safety, two-tier wages, and seniority, and it secured virtually the highest wage in the industry. It wasn't everything P-9 wanted, but that wasn't the point anymore. To Hansen, the point was: Did P-9 possess any leverage to force Hormel into a better offer? Hansen was convinced it did not. He sensed he was beginning to understand the company, and when he heard Nyberg reiterate that the plant would not sit idle indefinitely, the threat carried a new sense of urgency. He knew Knowlton's pride in the new packinghouse and that he was restless to get it running again. He knew there was a growing pattern in the packinghouse industry to "scab" a struck plant by hiring replacements and resuming operations without the union. The bluff-and-gruff game of bargaining at some point depends on at least one party from each side developing enough trust to believe they have reached the bottom line. Hansen now believed Larson when he said the mediator's proposal was the end of the line. Finally, he knew that at least some P-9 members were growing restless with their leadership, and he feared that the union would break ranks if Hormel reopened.

On December 20 Hansen mailed a carefully drafted six-page letter to the 1,422 P-9 households. He avoided an actual recommendation of the proposal, but he made his position clear in pained language:

> In a fight as tough as the one the members of Local P-9 have waged, it is never easy to accept less than you want and less than you deserve. By the same token, however, you must decide whether there is anything further to be gained by continuing this painful and demanding struggle.
>
> Speaking as one who assisted your local union leaders throughout the contract negotiations, it is very clear to me that nothing measurable can be won by continuing the struggle that has cost you, your families and your community so dearly.
>
> During my association with the members of Local P-9, especially during this long struggle, you have earned my great respect for your courage, idealism and tenacity. But despite this, it is my firm view that the company will not make any further changes from those in the proposal you will vote on.

Hansen went on to express his skepticism about the impact of the corporate campaign and about sending roving pickets to other Hormel plants. In case any of the P-9ers should miss his point, he added:

> I truly believe that extending the picket lines would only compound the suffering—not only for the UFCW members at the other plants who would be jeopardizing their jobs, but also for P-9 members. Therefore, I will not

recommend that the International Union sanction exten-
sion of picketing and the International Union will not
sanction such picketing regardless of the vote outcome.

Voting to accept this proposal is, in my mind, the best
hope that Local P-9 members will have to end the strike
with dignity and some hope for a better tomorrow.

Hansen knew he was burning the last bridge between the
UFCW and P-9: himself. And sure enough, that very day Guyette
angrily denounced him and accused him of placing his ambition
and his position with the UFCW above his principles. That day
the fury of P-9 turned on the UFCW itself. Hansen and Zack had
called a press conference in the Twin Cities to describe the mediator's proposal and explain their position. By noon more than a
hundred demonstrators from Austin had gathered outside
Hansen's office in Bloomington, waving the familiar placards and
chanting their opposition to the proposal.

Things got uglier a half mile away at the Thunderbird Hotel
when reporters began showing up for Hansen's press conference.
Blue caps wandered in from their chilly demonstration and began
prowling the labyrinthine hotel for the UFCW's conference room.
When they finally found it, they discovered that the UFCW had
posted five burly union staffers at the door who were admitting
only reporters. Inside the room Hansen and Zack were reviewing
Hansen's statement somewhat uneasily while television photographers set up their lights and tripods. Outside, the Austin contingent milled about, complaining about police state tactics and
trying to decide what to do. As more of them found the room,
they pooled into the narrow hallway outside and began pressing
up against the door. A shouting match erupted between one of
the guards and one of the blue caps. A short man at the back of
the crowd started yelling that the UFCW had threatened to call
the police on their own members. Suddenly the crowd surged up
against the door, pressing it open a foot. Three of the UFCW staff
reps put their shoulders to the door and nearly squeezed it shut.
For a moment both sides were frozen in a shoving battle that
tested the door's hinges. Reporters inside the room stared with
amusement and disbelief. Then Guyette appeared at the head of
the crowd, calming his members and asking for a few words with

Zack or Hansen. He argued that as editor of Austin's *Unionist* newspaper, he had press credentials and ought to be admitted to the room. Hansen and Zack weren't buying that, but they finally agreed that P-9 ought to be represented in the room. They said that if the blue caps would back off from the doors, they would admit representatives from P-9.

When peace was restored, reporters finally settled into their chairs, along with half a dozen P-9ers, including Guyette, Huston, and Marilyn "Mike" Jensen, another of Guyette's vocal supporters. Hansen began by saying the UFCW had called the news conference because "there's a lot of confusion down in Austin" about the mediator's proposal. He defended the UFCW's decision to hold a mail ballot, which he said would be collected at a Twin Cities post office and counted by an accounting firm or federal mediator. "This is a time for the most careful and reflective actions by the members of Local P-9," Hansen added, hinting that the circus atmosphere of P-9's union hall was not conducive to calm deliberation. He repeated that he was not endorsing the proposal but said, "Speaking as a person who assisted the members of Local P-9, I can tell you that the mediator's proposal is a compromise. We're there. We're at the end."

The reporters were still scribbling notes when Jensen shot to her feet and began lambasting Hansen. Why did Hormel have more input into the proposal than P-9? Why didn't the UFCW trust P-9 to conduct its own vote? How could the parent union drop such a proposal on Austin and leave P-9 members "cold and hungry"? Hansen repeated that he wasn't enthusiastic about the offer but that he thought it was the best P-9 could get. As Jensen fired another question, Hansen looked for questions from the mainstream press. Reporters seemed uncertain whether to intercede or let the confrontation proceed. Finally Hansen lost his composure, and the press conference threatened to turn into a shouting match. By the time Zack stepped in to adjourn the session, more blue caps were trickling in the back door. Rogers was standing at the back of the room, stabbing his finger angrily at Zack and Hansen and calling for an impromptu debate. Hansen and Zack pushed through a gauntlet of angry blue caps outside the room and made their way down a narrow hallway, to a chorus of insults and taunts.

As reporters packed up their notebooks and cameras, Rogers announced that he and Guyette would hold their own press conference in a room next door, where the 150 P-9ers could sit in. In a room packed with his supporters, steamy with body heat, and thick with cigarette smoke, Guyette faced a bank of reporters and calmly laid out his objections to the mediator's proposal. He said P-9 would abide by its own vote, not by the UFCW's mail ballot, and announced that P-9 was prepared to fight on.

"There's no question," he said as the cameras rolled under the hot bright lights, "that we can get a better contract."

The next day Guyette and the executive board went before their members again to give a detailed critique of the mediator's proposal. They described it as "an extreme change from our previous contract," which it certainly was, but said it was inferior to the contracts at other Hormel plants, a debatable proposition. They reported that the executive board had voted to recommend its rejection.

In the remaining days before Christmas, the Austin Labor Center was busier than ever. Down in the basement Santa's Workshop went into full production, turning out wooden airplanes and stuffed teddy bears for strikers' children. At a row of phones installed for the purpose, Support Group volunteers called P-9 members urging them to reject the mediator's proposal. Guyette, Winkels, and Huston made themselves available on Monday and Tuesday, Christmas Eve. Yes, they assured their members, Hormel could be forced to offer a better contract.

Rogers, meanwhile, was busy reassuring the rank and file and the public. He told reporters about the weeks that P-9's volunteers had spent in Ottumwa, Fremont, Algona, Beloit, and the other Hormel towns, building support for a sympathy strike in case P-9 needed to shut down all of Hormel. He said P-9 would renew its picketing at First Bank branches and go to the Minnesota legislature to lobby against an interstate banking bill that First Bank sought. He said P-9's ranks were solid, predicting, "You don't have five hundred people out there who will run across the picket line." He said P-9 also had built solidarity among area farmers who might otherwise be tempted to take the union members' jobs if Hormel tried to reopen. He hinted at the possibility of hundreds of P-9ers engaging in civil disobedience. "It's not how long can the workers stick it out," he insisted. "It's how long can the company stick it out."

On Thursday and Friday the P-9ers filed into their union hall once again to vote on the mediator's proposal. To allay the UFCW's suspicions, Guyette had recruited four Austin clergymen to watch the balloting and attest that there were no irregularities. It was little comfort, however, to John Morrison. He had developed a bad feeling in his stomach ever since he saw that Santa's Workshop was cranking up production for Christmas. It was as if his union existed not to negotiate a contract but to tide the members through a war of indefinite length. When the votes were counted on Friday night, P-9's members had rejected the mediator's proposal by a three-to-two margin.

On the afternoon of Friday, January 3, 1986, Zack, Guyette, and one hundred P-9 loyalists were back at the Thunderbird Hotel in Bloomington to observe the counting of the UFCW's mail ballot. Hansen had hired an accounting firm, rented a small meeting room, and invited representatives from the clergy, the press, and the Minnesota legislature to watch the tally. In the center of the room several long folding tables had been set up in a big rectangle. The accountants sat in teams of two around the outside; observers appointed by P-9 and the UFCW sat in teams of two around the inside. Each team of accountants and observers would get a batch of ballots, complete their count, then pass the batch along to the next team. At the back of the room were thirty chairs set up in rows for observers. With a settlement or continued bitter strike hanging in the balance, the room had the appearance and the tense air of a high-stakes auction. After Zack made an initial statement describing the counting procedure, it became clear that there would be no results for hours, and the observers began drifting out of the room.

Immediately outside the door P-9 loyalists in their blue caps and blue jackets milled around in a long hallway, smoking cigarettes, chatting with reporters, giving interviews to filmmaker Barbara Kopple and accosting UFCW officials whenever possible. The most loyal of the strikers and retirees had spent so much time together by this point that they seemed to think and move as one, flexing and shifting up and down the hallway almost like a single organism, relaxing during the slow spells, then coalescing toward any sign of excitement. At one point, State Senator Pat Piper, a Democratic-Farmer-Labor legislator from Austin, left the counting room to talk with a handful of P-9ers. Before long the chat turned into a debate, and soon an audience of forty blue caps joined in. When a well-known Twin Cities television reporter stopped Guyette to ask a few questions, their interview attracted a crowd, which attracted a bigger one intent on not missing anything.

Finally, as winter darkness was beginning to fall outside, rumor trickled out of the counting room that the tally was nearly done. Inside, accountants and UFCW aides were collecting the team subtotals. One of P-9's supporters was scurrying around the table just ahead of them, keeping his own running tally. Just as aides were briefing Zack on the total, word shot out among the blue caps who had crowded into the room: The proposal had lost by a three-to-two margin.

Zack cleared his throat and announced the total: 540 yes, 775 no. A cheer erupted among the blue caps. The UFCW aides in the room wore pained expressions. Reporters bustled toward Zack, who explained that the UFCW would continue to pay strike benefits "so long as there is a reasonable prospect of arriving at a settlement." Hansen would withdraw from future negotiations and give P-9 a free hand, he said. In the hallway outside, reporters swarmed around Guyette, who gave another impromptu press conference. Yes, he insisted, P-9 would bargain for a better offer because it planned to raise the stakes even higher. He declined to elaborate. "We've telegraphed enough in the past. In a war situation the niceties go out."

Back in Austin that evening, Dave Larson was stunned by the vote. Larson had counted himself among the "doves" in Hormel management. He was the one who believed in collective bargaining. He was the one who had lobbied Knowlton to let company negotiators stay at the table and keep hammering away. He was the one who had argued that P-9's rank and file would come around after four months of fruitless strike and accept the mediator's proposal. Now he told Knowlton that he, too, had had "a bellyful."

The next morning, Saturday, January 4, Larson, Nyberg, Arnold, and a handful of other executives convened in a conference room at the packinghouse to plan the step they had always known was on the horizon but had delayed so long: to reopen the plant and call P-9's hand. Nyberg had already laid out Hormel's alternatives to the executive committee, which consisted of himself; Knowlton; Bill Hunter, vice-president for operations; Jim Silbaugh, vice-president for meat products; Jim Hall, vice-president for prepared foods; and Donald Hodapp, group vice-president for administration. The alternatives made a short list: Either P-9 accepted the mediator's proposal or Hormel reopened the plant. To postpone reopening now would mean giving P-9 power to keep the plant shut indefinitely, Nyberg argued. The committee agreed. With or without a settlement, the plant was going to reopen.

Now the executives faced a new series of questions: How fast should we gear up? What if nobody came back to work? Should we hire replacements? If replacements are hired, should they be temporary or permanent? Finally, what if violence broke out on the picket line? The last question in particular prompted a long and sobering discussion. These were men who had grown up in Austin or towns like it and who planned to live in Austin a long time. Their families shopped on Main Street and attended Austin schools. Much to their discomfort, they already were going down in history as participants in one of Minnesota's most celebrated strikes. Violence would surely reflect on them, too.

But the company officials decided there was no reasonable prospect of P-9's accepting any offer they intended to put on the table. If they were going to reopen, they might as well reopen as soon as possible. They decided on the first Monday feasible: January 13. If nobody came to work, they would hire replacements. Since those people were unlikely to breach a picket line for temporary jobs, the executives decided that the replacements would be permanent. If violence broke out, they would have to rely on local and state authorities to keep the peace.

Nyberg also had taken time to brief the executive committee on a point he considered vital: Under the latest labor law precedents, a company that hired replacements and promised them permanent jobs was obliged to keep them on the payroll, even if the strikers eventually offered to come back to work. It had been a terrible sticking point in the settlement of some recent strikes.

The repercussions could be particularly nasty in a small town like Austin if P-9 members eventually offered to return to work and their jobs were taken by outsiders. But the committee decided that its first obligation was to open the plant and serve its customers.

The executives wanted to notify their employees before releasing the decision to the press, so their public posture remained simply that the plant "would not set [sic] idle indefinitely." Later on Saturday, when a reporter asked Deryl Arnold for proof that Hormel was not bluffing, he simply responded, "This company has not made it a habit to make idle threats. This is not a threat. This is a business decision." That afternoon Hormel dropped 1,422 letters into the mail announcing that the plant would reopen in nine days.

The letters began arriving in homes around Austin and along the rural delivery routes on Monday morning. In Arnold's typically direct language the letter began: "The strike by Local P-9 has now dragged on for over 20 weeks. The time has come to reopen the plant and make work available for those who want to work. We do respect the dignity of each of our employees and no harassment campaign will change that. That is one reason why we have waited so long to make this very difficult decision. Returning to work may be a difficult decision for you, however we urge you to make that decision for yourself and your family."

The letter described the procedure for returning to work and included a registration form. It warned employees that they might see help-wanted newspaper ads but promised that no replacements would be hired until after January 20.

It concluded: "As we have said many times, the Austin plant was not built to set [sic] idle. We are committed to running this plant. We want you to be a part of that operation."

From the Austin Labor Center to the governor's mansion in St. Paul, Arnold's letter jerked everyone to attention. On Monday morning in Austin the blue caps had returned to the packing-house for a dawn demonstration, twenty-five of them rallying at the main gate and dozens more driving in a caravan around the plant's perimeter.

In St. Paul Governor Perpich decided it was time to intervene again. He had withdrawn some months earlier, convinced that

Hormel and P-9 were unwilling to compromise. But on this day his secretary had been fielding a steady stream of calls from frightened P-9 members. They insisted that they hadn't realized Hormel would actually reopen if they rejected the mediator's proposal. They wanted another shot at a settlement. The governor asked state mediator Paul Goldberg to call Guyette and tell him that Perpich wanted to see the executive board right away. That afternoon P-9's leaders arrived at the governor's reception room in the Capitol, an ornate room of carved wood and historical portraits. Perpich began the meeting by reminding the executive board how serious the situation was. He had no doubt that Hormel really intended to open the plant. The consequences could be violence, loss of jobs, and even loss of the union. Veteran Floyd Lenoch took the lead. Hormel wasn't the same company it used to be, he said, and it was time P-9 did something about it. The others chimed in: Hormel had taken away the workers' dignity; the plant was unsafe; P-9 had a national ground swell of support; if it didn't stand up against wage cuts, who would?

Perpich, himself the son of an iron miner and union member, listened but soon got restless. Finally after twenty-five minutes, Goldberg cut them off. He reminded them that he and the governor had a date the next morning with Knowlton and Nyberg to try to avert this tragedy. What did P-9 want them to ask for? Goldberg asked them to name their top six issues. Guyette said it was impossible to boil the dispute down to six issues and started ticking off P-9's complaints. When he got to number eighteen, an incredulous Goldberg cut him off again and adjourned the meeting. On the way out he grabbed Guyette, Winkels, and Huston, pulled them aside, and demanded that they give him permission to call Ron Rollins that night. Goldberg wanted to confer with Rollins to see if they couldn't narrow this list down to something that could be presented to Knowlton the next day. The three agreed to let their attorney and Goldberg have a go at it.

The next morning Perpich and Goldberg drove to downtown Minneapolis to meet Knowlton, Nyberg, and Larson at Hormel's lawyers' offices in the Piper, Jaffray skyscraper. Goldberg presented what he thought was a short list of P-9's key issues: seniority; safety; procedures for resolving grievances. The executives listened politely. Then Knowlton responded with what had become Hormel gospel: There was scarcely a packinghouse in the country paying more in wages and fringe benefits than Hormel. Other meat-packing executives were actually calling him irresponsible for leaving Hormel wages as high as they were. Larson and Nyberg were willing to discuss safety and seniority arrangements, but they didn't see any hope of P-9's settling for anything the company could realistically put on the table. Then Perpich took over, noting forcefully that everyone feared violence if the packinghouse reopened. He said Goldberg had an idea for one more crack at resolving the contract dispute, and he asked Knowlton to give them one more week. Knowlton agreed: Hormel would postpone the opening.

John Morrison, too, was shaken by Hormel's plan to reopen the plant. Going on strike for five months had been bad enough; it had cost Morrison and every other P-9 member more than eight thousand dollars in lost wages. Now, he thought, it was going to cost them their jobs and very possibly their union. Morrison contemplated the bleak alternative: to cross his own union's picket line. To make matters worse, he was convinced that the rank and file didn't know what really was in the mediator's proposal thcy had rejected. He thought Arnold was right in his telegram to Guyette: The P-9 leadership had misrepresented the proposal. His phone, too, had been ringing like crazy. P-9 members were frantic that this was not another bluff and they were not going to get another contract offer. He and John Anker and Chad Young made one last stab at reaching their fellow union members by placing an ad in Tuesday's editions of the Austin *Daily Herald.* "If anyone feels they did not understand that . . . the company would reopen the plant with or without union members, then the time to act is now." It called on P-9 members to show up at the Wednesday night union meeting and demand another vote on the mediator's proposal.

Another crack at the mediator's proposal was exactly what Paul Goldberg had in mind. He was convinced that at least some of the P-9 members had misunderstood the proposal and that many more thought Hormel's threat to open the plant was a bluff. But he also knew that Guyette and the executive board would refuse to hold another membership vote unless Hormel put something new on the table. He thought he had concocted a solution. On Wednesday a courier appeared at the corporate office in Austin and at the Austin Labor Center with a proposal from Perpich. The governor wanted to appoint a panel of distinguished neutral Minnesotans who would search the country for a labor expert familiar with contract disputes. This person would serve as a neutral fact finder who would review the mediator's proposal, meet with both sides to review their positions, and then issue a report clarifying any misunderstandings or disagreements. If P-9 and Hormel could use the fact finder's report as a basis for settling the dispute, so much the better. In the meantime, Perpich formally asked Hormel to delay the reopening and urged P-9 to hold off on roving pickets.

In a letter designed to chasten both sides, Perpich wrote, "I am incredulous at the wide variations in your respective descriptions of the recently rejected settlement proposal. I am also troubled by the calls and reports which I have received concerning the accuracy of understanding by P-9 members prior to their recent vote."

Once Larson had looked over the proposal, he took it in to Nyberg and explained it to him. Together they walked down a short corridor into Knowlton's office and recommended giving it a try. Larson called Goldberg that afternoon and said Hormel was on board if P-9 was on board.

In fact, P-9's position on another vote was a matter of intense internal debate. That evening, even as Larson and Nyberg were preparing for a session with a fact finder, Morrison, Young, and Anker were girding for a showdown at the Wednesday night rank-and-file meeting. They were convinced that the rank and file hadn't correctly understood the terms of the mediator's proposal, and they were equally convinced that Hormel would not make a better offer. Long before the meeting started, P-9 members started turning up at the Austin Labor Center, their cars and pickup trucks lining the curb for blocks along Fourth Avenue. By the time the meeting started, the center's big meeting room was packed with perhaps eight hundred members, crammed into the rows of chairs, standing two and three deep along the side and back, spilling into the aisles between the ranks of chairs. As the meeting got under way, Russ Vaale, a P-10 supporter, moved to a microphone and proposed a change in the agenda so that the members could discuss taking another vote on the mediator's proposal. The hard-liners started shouting their disapproval, and the P-10ers hollered back that they should hear Vaale out. When order was restored, Young tried to second the motion. Guyette, chairing the meeting, said that he didn't hear a second and that the agenda would stand. That drew more yelling from the P-10ers. Members of the two factions glared at each other. Morrison sensed it was time to step in to save Vaale's motion. He moved to a floor microphone and asked that the members be polled on whether they had heard the motion seconded. Guyette slammed down his gavel and repeated that he did not hear it. Morrison refused to yield the microphone and kept insisting on a vote.

At that point, pushing and shoving broke out on the floor. When Morrison turned around, he saw Duke Schaefer, a P-10er, lying flat on his back in an aisle halfway up the room. Hagen had assigned a guard to Schaefer when he showed up at the hall, sensing there might be trouble because Schaefer was known to speak his mind. Somehow Schaefer slipped away, and when he came into the hall, he started yapping and someone punched him. Morrison could tell that Duke was in no position to fight for himself, so he started pushing his way toward Schaefer. There was more pushing and shoving, and within two minutes Morrison found himself nose to nose with Guyette, who was screaming in his face, "Don't do it! Don't do it!" Morrison thought, Don't do what? He had told himself before the meeting that he wouldn't throw any punches, that he didn't want to get kicked out of the meeting. But now people were grabbing at him, trying to restrain him. Suddenly, out of the crowd, an overhand punch caught Morrison in the mouth. He saw who did it but couldn't get at him through the swarm of bodies. The tussling continued until a shout went up that Austin police had arrived. The room calmed down quickly, the union members took their seats and straightened their clothes. Guyette disappeared into a conference with police for several minutes.

When he emerged, he said that the meeting would continue but that Morrison had to leave. Morrison felt powerless. He walked out of the union hall to the hoots and shouts of blue caps. He walked a few blocks south to Riverside Arena, the municipal hockey rink. He had been scheduled to referee the hockey game that night, and he figured he might as well watch the end of the game. He had given up a $125 night of refereeing and his last hopes of peace in P-9 for a ten-minute union meeting.

That evening Guyette issued a statement that P-9 also would participate in the fact-finding process and would conduct another membership vote, but only on the condition that Hormel return to the bargaining table and produce a better offer. "We've already voted on the mediator's proposal," Guyette told a reporter that evening. "We've rejected it, and we need to sit down with the company face-to-face."

When Nyberg learned of P-9's position on the mediator's proposal, he fumed. "We are talking about the mediator's proposal and nothing else," he told a reporter calling to get the company's latest reaction. "Guyette is telling the governor, 'Thanks, but no thanks.'"

The next day Nyberg issued a statement reaffirming Hormel's plans to open on Monday. In St. Paul, at the state mediation offices, Goldberg's heart sank. Privately he fumed at P-9 leaders for attaching conditions to the fact-finding process that they should have known would make it unacceptable to Knowlton and Nyberg. Publicly he remained neutral as reporters pestered him all day. What exactly had Perpich meant with the fact-finding? Was it mediation or not? Was it fair for P-9 to demand further concessions as part of fact-finding? Goldberg gave the ambiguous responses of a diplomat trying to prevent war between two belligerents.

But the week's melodrama wasn't over. On Friday night Guyette and Nyberg were scheduled to square off live on a weekly public affairs program on Minnesota public television. It was the first time they had seen each other in weeks, and they showed up at the St. Paul studio distinctly wary of what the other might say. The show's producer kept them in separate waiting rooms while a few reporters filed downstairs to the studio and into a soundproof production booth.

After Guyette and Nyberg had taken their places under the lights and the cameras came on, they spent a few minutes sparring over who had misinterpreted the fact finder proposal. Nyberg accused Guyette of blatantly adding a condition that was not contained in Perpich's proposal. Guyette responded that to participate under Hormel's terms would mean giving up the union's right to bargain. He said again that P-9 would not vote again on the mediator's proposal, saying that Hormel and the UFCW "want us to keep voting till we get it right." But much of the debate centered on Hormel's willingness to meet with P-9 and bargain. Guyette repeated his charge that they hadn't met face-to-face since November and said Hormel didn't have anyone at the table with the authority to settle the strike. Nyberg responded that Hormel negotiators had met with P-9 more than a dozen times face-to-face during the summer and countless times more through the federal mediator. He said the mediator's proposal was proof of Hormel's willingness to compromise and again accused Guyette of distorting the proposal. Guyette replied, "If the company's still confused about the proposal, we'll certainly sit down, because that's the only way this dispute can be resolved."

Finally the time was up, the lights came down, and reporters rushed onto the set. Nyberg and Guyette continued debating, and their discussion turned into an impromptu press conference. Nyberg denied that Hormel was unwilling to meet with P-9 negotiators, but Guyette kept pressing the point. Finally Nyberg relented. He agreed to round up the Hormel negotiating team at ten o'clock the next morning at St. Edwards Church in Austin if Guyette could bring his team. The two shook hands and walked off the stage.

To no one's surprise, the Saturday meeting was a disaster. Guyette and Winkels came in with a surprise proposal that their members go back to work without a contract, pending an interpretation of the mediator's proposal by the governor's fact finder. But they insisted that P-9 was not giving up the right to negotiate further, and they held out for wages above ten dollars and fringes restored to their 1978 level. Larson rejected the proposal out of hand. If P-9 wanted to come back to work, he said, the company demanded a signed contract. And Hormel was going no further than the mediator's proposal. Before they broke off that morning, however, there came a knock at the door. It was a state highway patrolman, with yet another request from Governor Perpich. If Hormel would consider postponing the Monday morning opening, Perpich would intercede once more with P-9 and urge it to take another membership vote or accept the fact finder. Larson told the patrolman to tell the governor: No contract, no postponement.

That evening there was another knock on the door. This time it was the Reverend Donald Zenk, St. Edwards pastor. Could they please wrap it up? Mass was due to start, and the church needed the space. As the negotiators packed up their briefcases and put on their jackets, Larson was approached by a new P-9 lawyer, Dave Twedell, who had taken over for Ron Rollins. Twedell, from Texas, was the son of a UFCW officer Larson had negotiated with several times. In fact, Twedell was himself a former UFCW regional officer who had left the union after a falling-out over the UFCW's direction. Now he approached Larson and asked for a word. If Twedell could get Guyette to come back to the table that evening, would Larson be willing to return to the church after mass and have an informal talk? Twedell said he was confident the dispute could still be settled. Larson was skeptical but agreed to ask Nyberg. He warned Twedell to run the ground rules past Guyette. Twedell called Guyette over. Larson told Guyette that he would send his committee home if Guyette would do the same. Guyette said he intended to bring the whole executive board. Larson practically growled. He repeated Twedell's view: If the negotiators were going to get anywhere, this would have to be a small-group session. Guyette said he wasn't interested in any closed-door secret meetings. And so it broke off.

On Monday morning, with a crowd of demonstrators watching peacefully from a snowbank across the street, Hormel reopened the packinghouse. The P-9ers were somber as they began to gather in the sub-zero darkness about 5:00 A.M., but there was an air of tension and expectancy, as if something historic was about to happen. Fifty yards from the plant's south gate, sympathizers and reporters parked on a side street, then drifted past an abandoned railroad siding that stood on a slight rise across the street from the south gate. Television reporters moved in and out of a big satellite remote-broadcast truck. P-9 members and their supporters, dressed in snowmobile suits and stocking caps, arrived in threes and fours from the union hall and took up positions behind a string of barricades that police had set up on the snow-covered curb across from the gate. Larry Long, a Minneapolis folk singer, roamed the street in front of the crowd, rubbing his bare hands, then strumming his guitar and leading the crowd in union songs. "I'll show my card to the National Guard," he sang. "I'm sticking with the union." Reporters and demonstrators alike, bundled to the ears in snowmobile suits and parkas, prowled the rail siding, not knowing what to expect but agreeing it would be important.

For the meat-packers the morning would test the loyalty of their ranks. They were out to see who was going to drive across that picket line. For reporters the morning would test all the crucial questions: Did Rogers, the master strategist, have a plan to keep the packinghouse shut down? Was Hormel correct—that its wage offer was so generous that hundreds of workers would take it even if P-9's leadership rejected it? Could Hormel call what was now a year-old bluff and break the strike and the corporate campaign? Finally, at the back of everyone's mind, would there be violence?

Across the street three Austin policemen and three P-9 pickets paced watchfully against the backdrop of a steel fence and a floodlit parking lot. In the distance behind them the great packinghouse almost glowed in the predawn darkness. The officers and pickets looked a little lonesome, with the crowd across the street on top of a snowbank and the plant's perimeter road virtually deserted. As the sun began to crack the horizon and the crowd of demonstrators swelled to three hundred, a beat-up black pickup truck with two men in the front seat drove slowly past the gate, then moved on. A few minutes later the truck returned, having completed a tense lap around the plant so its occupants could gauge the crowd. It slowed as it approached the gate again. The demonstrators across the street shook picket signs and started hollering, "Lowlife! Scab!" The driver slowed a little more, then turned into the driveway and stopped. A policeman checked the passengers' Hormel ID cards. The truck rolled past the pickets and into the packinghouse parking lot. Hormel had its first strikebreakers.

A few more cars and trucks followed during the next hour,

each one performing much the same ritual: a slow cruise past the gate and the demonstrators; a return lap for the plunge into the driveway and through the gates. By the time the sun was fully up and the demonstrators began dispersing, Hormel had about twenty of its old employees back for the day.

On Tuesday morning the scene turned more tense as Hormel began handing out job applications. The trickle of curious drivers grew into a slow stream, and in the three hours before and after dawn several hundred cars and pickup trucks passed through the south gate. The demonstrators responded with more volume and occasional fist shaking. "Keep it moving. This isn't scab town!" a demonstrator yelled at one slow-moving car. "We got your number, scabs!" shouted another as he made a note of the car's license plate. But the scene remained nonviolent. Apart from clogging traffic from time to time with their own vehicles or pressing past the police barricades to pound on an occasional car fender, the members of P-9 did little to stop strikebreakers. Instead, they watched from the snowbank, dismayed at the flow of traffic. But they were too startled to know what to make of it and recoiled from what seemed to be their only alternative: violence.

"It's not us against them or them against us. The company's making profits from both sides," said Al Wesely, a former carpenter who had gone to work for Hormel in 1982 and become one of P-9's most active volunteers. "I just hope they realize that the name being put on them today is something they're going to carry for life."

The scene was repeated on Wednesday and again on Thursday and Friday. By 9:00 A.M. Friday the plant's big south parking lot was half full, and still traffic trickled through the gate. One demonstrator turned to walk back to his own car, giving a last look through the fence to the parking lot.

"We got 'em right where we want 'em now," he said.

CHAPTER

12

When Jim Guyette called the rank and file to order at seven o'clock on Friday night, Local P-9 had its back to the wall.

Five tense days had passed since Hormel reopened the packinghouse. An estimated fifty union members had abandoned the strike and crossed the picket line with impunity. Hormel's newspaper advertisements for job applicants had attracted nearly two thousand men and women from all over southern Minnesota and northern Iowa, eager for the eight-dollar-an-hour jobs of remaining strikers. The company had pledged to start hiring replacements the following Monday. While Guyette loyalists remained committed to the fight, a growing segment of union members, led by the P-10ers, was confused, angry, and fearful that they might lose their jobs altogether.

As the small auditorium in P-9's cramped union hall filled up that evening, questions raced through everyone's mind. If Hormel could staff the plant and keep it running, P-9 would lose its economic leverage to bring the company back to the bargaining table. The high level of automation in the plant would make it easier for even untrained workers to run product lines and become proficient at their new jobs. Worse, under federal labor law it appeared that Hormel could give away the strikers' jobs permanently. In the 1960's and 1970's such a move would have been unthinkable, but with the Republican Reagan administration, busting strikes with replacement workers had become more common. While their faces said otherwise as they looked around the room, the strikers had to know that Hormel had taken its gamble and apparently won. Now it was up to P-9 to make the strike work.

Two tactics were on the agenda. First was shutting down the packinghouse again, this time against the company's efforts to keep it open for returning workers and replacements. This was the meat-packers' first impulse because despite their joking swagger, it would agonize them to watch fellow workers cross their picket line and take their jobs. If Hormel could run its Austin plant, capable of making every Hormel consumer item in large quantities, it would spell defeat for the P-9ers, no matter how many spirited labor rallies they held, no matter how much publicity they generated. Yet to shut down the plant, now that Hormel had thrown open the plant gates to all comers, would bring human confrontation and, almost certainly, violence.

Despite the anger and gruff demeanor of some strikers, and the fond recollections of old-timers who remembered the riotous strike in 1933, the great majority of the P-9 rank and file seemed genuinely to abhor violence. Rogers preached nonviolence, too, knowing full well the negative impact on a fickle public watching fistfights, rock throwing, and shootings on national TV. For a year he had held the rank and file's emotions in check, channeling their energies into useful projects that had kept them busy building the campaign's support network. To be sure, there had been a growing number of incidents of vandalism, threats, and the like against company executives and their families. But there had been only one arrest, for telephone death threats to Knowlton shortly after the strike began. Company officials admitted that there seemed to be no direct link in the case to strike leaders, but Nyberg used the occasion to scold Rogers and the leadership for setting in motion "a chain of events that foster violence, whether they publicly accept responsibility or not." Rogers's military analogies about "total annihilation" of the company, and the War Room name he chose for the main meeting place in the union hall, made his critics fear that a bloodbath was imminent. Every group has its rowdies and crazies, and P-9 was no exception. Whip them into a frenzy, and no matter how much you guard against it, somebody could do something stupid and incite a riot. What would happen if a couple of buddies showed up drunk on the picket line one morning and started blasting away with shotguns? One person, on either side of the picket line, could ignite bloodshed with a "fuck you" and a flip of the middle finger.

The second strategy was to expand the strike by means of roving pickets, who would flock to Hormel plants in other states, set up picket lines, and try to turn perhaps three thousand workers away from their jobs. This was P-9's flanking action, and it had tremendous appeal among workers who saw it as the ultimate act of solidarity and unionism. Hormel was getting about two thirds of its production from a dozen other plants, primarily in Iowa, Nebraska, and Illinois. In addition, Hormel was getting hundreds of hogs slaughtered every day at FDL Foods' two big slaughterhouses in Dubuque, Iowa, and Rochelle, Illinois. It was this production that had carried the company through the strike's first five months. If the P-9ers could cripple the other operations and keep Austin out of production, their reasoning went, it would send a heroic signal across the nation, broadcast on the nightly network news, that grass-roots labor had pulled off the impossible. No way could Hormel hire enough workers fast enough to replace those honoring the picket line. Under excruciating financial and moral pressure, the scenario concluded, Hormel would crawl back to the bargaining table with an open checkbook and begging for mercy.

But dispatching roving pickets posed three big problems for the union, two of them sticky legal questions. For starters, it was not clear that Hormel's union employees in other towns could legally honor picket lines sent from Austin. All but the Ottumwa plant had contractual obligations to keep working through such a strike, and even in Ottumwa the workers could be permanently replaced if they honored such a picket line. There were two thousand to twenty-five hundred workers under union agreements at other Hormel plants, but asking them to join the strike could get them fired. That would raise the strike's toll, and getting them back to work would simply be one more thorny problem at the bargaining table.

Secondly, federal labor law was unclear about P-9's right to picket other Hormel plants. If Hormel challenged the move and won before the Reagan administration's National Labor Relations Board, as it already had done with secondary-boycott charges involving the corporate campaign, it would only add to P-9's legal woes and further drain its financial war chest.

Thirdly, and perhaps worst of all, to send the roving pickets would be to fire the last arrow in P-9's quiver. Throughout the yearlong campaign, as Rogers laid out his plan, he had always promised that after the current step lay another, more powerful, more daring, and more controversial. But after roving pickets, there was nothing new to try. There were plans to boycott Hormel products, but there was nothing novel in that. Unions had been trying it for years, but the track record was spotty at best and it took years to produce results. The fund raising and coalition building would help, too, since they extended from coast to coast. But those efforts had been in place for months, and it was unclear what more they could do to turn the tide in Austin. As badly as the P-9ers wanted the roving pickets to do the trick and shut down the company completely, what happened if the gamble flopped? What if nobody honored the picket lines? And if they stayed out one day, how would you keep them out if Hormel started hiring replacements? Then what would P-9 do?

In short, it was time for some hard decisions by P-9's leaders. By this time, however, a kind of paralysis was beginning to grip the executive board members. For one thing, they never got any peace of mind to deliberate on their prospects. If the Labor Center was a place of bustle and high morale, it also was a chaotic place for the board to conduct business. The building was constantly packed with rank-and-file volunteers, reporters and photographers, sympathizers from the outside, and friends and relatives. It was difficult for Rollins and the other attorneys to get the full executive board together for any length of time to reflect on strategy without interruptions. Guyette and Winkels were chronically late for executive board meetings, and the other members had plenty of distractions looking after financial matters, picket assignments, police relations, and inquiries from the press.

There was also tremendous confusion about the state of picketing. The executive board was getting legal advice to stay away from the picket line, so that the union couldn't officially be held accountable in case violence broke out. But they were also getting requests from Chief Hoffman to come out to the plant each morning and calm the demonstrators. In fact, members of the executive board weren't always sure what the union's strategy was at the picket line. Two months later Jim Retterath testified at an NLRB hearing that he wasn't aware if other P-9 officers were encouraging mass picketing, didn't know if the union was violating a Mower County court injunction to limit picketing, and didn't even follow news accounts of the plant gate skirmishes.

Away from the picket line there was serious debate on the executive board as week one of the reopening drew to a close. Rollins had briefed the rank and file on the legal significance of permanent replacements: Hormel would be obligated to keep them on the payroll even if other issues in the strike could be settled. Now the executive board members had to consider how to keep out replacements. Retterath thought Rogers's proposals for civil disobedience were crazy; he was not about to lie down in front of a bunch of pickup trucks in twenty-below weather. Kathy Buck thought that this passive picketing was futile and that P-9 would have to be willing to break the law—possibly by returning to work and occupying the plant.

There was similar debate about the roving pickets. One of the doubters was Keith Judd, a thirty-eight-year Hormel lifer and the only Guyette opponent left on the executive board. He had served in various P-9 offices for years and thought it was foolish to defy the UFCW. He had grown more and more doubtful about the wisdom of the campaign and frequently spoke his mind to other board members. In fact, it got to the point where Guyette and Winkels would cut Judd out of key bargaining developments, and Huston had angrily called him a traitor to P-9. Still, he knew what solidarity meant, and he remained a strong supporter of the strike. But sending roving pickets without the sanction—and clout—of the international leadership was too much. He knew he had some support on the board, but he wasn't sure how deep it ran. During negotiations with the company he regularly gave Floyd Lenoch a ride home from the talks. One day when he pulled up at the curb in front of Lenoch's house, Floyd turned to him and said, "One of these days these kids are going to wake up and find themselves under a trusteeship." Judd shared the concern, but every time he raised it with the board, it seemed that Guyette, Huston, and Winkels were able to prevail on Lenoch and whoever else had doubts.

Lenoch was among the old-plant veterans who, as the dispute festered during the summer, confided to friends that common sense would prevail, that the proud Hormel Company would never take a strike at its brand-new plant. Later he made the same claim about its reopening: never without P-9 and the workers who made the company what it was. That he was wrong on both counts underscores how Lenoch had by that time become more of a symbol on the board rather than a forceful leader. To his colleagues, he was a bighearted father figure, knowledgeable about the past and a stabilizing influence for younger members. It was Guyette's turn to be president, he once said, so Jim ought to do the talking. Critics jumped on his penchant for philosophizing when it was time for serious talking at the bargaining table. He also was known to waver in his position on some of the union's strategies, and he shared Judd's concern about the roving pickets. But he, too, was loyal to the fight, a tireless worker who devoted countless hours to refurbishing the union kitchen, and no one doubted that his heart would always follow the dictates of the majority of the rank and file.

Kenny Hagen didn't like the roving pickets from the start. Part of the big hiring class of 1968, he initially took more interest in fast-pitch softball than in union meetings. But he started getting more involved as he and his workers started taking concessions. Shortly after the new plant opened, a furious Hagen called Dick Knowlton at home to air a list of complaints that had cropped up. Knowlton invited him over, and they talked for three hours. But Hagen remained a critic. His opposition to the wage cut in 1984 prompted a friend to nominate him for the executive board, and he won. He put himself among those embittered by Hormel's continual demands to take more from its workers. But on roving pickets, he also considered himself realistic. For as much hardship as the strikers were enduring in Austin, he reasoned, it was foolhardy to spread it around to workers at the other plants. Now that roving pickets were being put to a question, he maintained his opposition. Whether the other workers could legally honor the pickets was almost beside the point. The issue was whether it was right for P-9 to bring those workers into the strike and probably lose them their jobs. Hagen clearly didn't think it was appropriate. But he also knew that Guyette viewed it differently and that even though there were votes against the roving pickets, Guyette was a pro at bringing the board around to his point of view. That was the difference between Guyette and the rest of the board, Hagen said later. Everybody was inexperienced, but Guyette was inexperienced and had power.

At a board meeting on Friday afternoon, January 17, Judd finally vented his opposition, and Hagen and Lenoch joined him in voting against using P-9's final weapon under such circumstances. But a majority of the board decided to go ahead. That night they would tell the rank and file that the time had finally come to put this notion of support to the ultimate test.

Strikers began wandering into the Austin Labor Center around 6:30 P.M., and the big meeting room was soon packed mostly with blue caps, a smattering of P-10ers, and others who claimed no allegiance to either group. The crowds at rank-and-file meetings had been getting even bigger in the past two weeks, ever since Hormel had started recruiting new workers. By the time Guyette brought the meeting to order, it was standing room only, meaning that at least five hundred people had crowded in. Most were solidly behind the campaign, but everyone knew that a picket line showdown was inevitable when Hormel's recruits showed up Monday morning. The strikers wanted to know what Guyette and the other P-9 leaders were planning for the occasion. On top of that, how could they raise the ante against Hormel?

Accounts of the meeting differ, and reporters were kept outside in a small meeting room near the front of the union hall. Those who attended piece it together this way: After some initial discussion of the previous week's events, Guyette made an impassioned plea to send the roving pickets. Hadn't P-9's emissaries worked all spring, summer, and fall to build loyalty in Fremont, Ottumwa, Algona, Beloit, and Dallas? Wouldn't those workers finally see that P-9 was right, that the threat to Austin was a threat to them, too? Wouldn't they jump at the chance to join this new

265

wave of solidarity that was destined to rebuild the labor movement? There was no mention of the potential legal snares, of the
likelihood that workers risked getting fired if they honored
the lines, as Hormel had been warning since the strike began.
A recent telegram from Wynn refusing to sanction the roving
pickets was cast as yet another attempt to undermine their fight.
Besides, Guyette also had been telling the other workers for
some weeks now that the UFCW had never signed the labor
agreements in Fremont and the other towns, so there was no
contractual ban on sympathy strikes. He was wrong again. While
the final documents remained unsigned, UFCW negotiators had
signed the initial bargaining table agreements, and the NLRB
found that they were binding contracts. To Guyette, however, a
good trade unionist doesn't cross a picket line, and this was a
fight that transcended P-9.

The meeting displayed the young Austin leader at his finest.
Even his worst enemies in town, and there were plenty, gave him
credit for knowing how to rev up a crowd, say the right things,
and leave people feeling there was a wrong they must set right,
that theirs was an almost evangelical crusade. There was something about him that made him persuasive, even if you disagreed
with him. He was an unassuming master of rhetoric, not a take-
charge loudmouth. Rogers had clearly influenced Guyette as a
public speaker, making Jim more comfortable at the podium. But
Guyette maintained his slightly high-pitched voice, more convincing than innocent, which contrasted with Rogers's gravelly
East Coast bark. To his Austin supporters, Guyette simply said
what most of them felt, albeit with a finer point and a dizzier
spin. P-9 didn't have leaders, he would say; it had a rank and file
of leaders. In that vein he never grabbed the spotlight. Instead, he
seemed to position himself so it would find him at just the right
time.

As for the Austin packinghouse, Rogers unveiled a new plan.
Drawing lessons from the masters of civil disobedience, he would
have his troops drive to the big plant by the scores, clogging its
access streets without risking violent confrontation. The scabs
might show up for work Monday at dawn, but they would spend
the morning fighting traffic, not slaughtering hogs. It was all legal
and, if done right, completely without risk of punches and fights.

266

It was not the kind of stuff that might sour a national TV audience watching on the nightly news, or damage P-9's coveted image as a unique force in the labor movement.

Until that night Rogers had always telegraphed notice of his public demonstrations in Austin to the city's affable police chief, Don Hoffman. Whether it was leafleting First Bank Austin, canvassing door to door, or holding rallies at the high school, whenever P-9 drew a crowd in public, Rogers always told the chief when and where and about how many. It was Rogers's way of being militant without getting into trouble with the law. Hoffman, in turn, felt comfortable that despite all the union rhetoric he heard about destroying Hormel, organized labor wouldn't turn his quiet city into a war zone. In fact, Hoffman had taken to inviting Rogers, Guyette, and company officials to his small office at the Law Enforcement Center for pregame powwows about their plans. Each would outline his position about picketing or demonstrating. Hoffman would take it all down in a memo, then send a copy to P-9 and Hormel. There was nothing binding about the memo, Hoffman knew, but it had the psychological effect of an implied promise. With civil disobedience things were different. It was no secret that Rogers was fond of the tactic, but deploying it required an element of surprise. If the time came to block the plant with cars, no one outside the union, not even Hoffman, would know about it in advance.

After Rogers's presentation to the rank and file, discussion ensued for about ninety minutes. Only Austin Mayor Tom Kough spoke out in opposition to the roving pickets, but his plea went nowhere. Then reporters waiting outside heard a great cheer. The double doors swung open, and out poured once again pumped-up strikers, yelling and cheering. "Circle the plant!" yelled one. "Let's do the plant!" Dozens of men and women went out to their cars and drove to the plant, circling the darkened fortress bumper to bumper, honking their horns, yelling and cheering into the night. Back in the lobby of the union hall a coy smile crept across Rogers's face. A test run, he called it. The real thing would come later.

As the cars raced off toward the plant, Guyette and his executive board held a press conference to present their plans. Meetings with the press had become commonplace following big gatherings, and Guyette and Rogers usually were happy to oblige. They prided themselves on running an open campaign, making themselves, Winkels, or Huston accessible to the media—to a point. That night, as reporters from the Twin Cities and Austin waited for Guyette to make an announcement about the roving pickets, he began with an all-too-familiar refrain: "We are proceeding with our plan."

It was his favorite phrase. After rallies, arbitration defeats, negotiating sessions, strike votes, bank protests, regardless of the event or the outcome, the plan was proceeding. Guyette and P-9 were on a mission, and the details would be filled in as they moved along. But on this night the proclamation seemed at odds with the whirlwind pace that was developing around the strike. Board members were always running off to meetings out of town, six hours driving to Fremont, nearly the same to Ottumwa, two hours to the Twin Cities. Guyette was by far the board's most tireless worker, and he never seemed to need a break, but the others were feeling the strain. There were board meetings, rank-and-file meetings, sessions with lawyers, meetings with the company, Support Group meetings. The Communications Committee, which provided speakers who collected donations, was running low on volunteers. Bargaining sessions were becoming exercises in disorganization, with absolutely nothing getting accomplished. Not even customary hellos were exchanged between the two sides. Our own members are starving, Hagen thought later, but negotiators were too busy running around doing other things, seemingly unable to get serious about drawing up a decent contract that would eliminate the threat that loomed with the hiring of replacements.

On this night Guyette's plan meant that P-9 would indeed dispatch roving pickets, but to unnamed plant locations at undisclosed times. Coupled with the plan to blockade the plant, it marked the first time in more than a year that the campaign tried to assume a cloak of secrecy. "It becomes like a war situation," Winkels told the press. "On D-day everybody knew what was coming. They just didn't know where." The roving bands would receive their instructions the next day, but even those boarding the buses would not know their destination until they were on the road. The plan drew virtually no opposition from the rank and file, Guyette said, which approved it in a voice vote. And board members at the press conference disavowed reports of any disunity among themselves.

The plan was proceeding.

At 10:00 P.M., not long after the press conference ended, John Morrison flipped on the portable TV sitting on the dashboard of his brown Suburban truck. Time for the news on Channel 6, Austin's local station, and an update on what his union had decided earlier in the evening. Morrison had walked out of the meeting to take his 8:00 P.M. to midnight shift on the picket line. Sitting next to him on the passenger side of the front seat was Ron Bergstrom, one of Morrison's closest buddies and himself a P-10er. Together they drove over to the north side of the plant, backed the truck next to the locked gate in the driveway, and parked so they could watch traffic go by. Outside the air was cold, the night sky filled with silence.

On a Friday night it was even quieter than usual. Cars that gathered at downtown bars never got out by the plant. The only traffic past the north gate had to exit off the freeway overpass seventy-five yards away, and at night most cars zoomed past without giving the plant a glance. Motorists never saw the picket line, which on this night consisted of two guys in a truck quietly pondering one of the biggest decisions of their lives.

Even as Morrison focused on the small black-and-white TV, he already sensed the meeting's outcome. He remembered his last P-9 membership meeting, the night he got jumped and then thrown out. To Morrison and allies like Bergstrom, the ruckus was indicative of P-9 meeting conduct these days. Anyone who spoke out against the leadership was derisively shouted down by blue caps, who were strategically clustered at the microphones, in the front, at the back, wherever they could make the most noise, cause the most disruption, and intimidate people. Those who persisted in opposition were taking a chance on their physical well-being. The rank and file were hot, and criticism ignited the fuse. That's partly why Morrison was tossed out. Of the untold numbers of union members with serious doubts about Guyette's leadership, he was one of the few who refused to back down from the vocal militants. The husky thirty-five-year-old had broken jaws in Rochester bars and since high school had carried a reputation that he needed no help in handling himself.

Now that the plant was open, Morrison and his sympathizers had appealed again for some kind of help; their jobs and their union were on the line. The official line from the international advised them not to cross the picket line since it still had the parent union's sanction. In an attempt to get the rank and file to apply more pressure on Guyette to change course, International President William Wynn had sent him a mailgram in which he refused to sanction the roving pickets and blamed Guyette for prolonging a hopeless cause:

> Local P-9's courageous members stand at the edge of the cliff you led them to, and they need courageous leadership that will lead them away from a disastrous mass suicide with their dignity preserved. True leadership doesn't yell "jump" and it doesn't expose workers to unnecessary risks in the pursuit of unachievable goals, no matter how achievable those goals are. . . . Suicide is not an acceptable alternative. You may choose martyrdom for yourself, but as a leader it is your responsibility to make sure that 1,500 loyal and true union members don't also become martyrs. . . . You cannot achieve the total victory that has been your goal, but it is within your power to prevent the imminent total defeat. In the name of human compassion, I urge you to put a stop to the suffering P-9 members and their families have endured for five long months before it is too late.

The letter had simultaneously been released to the news media the day before the rank-and-file meeting on roving pickets, but it did nothing to jar Guyette. Considering the whipped-up emotion against Wynn in Austin, the letter came across like an overbearing brother trying to tell his kid sister to stop dating her boyfriend because the family didn't like him. Guyette had fired back an equally vicious letter, chastising the international for turning its back on requests for roving picket sanction for Fremont and Ottumwa and accusing Wynn of being out of touch with the rank and file:

Your latest mailgram probably would be best suited under a Geo. A. Hormel & Co. letterhead. Again and again
you have employed the word "suicide" to characterize
our effort to win a fair contract. . . . Given the steady
stream of rhetoric you have turned loose on us, perhaps
Hormel, rather than union members, should be paying
dues to the UFCW. . . . True leadership, you say, doesn't
yell, "Jump." But that is just what you and other so-called
leaders of the UFCW have been shouting at us for
months: "Don't think for yourself, just jump when we say
jump." I have felt for some time that different con-
ceptions of leadership are at the heart of our ongoing
disagreement. I ask you now: what higher standard than
democratic process is there? Just who are these leaders
who are so wise that they know the interest of the rank
and file better than the members themselves?

As the rhetoric heated up again, it seemed that efforts by the
P-10ers were for naught. All Morrison and Bergstrom could do
was sit in the truck on the picket line and watch the news in
darkness, waiting as their union made a do-or-die decision on
their future. Earlier in the night they had watched with some
amusement as the honking, hooting group of cars from the union
hall drove by, practicing their civil disobedience. Another Rogers
stunt to keep the blue caps busy, they thought.

Morrison had no delusions about the roving pickets. He knew
that workers in Ottumwa were bitter toward Hormel. The company had played a ruthless game of chicken with them in the
spring of 1984, laying off workers until the local approved a concessionary settlement. In recent weeks the Ottumwa rank and file
had elected an ardent Guyette supporter as chief steward over
one of Schaefer's cronies who campaigned as a moderate. But at
the other Hormel chain plants, Morrison figured workers
wouldn't jeopardize their jobs to win P-9 a contract better than
their own. He just wanted his job back. He'd seen the scabs going
in to fill out applications the week before, and it bothered him a
lot. He also knew many of his friends were thinking the same way
he was. He would have to cross the picket line despite what Anderson had been telling him. The way these clowns were operat-

ing, he thought, the sanctity of a picket line didn't mean much. Guyette and Rogers were nothing but a couple of egos that were too big to fit in the system, he thought. And they certainly didn't represent the union he had joined eighteen years earlier.

As the newscast ended at ten-thirty, Morrison flipped off the TV and paused to think for a moment. "Next week," he said to Bergstrom. Ron nodded in agreement. They didn't set a day. They didn't talk about going back in together. They simply knew there was no way out.

Chuck Nyberg, too, watched the newscast that Friday night at home in southwest Austin. He felt much the same way Morrison and Bergstrom did: There was no way out. He and Knowlton and Deryl Arnold had laid the plans to reopen the plant, and now they couldn't go back. So far the omens were good, but the week had added some new worry lines to Nyberg's face. He and Arnold had kept it a secret, but their plan was to keep hiring until the plant had the same number of people that it had when it opened for business on August 9, 1982. The company needed 1,050 people to run one eight-hour shift of hog slaughtering and processing. The overflow of applications during the past week assured Arnold of finding quality help. But they publicly and privately expressed a desire to have P-9 members come back. For one thing, the P-9ers were experienced and they were generally hard workers. More important, management had to live next to the P-9 members, shop with them, and go to church with them. The executives feared that many solid union people would eventually lose their jobs out of blind loyalty to the notion of solidarity. How many would come back to work was anybody's guess. Management refused to speculate publicly, especially since it had consistently underestimated the depth of Guyette's support in the months preceding the strike.

To keep the plant open, Hormel was relying almost exclusively on the law enforcement capabilities of the tiny Austin Police Department. The Hormel executives didn't like it; they couldn't quite believe that Hoffman could control hundreds of demonstrators with thirty-three sworn officers, but they didn't have much choice. So far Hoffman's faith that his "own people" wouldn't break the peace had been vindicated. Remarkably enough, so far he had been able to maintain order with only a handful of officers guarding the plant gates and approach streets. There were the usual complaints from strikers—cars not stopping at the picket line or not carrying license plates—but nothing confrontational. In fact, for all the ugly hollering, the pickets had been so polite to police that it was almost comical. A band of pickets would crowd behind one of the police emergency sawhorses, gradually pressing it two or three feet into the street as they gestured and shouted at the scabs' cars. After thirty minutes or so Captain Tom Steininger or Sergeant Larry Moeykens would come over, saying, "OK, let's back it up." The pickets would quickly oblige and move the barricade back a yard or two, set it down, and resume their hollering. It seemed to work fine during the first week, when P-9 defections were few and replacements were going in to apply for—but not yet take—the strikers' jobs. But how long could order prevail?

The roving pickets, despite their apparent significance in determining the outcome of the strike, were less of a concern to Hormel executives. Nyberg had alerted other plant managers and briefed them on the contract language at each facility. The only place where workers could honor the picket line without risk of dismissal was in Ottumwa, and then only if the UFCW sanctioned the roving pickets. Even if Wynn changed his mind and went along, however, Hormel could legally replace any employee who stayed away from work. At all the other plants—Fremont, Algona, Beloit, Dallas, Atlanta—workers who honored the picket lines could be fired on the spot. In addition, Dave Larson had been monitoring union sentiment through his negotiating contacts, and he doubted that the "P-9 virus" had spread far beyond Austin and perhaps Ottumwa. Just to make sure, Larson and Nyberg traveled to Fremont, Nebraska, and held a press conference at which they insisted that workers who honored such a picket line would be fired. Guyette had made his own plea for support a few days earlier, but the executives sought to avoid a repeat of Ottumwa at its only other company-owned slaughterhouse. For the most part, though, Nyberg didn't lose much sleep over the roving pickets. P-9 had telegraphed the move for months, and wherever and whenever they showed up, Nyberg felt the law was solidly in Hormel's favor. To the conservative-minded company, that was all the assurance necessary.

273

When Saturday morning came, the P-9 executive board was hammering out details about the roving pickets. In each city they would picket in the morning and evening and stay overnight with supporters. Outside Austin, Hormel's biggest packinghouses were in Ottumwa and Fremont, both of which employed about nine hundred people. Like Austin, the plants had slaughtering and processing operations, making them primary facilities for handling millions of tons of meat each year. The Ottumwa plant had been through its own labor strife in April 1984. Workers there were bitter, and P-9 had hundreds of supporters. Fremont was a different story. The local president was Skip Niederdeppe, chairman of the Hormel chain and a strong supporter of Lewie Anderson. He and other local leaders had been warning their members that honoring a P-9 picket line would almost certainly cost them their jobs.

There also were slaughterhouses in Dubuque, Iowa, and Rochelle, Illinois, owned by FDL Foods but connected to Hormel through an agreement by which Hormel marketed their products. P-9's support in Dubuque, FDL's biggest plant, was uncertain. FDL workers were making less than P-9 members before they went on strike and had taken pay cuts just to keep their jobs. Had it not been for Hormel, FDL probably would have folded or filed for bankruptcy, leaving many workers unemployed in a town already hard hit by the farm depression.

Finally, there were smaller Hormel plants producing sausage and other specialty products in Atlanta, Georgia; Houston and Dallas, Texas; Algona and Knoxville, Iowa; Beloit, Wisconsin; and several smaller cities. They were not make-or-break plants in terms of production, but P-9 had dozens of volunteers with little else to do with their time than drive.

Inside the union hall there was a renewed sense of excitement as the roving picket strategy took shape. By Saturday evening cars and vans packed with ardent P-9ers were pulling out of the union hall parking lot, rolling out to Interstate 90, and diverging for a dozen destinations all over the central, southern, and western states. Guyette and Rogers, who reveled in TV camera lights and reporters' microphones, suddenly disappeared from sight. Officers could not be found at home or the union hall. The always eager-to-help volunteers staffing the hall said that for once they didn't know what was next on the agenda. "We've tele-graphed everything until now," said Vice-President Lynn Huston, smiling his most inscrutable smile. "Now we're going to use the element of surprise."

The next afternoon Guyette showed up in St. Paul, this time at Tom Laney's UAW hall, speaking to a crowd that packed the meeting room and flowed out the doors. The hall was fast becom-ing P-9's second home, providing the renegade local with its clos-est and biggest showing of support. Guyette reminded the crowd that Monday would be Martin Luther King Day. For most of them, that meant a day off work, and what better way to commemorate the great civil rights leader than to drive to Austin and join P-9 on the picket line? Guyette asked supporters to join him at the Austin packinghouse at daybreak. Would this be the massive traf-fic jam and civil disobedience that Rogers hinted at on Friday night? No one would say for sure. All Guyette would say was that the previous week belonged to Hormel. The coming week would belong to P-9.

CHAPTER

13

Cars and pickup trucks rolled slowly through the early-morning massive, stalking the massive packinghouse like a caravan of hunters. More than a hundred vehicles, lined up practically bumper to bumper, exhaust streaming into the air, headlights beaming, were circling Hormel Drive. It was Monday morning, week two of the plant's reopening. During the night twenty-five carloads of union supporters had arrived from the Twin Cities, responding to Guyette's call for help. As they approached the plant, they joined other vehicles along with nearly three hundred men and women, bundled in heavy coats, snowmobile suits, and gloves, who braved the sub-zero cold to huddle outside the employee entrances at the south and west gates. Fires lit in fifty-five-gallon barrels burned brightly next to three pickets who stood vigil in each of the driveways. A large American flag anchored the masses as dawn began to lighten the sky and vehicles crawled to a stop around the plant. They didn't need to storm the plant; they would sit and wait for their prey. If anybody wanted to come to work for Hormel this morning, they would have to pass through a blockade to get there. Buoyed by the massive outpouring of supporters from other Minnesota unions, the mood on the picket line turned to cocky defiance. "I never liked working there anyway," one picket muttered.

Replacement workers and defecting P-9 members began

showing up just before dawn, and many got through the gates. But by 7:30 A.M. workers found themselves trapped in a bumper-to-bumper barricade and surrounded by angry pickets. "This is what a scab looks like!" roared one of the strikers, thrusting a huge hambone into the morning sky. As workers tried to drive through the crowd, angry demonstrators brought them to a halt, rocking cars and screaming at them behind rolled-up windows. "Go home, scabs! Bloodless scabs!" Police officers tried to keep demonstrators behind wooden barricades and out of the street, but they were badly outnumbered. Each time they turned their backs to escort one car through the crowded street, demonstrators spilled into the road behind them and surrounded another car. It became virtually impossible for cars to move, although one driver, panicked by the rocking and jeering, slammed on the accelerator and sped off along a snowbank, nearly crashing through a crowd of people. Angry union loyalists quickly gave chase in a pickup truck. Another driver, a photographer from the Hormel corporate office, made the mistake of climbing out of his car when he found himself surrounded by pickets banging on his fenders. He got into a melee and was kicked in the groin before police could extricate him and drive him to the hospital. On and on it went, a few workers trickling through the line, most turning away in fear or disgust. Even the company doctor was forced to turn away, despite a police escort. At midmorning company guards pulled the plant gates shut and police sealed off the entrance to Hormel Drive. Nobody was going anywhere. About 120 union members and 50 replacement workers had slipped into the plant, most of them before many demonstrators arrived. But as long as the crowd stayed put, those workers would get their initiation on the way out.

Downtown at the Law Enforcement Center, Police Chief Don Hoffman was starting to worry. He had packed his office with shortwave radios for reports from his field commanders, and he could tell from the chaos that crackled over the airwaves that his men were losing control. About ten-thirty A.M. Captain Tom Steininger reported back from the plant to Hoffman's office. "We've lost it," he said in exhaustion and frustration. Hoffman refused to believe it. Steininger was a spit-and-polish cop, a meticulous man who would actually brush his regulation boots while sitting in Hoffman's office. Hoffman wanted to hear the words from somebody a little more laid-back. Then Sergeant Larry Moeykens, easygoing Larry Moeykens, came in from the plant. "We've lost it," he told the chief. Hoffman got a sick feeling in his stomach. All his months of preparation, all his careful planning, all his efforts to handle the situation with restraint were crumbling in a mob scene just a few blocks away. He couldn't even maintain order in his own town. He called Guyette's house, then the union hall and almost pleaded with Guyette to get the people at the gates under control. Guyette replied that the action was spontaneous but that he would do what he could. Hoffman was doing his best to keep believing in people. But he was frightened at all the reports of outsiders coming down from the Twin Cities. He knew he sounded like a red-neck when he used the word "outsiders." But he likened them to businessmen at a convention: Grown-up men who wouldn't consider breaking the law at home might pull any shenanigans in somebody else's town. Hoffman pressed Guyette further, telling him that he was the only one who could bring them to order. "If anybody touches a match to it," the chief told him, "it would blow up."

Across the freeway at the corporate office, Hormel executives were not nearly as patient. They had feared trouble every time Guyette and Rogers put out the call for outside supporters to come to Austin. Like Hoffman, they trusted the local people because they knew their faces, but not the newcomers. At about 9:30 A.M. Knowlton called Governor Perpich in St. Paul and asked that he send out troopers with the Minnesota State Patrol to keep order outside the plant. Knowlton told the governor that local police were powerless to control what he described as mob rule. Perpich called Paul Tschida, his commissioner of public safety, who came to his office and conferred with the governor's chief of staff, Terry Montgomery, and his deputy, Lynn Anderson. At 10:00 A.M. Tschida and Montgomery called Knowlton and Nyberg and told them that Minnesota law prohibited the use of troopers in connection with labor disputes. They also advised the unhappy executives that use of the National Guard was not permissible simply because the company requested it. The call for help would have to come from local law enforcement officials, and only if they deemed the situation beyond their control.

Undaunted, Nyberg called back a few hours later with an update. He told Montgomery about the company photographer who was kicked. Even more troubling, police were saying that a shot had been fired at a truck leaving the plant. The demonstrators had set up another blockade at the corporate office, raising the possibility that top management, in addition to plant workers, would be stranded for the evening. Without outside help, company executives grew fearful that the Rogers veneer of non-violence could quickly peel away, igniting bloodshed that would fulfill his military sloganeering about "total annihilation" of Hormel.

Early in the afternoon Perpich gathered his top advisers in his office at the State Capitol. Among them were Montgomery, Tschida, state mediator Paul Goldberg, communications director Gerry Nelson, and State Senator Tom Nelson, who represented the Austin area and was familiar with the personalities involved in the dispute. During the past several weeks Montgomery, who was Perpich's chief strategist, had assembled a multipronged plan to guide his boss through political and legal minefields. Earlier in the dispute the footloose Perpich occasionally took initiative on his own, calling on the company and the union, offering to be of help. But during the holidays, as it became increasingly clear that a major confrontation could explode in Perpich's face, Montgomery went to work. Montgomery was known around the Capitol as a cool tactician who did his best work behind the scenes, thinking ahead to ward off surprises created by a governor who was prone to off-the-wall ideas. In this case he directed Goldberg to keep in touch with company and union negotiators, as he had been doing since February, exploring every possible angle to reach a negotiated settlement. If that didn't work, and there was a good chance that it wouldn't, Montgomery told Tschida to check out the state's responsibility and authority should it be asked to provide law enforcement assistance. That resulted in a legal opinion from the Minnesota attorney general's office, which had landed on the governor's desk ten days earlier.

As a student of Minnesota history Montgomery was keenly aware of the trouble that befell the last Minnesota governor who used the National Guard in a labor dispute. In 1959 then Governor Orville Freeman dispatched guardsmen when he declared martial law in Albert Lea and Freeborn County during a violent meat-packers' strike at the Wilson plant. But a three-judge panel later ruled that Freeman had abused his authority, and one year later he lost his bid for reelection. Now Perpich was in a strikingly similar situation. Another meat-packing plant, another Democratic governor with political ambitions, another nasty strike. Perpich, too, planned to seek reelection in the fall, and his top party foe was a popular St. Paul mayor who waited eagerly to pounce on his political missteps. Montgomery retraced the events of the Wilson strike and determined that a big reason for Freeman's mistake was that he had used snap judgment. That was one of Perpich's nemeses, too. He had cut his public teeth on the rough-and-tumble politics of Minnesota's Iron Range and drew as much support as criticism for his unorthodox, shoot-from-the-hip style.

This time, however, Montgomery was determined to follow a systematic process, a step-by-step procedure for handling every possible development, including worst-case scenarios. He urged Perpich first of all to do whatever he could do to bring about a negotiated settlement. That failing, he should be prepared to do what he felt was right in order to avoid loss of life and minimize violence in Austin. He should act decisively, and he would have to communicate clearly his strategy to the public. He also would have to alert his friends in the labor movement, including Danny Gustafson, president of the Minnesota AFL-CIO; Howard Fortier, head of the state's Teamsters' organization; and Bob Killeen, a regional officer of the United Auto Workers and a well-connected lobbyist. Montgomery knew that Guyette and Rogers had alienated the top brass of Minnesota's labor movement, but calling out the Guard would antagonize those in Perpich's backyard, the heavily unionized Iron Range. Unionists aside, Montgomery knew that if Perpich called out the Guard, public opinion would eventually turn against him, especially if the public wasn't informed about why he did it. Perpich had to keep the media fully briefed if he wanted to have a chance. At that point he would have to make the best of a bad situation.

As the afternoon wore on in Austin, streets around the plant remained in gridlock. Five hundred to seven hundred demonstrators were still blocking the entrances to the plant, preventing any movement in the area. About 2:00 P.M. Chief Hoffman called Perpich's office to request help from the National Guard. Montgomery told him that Perpich would take his call, but only if Mower County Sheriff Wayne Goodnature and Mayor Kough were on the line simultaneously—all making the same request. Montgomery didn't want anybody in Austin second-guessing Perpich a day or a week later. One hitch: Goodnature was in Quantico, Virginia, at an FBI training school.

Finally, at 3:00 P.M., Tschida received a conference call from Hoffman, Kough, and Goodnature. Together they requested that the governor dispatch the Guard to Austin. Hoffman said that as much as he had wanted to handle the disturbance without outside help, he knew that his thirty-three officers were nearing physical exhaustion from several days of picket line duty. There had been threats all day long, broken windshields, slashed tires, the assault on the photographer, and the apparent gunshot fired at the truck. To Hoffman, the situation was out of his control and the crowd had become an angry mob. Tschida asked him if he had tried to make any arrests. The chief said that in his judgment, such a move would provoke a riot. Tschida then asked Kough, a striking member of Local P-9 and Hoffman's boss, if he concurred. The mayor agreed, saying that the situation was beyond the control of local officials. Tschida asked Goodnature if there were other resources in the county to which he could turn for support. The sheriff replied that with mutual aid agreements between departments, the most he could round up would be another forty people, not nearly enough to get the area under control and maintain peace. Tschida was convinced. But as a precaution, he had each man repeat what he had said, to make doubly sure that they felt there was a serious threat to public safety that they could not control without help from the National Guard.

Tschida hung up the phone at 3:15 P.M., approached the governor, and advised him to grant the request. Tschida knew that on the basis of bloodshed alone, there was no justification for taking such action. One fight, some picket line vandalism, and a day full of yelling and shouting hardly seemed to warrant such drastic measures. But all the statutory thresholds had been met. With the Austin police running out of gas and unable to resolve the standstill, it seemed imperative that the state move quickly. Politically it would be safer to wait until blood flowed, he thought, but then Perpich would be condemned for being soft on labor and allowing violence to occur when he'd had a chance to prevent it. Tschida also feared that the chance for injury would be greater if assistance had to be called in during a mob scene. Better to get set up ahead of time, he thought, than have to fight a frenzied crowd of surly strikers. In the end Tschida, himself a Democrat whose father was a union member, figured that if he had to be wrong, he preferred to be safe than sorry.

It was not the news that Perpich wanted to hear. He was a liberal, a leader of the Democratic-Farmer-Labor party in Minnesota, proud son of a union family. He had counted on and usually got labor's support throughout his political career. But now he was faced with a larger issue that superseded politics and friendships: public safety on the streets of Austin. He knew what he had to do. But before he made up his mind, Perpich turned to Goldberg and told him to get Guyette on the phone.

Goldberg went into another room, picked up the phone, and dialed Guyette's office at the Austin union hall. One of the many supporters milling around the hall that afternoon answered the phone. Goldberg announced who he was and said that Perpich wanted to speak with Guyette. The striker replied that Guyette was busy, in a board meeting, and couldn't come to the phone. Goldberg exploded. He told the striker to tell Guyette that the governor of Minnesota wanted to talk. If Guyette was too damn busy, then he had better come to the phone himself and let the governor know. The flustered striker quickly summoned Guyette, who agreed to take the call.

Perpich picked up the phone in his office. He pleaded with Guyette to pull his people away from the gate, to give him more time to work toward a settlement. He reminded the young union leader that it was Martin Luther King Day, a day for nonviolence, not for confrontation. Guyette replied that the people were not under his control, that he couldn't simply whistle and call them away from the gates.

An exasperated Perpich tried one more time. He asked Guyette if he understood that he was going to force Perpich to take some action that the governor didn't want to take.

Guyette told the governor that the situation was out of his hands.

Perpich hung up the phone, his face sullen. He remained perfectly silent as he pulled his tall, angular frame out of the chair and slowly walked into another room where his advisers were gathered.

"We've got to do it," he said.

At 3:30 P.M. the National Guard was given the order to go to Austin. One half hour later, at a hastily called news conference in the State Capitol, Perpich told the press that four military units, six hundred people in all, were on their way. Two more units were put on standby. "As governor," he said, "I have a constitutional responsibility to protect the lives and safety of Minnesota citizens, and this action is taken to fulfill that responsibility."

By sundown advance commanders of the National Guard were pulling into Austin, and by ten o'clock that night, the first of the army green trucks and Jeeps were rolling up to the Austin armory. The crowds around the plant had dispersed by nightfall, allowing workers at the plant and corporate office to get home. But the guard commanders feared another demonstration and wasted no time in getting set up well before dawn. The guardsmen, clad in camouflage fatigues, visored helmets, and white boots, took to the streets in the misty cold darkness, marching double time into position around the north gate of the plant, then fanning out to the other two gates. Even though it wasn't light yet, several hundred demonstrators gathered to jeer at them, some humming the theme from the TV series *F Troop,* others urging them to buy P-9 buttons for a dollar. "This is Hormel, Minnesota, not Austin, Minnesota," bellowed burly striker Merrill Evans. Unfazed by the commotion around them, the guardsmen lined up shoulder to shoulder, elbow to riot club, gazing straight ahead as if seeing everything and nothing at the same time. Bright white banks of lights shone down from utility towers, making the plant glow in the morning darkness and illuminating an eerie standoff: civilian Minnesotans who had stepped out of their ordinary lives into military garb, standing in mute ranks against fellow Minnesotans who had stepped out of equally ordinary lives into a big-time labor war.

But there would be no battle Tuesday morning. In a series of phone calls during the night, law enforcement authorities persuaded company officials to keep the plant closed Tuesday to prevent violence. Part of the problem was that not enough guardsmen could get to Austin in time. Rogers delivered the news over a squad car loudspeaker to the early-morning crowd at the picket line, drawing a roar of victory. There were fewer demonstrators, perhaps only one hundred or two hundred, but despite Rogers's announcement, they kept the streets clogged around the south and west gates throughout most of the day, hinting at a confrontation that never came.

Instead, Tuesday's news was of a more tragic nature. A chartered helicopter carrying one of several network news teams assigned to cover the strike had crashed in a field south of the Twin Cities. Two ABC Television journalists, reporter Joe Spencer and producer Mark McDonough, were killed, as was the pilot, Curt Haugen of suburban St. Paul. Spencer and McDonough had stayed overnight in the Twin Cities Monday while their photographer and sound man drove to Austin. They planned to edit tape of the previous day's confrontation for Tuesday morning's *Good Morning America,* then leave for Austin about dawn. The helicopter crashed into a cornfield while flying low to navigate through the morning's dense fog. The news cast a pall over Tuesday's strategy sessions in Austin, but ironically, it gave many of the strikers a new sense of mission. Two months later they erected a memorial to the ABC journalists in the Labor Center parking lot.

On Wednesday Hormel reopened the plant again after agreeing to a 3:00 A.M. request from authorities to lock the usual south and west gates and route all traffic through the north gate, which was just yards from an exit off Interstate Highway 90. There guardsmen formed a human barricade shutting off traffic from side streets and cordoned off the short approach road from the freeway ramp so that workers could slip quickly through the gate and into the plant compound. This tactic seemed to catch the union by surprise, and by the time they recovered, hundreds of demonstrators were forced to stand in the snow nearly two hundred yards away, leaving only the three pickets allowed by a court order to stand at the gate. Unable to dent the Guard's presence at the gate, the P-9 force retreated to the union hall shortly after dawn for a new strategy session with Rogers and Ed Allen.

Later that morning Guyette issued a fiery denunciation of Perpich for turning the Guard into a taxpayer-funded Hormel escort service. Neighbors near the plant protested that the Guard's formation cut off access to their homes. A group of Twin Cities supporters demanded that Perpich pull out the Guard, shut down the plant and force the two sides to negotiate. But the only movement came from within the plant as some two hundred workers, P-9ers and replacements both, cranked up operations and began churning out Spam, bacon bits, and dry sausage.

The blue caps and the Support Group members convened at the union hall in the wee hours of Thursday morning, this time with a new strategy. If the Guard was going to turn Interstate 90 into an easy-access approach to the plant, the demonstrators would do what they could to clog the freeway with a motorized version of civil disobedience. Moving out again before dawn, the strikers backed up their cars several yards to the freeway and jammed exit ramps. Rogers had talked of clogging the plant gates with supporters lying down in front of trucks and cars trying to enter the plant, but in the middle of January in Minnesota, sitting in a locked car on a freeway ramp was a good deal more palatable. In addition to plugging the ramps, demonstrators frustrated authorities by stopping their cars on I-90, then starting up and driving away as tow trucks approached to pull them off the road. Once again Rogers's tactics had produced mayhem. Traffic was backed up for more than a quarter mile from the eastbound exit to the plant. Scabs unfortunate enough to get caught in the jam found their cars surrounded again by angry pickets. This time authorities responded with a more aggressive stance, smashing car windows to arrest eight strikers who locked their stalled cars and refused to leave. Guardsmen also brought two tank-treaded armored personnel carriers to the plant gate area after monitoring citizen band reports asking drivers of semitrailer trucks to join the blockade. The trucks never materialized, however, and Rogers railed against what he called "a police riot." Demonstrator Greg Bell appeared at a press conference later that morning to show facial cuts he said were a result of sheriffs' deputies pulling him from his car and throwing him to the pavement. But Sheriff Goodnature termed it use of "reasonable force." Whatever it was called, it was clear that police were taking control with a vengeance. And it didn't prevent three hundred to four hundred people from reporting for work.

Away from the picket line, the confrontations were more random and anonymous, taking the form of slashed tires, broken car windows, and telephone threats against union members who returned to work. The phone calls were unofficially traced to P-9 supporters from outside Austin, since union members generally recognized each other's voices. Shortly after midnight on Thursday someone fired BB-gun pellets at the rural home of Richard Cummings, a Mower County commissioner and P-9 member who had returned to work. The pellets shattered a window of Cummings's six-year-old daughter's bedroom. Another elected official, council-member-at-large Bob Dahlback, received a telephone threat on his life. Later the word "scab" was twice burned into his garage siding and once into his jacket. Shortly after the Guard arrived in Austin, police were called to Lefty's Bar to break up a fight between several P-9ers and Tom Tschida, a big former P-9er (not related to Perpich's public safety chief) who took to taunting demonstrators when he arrived for work and who was among the few headstrong enough to venture into the blue-collar hangout. Strikers were still smarting from Tschida's first day back, when he told reporters that he had visions of doing his own version of the "Super Bowl shuffle" as he sauntered across the picket line.

But most union members who went back were more remorseful than strident, and they certainly weren't in the mood to show their faces at Lefty's. More often than not, they crowded into station wagons and aging sedans before heading to work, taking comfort in their numbers. For the first several days many congregated at the Union 76 truck stop, at the first freeway exit east of the plant, before heading en masse to cross the picket line. They did not view themselves as scabs but as people reclaiming their jobs. As carload after carload drove across the line, their faces were grim, their mouths closed, their eyes trying not to focus on longtime friends and neighbors bitterly staring at them out of the dark through the frosted windows. They heard the cussing and insults and tried to brush them off. But they couldn't ignore the chill as they hurried home at night past neighbors still on strike, people who had always waved hello but now only stared or refused to acknowledge them at all. Most wouldn't go out after they went home, including Dahlback, a rugged ex-jock from Austin High with eighteen years in the plant and holder of the city's second-ranking elected office. Dahlback's only night out was for the bimonthly council meeting, when he was vociferously booed and jeered by P-9ers as soon as he entered the council chambers, whenever his name was mentioned, and every time he opened his mouth to speak. It was nearly a month after he went back to work before he ventured out socially, joining his wife, Bev, and four others for dinner at a restaurant six miles outside of town. When they were seated, another council member, Peter Grover, made sure that Dahlback was seated with his back to the rest of the diners to reduce the chance that he would be seen.

It wasn't any easier on Larry Jensen's side of the picket line. His son-in-law had returned to work for a day, giving up the strike for lost. That night Jensen had a long talk with him and convinced him to stay out. Even though the veteran was having his own doubts about the union's direction, he knew one thing: The law is there to be obeyed, whether it was the Ten Commandments or a traffic signal. And in a labor union the law was that you didn't cross a sanctioned picket line. Yet he also knew that many people he had known for a long time were sitting at home getting sick to the point of vomiting, agonizing over whether to go back. Some people seemed to have little choice. The financial pressure was enormous on everyone; but for some with illnesses or children to care for it was even greater, and not even the Adopt-a-Family program could tide them over. In many cases the difference between those who returned out of necessity and those who stayed out boiled down to a question of inner strength and stubbornness, Jensen thought. Once he got back in the plant, he figured he would be able to work with those people and talk to them. But then there were the cocky young guys who abandoned the strike as fast as they could to grab plum jobs that normally took thirty-five years of seniority to get. Even mild-mannered, law-abiding Jensen could not bring himself to work side by side with those jerks. To him, that was like taking the gold out of your mother's teeth before the lid was closed on her coffin.

By Friday afternoon, however, it was clear that P-9's strategy to keep the plant shut down was generating more publicity than real success. Try as they did to frustrate workers with road blockades, harass replacements with scare tactics, and plead with fellow union members on the telephone until all hours of the night, the strikers were unable to stop the hiring, much less keep their own ranks intact. About three hundred nonunion replacements had been hired, and more than one hundred P-9 members had accepted the company's offer to return to work. Even more troubling, Hormel was hiring replacements at a rate of fifty a day, hoping to fill the 1,050 jobs that were needed to run a full shift of plant operations. Despite calls for more aggressiveness on the picket line, Rogers continued to preach nonviolence and civil disobedience. He knew that he had succeeded in attracting dozens of national reporters and all the major TV networks to Austin and that a bloody confrontation would not play well on the news. The media were growing skeptical, too, hopping from press conference to press conference, from the Labor Center to the police station to the corporate office, often getting conflicting versions of the number of people reporting for work. That made it nearly impossible to assess which side was prevailing. Further defusing P-9's attack was the refusal of the international union to sanction roving picket lines. To the media, to almost everyone who watched the drama unfold on TV, and to those who were living the story in Austin, the question became quite simple: How was P-9 going to win this thing if it couldn't keep its own plant shut down?

Paul Wellstone, the college professor from nearby Northfield and one of P-9's earliest supporters, asked himself the same question. If Plan A wasn't working, where was Plan B? How were the strikers going to stop the scabs? How was P-9 going to regain control of the plant? In one swift gubernatorial order Perpich had tipped the state's previous position of neutrality decidedly against the union. Without a way to get the plant back, P-9 was on the verge of losing it all, a thought that had lingered deep in Wellstone's mind almost since he first became involved in the crusade nearly ten months earlier. It hadn't stopped him from becoming one of P-9's most upbeat and inspirational supporters. Diminutive next to the strapping meat-packers, the political science professor was a popular speaker at rallies, passionately urging on a group of workers who were fighting an important struggle for justice, led by a man of refreshing integrity and conviction.

For all his early speechifying on P-9's behalf, Wellstone later conceded that it was difficult to sort the rah-rah from the message. He wanted P-9 to fight but not to commit suicide. He did try to express his concern in private. In early October Wellstone volunteered to drive Guyette to Duluth, where he was scheduled to address a gathering of state, county, and local government union workers. It was a rare chance to talk to Guyette alone, a three-hour drive from St. Paul, and Wellstone took the opportunity all the way up and back. He told Guyette that he admired his rare courage and willingness to stand up for what he believed and to fight for justice. He had become an important symbol to people all over the country. P-9 had lit the candle. "You have to make sure that you can't let them destroy you," Wellstone pleaded. Guyette, sitting quietly in the passenger's seat, looked at Wellstone that afternoon and flashed a trademark smile that simultaneously expressed his own confidence and seemed to tease his companion for doubting him. "Don't worry," he said.

Despite Guyette's demeanor, Wellstone remained rather uneasy about just how P-9 would avoid getting killed. That prospect became painfully real when Wellstone saw the guardsmen lined up outside the plant on Tuesday morning. He was furious at Perpich for making the move and later drove to St. Paul to vent his anger at Montgomery in a back room of the governor's office. But the more pressing problem was in Austin. Wellstone saw no strategy for stopping the scabs. What about a mass return to work? They could start a sabotage campaign to pressure Hormel from the inside. At the very least they would save their jobs and continue negotiations while collecting a paycheck. One thing was clear: Rogers's campaign to jam traffic with hundreds of cars wasn't doing the job. Now what? As angry as strikers were at their Democratic governor for calling in the militia, they had nothing in their carefully crafted strategy to counteract such a move. For all the newfangled tactics engineered by Corporate Campaign, they had produced nothing more than a classic standoff from the past. They had tried impassioned and sometimes threatening phone calls to dissuade their own members from crossing the picket line. And they had viciously shouted their defiance on the picket line. Rogers preached more civil disobedience, but neither their voices nor their bodies could stave off the realization that they had lost control of the plant.

The day after the Guard came to Austin, Wellstone stood up at a Metro Area Support Group meeting in the union hall and painfully expressed his concern about what he felt was going to happen if the plant remained open. "People are going to be destroyed," he told the crowd. Rogers tried to cut him off, but Laney interrupted, telling the group that Wellstone had something to say. The professor tried to make it clear that the replacement workers were permanent, that Hormel wouldn't replace them unless they quit on their own. It was a fine legal distinction that couldn't be ignored. Some of the leftist group members glared at Wellstone and started to shout him down, outraged by what they heard. Wellstone thought that if one of them had had a gun, he would have been killed.

Rogers did not seem the least bit concerned about whether the replacements were permanent, and he certainly never dwelt on the legal technicalities. On Friday morning, the Guard's fourth day in Austin, he told a pensive group of strikers and supporters that company claims about union members losing their jobs to permanent replacements were simply not true. His rationale appealed squarely to their emotions, not the legal issue. "If the union loses, and you have a weak union," he shouted into the microphone, "yeah, you lose your job. If the union is strong and the union wins, then you turn everybody out of that plant that doesn't belong there, including all the people that crossed the picket line that were your own members." A massive cheer erupted in the hall as Rogers provided reassurance to worried P-9ers that they still controlled their own destiny.

The Support Group meeting effectively ended Wellstone's relationship with Rogers. Wellstone had lost faith in the organizer and was suspicious of his unwillingness to tolerate criticism, even when it was offered constructively and not in an attempt to undermine the movement. Wellstone did not publicize his skepticism, however, and sought to remain close to Guyette, Winkels, and Huston. But he clearly kept his distance from key parts of their strategy. Huston later called him about speaking in other states where the roving pickets were headed, but Wellstone wistfully turned him down. He told Huston that he believed in P-9's struggle, but Wellstone couldn't ask people in other states to lose their jobs.

Wellstone was not the only one starting to express doubts. Each day more and more union members were wandering into Guyette's office or Rogers's strategy room after the morning rank-and-file debriefing sessions to ask if their jobs weren't in jeopardy. Rogers insisted that the big packinghouse couldn't be running very efficiently with a bunch of rookies on the line. If Hormel wanted to use scabs, he reminded the rank and file, P-9 would unleash its ultimate weapon: roving pickets to shut down the rest of Hormel's plants. Guyette reassured his members that Hormel had a ninety-day probation policy; it could fire the replacements and rehire the members of P-9 as soon as it saw the wisdom of signing an acceptable agreement. As for the roving pickets, he was confident that Hormel employees at other plants had every right to stage sympathy strikes because the UFCW had never signed the 1984 chain agreement that contained a no-strike clause. It turned out he was wrong—a National Labor Relations Board investigation later found that the UFCW had signed the agreement—meaning that P-9 would place hundreds of workers at risk of losing their jobs.

P-9 had begun "testing" the roving pickets on the first day the Guard took up its position in Austin. The results were cause for celebration and concern. About sixty strikers had set up a picket line at the Hormel plant in Ottumwa and persuaded most of the five hundred-plus day shift workers to honor it until it disbanded at 9:30 A.M. It was a strong sign of support from workers who were probably the most sympathetic to P-9 of any Hormel employees. The work force was young and embittered at Hormel's tactic of laying off workers during contract talks in the spring of 1984. In response to their refusal to work that morning, Hormel quickly filed a lawsuit accusing the Ottumwa local of breaching its contract. But the company backed away from its threat to fire anyone who honored the picket lines.

On Wednesday morning the pickets moved on to Algona, where they set up a picket line outside Hormel's pepperoni plant. This time, however, most of the eighty employees on the first shift ignored them and reported for work. The strikers claimed a partial victory in convincing three dozen workers to show up ninety minutes late, but company officials said only seven or eight workers were tardy. Unlike their counterparts in Ottumwa, workers in Algona had been told by their union steward, Paul Fortune, that they were obligated to cross the lines and report for work.

Another attempt was planned for Friday morning at Hormel's number two plant in Fremont, Nebraska, but the mission was to be aborted by events that almost no one could have anticipated. In fact, with the Guard in Austin and the roving pickets heading everywhere, events were starting to move at a pace that even Rogers and the P-9 executive board were having trouble keeping up with. On Wednesday Perpich, under pressure from Wellstone and numerous other strike activists to lock both sides in a room until they settled, tried once again to get P-9 and Hormel to sit down with a neutral fact finder. While he didn't have the legal authority to order them to meet, this time the governor's insistence paid off. The next morning P-9's executive board and a handful of Hormel negotiators, including Dave Larson, drove to St. Paul to meet the fact finder, a Boston attorney and Harvard instructor named Arnold Zack (a distant cousin of UFCW spokesman Al Zack—a fact neither man knew until P-9 brought them together). Guyette was hopeful that he could persuade Zack to consider union objections that went beyond the mediator's proposal, but Larson was stony and noncommital. He had good reason.

Under Perpich's plan, Zack would ask both sides to explain their positions on the mediator's proposal. He would next summarize their views and his interpretation, then give them a report within forty-eight hours to use as a basis for a settlement. Technically this was not mediation. Both sides were required to do no more than state their positions and let Zack find any misunderstandings. If Zack or Goldberg could find a little room actually to mediate—that is, to encourage either side to budge a little—so much the better. The main point, however, was to throw a lifeline to P-9, hoping that the union's embattled leaders might use Zack's report as an excuse to let their members vote again, this time with the image of a failing picket line fresh in their minds. It wouldn't be the first time that mediators had given negotiators a face-saving way out of a tight corner. There was just one hitch. No one explained to Guyette and the executive board that fact-finding was a face-saving device, that this was another chance for his membership to change its mind. Guyette certainly wasn't changing his. "Our members have voted down this proposal twice," he told reporters during a break in Thursday's session at Goldberg's office above a bank in St. Paul. "Are we supposed to keep voting till we get it right?"

Zack found himself highly frustrated. He had handled tough showdowns before, including the Professional Air Traffic Controllers' dispute in 1981. But never had he encountered such entrenched negotiators. At first he and Goldberg couldn't even get Hormel's negotiators to sit down face-to-face with Guyette and the executive board. Nor could they get Guyette, Winkels, Lenoch, and the others to give them any succinct summary of their demands. They kept working on the two sides all day, asking that both at least preserve the status quo. Would Hormel agree to interrupt the hiring of replacements if P-9 would agree to hold its roving pickets in check? Finally, as the parties broke for a late dinner about 9:00 P.M., Zack and Goldberg got Larson and his team to agree to sit down in the same room with P-9. A mediator on Goldberg's staff went to give Guyette the good news and ask if he could stay late. Guyette said no because he had been invited to debate Lewie Anderson on Ted Koppel's *Nightline* program that night, and he was due at the ABC affiliate in St. Paul a little after 10:00 P.M. Zack, a balding intellectual given to bow ties, flew into a rage. What was more important, he demanded to know, settling this dispute and saving jobs or getting in another lick on television? Guyette told him that *Nightline* was an invaluable opportunity to spread his message about fighting givebacks and unionism.

Nightline opened that night with a shot of demonstrators outside the Austin plant, while Koppel intoned, "At this meatpacking plant in Minnesota, the battle is over what may be the key labor issue of our day." Strikers shouted their now-familiar refrain: "They say give back, we say fight back!" With a national audience watching, Guyette hammered home the P-9 line with Anderson in Chicago and U.S. Labor Secretary William Brock listening from Washington. Even Koppel, undoubtedly one of the best confrontational inquisitors on live TV, could not fluster the unflappable labor leader from Austin.

"Mr. Guyette," Koppel began, "if I said to you, you seem to be out of step; you and your parent union are in disagreement; you and your company are in disagreement, and it seems as though you're out of step with the times, because givebacks are becoming a part of the economy these days."

"Well, that's exactly the problem," Guyette said. "Givebacks for the Hormel Company, the most profitable company in the meat-packing industry, are just not necessary at this time. We've given givebacks to this company sixteen out of the last twenty-three years, and now the company's experiencing the highest profits in their history, and they still want more from their workers."

"And every other plant and every other local is wrong, and you guys are right," Koppel said.

"Well, first of all, we need to stabilize the wage rates for the profitable employees in the meat-packing industry and bring the others up to a level," Guyette said. "But what we have is a downward cycle in the meat-packing industry that'll only stop at minimum wage levels."

Koppel then bore into Anderson, noting that in the old days a split between a parent union and a local would have been unthinkable. "Why aren't you guys backing them?"

Anderson replied that the meat-packing industry was in turmoil, with jobs often hanging in the balance of union decisions about whether to fight concessions. The international's strategy was to forge coalitions, educate memberships, and gradually bring wages back up again. The key, he said in a backhanded slap at what he perceived to be Guyette's selfish motives for P-9, "is to accomplish the greatest amount of good for the greatest number of workers."

Koppel interrupted. "But what Mr. Guyette says is exactly correct . . . Hormel has been doing very well; it's making money. Big profits."

Anderson concurred but explained that Hormel had developed a new low-wage front through its FDL subsidiary to handle hog slaughtering previously done in Austin. FDL workers were earning two dollars an hour less than Hormel was proposing to pay in Austin. The split underscored the need for a national wage rate to prevent companies from whipsawing work from top-dollar plants to lower-wage operations. "If you have a group of workers that gets so much further ahead than the rest, what happens is the employers subcontract that work out to a lower-wage operator," he said.

Later Koppel pressed Guyette on the urgency of resolving the dispute since within a short period of time strikers risked being out of work for good. Guyette acknowledged the meetings with Zack, but he insisted that "ultimately this company has to understand that they have made promises to the workers in the past; the workers have cooperated. And we've tried to guarantee the company a profit level or we'd take a cut in pay. But they simply want more and more out of their workers. They don't seem to care about the injury rate in the Austin plant, and we've felt that we need to put a stop to it now."

Guyette was at his best. He criticized Hormel for using layoffs to pressure workers into taking concessions and pitting workers against each other in bargaining. While portraying workers as willing to take cuts if the company wasn't doing well, he pointed out that Knowlton had received a 68 percent salary increase. He also accused the international of turning its back on P-9, criticized its organizing efforts, and cited Anderson for essentially advocating that workers take wage cuts "whether we work for a profitable company or an unprofitable one."

Anderson responded that a strategy of pushing for more would only continue the downward wage spiral caused by employers shifting work from high-wage to low-wage plants. He also cited Guyette's complaint about Hormel as evidence of the need to maintain an overview of the industry, to figure out how to move all workers forward when employers have the tools to destroy them.

But it was Brock, a savvy Washington insider and President Reagan's chief labor administrator, who offered the most telling commentary of the evening.

"The tragedy of Hormel—and it is a tragedy—is that this is a failure of collective bargaining, with a company and a union that have had a remarkably good record of labor-management relations and cooperative collective bargaining," he said. "For fifty years there hadn't been a strike in that organization. Now because of the pressures, because of the difference between that local circumstance and the national, you have something that looks extremely difficult to solve, and that's tragic for those individuals, but for all of us, I think, too."

But while Guyette debated Anderson, one of the strike's most significant subdramas was unfolding in a manner that showed just how much pressure was coming to bear on P-9's executive board. All day long Goldberg's staff had hammered away at the union officers and the executives at least to keep matters from getting worse. They knew that with every replacement worker signed onto the Hormel payroll, a junior member on P-9's seniority list was probably losing his job, making it harder and harder to settle the dispute. They knew that if P-9 sent out its roving pickets again Friday morning, they could create further chaos and endanger more jobs. They asked both sides to preserve the status quo. Larson was considering the request, for he, too, knew that the issue of permanent replacements would become the biggest obstacle to a settlement now. Winkels, Lenoch, Hagen, and the others also understood Goldberg and Zack's message of conciliation. But a caravan of eighty roving pickets already had left for Fremont for a crucial test of support. Not only was Fremont a big plant for production, but it also put P-9's feud with the UFCW on center stage. The president of the Fremont local, Skip Niederdeppe, was a loyal Anderson ally and opposed to the campaign. If the roving pickets could convince the rank and file to stay out, as they seemed willing to do in Ottumwa, P-9 would have convincing evidence that the UFCW had been wrong all along.

That night, even before Guyette had finished squaring off with Anderson on national television, board members were in their St. Paul hotel getting nervous phone calls from Austin. A feeling had set in among some of the members and wives that if talks were going on, it made sense to let them progress without interruption. The board, always sensitive to the concerns of its rank and file, hastily convened a meeting in a hotel room, with Guyette and Huston absent. Members also heard that one of their strongest supporters in Fremont, who formerly worked in Austin, was getting cold feet about honoring the picket line. If he crossed and other would-be P-9 sympathizers followed him, it could turn into a fiasco. All that made Zack's plea for maintaining the status quo seem more attractive. The board agreed to pull back the pickets and phoned Austin with new orders: When the pickets called in from Fremont for last-minute instructions, they should be told to return to Austin.

Sure enough, when the strikers pulled into a McDonald's parking lot in Fremont about 3:00 A.M., they phoned strike control and were told to turn around and come back. They were stunned. They called Ray Rogers, who was at his basement apartment near the packinghouse getting his first full night of sleep in three weeks. Rogers, too, couldn't believe it. He demanded to know who gave the orders. He was sure there was a breakdown somewhere. He told them to call back in two hours and not to budge in the meantime. Rogers wasn't an executive of the union—he wasn't even a member—and he couldn't countermand orders that must have come from one of the officers. Rogers called the hotel where board members were holding an all-night session to prepare for Friday's fact-finding. By the time Rogers got through and argued that this was a strategic blunder, it was too late. Dawn was breaking in Fremont. The only pickets were a dozen or so from Austin who forgot about the McDonald's rendezvous and never got the orders to turn back. Some five hundred Fremont workers, already warned not to take P-9 seriously, saw the feeble effort at picketing and decided that P-9 was not the juggernaut everybody said it was. They poured through the gate and into work. The roving picket strategy had suffered a disastrous setback.

For all the overnight chaos, day two of fact-finding didn't go any better. Guyette was emboldened by his effective appearance on *Nightline.* Larson had been unable to persuade his superiors to stop hiring replacements that morning. The executive board was racked with uncertainty over the roving pickets. Huston was so exhausted from the all-night discussion that after about twenty minutes he stretched out on the floor of the conference room and fell asleep. When Zack emerged from the final fact-finding session at 5:45 P.M. on Friday, he was noncommittal at best. "We resolved a lot of confusion," he told reporters. Would his report lead to a settlement? "I don't know what the trigger event is," he replied. Neither company nor union negotiators voiced much optimism as they departed. They had not discussed new proposals, only new ways of looking at the mediator's proposal. As the despairing mediators trudged out to their cars in a light snow, a reporter said good-night and wished them good luck. "Thanks," Zack called back. "That's what it's going to take."

In reality, it would take much more than that. The next night hundreds of rank-and-filers braved cold, windy conditions to attend a meeting at Ellis Middle School, named after union patriarch Frank Ellis, on the east side of Austin. For many neutral observers of the strike, this was the most crucial union meeting to date. Zack's report was due the following day, reflecting the urgency brought about by Hormel's rapid hiring of replacements. If the meeting produced rank-and-file pressure to get back to work, the report could become the much hoped-for bridge to a settlement. But if union leaders gave a negative assessment of the meetings with Zack, Guyette's supporters at the meeting would likely prevail and P-9ers might never get a chance to vote again. If Zack recommended another vote on the mediator's proposal, it would have to be done fast, before Hormel had completed its hiring, if there were to be any jobs left. Moreover, the issue of the replacements would have to be addressed by any such settlement. Nyberg was adamant about refusing to lay them off or fire them to make room for P-9ers.

The meeting ran for nearly two hours. But several members left early, their emotions and hot tempers reflecting the frustration many felt at the inability to move the dispute off center. Outside the back of the room a group of fifteen to twenty strikers crowded around board member Kenny Hagen, pleading with him to do something to get them back to work. But it didn't help. To reporters waiting in the lobby, it became clear, from several bursts of boisterous applause, that Guyette's supporters remained in control. As workers poured out, they vowed to escalate the battle. Roving pickets would be dispatched even as union leaders discussed Zack's report. They issued a call to have union supporters from across the country come to Austin to help shut down the plant later in the week. They urged union members thinking of returning to work to refrain. A nationwide boycott call was sounded. And finally, a meeting was tentatively set for the following Saturday to consider the leadership's recommendations about the fact finder's report.

At a press conference back at the union hall Guyette made it clear that he expected little from Zack. "We're not interested in voting until we get it right," he said as a group of blue cap supporters stood in the back of the room, looking on approvingly. Vice-President Lynn Huston added that with the purging of the small P-10 faction of members who had returned to work, the union was more united than ever. "It isn't P-9 anymore. It's the entire labor movement around the country," he said.

On Sunday morning Larson was relaxing at home, listening to his favorite sports talk show from the Twin Cities. But he couldn't help thinking about what he had heard about the union meeting the night before. And he was troubled and perplexed. For all the urgency in Perpich's forty-eight-hour deadline for Zack's report, P-9 was certainly taking a relaxed, even cavalier approach to it. What were these guys thinking? If members waited until Saturday to vote on whether to consider it, there probably wouldn't be any jobs left. The meeting made it even clearer to Larson what he suspected all along: that P-9 simply had a different agenda than resolving the dispute. But just what was on the agenda? Starting a new union? A coalition of militant unionists from across the country seemed to be adopting P-9 as a rallying point. What about a new Hormel chain? On the other hand, Rogers was keeping people involved and getting them exposure on national television, the kind of attention that most people in Austin would not see for the rest of their lives. And it certainly had to be a lot more fun than slaughtering hogs. As long as members were led to believe they still had time to maneuver, why stop now? But the reality was that they had very little time left. They had twice rejected the mediator's proposal, and if they turned it down again, well, to Larson's way of thinking, three times and you're out.

That afternoon Zack picked up his telephone in Boston and dictated an eight-page single-spaced report to Goldberg's office in St. Paul. Once it was typed up, Goldberg jumped in his car and rushed the document to Austin, where he delivered copies to Larson and members of the P-9 executive board that night. The report, without making new recommendations, sought to clarify the most divisive issues. To clear up seniority questions, Zack reiterated that the language would follow the terms negotiated in Ottumwa, with the thorniest issues to be handled by a joint company-union seniority board. The wage would be ten dollars an hour for production workers, eleven dollars for maintenance workers, and the two-tier system would be eliminated. He also spelled out terms of the thirty-six-hour weekly guarantee, time and a half pay after forty hours, and a cap on the number of temporary hires. On the troublesome safety question, Zack noted that a study would be done by an expert chosen by P-9, with Hormel to implement "those recommendations that are reasonable and economically feasible." Overall, Zack described the mediator's proposal as an improvement over Hormel's last contract offer. He found that there clearly had been confusion about the meaning of the mediator's proposal, and he recommended another vote on it. He urged P-9 leaders to take action on the report within forty-eight hours.

But Guyette was unimpressed. He saw the same problems with Zack's report that he saw in Bell's proposal. He seemed especially bothered that the safety provision left too much discretion to the company. He said it would take until the following Saturday to distribute copies and have the leadership consider the document. Another two days would be needed to conduct a secret vote if necessary. In the meantime, a bus with an estimated fifty P-9 members was heading to Fremont that night, and this time there would be no turning back. A second bus was on its way to Ottumwa. The war was on.

That same Sunday night Laney and Wellstone drove to Austin intent on having a meeting with Guyette. Since the Guard's arrival, the sight of a growing number of replacements streaming into the plant was making already nervous strikers downright panicky. After Saturday's meeting there were reports that hundreds of union members were going to cross the picket line Monday morning out of fear that their jobs would be lost for good if they didn't act fast. The rumors intensified when word spread that the leadership viewed the fact finder's report as a rehash of the mediator's proposal and would not endorse it. Scores of people had been calling the international offices in Washington and

Bloomington, seeking advice on whether to go back to work. Each time the answer was the same. As critical as it was of Guyette and Rogers, the parent union stood by its sanction of the picket line. Union members were told they were not supposed to cross it. The international was, in effect, sacrificing jobs with the hope that it could salvage them later.

As Wellstone and Laney walked through the doors of the Labor Center, they saw the worried looks. Strikers were milling around, looking scared and confused. They wanted answers but Wellstone told them he didn't know what to say. He and Laney went into Guyette's office, where they were joined by a young P-9 member and, for part of the time, Pete Winkels. Wellstone felt thankful that Laney was there. No one could question Laney's credibility as a labor leader or accuse him of being a bureaucrat. Unafraid of the labor power structure, he was P-9's first and most vocal outside supporter. Laney embodied unusual courage, Wellstone thought, and shared a deep willingness to fight for just causes. Now the militant and the populist had to convince Guyette, an equally principled leader under immense pressure, that the time had come to go back to work and live to fight another day.

Laney couched everything in terms of a victory, hoping Guyette would understand that they remained concerned and were not betraying the fight. He urged Guyette to lead his people back to work unified, to continue the battle from the shop floor, where the union would be in solid control. Look at the gains: P-9 had become an internationally known force in the American labor movement. Its members had captured the imagination of people everywhere, translating anger into can-do idealism. They could continue the fight at the bargaining table the following year, and no one would call it defeat. It would be a stirring success, a unified rank and file that had shown the world how to fight corporate America in the 1980's, when everyone said it couldn't be done. For nearly two hours they talked in relay, urging Guyette to act before the rank and file became irrevocably fractured. But Guyette was immovable. He reminded them that a majority had voted the night before to continue on the same course. He took that as a strong sign that workers wanted to fight and did not want to go back. Besides, he said, what would stop

Hormel from finding ways to fire P-9's militants if they returned to work without a contract? And what would become of the P-9 members whose jobs already had been taken by replacements? No, he said, P-9 needed a contractual victory.

Finally, the normally talkative Wellstone got tersely blunt: "Jim, I think you're going to get wiped out."

After a moment of silence the young striker spoke up. He pleaded with Guyette to listen to what Wellstone and Laney were saying. Tomorrow a lot of people would be crossing the picket line, he said, their hearts spilling out. The young striker promised not to be among them, but he posed a heart-rending question that was being repeated in various forms in living rooms, kitchens, and bedrooms all over town that night. "I have two children, a seven-year-old and a nine-year-old," he said. "What's going to happen to them?"

Wellstone was speechless. Never since he first got involved with P-9 had he heard a more powerful statement. Even before the words sank in, he felt convinced that Guyette, whom he had come to admire greatly in the short time they had known each other, would make the right decision when the moment came. Some of the best people in the local, including active supporters of the campaign and strike, were on the verge of losing their jobs. Surely he could not let that happen. A unified return to work was a logical next step, and Guyette had a chance to take it not only with dignity but with a huge victory in his pocket.

Guyette repeated that the members had spoken the night before and the strike would continue.

Wellstone left Guyette's office and ran into Winkels later that night in the union hall. "The criticism is out of love," the professor said. "I just can't see people getting crushed." The look on Winkels's face told Wellstone that he was worried, too.

The next morning P-9 gave its ultimate test to the months of grass-roots canvassing at the other Hormel plants. About 200 strikers set up picket lines at plants in Ottumwa, Fremont, Dallas, and Houston and at a plant run by the company's FDL Foods subsidiary in Dubuque, Iowa. Without the sanction of the international union, they were, in effect, asking people to risk getting fired by not reporting to work. In Ottumwa, 486 of 500 day shift workers honored the lines, effectively shutting down what had been the company's second-largest plant without Austin in full operation. In Fremont, the only big plant with slaughtering and processing operations, about 65 out of 850 workers honored the line, the rest heeding their local president, Skip Niederdeppe. Unlike the more radical leadership of the Ottumwa local, which shared Guyette's disdain for the international, Niederdeppe told his workers that they were contractually obligated to report to work. Workers in Dubuque were told the same thing by their leaders, and although absenteeism was unusually high, most of the plant's 900 employees showed up for their shifts. At a small smoked meats plant in Dallas, about half of the forty-member day shift honored the lines. But at a hot dog plant in Houston, where Hormel planned to hold its annual meeting the following day, the pickets were largely ignored.

Hormel, which had warned workers during the roving pickets' test runs the previous week, fired everyone who stayed away from work—more than 500 people that day. It was a swift, stunning move that, in most labor disputes, would have brought the union to the bargaining table, desperate to settle. Up to three fourths of Hormel's union workers had ignored P-9's call, and the rest had suffered terribly for it. But as had been the case so many times before, a dramatic showdown that Hormel appeared to have won did virtually nothing to bring an end to the battle. In fact, it did just the opposite.

As reports of the roving pickets' efforts trickled back to the union hall in Austin, Guyette and his supporters took delight in what they were hearing. They had spread their fight, and the workers had responded, particularly at Local 431 in Ottumwa. They expressed little surprise that Hormel had fired all those who stayed out, including workers in Fremont and Dallas. To P-9, it simply meant that more people were on their side and that Hormel's biggest slaughter plant outside Austin was crippled. In Washington the international took an I-told-you-so position and laid out a completely opposite view of the firings. Rather than increase Austin's leverage to shut down the company, the hundreds of people who had lost their jobs would make things even stickier at the bargaining table: What was P-9 going to have to give up in order to get the Ottumwa workers their jobs back?

By contrast, the picket line in Austin was stopping no one

Monday, as the Guard provided unfettered access for about five hundred workers, including another twenty replacements and eighty returning P-9ers since Friday afternoon. Perpich, under increasing fire from union supporters for deploying the Guard, made a plea for a forty-eight-hour cooling-off period. In a hand-delivered letter to Guyette and Knowlton, the governor asked Hormel to stop hiring replacement workers, asked Guyette to "stabilize" strike activities, and urged both sides to "give additional serious reflection to the likely consequences of a continuation of this dispute." The people of Minnesota, especially those in Austin, would like it settled, he wrote. Knowlton, always deferential to the governor even when he was livid about his actions, replied in a letter that Hormel was in agreement with Zack's report and would accede to his request to stop hiring on the condition that the union hold up its part of the deal. But Guyette refused, noting that Hormel had continued hiring replacements during the two days of meetings with Zack, when P-9 pulled back its roving pickets. He also turned back Perpich's request to respond within forty-eight hours to Zack's report and reiterated his belief that it differed little from the mediator's proposal.

The level of distrust had sunk to a new low. In the absence of any efforts toward a settlement, and with Zack's report apparently headed for sure defeat, Hormel and P-9 were following separate agendas. Hormel wanted to run the plant with anybody willing and able to do the work. P-9 wanted to run the strike with anybody willing and able to provide support. To judge by the confidence on both sides, there was plenty of help in each camp to run its operation effectively. The problem was, the fifty-three-year-old link between them was gone. And within a matter of days Hormel would no longer need P-9 to survive.

CHAPTER
14

Dave King rose from the audience of stock-holders and made one thing clear: Even though he had spent the past two weeks watching hundreds of people, including longtime co-workers and friends, cross his union's picket line he had not hollered the word "scab."

At least not yet. Attending Hormel's annual meeting in Houston on Tuesday afternoon, January 28, 1986, King hardly looked like a picket-line rowdy. Dressed in a tan suit, light shirt, and dark tie, with glasses and neatly combed dark hair, he was indistinguishable from the Texas shareholders who did not share his membership in Local P-9. Like them, he was proud of his company, even if it had posted a record 1985 fourth quarter without him. He listened quietly as Dick Knowlton, three years his junior at Austin High School and a fellow lifetime Hormel employee, outlined the past year's performance. While it might have been hard for King to detect from the packinghouse floor, Hormel had nearly completed a dramatic transformation. From a stodgy meat-packer captive to volatile hog prices, Hormel had transformed itself into a high-powered food company equipped with the latest technology and flush with new microwave gro-cery items, backed by escalating marketing programs. One Houston shareholder was so impressed that he wondered out loud if it was time for Hormel to shed its traditional meat-packing operations altogether, since the scope of the company had become so much broader than its reputation for Spam, bacon, and ham.

King wanted to talk about the old Hormel. He had toiled in the Austin packinghouse since the presidency of Franklin Roosevelt, rising to the coveted skilled position of machinist. He had taken home more than five hundred dollars a week, making him one of the best-paid workers in the plant, until a hand injury a year before the strike put him on workers' compensation. He was, in Knowlton's words, one of Hormel's many good, rock-solid employees. When the new plant was constructed, he proved his loyalty by working eighty-hour weeks to build the facility that his boss so desperately wanted. To keep construction on schedule, King and his compatriots had labored so long into some Sunday nights that they couldn't report to their regular 7:00 A.M. duty on Monday because union rules required an eight-hour break between shifts. In thirty-eight years he had never received a faulty work slip. Far from being a militant, he was a very wealthy man, thanks to Hormel and hard work. Like many veterans, he had taken advantage of the company's stock purchase program, making weekly purchases for the past fifteen years. Scanning the holdings listed in the company's proxy statement, he figured that he owned more stock than at least half the twelve-member board seated in front of him at the meeting in the Hyatt Regency West Hotel.

But as King stood up at the microphone and told his story to an unfamiliar audience of Texans, he spilled out the hurt of a man betrayed by a trusted friend. His tale was as succinct and powerful as anything produced by the corporate campaign to date. Back in 1978, after twice voting no, he voted to approve the contract to build the new plant in Austin. He changed his mind only after being told by Knowlton and Hormel Chairman I. J. Holton, in remarks televised on Austin's Channel 6, that under the new arrangement workers would never make any less than they did in the old plant. Fair enough. But King hadn't seen a raise since 1980, despite a steady rise in the cost of living since then. Then, in 1984, while his company was doing well and its executives were getting raises, his wages and benefits were cut back. Something wasn't right. He reminded Knowlton of the wills left behind by George and Jay Hormel, who set up the Hormel Foundation and stipulated that the company would always conduct itself for the benefit of Austin and the surrounding communities. "Do you think what you are doing in Austin," he asked, "that you are living up to that trust?"

Knowlton replied that his personal drive for a new plant in Austin at a time when other board members urged building elsewhere was evidence of his commitment to the town. Like King, Knowlton had never worked anywhere but Hormel. "If it were not to be successful," Knowlton said of the plant, "I would feel a personal sense of failure. There's nobody in this room or this company who can tell you that they have more interest in Austin, Minnesota, than I can."

He went on to explain that the 1978 agreement was designed to provide a supplemental wage payment, a financial buffer to compensate veterans for the loss of incentive pay once they made the move from the old plant to the new one. Workers agreed to put future wage or cost-of-living increases into interest-bearing escrow accounts that would be paid back to them in weekly sums once the new plant opened. The theory was that inflation would keep wages rising until workers made as much without the incentive system as they had with it in the old plant.

But the agreement didn't anticipate the rapid slowdown in inflation in 1981 and 1982 or that industry wages would plummet after fifty years of increases. Knowlton said he was tormented by the prospect of asking for wage rollbacks, that there were times when he lay awake at night wondering what to do as his financially troubled competitors slashed their rates. In the fall of 1984, after workers had threatened to strike company-wide, he had told Larson and his negotiators to fashion a wage package offering nine dollars an hour that year and ten dollars in 1985. That triggered angry phone calls from other meat-packing executives who were struggling to pay eight dollars an hour while competing with nonunion firms paying as little as five dollars. Still, he felt his workers deserved to be at the top of the industry pay scale. They were right, Hormel could afford to pay more than less successful packers. But the wage gap had grown too wide, and Hormel needed concessions to keep it from growing wider.

"You know," he told King as his gravelly voice cracked

slightly, "we'd like to be a little bit proud of the fact that we're out there in front, that we are providing the best wage and fringe program in the industry. And I know it's an adjustment, I know full well, but when—"

"You don't know that!" King shot back. "You don't know it's an adjustment!"

Knowlton continued, pointing out that fifty miles south of Austin in Mason City, Iowa, Armour was paying nonunion meat-packers a base wage of $6.38 an hour. At Worthington in south-western Minnesota, Swift Independent Packing was paying union workers $7.25 an hour and outbidding Hormel for hogs. Right next door, Farmstead workers in the old Wilson plant in Albert Lea had just ratified a three-year agreement starting them at $8.50. Yet Austin had refused to consider the $9 and $10 offer in the fall of 1984, even after the rest of the Hormel chain had agreed to it. "We know about what we think we can commit to," Knowlton said. "While some would say it is not the key point at the moment, ten dollars was the key issue when we started out. Whether it is or not now, we'll never find out."

"It's one of the issues, but you're comparing a highly profit-able [plant]," King quickly retorted. "I think you're doing great, but let's share that with the workers. You say you know what concessions are. What concessions have you made? Yourself per-sonally? I have! All our workers have! You haven't, so how do you understand what it's like when you bring back home a hundred less a week and you got all these payments to make? You don't know what it's like. I don't think you can understand that."

"Well, I'm sorry you feel that way, but I do and I can, and you will not change that," Knowlton responded matter-of-factly. "I can only say that given the circumstances with everyone in this industry, do you think I'd be a responsible executive if I sat there and approved of something that was going to take us down?" True, Hormel was profitable, but its profits from 1979 to 1984 had been essentially flat. Moreover, the company's return on eq-uity was only 13 percent, respectable among packers but well behind the Pillsburys and General Foods that the meat-packer was coming to regard as its competitors. It was no longer good enough for Hormel to be a sleepy small-town meat-packer, a breed that was becoming extinct. If Hormel were to prosper, it would have to mold itself into an aggressive consumer food company with high-margin brand-name products. Firms in that niche were generating 16 to 20 percent returns on equity and more. In other words, an investor choosing between the stock of Hormel and Pillsbury could earn a significantly better return by buying Pillsbury. And that limited Hormel's ability to raise funds for new plants, machinery, new products, and other improvements needed to maintain and expand its presence on the supermarket shelf. "Just because everybody else [in meat-packing] is failing doesn't mean that we're doing all that great a job," he said. All together, the $10 wage offer in Austin was part of a total compensation package valued at $19.60 an hour. Company-wide, labor was Hormel's second-largest expense after the cost of hogs. Hormel could not help paying the going rate for hogs, and sooner or later its higher labor costs would squeeze profits. "How good do you think we are?" Knowlton asked his fellow Austinite. "How long do you think we can go with that kind of a premise and not be jeopardizing the future of the company?"

King wasn't convinced, but the exchange had lasted more than ten minutes, and Knowlton tried to bring it to a halt so others could ask questions. King was through asking questions, but there was one more thing on his mind. He wanted to read from a statement he had prepared. Knowlton nodded his approval.

"This strike can go on longer. You can hurt us more and we can cost the Hormel Company more, by picketing other plants, as you can see. But let's not do that," King stammered. "I hurt every day when I see what is happening in our town and to its people, pitting neighbor against neighbor, friend against friend, and worker against worker. I think if you, Mr. Knowlton, have the power to tell your negotiating team to sit down and negotiate a just contract with our union, we can save this company a lot of money, we can get our good image back, and I can once again be a happy, loyal Hormel worker." He concluded by urging that the big slogan on the wall of the union hall—"United We Stand, Divided We Fall"—ought to apply to P-9 and Hormel together. The stockholders joined P-9's seven members in polite applause.

"I couldn't agree with you more, and I would like to have it that way," said Knowlton. "Our people feel that we've tried to get this resolved, and we don't see a willingness to find an end to it because the positions that were advanced before you went on strike included some things that just could not be tolerated. I can tell you honestly that I would rather have given you the keys and said, 'Here, go have fun,' rather than try and operate that plant with the proposal that was left."

"We don't want the world," King implored. "Just sit down and talk. Back and forth. Maybe take a week or two, but we'll come up with something. We don't want the world. Just sit down and talk, please!"

Then it was Guyette's turn. Dressed in one of his familiar cardigans and toting his ever-present yellow legal pad, he pressed Knowlton on the 1978 promise cited by King that Austin workers would never earn less than they had in the old plant. He said that the money workers had deferred in wages for the escrow accounts amounted to an interest-free loan that had helped the company finance the plant's construction.

Knowlton responded that Hormel paid a passbook savings rate of 6 percent compounded daily on money accumulating in escrow accounts. In fact, Hormel wound up paying workers back more than they collectively put in because wages still hadn't risen enough to compensate for their lost incentive pay.

Then Guyette asked how much Hormel was paying Thomas Krukowski, Hormel's attorney from Milwaukee. Krukowski's presence had become a fixation for P-9 members, who saw him as proof of the new, meanspirited Hormel bent on crushing the union. They also cited him to answer those who criticized the presence of an outsider like Rogers in Austin. If Hormel can get advice from a Milwaukee attorney, their logic went, why can't we hire a labor consultant from New York?

Knowlton said he didn't have the figures, adding that he didn't think it was important to stockholders anyway.

"I think it's very important," Guyette replied.

Knowlton's direct contact with Guyette had generally been limited to annual meetings. As much as he detested the union leader for his strategy, Knowlton tried to avoid publicly attacking his character, and never by name. The closest he came to faulting Guyette was in a newspaper story three months before the strike, when Knowlton called the P-9 leadership unenlightened. He was no Lee Iacocca, but now, with Guyette accusing the company of breaking the union, Knowlton had an opportunity in front of a friendly audience for a little lecturing. Had he accepted either the company's original offer or the mediator's proposal, Knowlton told Guyette, there would be a union contract in the Austin plant. "This is not a union-busting company," he declared, to the hearty applause of stockholders.

Guyette straightened his face and pressed on. Krukowski, he said, had a well-publicized reputation for busting meat-packing unions, and Hormel had sought him out in 1983. The cost for his services "is relative to the amount of damage that's been done today," Guyette said.

Knowlton responded that "it would be so infinitesimal compared with the damage that I think the leadership of P-9 has caused the company that it would not be worthy of the stockholders' time to examine it."

"Well, I'm a stockholder, and I would like to hear it," Guyette calmly replied.

Knowlton, growing increasingly frustrated, steered the question to Nyberg, seated at a table to his right. "Your premise is entirely wrong," the lawyer began. Krukowski, he said, was hired to provide legal help after P-9 had challenged the company's interpretation of the me-too clause that started the whole dispute in the fall of 1983. The clause directly addressed the notion, widely held by King, Guyette, and other veterans from the old plant, that they were guaranteed that wages in the new plant would never fall. However, an arbitrator ruled five times that Hormel's reading of the clause was right, that by contract with P-9, it had the right to reduce wages and benefits in accordance with industry patterns. "That's what the contract meant," Nyberg said. He also denied that Krukowski was hired to set up a union-busting plan. Turning the tables on Rogers, who was not at the meeting, Nyberg told Guyette, "You have retained a harassment, intimidation, and threat expert who has no peer anywhere in this country. I will refrain from calling him a company buster if you will refrain from calling our attorneys union busters."

Guyette kept plugging. "All right, irrespective of what they were hired for, how much is the company outlaying to that firm?"

Nyberg said he hadn't computed the figure, that the company

paid for its services by the hour to cover arbitrations, NLRB hearings, and court litigation.

"If I can't get the information at a stockholders' meeting, how can I get it?" Guyette asked.

"Well, I think it is totally irrelevant to what you're saying because we don't have any layout of any kind of any plan to bust the union," Nyberg said.

"Don't call it a plan to bust the union then, call it whatever you like," Guyette said, still showing patience at the mike. "How much has the company outlaid to that particular firm for services?"

"I cannot tell you that. I do not have it with me," Nyberg said.

"Does anybody have it?" Guyette asked.

"I'm sure that we've got figures someplace," Nyberg replied.

"Well, I'm sure that there's enough people here that could come up with the figures," the union leader said, looking around the room at board members and top management seated in the crowd. "I see all sorts of brass around here. I'm sure somebody's got the numbers someplace."

Nyberg threw up his hands and said nothing. Knowlton interjected, "Let me assure you, I don't."

The exchange ended with a smattering of laughter from the crowd. But that didn't diminish its significance. In fact, the confrontation went a long way toward explaining the stubbornness and distrust that had baffled even professional intermediaries like Paul Goldberg. A Hormel veteran like King could implore Knowlton to settle the strike personally, as if two old high school chums could end the dispute with a firm handshake. Knowlton, for his part, refused to put hometown sentiment above what he viewed as his company's survival. One hundred and sixty-five days into a strike that was tearing apart his union and his town, Guyette could use one of his only face-to-face meetings with the company chairman to press for a bookkeeping figure as if he could humiliate Hormel into changing course. Equally telling, the company refused to give a number and instead used the occasion to undress Guyette's logic.

A short time later up to the microphone stepped Don Erickson, who had felt compelled to travel eleven hundred miles to Houston to see a man that he didn't want to talk to. Knowlton and Erickson had been friends in Austin for a long time. When he wasn't working in the packinghouse, Erickson was a painter. Knowlton's wife,

Nancy, an art critic, had bought two of his earliest works. The Erickson family included five Hormel employees who had logged a collective 188 years of service to the company. One of them was his daughter, who came home with proud tears in her eyes on the day that she and her gang killed the two millionth hog in the new plant. The scene touched her father and made him realize that the good feeling about Hormel had been instilled in another generation. Like Dave King and other longtime employees, the balding, pleasant Erickson took pride in telling people he worked for Hormel. But the strike was changing all of that. When it was his turn to speak, he confronted Nyberg, who had been quoted a few weeks earlier as saying that P-9 members were like the "Jim Jones cult" that committed suicide in Guyana. "That hurt me," a shaken Erickson told the quiet crowd. "That would hurt every union man in the United States. Why would you say that?"

Nyberg, always measured and sure-sounding in fielding questions from the press, tried to explain himself. He told Erickson that as best he recalled, he had been asked how he could account for the tenacity and length of the dispute, the bitter raw feelings in Austin, and the staying power shown by followers of Rogers's corporate campaign. "And I said, 'I can't explain that. Neither can I explain why Jim Jones had a following in Guyana.' If that reflected adversely on you, I apologize for that, Don, because I wasn't referring to you. And I apologize to anyone who might have been offended by it. I guess if I had to do it over again, I would retract that statement. It was a strongly felt feeling at the time, I guess."

"Do you realize," Erickson went on, "what is happening to the employees that have crossed the picket line? The scars that are going to be left in the families and the children that have crossed over? They're a scab as far as the union's concerned, and that will live with them the rest of their life."

"Don, you refer to them as scabs—" Nyberg intoned.

"They are scabs!" he snapped back.

"We refer to them as our employees," the lawyer continued. "We pay their checks, we pay their benefits, and we care about them. And we care about you. Believe me, when somebody says they are not going to cross a picket line because there's some name of scab that's going to hang on them the rest of their lives, I regret that, too, because I wouldn't have any employee in that plant suffer if I had anything to say about it. But we didn't elect to go out on strike. We didn't elect to withhold our labor. You elected to withhold your labor. And you can elect to come back in. Those people who crossed that picket line to come back, I will say personally, I'm glad they're there. I hope that I am part of a rebuilding process in that plant, and I would hope that you would be, too. And again, I apologize if I offended you in any way."

"Well, you did offend me," Erickson replied. He also rebuked the company for complaining about not being able to get out of the corporate office for a hot meal because of the demonstrations. "That's part of this confrontation," he continued, "and only you, Dick, can solve it. We were on speaking terms, and I hope someday that we can get back."

"I hope we still are, Don," Knowlton answered. "I certainly don't have any personal offense in this."

A short time later Bruce Davidson, a Minnesota-born stockholder living in Houston, drew the day's loudest round of applause after congratulating management for its performance on and off the labor field. That prompted Erickson to get back up to the microphone.

"You know, we're not all bad," he said, smiling. "There isn't anybody any prouder of our company than we are. Or was, before this all happened. You know that yourself, Richard. We were proud. We were the best advertising you ever had." Then, gesturing around the room, he said, "This is our plant. I hope that we can overcome this. It's not insurmountable. We're a long ways away from each other, but it can be done. Thank you."

The shareholders applauded. "Good comment," said Knowlton.

An emotional King picked up on the same theme as he got in the final word.

"I believe in Hormel, and I've been Hormel for thirty-eight years," he told the shareholders. Then, to Knowlton: "I want you to direct those people . . . just sit down and talk with them," he said, pain showing in his voice as he threw up his hands. "You gotta start someplace, we're so far apart. Just sit down. Just talk. Thank you."

"Thank you, Dave," Knowlton said softly.

Even as King, Guyette, and Erickson were carrying the union's cause to Houston, more and more P-9 members back in Austin had decided that the cause was lost. The time had come for them to act on their own. With the fact finder's report drawing unflattering reviews and no new talks planned, that morning three hundred P-9 members crossed the picket line to return to work. If Austin was suffering from five and a half months without Hormel paychecks, the real and more enduring trauma was only beginning. The union that had once organized Austin "wall-to-wall" and brought home some of the fattest blue-collar paychecks in the nation was breaking apart before the omnipresent TV cameras. The same chasm that had opened between Dick Knowlton and Don Erickson was, in the few seconds it took to drive across a picket line, spreading all over town, straining relationships between schoolchildren, brothers and fathers, hunting partners, neighboring housewives, and hobbling retirees. "It is one thing to meet your opponent across the bargaining table," wrote resident sociologist Terry Dilley, who had taught nearly one third of P-9's members at the community college, "[but] something else to face an enemy across the supper table."

Two among the three hundred who crossed that morning were John Morrison and Ron Bergstrom. Five nights after pulling picket duty together in Morrison's brown Suburban truck, they had spoken again and made plans to return to work the next day. For both men, the decision capped a period of agony since Hormel had announced its plans to reopen. Morrison was by this time well known as a leader of the opposition, and his phone rang constantly with shaken P-9 members wanting to know if he planned to cross the picket line. Some of the callers urged him to organize a mass crossing. Others simply asked for his opinion, as if it would lend moral authority to their decision. He refused to organize anything and refused to give the callers any advice. From a practical standpoint, the last thing he needed was an opportunity for Guyette and Winkels to accuse him of busting the strike. From an ethical standpoint, Morrison knew this was a decision each union member must make alone.

So Morrison consulted his own heart, drove around Austin, hung around his house, and imagined his future without a job in the packinghouse. Morrison had run for union office in the past and aspired to try again. In that respect, to cross a picket line was suicide. And yet if he did not cross, and if no one else from P-9 crossed, there would be no picket line left. The packinghouse would fill up with farmers and transplants from Iowa, and he would spend the rest of his life knowing that somebody else was opening his locker every day just a mile away, doing his job, taking home his paycheck—all because of a bunch of union leaders he did not vote for, did not agree with, and could not stop. One day he came home so mad about the union and so frustrated about his own future that he lay down on the living-room couch and cried.

That night he wrote: "I may have to choose between a job that is easily replaced and my loyalty to unionism. I haven't lost hope that between now and the end of the week the union will take whatever action is necessary to save the union and our jobs. If the week should pass without some sort of compromise and the company starts to replace us, we will have lost more than our jobs. The threat of a non-union shop at Hormel would be almost a certainty. . . . Our local leadership and Ray Rogers are desperately clinging to a strategy that has failed."

He told himself this wasn't really a picket line in any meaningful sense. It was engineered by leaders who flouted their own union and fed on suicidal impulses. To cross this picket line would be to do the labor movement a favor and save Local P-9. And yet he didn't really buy it. How many other scabs in how many other strikes had rationalized their decisions the same way? He was doing this to save his job, his home, his family, and the life they had built.

Before dawn on Thursday, January 23, Morrison peered out his living room window to see Bergstrom and two old friends pull up. The four climbed into Morrison's wagon and drove across town to the packinghouse with filmmaker Barbara Kopple riding in the back seat. They dropped off Kopple at the freeway exit and headed down Fourteenth Avenue past a row of guardsmen and a phalanx of pickets. As they neared the gate, several people recognized Morrison and pleaded with him through the glass not to go through the line. He rolled down the window and shouted back that they would be better off coming in with him. They eased past the picket line and through the plant's north gate, trying to shut out the shouts of "Fucking scab!" hurled at their backs. When they had parked the truck and started across the big parking lot to the packinghouse entrance, Bergstrom could see a handful of supervisors standing in the doorway. He and Morrison reached the door, and the foremen patted them on the back and said they were glad to have them back. He glanced at Morrison and saw tears streaming down his cheeks.

Bergstrom didn't feel remorse that morning so much as anger at Guyette for putting him in this position. But anger didn't make his decision any easier. For Bergstrom, the stakes were personal as well as professional: When he when back to work, he left his brother R.J. on the other side of the picket line. Ron and R.J. had parted ways some years earlier. Ron enrolled at Mankato State University, seventy miles northwest of Austin, and spent four years earning a degree. R.J., two years behind Ron at Austin High, got his diploma, went into the U.S. Army, and then to Vietnam. While Ron got a good job dropping heads in the hog kill, R.J. came home from the war and kicked around in a series of construction jobs. When R.J. got hired at Hormel in September 1982, Ron felt relieved that they were back on the same footing. They remained hunting and hobby partners: R.J. helped Ron remodel his kitchen, and Ron made a hutch, a trestle table, and a pair of benches for R.J.'s kitchen. They went pheasant hunting together in the fall of 1984, but it was clear that they didn't see eye to eye about their union. R.J. thought Ray Rogers promised a way of teaching Hormel a lesson. Ron was skeptical of Rogers and thought it foolish to flout the UFCW's advice.

Then one day, Ron discovered that R.J. was becoming a regular in the corporate campaign ranks. The pair of coveralls R.J. had plastered with HORMEL UNFAIR bumper stickers had made him something of a celebrity; he became a walking picket sign who turned up in countless newspaper pictures and television clips. When the plant reopened, a reporter learned that the highly visible R.J. had a brother who had crossed the picket line, he talked R.J. into giving an interview. That night Ron watched as his brother disowned him on national television.

On R.J.'s part, the strike had been especially difficult. He didn't have the long years of Hormel paychecks to build up a nest egg. Now one of his neighbors had crossed the picket line, and R.J.'s oldest daughter had to ride the school bus every day hearing the neighbor girl talk about the family's new car and VCR. R.J. thought he was going to throw up the day he learned that Ron crossed the picket line. Getting up every morning and eating breakfast on the table his brother had built didn't make things any easier.

Their feud hadn't mellowed even three months after Ron first returned to work. One Sunday morning near Easter Ron looked out his window to see R.J. pulling up the driveway with a load of furniture in the back of his pickup truck. It was the trestle table, hutch, and benches Ron had made for him. R.J. climbed out of the truck and told Ron he didn't want the furniture in his house anymore. Ron asked if R.J. wanted a hand unloading them. R.J. replied that he'd better help, unless Ron wanted them dumped on his lawn.

Gerald Henricks was grappling with the same dilemma as Morrison and Ron Bergstrom. On the contract issues Henricks believed in his union's position. The work pace, job standards, safety, wages, and attitudes between labor and management—all needed improvement from what had been proposed before the strike began. But after Hormel sent out letters in early January telling workers that the plant was reopening, the eighteen-year employee started asking himself questions. "Is the corporate campaign succeeding? Is there any hope that it will succeed? Are union negotiators making realistic demands? Are they making any progress? Is the company showing any sign of being influenced by Rogers or Guyette? Is there any way I'll be able to keep my job?" The answers kept coming back in the negative. Henricks asked himself, "Is Guyette going to make any changes in his strategy?" On the basis of his view of the union leader, he thought the only plausible answer was no.

Henricks had been cool toward the campaign since Rogers first showed up. Still, he knew the meaning of democracy and majority rule, and he kept his dissent to himself. As an Austin City Council member, he felt he had to remain neutral. A month after Rogers's arrival, he went so far as to author a council resolution urging Hormel and P-9 to meet with a federal mediator to resolve their differences. During the strike Henricks stayed away from picket duty, instead volunteering behind the scenes in the union's kitchen and helping process unemployment applications.

He had looked for other work, but turned up little. He was forty-one years old, armed with a bachelor's degree in business from Mankato State University that he earned the past June. Now it was January, and he had to consider his own situation. He had three children, all excellent students, and hoped to put the eldest in college in three years. The past five months had consumed most of the family savings from what had been a $25,000-a-year job packaging grocery products and a $3,000 annual salary as a council member. Despite his new academic credentials, the only person who would hire him during the holidays was his wife, who paid him $3.35 an hour to help her run a Hickory Farms gift kiosk in Oak Park Mall. They discussed looking for work in California or Arizona because as much as they wanted to stay in their hometown, they were getting realistic, too. Jerry planned a western trip for the first week of January but scrapped it when the mediator's proposal surfaced as a possible settlement.

If they stayed in Austin and he went back to Hormel, there were other considerations as well. Henricks's father had worked for Hormel for forty years, a time during which he and his union co-workers had built up some of the best packinghouse contracts in the industry. The thought of abandoning that union, where Henricks himself had served as a department steward, sickened him. The implications for getting elected again bothered him less. In 1984 he had run for mayor but been defeated by Kough. Going back to work would destroy any chance of holding public office. People would look at him as betraying a concept, he thought, as someone who couldn't be trusted. As he talked it over with his wife, Susan, however, he concluded that his political career was not nearly as important as his family's survival.

If Henricks had any doubt at all about what to do, it was clinched by the sight of Morrison getting slugged and thrown out of the union meeting on January 8. As the strike had worn on, Henricks quietly aligned himself with the Morrison-led P-10 faction. Now he was convinced that if someone could not express an opposing opinion during a union meeting without being accosted, then freedom of choice was gone. The democratic process was not working. He and the other P-10ers were openly frightened by the intimidation, interruption, hissing, booing, and physical confrontations inspired by rowdy Guyette supporters. Few had Morrison's guts to take them on physically, and no one thought more confrontation would settle anything. Certainly a union that believes in collective bargaining could tolerate diversity of opinion, he thought, but apparently this one could not.

Less than a week later, on the third day after the plant reopened, Henricks joined a car pool of P-10ers and rode to the picket line. He was going back to reclaim his job, he rationalized, not take someone else's. He did not try to hide his face. As he neared the gate, he was immediately recognized by friends, coworkers from his department, and other good people whom he had grown to respect. As he passed through the line, they swore at him, yelled insults, and cussed at him some more. Henricks, a Sunday school superintendent at Faith Evangelical Lutheran Church, tried to remain proud. Though the insults stung, he felt no shame or urge to apologize.

In the days that followed, he drew icy stares from longtime P-9 friends and drinking buddies around town. To them, Henricks was the lowest form of life. Henricks tried not to hold a grudge against them. They were committed to their philosophy, and he respected them for that. "Their opinion is that they're winning; my opinion is that we are not," he said several days later. "We have that right to differ."

With the departure of union members like Morrison, Ron Bergstrom, and Henricks, pressure intensified on those who stayed on strike but who also had doubts about P-9's strategy. In the absence of a total collapse by Guyette's supporters, which seemed unthinkable at the time, there were now a dwindling number of critics left on the inside to marshal support for a new direction. As a result, P-9 seemed to grow more unified even as its ranks—and the town—were splitting in two.

But looks within the union were deceiving. If the P-10ers represented a minority of union members, so did the loudest and most visible advocates of the union's all-or-nothing course. Somewhere in the background, usually out of sight of the TV cameras and press conferences, the rest of the union members weighed their options in silence. They quietly pulled picket duty, gathered to drink coffee and tell stories in living rooms and kitchens, anguished for hours on the telephone, hung out in mechanics' garages during the day, and dropped in at the union hall for moral support. Many joined "The Pepsi Club," a group that met every morning at Lefty's for soft drinks and conversation about anything on their minds. Their hearts were undoubtedly on the sanctioned side of the picket line, but their minds longed to be back at work. They were not a united group at all, and their numbers were difficult to assess; but it's safe to say that they probably accounted for the majority of those still on strike.

Some were aligned in their bitterness against Wynn and the UFCW, which seemed to be choking them off by sanctioning the Austin picket line but doing nothing either to support the roving pickets or to keep the local from splintering. As they saw it, the UFCW authorized the strike, allowed four months to pass, and then helped negotiate an offer that wasn't even good enough to recommend for approval. Instead of forcing Hormel back to the table, Wynn was publicly ripping Guyette and Rogers, further alienating himself from the rank and file. If the Washington bigshot was so concerned about the people in Austin, why was he letting them bleed instead of stepping in to take control before all the jobs were gone?

Others vented their anger at Hormel for forcing a showdown that had poisoned the community. After acceding to a city request to house the National Guard, St. Edwards Catholic Church was dubbed Fort Edwards. Two dozen union families stopped attending Sunday mass. A walkout by students at Austin High School and Ellis Middle School drew charges and countercharges from parents protesting and supporting the idea of dragging children into the fight. Shoppers changed aisles to avoid passing each other in grocery stores. Women supporting the strike hissed "scab" at retirees' wives who bought Hormel hams and bacon. One striker stopped to pull a stranded motorist out of a snowy highway ditch, then drove away without helping when the driver told him he was a replacement worker. The Austin *Daily Herald* was filled with screeching letters attacking everyone involved in the strike. City council meetings exploded into tense showdowns between boisterous strike supporters wearing their blue hats and P-9 buttons and a frightened band of white-collar residents sporting stickers on their shirts and jackets proclaiming HERE WE GO! AUSTIN! Strikers posted signs at the plant gates designating various returning P-9ers as "Scab of the Week." As much abuse as the returning workers and replacements endured, those loyally pulling picket duty became the targets of nasty intimidation as well, drawing taunts and jeers from cocky workers backed by guardsmen. The most ardent P-9ers quickly identified bars that served scabs, designated them for boycotts, and organized occasional "bar-cleaning" missions to chase out replacement workers.

Another loosely organized faction took on Guyette and the board, urging them to change course and mend their split with the international before the battle was hopelessly lost. To them, it simply was not good unionism to bash fellow members in public, especially when it deflected attention away from the common enemy, Hormel. While these strikers certainly had no love for the UFCW's approach to the strike, they had grown equally frustrated by the board's inability to make Hormel negotiate. Late in the fall they actually urged some board members to bring in a fresh bargaining committee, a team of relief pitchers to help overcome the company's open disdain for Guyette. But the suggestion received a chilly reception from those who feared it would show weakness within the union. The nine-member board was seldom unanimous, but the skeptics, led by veteran Keith Judd, never mounted a serious threat to the Guyette-Rogers strategy.

As the strike wore on, P-9 also had developed a faction that wanted to dump Rogers. Early on they were tolerant and even supportive of his gutsy approach, and they never doubted that he had given P-9 its money's worth. But now they feared that he had overstayed his usefulness, that the corporate campaign was failing or, even worse, had become a deterrent to progress in negotiations. Critics saw Rogers looking more and more like a businessman first, their friend second. Especially frustrating was his use of sixties-style civil rights techniques that seemed to bring him more attention and cause P-9 more trouble. Rogers had delivered beautifully on his promise to make P-9's fight a nationally known cause. But now there was a contract to settle, and like it or not, Hormel had made him the main obstacle. Under those circumstances, these quiet skeptics saw little remaining leverage in Rogers's approach, especially when he was telling them to lie down on an icy street and dare cars and trucks to run them over.

To Larry Jensen, division within the ranks was no way to fight a battle on behalf of the entire labor movement. And it certainly was not going to win a good contract in Austin. Once the plant reopened, Jensen brought a handful of members in to see Guyette and urge him to save the union and their jobs before it was too late. Dozens more were too scared to say anything. One man who proposed at a union meeting that P-9 patch up its differences with the international was showered with boos. A group trying to force a vote on the fact finder's report got into a shouting match with Guyette. Critics were labeled assholes and Communists. As supporters from Europe and across the country poured into Austin, the strike became a battle against oppression in South Africa and Afghanistan. The pay hike and improved working conditions for which Jensen had gone on strike were getting shoved into a corner.

In reality, the differences of opinion within P-9 were so blurred and so mercurial that they scarcely could be recognized at all. The common denominator was bitterness. Despite their differences, all the remaining strikers had made the decision to honor the picket line. It might cost them their jobs, but they simply would not cross the picket line as long as it was sanctioned by the international. Whether out of loyalty to the union or fear of retribution, they appeared as solid as Guyette's core followers. But almost six months into the strike they were tiring of speeches by out-of-towners and soup lunches in the union hall. They wanted to see whatever it would take to get movement at the bargaining table that would save their union and get them back their jobs.

It seemed so simple. But it was impossible. With their convictions being held under a national microscope, Hormel, P-9, and the international were not going to back down. The people getting gored were all over Austin, like Jensen, unable to retreat, unwilling to surrender.

The picket line in Austin offered mixed signals about who was winning. With replacements getting hired at a rate of fifty a day, the work force had grown to more than six hundred by the last week in January. The day after the annual meeting, Hormel announced plans to stop hiring when employment hit 1,025, nearly the number of workers it had when the plant first opened in 1982.

But the rules at the gates were about to change. As P-9 turned its attention to picket lines at other plants, the disturbances in

Austin grew quiet. The sight of dozens of helmeted guardsmen taking their shifts alongside three or four peaceful strikers smacked of overkill. In St. Paul Governor Perpich was under mounting pressure from political friends in the labor movement to call off the Guard. They may have disagreed with P-9's strategy, but they couldn't stand by while replacement workers were escorted across the picket line. Each morning about a dozen P-9 retirees camped out in the governor's reception room at the State Capitol, vowing to continue their vigil until the Guard was gone. Other Twin Cities supporters held noisy protests outside the governor's mansion on St. Paul's fashionable Summit Avenue. Perhaps the most legitimate complaints came from residents who lived near the plant but had no connection to the strike. Because the Guard had cordoned off several streets, these homeowners were in effect held hostage in their own driveways, unable to leave home without taking a Byzantine detour through the north side of town.

Most of the outcry in Austin was directed at Mayor Kough, who had been roundly criticized by some of his own members for his role in calling for the Guard. His kitchen telephone rang constantly day and night as frightened and angry constituents pleaded with him to do something. P-9 members implored him to get Perpich to remove the Guard, while others who feared a union outburst demanded that he place public safety ahead of his union loyalties. Kough knew he couldn't make everyone happy, but he was determined to press for something that would clear the streets at least so residents nearest the plant could move about freely.

On Monday, January 27, Kough drove to St. Paul to meet with legislators and press his case to have the Guard removed. The next day he delivered a letter to Perpich requesting that the Guard be moved "from blocking the city streets which infringe [*sic*] upon the rights of our citizens." He also wrote that "under no circumstances am I asking you to remove the guard at this time."

That same day Perpich met with Public Safety Commissioner Tschida and several key legislators. At 5:00 P.M. Kough called and reiterated his request. According to Perpich aides, Kough made it clear that he wanted the Guard away from the plant gates. Kough later said his only intention was to clear the streets so that residents near the plant could move freely. Whatever the intent, a frustrated Perpich decided that night to honor Kough's request and withdraw the Guard to the Austin Armory and St. Edwards School. The decision was not made public until 7:00 A.M. on Wednesday, when guardsmen quietly cleared the plant gates and drove away. For the first time in eight days Austin no longer looked like a town under siege.

But any sense of calm that may have been inspired by the move was embroiled in controversy before the morning was over.

Sheriff Goodnature lashed out at Kough for trying to assert authority that legally belonged to the county's top cop—namely, Goodnature. Police Chief Hoffman feared a repeat of the demonstration that triggered the Guard's presence in the first place. He knew that before the Guard was pulled back, Guyette had issued a call for union supporters nationwide to converge on Austin for a massive show of support. The chief also knew that when Guyette and Rogers asked for support, they got it. Kough claimed Perpich had misunderstood him. The mayor said later that he wanted troops left at the gates, while still allowing residents easier access to their homes. But Perpich, miffed by Kough's equivocations, refused to change his mind and left the gates in the control of local officials.

The lawmen's consternation, however, paled in comparison with the howls of protest from Hormel executives. Arnold blasted Kough for letting his union sympathies interfere with his duties as mayor. Knowlton went to St. Paul to meet with Perpich and Paul Tschida to vent his personal opposition to pulling back the guard.

As pickets in Austin prepared to receive outside reinforcements that same week, the roving pickets fanned out to nine Hormel plants, from Iowa to Texas and up through California and Washington. They remained most effective in Ottumwa, where most of the plant stood idle because half of 900 workers stayed out—and lost their jobs. In the 950-employee Fremont plant, the hesitation shown by the roving pickets a week earlier continued to plague P-9, as support slipped from 68 workers who honored the line on Monday to about 50 by the end of the week. At FDL

Foods in Dubuque, 90 of 1,200 employees stayed out on Monday, but the figure dropped to 40 later in the week. The pickets had only sporadic impact at smaller plants in Houston; Dallas; Seattle; Beloit, Wisconsin; Algona, Iowa; and La Miranda, California.

On Thursday, January 30, three days after Hormel announced the massive firings, another fifty P-9 members returned to work in Austin, uncontested by pickets. With the Guard pulled back, the gates were patrolled only by Austin police. But word had spread through town that a huge demonstration, "a special kind of early-morning rally" Rogers called it, was percolating for early Friday. With waves of union supporters expected from out of town, Arnold advised workers to listen to the radio for instructions about reporting to work, and to return home if the situation turned ugly. Goodnature, Hoffman, and Kough repeated their joint plea for the Guard. But this time Perpich, under pressure from labor leaders and state legislators for his actions the week before, turned them down.

At the same time international President Wynn released a letter to the media that blasted Guyette for jeopardizing the jobs of union members in Ottumwa, Fremont, and Dallas. But with a twenty-thousand-dollar donation from the Minnesota Teamsters coming in, and a ten-thousand-dollar food caravan from Oscar Mayer workers in Madison, Wisconsin, Guyette dismissed such analysis from someone he described as an armchair quarterback. To give up now, he told reporters, would be a tragedy.

True to predictions, Friday morning turned into another massive demonstration. By 5:30 A.M. five hundred supporters, half from other unions in Minnesota, South Dakota, and Wisconsin, had blocked freeway ramps and gates to the packinghouse and corporate office. Authorities chose not to confront anyone and withdrew. Most employees stayed home, so the scene was mostly devoid of violence or confrontation. But it infuriated Hormel executives. Only about fifty of six hundred corporate office employees made it to work before the demonstrators arrived. One woman scrambled over a chain-link fence, company officials pulling at her arms while pickets grabbed at her legs. A group of P-9 wives stood at the locked gates and demanded to have a letter delivered to Arnold, but no one from the company came out to accept it. The gates remained locked most of the day because police and sheriff's deputies felt they were unable to guarantee safe passage. Hormel officials angrily denounced the scene as "every man for himself." Goodnature blasted Perpich for letting politics permit what he called mob rule.

Perpich had seen enough. After conferring with Minnesota's top labor leaders that morning, he summoned the P-9 executive board to a closed-door meeting in Goldberg's office at eight-thirty on Friday night. The membership was scheduled to consider voting on the fact finder's report the following night, and Perpich wanted one more shot to push it through and avoid catastrophic job losses. He brought along one of the state's biggest labor guns, Bob Killeen, subregional director of the United Auto Workers, hoping his presence would sober up the executive board. Also attending were the UFCW's Joe Hansen; state mediator Paul Goldberg; Jill Leeds Rivera, his principal mediator; Terry Montgomery, Perpich's chief of staff; and Gerry Nelson, the governor's communications director. A heavy snowfall made for difficult driving from Austin, and only a partial contingent of board members—Guyette, Winkels, and newcomers Kathy Buck and Carl Pontius—showed up by nine o'clock.

Perpich opened the meeting by telling of his family's labor history on the Iron Range and how his father, a union member, was beaten up for standing up for his beliefs. He laid out his pro-labor record as a legislator and governor, citing his involvement in reaching settlements at Northwest Airlines and the Boise Cascade lumber company. He also talked about his losses as a politician, from his days as a school board member in Hibbing, Minnesota, to his embattled tenure as governor. He talked about hardship on the range, where steel industry cutbacks had left thousands of union laborers without jobs, creating depression that rivaled the woes in the Rust Belt. Along with Guyette's members, they were once the best-paid blue-collar workers in America, but now they had nothing. P-9 members still had a chance. Perpich pleaded with the board to avoid a similar fate. He told Guyette that he was a leader, someone on whom people depended, and that he had to put his personal feelings aside and do what was best for his members. There comes a time, he said, when you accept what is, go back to work, and live to fight another day.

Guyette replied that there was nothing to settle, that Hormel's proposal was worse than nothing. With Hormel refusing to budge, the union had only one choice: shutting down the company and forcing it to negotiate. The union's position was right.

Perpich replied that he didn't want to hear about what was right and what was wrong. P-9 was past that point.

Then Killeen jumped in. He told Guyette that there were times when he didn't have to be a winner, times when he had to figure out how to get his people back to work. He urged Guyette to lead his people back, even without a contract, and work out the problems later.

But one by one, Winkels, Guyette, and Buck defended P-9's position. Support for their battle was building, as evidenced by the shutdown at Ottumwa and at other plants. Coupling those with the shutdown at Austin that day, Guyette claimed that P-9 had shut down 75 percent of Hormel's production capacity.

Finally, Hansen couldn't take it anymore. Either P-9's roving scouts were calling in false reports from Fremont and the other plants, he said, or Guyette was making it up. This led to a testy exchange between Hansen and Guyette over whether Ottumwa was actually shut down. Hormel had not yet started rehiring after the mass firings. By the end of the week, however, the company claimed the plant was running at 33 percent of capacity, without the labor-intensive and often unprofitable kill-and-cut operation. To make up the difference, all Hormel had to do was buy raw pork cuts from other packers, most of them paying workers less than Hormel paid in Ottumwa. Moreover, Hormel had shown during the fall that it could turn record profits, even without Austin, by relocating equipment and stepping up production at other plants. For the first time in the long dispute Hansen completely lost his temper. He denounced Guyette as a union buster for, in effect, costing hundreds of UFCW members their jobs. Guyette's face turned red, and according to those at the meeting, he came as close to losing his cool as at any time in the long dispute. But he stood his ground.

The meeting adjourned shortly before 11:00 P.M. Perpich emerged looking somber and weary. "We'd just like to see the issue resolved," he told a reporter waiting outside the office. He termed the next seventy-two hours critical but said he didn't have a clue to whether P-9 would heed his plea to accept the Zack report. Goldberg had handed the union leaders several NLRB rulings as well as a Supreme Court decision upholding the hiring of permanent replacements. But he was equally perplexed. "Progress, movement, I'm not sure what those terms mean at this point," he said with a look of resignation. "They were deliberative, they listened well, and I don't know what more we can ask."

Guyette was not persuaded. He made it clear that his feelings about the fact finder's report had not changed. It simply didn't address the union's concerns. P-9 would press its battle on the national stage, with a goal of disrupting Hormel's marketing. No longer was it a fight over sixty-nine cents an hour, he said. If Hormel was intent on destroying its work force and the union, P-9 would fight until it had a fair contract reflective of the most profitable company in the industry.

It quickly became clear that neither side was interested in Perpich's efforts at conciliation. The next morning, smarting from the loss of plant operations on Friday, Hormel reopened the packinghouse. A Saturday shift was a common practice during normal times, but in the heat of the strike it struck Tschida as an unnecessary provocation. P-9 was happy to fight back. Austin police didn't expect a confrontation, with the plant not slated for weekend operation during the strike, so about seventy-five demonstrators faced little opposition as they pounded on cars and slashed tires of workers who tried to cross the picket line. When police reinforcements arrived nearly an hour later, officers had to drag people out of the street. The small rowdy group did more damage than all five hundred people had done the day before. Afterward, Hoffman promised that local authorities would start using stronger tactics to combat picket line intimidation.

That night nearly a thousand union members turned out at a rank-and-file meeting and, in a voice vote that Guyette proclaimed an overwhelming majority, rejected Zack's fact-finding report without putting it to a secret ballot. There would be no third vote on the mediator's proposal. The jubilant strikers emerged from the meeting poised for more battle. With all the P-10ers out of the union, they gave every appearance of a union united and confident of victory.

With the splintering of P-9 virtually complete, the potential for trouble on the picket line looked greater than ever. Tschida went down to Austin on Sunday to meet with Neil Haugerud, a former legislator in the area who was now one of his top assistants in the Department of Public Safety. Haugerud had been stationed in Austin since the National Guard's second day, mixing with people in the union hall and corporate office and acting as Tschida's personal representative. Haugerud and the police were turning up rumors of another demonstration brewing for Monday morning. The speculation apparently came from union members who were convinced that Perpich, under escalating pressure from his Iron Range constituents, would not call out the Guard again. Even more troubling, however, that night rumors began circulating that returning workers, fed up with the abuse they took from the strikers, were arming themselves with baseball bats and planned to fight their way into the plant if necessary. The rumor seemed even more plausible when authorities verified that one of the workers had a lathe set up in his basement that could turn out wooden clubs. There also were reports that workers had been sighted loading their car trunks with shotguns and rifles.

It was well past midnight Sunday when Tschida and top officials sat in the Law Enforcement Center and mulled over the possibilities. Did they have to wait until violence broke out? If the demonstrators took the gate, how much blood would be shed to get it back? How real were the ones? Separating fact from fiction was nearly impossible in the gossip-ridden town, but authorities felt obligated to take rumors seriously and check out what they could. Sometimes they turned up bizarre ones, including a report that a guerrilla team would storm the corporate office to damage Hormel's computers and sabotage its marketing. But baseball bats and shotguns were easier to believe, and Tschida decided that enough of what he had heard was real. At 4:00 A.M. three hundred national guardsmen were dispatched from their command post at the armory back to the north gates of the plant. When daylight broke a few hours later, hundreds of workers streamed across the picket line uncontested.

CHAPTER

15

If January was the month of agony in the union households of Austin, February was the month of agony for Joe Hansen a hundred miles north at the UFCW regional office in Bloomington. The plant gate skirmishes continued, but Hansen could see that they were becoming futile exercises in spite. With the return of the Guard on Monday morning, February 3, the plant opened successfully and would remain open. Later that day Mower County Judge Bruce Stone found Guyette, Rogers, and Corporate Campaign guilty of contempt of court for violating his order to limit pickets at the packinghouse. If they didn't obey, Stone said, he would impose fines and jail sentences. Three days later the strikers staged another demonstration. Police arrested Rogers and twenty-six others, hauling them away in handcuffs. Most were slapped with minor charges relating to civil disobedience, but Rogers was charged with criminal syndicalism, an obscure felony left on Minnesota's law books since a red scare in 1919. (It was another historical irony of the strike: Frank Ellis had been jailed on a similar charge in Nebraska in the 1920's. He, too, thought unions could win by packing jail cells full of protestors. In Rogers's case, the law later was found unconstitutional and repealed by the 1987 state legislature.) And a few days later, reinforced by supporters from around the state, the strikers

staged another demonstration, this time with 120 vocal supporters.

But the demonstrators simply were no match for the National
Guard, and with Rogers preaching nonviolence, they did little
more than slow traffic and holler new insults. It was clear that
Perpich, exasperated by Guyette's insistence on total victory, intended to keep the Guard in Austin until Police Chief Don
Hoffman and County Sheriff Wayne Goodnature could maintain
order. At a cost of fifty thousand to sixty thousand dollars a day,
taxpayers wouldn't support the Guard's presence indefinitely,
however, so he directed local officials to devise a plan to handle
future demonstrations on their own. Meanwhile, P-9's appeals in
Austin and the surrounding communities were widely ignored.
Hundreds of workers from southern Minnesota and northern
Iowa flocked to the plant for a chance to earn eight dollars an
hour. By this time they weren't as frightened of the crowds, and
they certainly weren't ashamed of their actions. "If they don't
want to work for eight dollars an hour, I sure do," a young farmer
said into a television camera one morning on his way into the
plant.

Indeed, some farmers around Austin were hoping quietly that
the union would hold out longer so that more hard-pressed farmers could take the jobs. That hadn't been the case in 1933, when
the fledgling union forged alliances with farmers struggling
through the Depression to keep Hormel from hiring scabs. But
this was 1986, and while unions had made tremendous economic
strides to raise the workers' standard of living, many farmers
were still fighting to make it. The P-9ers did get support from a
hundred farmers who drove their tractors to the picket line
during the Guard's first week in Austin. Like most of the union's
demonstrations, however, the farmers made for good video but
did little to stop the rehiring. They were mostly members of
groups aligned with the radical American Agriculture Movement,
a populist farm organization that caught the nation's attention in
the mid-1970's by dumping milk in Washington, and in the
eighties with Depression-style rallies to stop farm foreclosures.

P-9's leaders, however, kept plugging away. Buoyed by their
members' spunk, they were convinced that they had more leverage than Hormel, the UFCW, and the media gave them credit for.

On February 11 Guyette and the executive board sat down briefly with Hormel's negotiators for one last stab at a settlement. They were prepared to give ground on wages and said they would settle for $10.05 an hour, just a nickel more than the company had offered. But they attached a dramatic condition: Hormel must rehire all the strikers immediately, as well as the 480 people fired in Ottumwa. It was an utterly perplexing move, considering that the strike was six months old, Hormel had hired hundreds of permanent replacements, and P-9's bargaining power was down to zero. Lewie Anderson and Al Zack were beside themselves. If P-9 had made that offer in the summer of 1984, they calculated, the strike could have been avoided, the Ottumwa workers would still have their jobs, and perhaps the whole chain could have settled together. Dave Larson viewed it more suspiciously. He saw it as a deliberate attempt to malign the company and garner more ammunition for a mass union solidarity rally the following Saturday at the high school. Union members could climb on stage and crow to the labor world that P-9 had offered to go back for Hormel's wage offer and the company still refused to budge. He didn't know whether to laugh or cry. "It's a little late, fellas," he told the board members. "We don't have any jobs left."

Two days later, one full month after reopening the packinghouse, Hormel announced that it had reached its hiring goal of 1,025 workers and that no jobs remained. Approximately 460 P-9ers had crossed their own picket line. Hormel had hired another 565 replacements. While the work force was at least 400 workers below the level when the strike started, it was almost identical to the work complement Hormel had specified in its original labor contracts for the new plant. With Hormel moving out equipment to replace lost production during the strike, some 400 jobs had disappeared from Austin. For all practical purposes, with the plant in full operation, the strike appeared over.

The defeat was not lost on outside observers. In an editorial published on February 14, 1986, *The New York Times* wrote, "The sad and highly publicized failure of a strike by Minnesota meatpackers against Hormel is costing most of the workers their jobs. Less a labor action than a defiant shaking of fists at large economic forces, it resembled the demonstrations by farmers trying to keep banks from repossessing their land. It was no more effective."

The very next day in Austin, however, it was hard to believe that the newspaper was talking about the same union. More than three thousand P-9 supporters from across the country marched from the Labor Center down Main Street to a stirring rally at the high school auditorium. Led by a full color guard, a grand marshal, and Austin Mayor Tom Kough, they carried signs, flags, and banners representing health care and communications workers from New York, steelworkers from Pittsburgh and the Iron Range, bakery workers from Detroit, autoworkers from Pontiac, Michigan, and St. Paul, electrical workers from Philadelphia, flight attendants from San Francisco, and musicians from Los Angeles. These weren't just token representatives, but dozens of people sporting union jackets and P-9 buttons, East Coast accents mingling with midwestern drawls, united under the leaden gray skies, their nonstop chants of "You say give back, we say fight back!" resounding through the otherwise silent streets. Stenciled black-and-white signs read JAY HORMEL CARED, while others took aim at the new work force in the plant: PICK A SCAB, MAKE IT BLEED. Once the crowd had entered the old auditorium, the walls thundered with standing ovations and chants of "P-9! P-9! P-9!" as speaker after speaker delivered emotional accolades and blasted all the institutions—the courts, the police, the media, the governor, and the international—that had betrayed P-9. "This rank and file is the litmus test for all of organized labor," called out Henry Nicholas, president of the National Union of Hospital and Health Care Employees in New York. "I didn't come here for a wake," bellowed Ron Wiesen, a stocky steelworkers' president from Pittsburgh. "If it wasn't for the National Guard, this strike would have been won," Bob Brown, an electrical workers' vice-president from Philadelphia, told the cheering throng. When one speaker mentioned the five hundred workers fired from Local 431 in Ottumwa, the graceful old theater exploded with the loudest ovation of the afternoon and chants of "Four-three-one! Four-three-one! Four-three-one!" A Los Angeles musician vowed to line up John Cougar Mellencamp for a benefit concert. Nicholas called the P-9 fight "the crucifixion that will later become a resurrection that will redirect the labor movement."At the end of the rally there were a dozen union leaders on the old wooden stage, representing workers from across the nation, their hands clasped, arms triumphantly upraised, with Jim Guyette in the middle in his ever-present cardigan and cowboy boots, smiling broadly. In the wings of the stage stood Ray Rogers looking equally pleased with the emotional outpouring of support.

But that same weekend in Bal Harbour, Florida, Bill Wynn denounced P-9's strategy as a con consisting of "rallies, balloons and lots of hot air" in a letter circulated at a meeting of the AFl-CIO's executive council. P-9's members "have become cannon fodder for a self-proclaimed master strategist bent on attaining symbolic victory or glorious defeat at the expense of hundreds of workers' jobs, divided families, a broken community and labor solidarity," he wrote. "Never in my experience as a union representative has a better group of members been so poorly served by inexperienced, inflexible local union representatives." During the course of the convention Guyette demanded and received a personal audience with AFL-CIO President Lane Kirkland. But Kirkland denied Guyette's request for a meeting with the federation's executive council, saying the dispute was an internal matter for the UFCW to decide.

Hormel's announcement that the plant was full only increased the agonizing for Wynn, Lewie Anderson, and Joe Hansen. A fully staffed packinghouse in Austin changed the stakes of the battle. Until January P-9 was simply a rogue local pursuing ambitious goals and disagreeing vocally with the UFCW leadership. Now P-9 was costing the UFCW real losses. Nearly a thousand UFCW members had lost their jobs in Austin, apparently for good. Another five hundred were out of work in Ottumwa and Fremont, also for good. Perhaps worse, union members were now a minority inside the Austin plant, and the UFCW was in danger of losing representation rights there. Under federal labor law, a union earns bargaining rights by demonstrating that a majority of employees wants its representation. It retains those bargaining rights by maintaining a majority and keeping them under a signed labor contract. But if the labor contract expires, employees are free to petition for an election to decertify the union. Although Hormel had imposed its own work rules and wages in the plant, there was no signed labor agreement, and the UFCW was vulnerable to a decertification.

The prospect made Wynn, Anderson, and Hansen nervous. The UFCW could lose the biggest packinghouse of the most profitable employer in the pork industry. In fact, rumors were sweeping the plant that someone was actually circulating a "decert" petition. The nonunion replacements, heckled and threatened on their way across the picket line each morning, made no secret of their bitterness toward unions. Others were getting phone calls at home in the evening inviting them to sign a petition that would pull P-9 out of the UFCW. Suddenly Wynn and Anderson could imagine a disastrous scenario: Austin goes nonunion, leaving Hormel to impose lower wages, streamlined work rules, watered-down seniority and grievance procedures, and reduced fringe benefits. With the Austin plant running under a management-imposed contract, Hormel would have enormous leverage going into negotiations with its six other chain plants in the summer of 1986. If the other packinghouses went on strike, Hormel could double the production levels at Austin and essentially starve out strikers at the other plants. Hormel could then drive down wages and working conditions throughout the chain. The whipsawing effect would leave the UFCW facing new concession demands from less profitable packers such as Morrell, Wilson, and Swift.

For Hansen, the agony was much more immediate. Every day he fielded phone calls from frantic P-9 members in Austin. It was always the same question: "Can't I cross the picket line and get my job back?" After all, the callers reasoned, the UFCW didn't support Guyette and Rogers; this was scarcely a sanctioned picket line. Hansen was in a box. A strike is a union's ultimate weapon, and a picket line is the only way to enforce it. As a career union officer he could not tell his members to cross a sanctioned picket line. Yet telling them to honor it was dooming them to the loss of their jobs. It was the opposite of everything that had led him into the labor movement in the first place.

Hansen later called it the most frustrating experience of his life. He was no fan of Hormel, and he respected the militance of P-9's members. At the same time he had never seen a union local defy its parent union so brazenly and so capably. Now his members in Austin were losing their jobs. Incredibly enough, the UFCW could lose Hormel. The UFCW had lost most of its support in Austin. The militants despised Hansen as a sellout; the moderates were upset that he didn't do more. Those in between—who honored the picket line even if they weren't fans of Guyette—could only wonder why he was leaving them in limbo. One of the biggest packinghouse locals was spinning out of control, and yet the UFCW was flummoxed.

The UFCW stepped up its counterattack against P-9. As a first step, Wynn loosed publications director Al Zack as a sort of attack dog on P-9. Zack was a veteran labor reporter and public relations officer whose father had done public relations for George Meany at the AFL-CIO. He quickly recognized that Guyette was capable of turning every UFCW announcement into a counterattack on the international union. He familiarized himself with the news deadlines of the Austin *Daily Herald* and Austin's television and radio stations. From that point on, whenever he released a new UFCW broadside against Guyette and Rogers, he made sure it arrived in Guyette's hands just minutes—if that—before it arrived on reporters' desks, and that was just enough before deadline so that reporters had little time to get P-9's response.

On February 17 the UFCW released a sixteen-page "special report" on the Austin strike, an unprecedented effort by an international union to discredit one of its own locals. It recapped ten years of bargaining history in Austin and answered thirteen so-called myths about the strike and the UFCW's role. In his cover letter, Wynn wrote: "The courage and sacrifice of the Austin members would be the stuff of which labor legends are made, if it were not for the imminent tragic destruction of 1,500 union jobs, the polarization of a local union, and the economic and social breakdown of a community. The P-9 tragedy is a story of inexperienced, misguided leadership and false prophets. . . ."

Wynn also took steps to cut off the flow of contributions to Austin. In December he had issued a letter to the presidents of other international unions, warning that their local affiliates might receive appeals from P-9's United Support Group for the Adopt-a-Family fund. He noted that the UFCW was providing strike benefits to P-9's members and that he had not sanctioned any other appeal in the labor movement. He went on to say, "We certainly have no problem with contributions if they are made through our regional office" in

Bloomington. Now Wynn's office received a check for ten thousand dollars from Local Lodge 780 of the International Association of Machinists in Bloomington. It came with a letter asking Wynn to forward the money directly to P-9 in Austin and asking him to return the money if he couldn't comply. Wynn sent the check back, writing, "If . . . you wish to act contrary to our request, please do it yourself. Also, next time you want to stick it to the UFCW, please don't ask us to bend over and cooperate."

On February 27 Wynn called a meeting with Hansen, Anderson, and Doug Dority, the UFCW's vice-president of organizing, at UFCW headquarters in Washington. It was time to consider an end to the strike. The obvious step—and a possibility rumored for weeks around the Austin Labor Center—was trusteeship, a legal measure by which Wynn could remove Guyette and the others and appoint his own deputy to temporarily run P-9. In fact, Lewie Anderson had been privately considering the step for months; he had long since been convinced that Guyette and Rogers had some unattainable goal that had nothing to do with the UFCW's interests. Now it seemed the only way for the UFCW to regain control of a local that was slipping out of its grasp. Hansen, too, was now leaning toward a trusteeship. He was beginning to feel the UFCW should have trusteed P-9 back in January when the packinghouse reopened. It might have caused an ugly court battle and turned Guyette into a martyr, but it could have saved more than a thousand UFCW jobs. Even Jay Foreman, a Harvard Law graduate and the UFCW's resident intellectual, was beginning to come around.

And yet a trusteeship is a desperate measure for any international. In March 1986 only two UFCW locals out of several hundred in North America were operating under trusteeships. In the entire nation, out of more than 55,000 union locals, only 421 were under trusteeships. Trusteeships also had an ugly history in the labor movement, which had prompted Congress to impose strict regulations. In the 1950's trusteeships became associated with the enforcement of graft and the suppression of political dissent when they were imposed on several locals of the Teamsters' and Longshoremen's unions for long periods of time. In 1959 Congress passed the Labor-Management Reporting and Disclosure Act (Landrum-Griffin), imposing new rules on trustee ships, placing strict guidelines on the financial management of unions, and giving the Department of Labor the power to regulate trusteeships. The law gave the benefit of the doubt to an international union that imposes a trusteeship, but it allowed the trusteed local to challenge the measure before federal regulators. The law permitted trusteeships "for the purpose of correcting corruption or financial malpractice, assuring the performance of collective bargaining agreements or other duties of a bargaining representative, restoring democratic procedures, or otherwise carrying out legitimate objects of such labor organizations."

So when the trusteeship debate started, Wynn kept one ear to his lawyers. He wanted an airtight case. True, the strike had cost hundreds of UFCW members their jobs. True, P-9 had sent roving pickets without permission from the UFCW. True, P-9 had spent more than a hundred thousand dollars on Corporate Campaign against the UFCW's advice. But Wynn did not want a protracted debate—in the press or in court—about solidarity, labor tactics, and union democracy. The dispute between P-9 and the UFCW represented, in part, a legitimate disagreement over philosophy and tactics that was widespread in the labor movement, and P-9's lawyers could make this look like political suppression. His lawyers observed that hundreds of P-9 members had turned on the UFCW, so that enforcing a trusteeship could get ugly if the meatpackers defended the union hall. In addition, the long string of letters and telegrams from Wynn to Guyette could establish a "history of animus" that might make a trusteeship look deliberate and vindictive if P-9 took it to court. The UFCW already had been through two messy court battles over trusteeships, one against a local in Los Angeles in 1972, another against a local in Hartford, Connecticut, in 1980. The last thing the big union needed was a trusteeship that flopped. If the UFCW was to impose it, the lawyers said, it had better stick. They counseled Wynn to take over P-9 only if the local defied a direct order.

The UFCW constitution, like those of most unions, requires that local affiliates obtain the permission of the international union to strike—for just the kind of reason exhibited in Austin. If Wynn lifted the strike sanction, it would cut off strike benefits of sixty-five dollars per week per member and turn P-9's strike into a "wildcat." But it would also make the 800 strikers eligible for unemployment compensation. (Under Minnesota law, workers who deliberately go on strike cannot collect unemployment benefits. But workers who offered unconditionally to return to work stood a good chance of collecting benefits if Hormel said it had no more jobs.) More important, lifting the strike sanction would remove the ideological barrier for remaining P-9 members who wanted to go back to work but refused to cross a sanctioned picket line. It was a little late for that now since Hormel took the position that the packinghouse was full. But the grueling nature of packinghouse work causes high turnover, and no one believed that all of Hormel's 565 new replacements would stick it out. Then there was always the chance that Hormel would gear up again to its prestrike staff levels of 1,400 to 1,500 people, even as high as the 2,100 once hinted at by Knowlton before the feud erupted. Finally, lifting the strike sanction would give Guyette and the executive board one last chance to come around to UFCW policy as well as demonstrate the international's good faith in case a court fight erupted later. If it backfired, however, it would surely touch off another fire storm in Austin and drive Guyette's loyalists deeper into opposition toward the UFCW.

Back in Austin, meanwhile, some of the strike's tireless rank-and-file supporters were leading a grass-roots effort to bring the warring factions back together. Charlie Peterson and Larry Jensen could see that with five hundred union members back at work, P-9 was breaking apart. Both men had resigned from the Communications Committee, whose fifty members had dwindled to a dozen by January. The grind of four to five speaking trips a week was straining families. Peterson offered his resignation when he felt he could no longer ask more of his workhorses, who had raised several hundred thousand dollars for P-9 families in just five months. Jensen ended his involvement at about the same time amid growing doubts about the strike's real intent. He joined a small group of union members who began pressing Guyette to get it settled before their jobs and the union were lost. Each plea, however, drew accusations from Guyette supporters that he was trying to undermine P-9's goals.

Peterson and Jensen knew that P-9 could not continue to war with the UFCW and Hormel at the same time. Yet neither was enamored with the UFCW, which had shown no inclination to work with P-9 since the mediator's proposal was rejected. So they tried to position P-9 for a move toward reconciliation. At a rank-and-file meeting in early March, Peterson stood up and read a motion that called for the executive board and the international to iron out their differences and go after Hormel. The motion touched off a host of jeers and boos. Guyette and his supporters didn't want to tie themselves to a big union that had refused to back them and turned on them with such a vengeance. Nonetheless, Peterson had touched a painful point that many people, even those bitterly opposed to the UFCW, could no longer ignore: Labor can't fight itself and expect to beat management. P-9 members had proved that they were fully capable of raising the money they needed without the international's assistance. But they could ill afford a bloodletting that caused both combatants to lose sight of the common enemy. As the debate raged on, Peterson stood his ground, and gradually his rationale began to prevail. In two days of secret balloting, March 11 and 12, the resolution passed, 345–305, marking one of the few times that the membership went against the recommendation of Guyette and the board.

By this time, however, the UFCW was well along with its plans to end the strike. On Thursday, March 13, Wynn convened the UFCW executive committee to lay out reasons for pulling the strike sanction. When it came time to vote, he abstained to avoid the appearance that his personal feud with Guyette and Rogers was a factor in the decision. The committee voted unanimously to pull the sanction and bring the strike to a formal end. That night Anderson and Zack stayed at the office till nearly midnight, conferring with the lawyers and drafting the directive to P-9. They went home to get a few hours of sleep before the storm they knew would erupt the next day.

On Friday a courier delivered the UFCW's packet to the Austin Labor Center. Inside was a directive ordering Guyette and P-9 to call off the strike. It read: "Progress towards a contract is nonexistent and, in fact, the bargaining situation today is further from resolution than at any time since . . . 18 months ago. To continue to sanction or authorize the strike can only lead to further division, further suffering, and further loss of jobs for good union members." The directive ordered Guyette to halt the strike, withdraw the roving pickets, call off the boycott of Hormel products, and inform Hormel that P-9's members were ready to return to work. It said the UFCW would continue to pay forty dollars a week in "post-strike assistance" to P-9 members who remained out of work, but only if they complied with the directive and applied for their jobs at Hormel.

The word raced through the union hall with the impact of a divorce decree after a long and nasty separation. A pack of blue caps swarmed through the corridors as if patrolling the halls against some hostile invasion. "If we're on a suicide mission, then they're committing murder," one P-9 member told a reporter. Others wondered how they were supposed to end a strike when Hormel wasn't hiring. Those most bitter lashed out at reporters for what they felt was slanted coverage. Others cussed at Wynn, repeating the now popular theme that he was more interested in his jewelry than in his members. After all, he was the one who had sanctioned the strike in the first place; now he was telling them to quit for a contract that almost everybody, even the P-10ers, had voted against in August. With Guyette in New York for a labor rally, Winkels called a press conference and issued a response: "Our members voted to go on strike, and we represent our members. The strike goes on." More than a hundred supporters at the back of the room cheered. Two days later they met at St. Edwards Church and formally voted to defy the order and announced plans to file a thirteen-million-dollar lawsuit against the international for undermining the strike.

For others, however, Wynn's action removed the psychological barrier between their unwillingness to cross the picket line and their knowledge that the strike had been over for weeks. Within a month 114 P-9ers had signed up on a preferential hiring list, hoping for a shot at a job when replacements quit or Hormel started hiring again. Executive board member Kenny Hagen resigned on March 19 and took a job two weeks later as a high school janitor. He had written a letter of resignation two weeks earlier but had torn it up after Guyette talked him out of it. This time, during a meeting at Lenoch's house, Hagen asked Guyette for his pen and a sheet of paper from his legal pad. Hagen scribbled out his resignation, signed and dated it, and had Guyette sign it. Then he went to the bank, cut his name off the rubber stamp used to endorse union checks, and went home. He also admonished the women who ran the Support

Group's finances to cover their tracks: After every strike, he warned, there was an audit.

For Guyette's loyalists, however, the UFCW announcement was new cause for bitterness. Until now P-9's members could tell themselves they were the conscience of the UFCW and the cutting edge of the labor movement. Now they realized that they were the UFCW's enemy, its outcast, and its nemesis. Several weeks earlier, when Wynn refused to sanction P-9's roving pickets, the ever-literate Winkels replied with a quote from America's ultimate misanthrope, Henry David Thoreau: "Any man more right than his neighbors constitutes a majority of one." Now P-9 was alone in the bunker. The months of rallies, the outpouring of letters and donations, the massive press coverage, all began to fall away as P-9's leaders realized that the nation's working people would not rally around the cause in Austin, that P-9 could not touch off a spontaneous conversion of the nation's working class. P-9 would have to fight this one alone, withdrawing and fortifying, a majority of one.

At the press conference where Winkels vowed that P-9 would press on, he had accused the UFCW of turning its back on P-9 and on unionism itself. Now he began to reflect on the meaning of unionism and on P-9's history. He had been one of the P-9 officers to recognize in January that the odds were growing slim, that the strike and the campaign were not bringing Hormel to its knees. But to him that didn't make the fight any less worth fighting. It was as though the militants of P-9 were the last vestige of the 1930's, men and women who still worked hard at physical labor, played hard in Austin's roughest bars, spoke the coarse language of the packinghouse, stood and fought when somebody tried to take what was theirs. Well, if the 1980's had forgotten all that history, the militants of P-9 had not. What did they stand to lose? A job—a stinking, dangerous, difficult job. A life of security and new cars and regular payments on the mortgage. Winkels could live without them.

Still, Wynn and Guyette sought one more effort at reconciliation. By this time the staff at UFCW headquarters had developed a running joke to vent their frustration over the repeated efforts at reconciliation with P-9. One after another, the joke went, UFCW officers "mounted the white horse" of optimism to meet with Guyette and the others and hammer out a compromise. But one by one, Anderson, Foreman, Hansen, and Wynn found the "white horse" shot out from under them as they discovered there was no trust and no common ground. Now it was the turn for Bill Olwell, a big, smiling man who served as the UFCW's director of collective bargaining and who still retained a measure of sympathy for P-9 members. He found Hormel's wage cuts as objectionable as they did, and he was glad the UFCW had local members who were so willing to fight. He urged Wynn to have one more meeting; perhaps he, Olwell, could achieve some reconciliation.

On March 21 the P-9 executive board members once again drove to Chicago, and once again they gathered around a big table with UFCW officers from Washington. Foreman was the senior official at the meeting, so he acted as chairman. For about ninety minutes they debated the status of the strike, P-9's reasons for continued hope, the UFCW's reasons for ordering the meatpackers back to work. Olwell and Foreman kept asking Guyette, Winkels, and the others if they intended to obey the international's back-to-work order. Guyette and the board responded with their own questions, a series of curiously legalistic queries about the UFCW's intentions. Then Anderson noticed something peculiar about a sheaf of notebooks in front of Huston. He whispered in Foreman's ear that he thought Huston had a hidden tape recorder. Foreman abruptly stopped the discussion and confronted Huston. The P-9 vice president pulled it out, saying P-9 didn't trust the UFCW any more than the UFCW trusted P-9. Foreman said he was outraged that one UFCW member would secretly tape-record another. "You'll get over it," Huston joked. Foreman flew into a rage, slammed the table with his fist, and called the meeting to an end. As they filed out, Al Zack smiled at Anderson and said, "Who shot the white horse?"

Five days later, on March 26, the UFCW announced that the fight was over; it would begin proceedings to place P-9 in trusteeship. Wynn said he would appoint a UFCW officer from another part of the country to conduct a trusteeship hearing. Hansen would present the international's case that P-9 had defied a direct order from Wynn. P-9's executive board could present the local's case. The hearing officer would write a report to

Wynn, and the UFCW executive committee would vote whether to take control of P-9. In a letter sent directly to P-9's members, Wynn wrote, "After more than seven months of strike, Local P-9's leaders still do not have a plan to regain jobs. They continue to rely on more publicity stunts, more arrests and more firings. These activities cannot and will not regain any jobs." Wynn urged the workers in Austin to disregard their local leaders and apply directly to Hormel for their jobs. He said the UFCW would cut off poststrike assistance to anyone who failed to fill out the return-to-work application or who continued picketing and boycott activities against Hormel.

Much as Wynn and Anderson expected, the announcement touched off a vigorous debate in the labor movement. Even groups that had not supported P-9's strike or boycott could sympathize with an apparently democratic local caught between a large, powerful international union and a large, powerful corporation. *Labor Notes,* a Detroit-based newsletter that serves as a nexus for hundreds of progressive union activists around the country, blasted the UFCW for its style of "bureaucratic business unionism," its failed national bargaining strategy in meat-packing, and its attack on P-9. Stanley Aronowitz, a former labor organizer and a sociology professor at the City University of New York, wrote in the *Village Voice:* "[T]he strike's focus has shifted to its poetry, its chance of becoming an emblem for the appearance of a new labor movement. Surely victory or resurrection are [*sic*] not around the corner. Meanwhile, thanks to the workers of P-9, a lot of trade unionists have been wakened from their restless sleep."

But the left was not unanimously behind P-9. Bill Dennison, labor reporter for the Communist party of the USA's *Daily World,* wrote that the UFCW was one of the nation's more politically progressive unions and that its packinghouse division represented a long history of industrial militance. He faulted Ray Rogers's analysis of Hormel and said that Rogers and P-9's leaders had led the local into a "quagmire of separatism and isolation." Lance Compa, a staffer for the United Electrical Workers (which itself had left the AFL-CIO years earlier in a red-baiting controversy) and a member of the National Lawyers Guild, went even further. He accused P-9 of engaging in "enterprise unionism," an effort to better its own lot because it happened to represent workers at a profitable company. Compa wrote that the labor movement's great achievement of the twentieth century was industrial unionism that established class solidarity across craft and corporate borders; he said P-9's effort to stay ahead of other packinghouse workers threatened that solidarity. He added, "Their belief that the modern, productive, profitable Austin plant compels Hormel to pay more to P-9 members than to other Hormel workers in older plants is the wrong starting point. That is why the entire effort has flopped in spite of its marvelous tactics."

In short, the trusteeship announcement made the strike more of a national cause than ever. Rogers and Guyette decided the time was ripe for one more demonstration that P-9 wasn't going to quit. That week P-9 and its Twin Cities Metro Area Support Group mailed thousands of leaflets across the country inviting their supporters to Austin for an event billed as a "Shut Down Hormel National March and Rally" on Saturday, April 12. The leaflet included a reservation form and asked supporters to check off the date they expected to arrive so that Rogers and Guyette could gauge the depth of their support. "Travel to Austin Early," it urged. "Bring sleeping bags and plan to stay at workers' homes, in campers or on union hall floors."

Supporters began to trickle into Austin on Wednesday, April 9, and to pour in on Thursday. About 350 demonstrators rallied at the plant's north gate on Thursday morning, but nearly 60 Austin policemen and local county sheriff's deputies kept them at bay. By Thursday afternoon it was apparent that the long weekend was going to include fireworks somewhere in Austin. Although none of the outside groups took credit for it publicly, antimilitarism and anticapitalist organizations had organizers in Austin that weekend to advise on tactics and plan a plant gate demonstration for the next day. It was destined to be the event of the year for labor's militants.

By dawn on Friday Austin police and state troopers had again cordoned off all approach streets to the plant. To get in, drivers would have to approach along Interstate 90 where it passes just north of the packinghouse, drive down the exit ramp, and turn right onto a short service road that links the freeway exit to the plant's north gate eighty yards away. But the authorities arrived too late. In the wee hours of the morning a group of blue caps and their supporters had driven to the plant and parked their cars in the middle of the short street that connects the freeway exit to the plant's service road. At dawn, some three hundred strikers, retirees, spouses, and supporters from coast to coast were crowded in and around this ring of cars, waving the American flag and singing songs of victory. The road was utterly impassable.

Twenty yards away, at the bottom of the freeway ramp, law enforcement troops from the Austin Police Department, State Highway Patrol, and several neighboring counties were readying riot gear. Shortly after 6:00 A.M., with the sun rising on a chilly but bright day, Austin Police Sergeant Larry Moeykens spoke through a police car bullhorn and told the demonstrators they were breaking the law and would have to disperse. He was greeted with raucous shouts of refusal. He waited several minutes and gave the warning a second time. He paused a little longer, then warned them again. The demonstrators hollered back derisively and linked arms to form a human chain. The officers began moving in on the crowd. First they linked their own arms, creating two human walls along either edge of the pavement and forming a gauntlet between their cars and the demonstration. A small pack of officers moved down this human alley and grabbed the first protester they came to. Pandemonium broke out. Other demonstrators tried to pull their compatriot back from the police. A hail of gravel and pebbles rained down on the officers. Arms flailed in the pack of bodies. Suddenly the officers tore one demonstrator free from the group, then a second and a third. They dragged them, stumbling and twisting, back up the short street to waiting vans.

Both sides paused for several minutes, wiping bloodied noses and straightening their coats. Then the officers came back for more. Again there was chaos. A small projectile whistled through the air, landing on the asphalt in the officers' midst and giving off a plume of red smoke. One demonstrator ran for the grassy ditch below the freeway exit. Three officers wrestled him to the ground and handcuffed him. The officers pulled more demonstrators from the pack and dragged them away. The police fell back again, several wiping a brown liquid from their eyes. Moeykens ordered his officers to fall back.

This time there was a longer wait. The officers regrouped around their cars. Officers conferred over police radios. The demonstrators checked each other for injuries and took stock of the arrests. The cars were unmoved; the human ranks refused to budge. More minutes passed. Just before 7:00 A.M. Moeykens came back on the bullhorn to announce that because of the rock throwing and the spraying of homemade chemicals, the police were declaring the demonstration a riot. Subsequent arrests would be considered felonies. "We're going to disperse this crowd with chemicals," he warned. Police and deputies could be seen behind the squad cars donning gas masks. That drew more derisive hooting from the crowd. Near the back, a handful of men and women circulated with strips of gauze and buckets of water. They doused the cloths in water and handed them out among the crowd. "If they use tear gas, put this over your mouth and nose and use it to wipe your eyes," a young woman counseled several demonstrators. Moeykens issued another warning. Then, quickly, the police moved forward, tossing tear gas canisters into the crowd and pressing people back with riot clubs. Chaos broke out again. Smoke billowed across the road in yellowish clouds. One canister came sailing back out from the crowd and landed at the feet of two policemen. A few dozen protesters scattered down a side street away from the plant gate. Others fell to coughing, gagging, and wiping their eyes. Still others ran into a grassy gully between the service road and the freeway. Police moved into the ring of cars, grabbing demonstrators, shoving some to the ground, and pressing others back up the street. Within minutes the mob had dispersed in two directions, one west down the street toward the plant gate, the other east down the same street toward the end of the Hormel property. The police formed a human barricade and began pressing the crowd back down the street while a fleet of tow trucks moved in behind them and began hauling cars from the blockade.

By seven forty-five police had cleared the road and Hormel's workers were driving into the packinghouse parking lot. The demonstrators, now powerless and backed down a side street, regrouped for a march back to the center of town. They wound their way to the Law Enforcement Center, a bunkerlike building attached to the Mower County Courthouse just off Main Street, where about two hundred flag-waving and placard-carrying demonstrators marched around the block, singing songs and shouting to their imprisoned compatriots.

A short time later inside the Law Enforcement Center, Police Chief Don Hoffman and County Sheriff Wayne Goodnature held a news conference. Reporters filed through a series of security points into a stark basement room, where Hoffman and Goodnature displayed a smoke bomb and a batch of fist-size chunks of asphalt that they said had been thrown at their officers. Both men were incensed, not surprising, for the hot-tempered Goodnature but a rare display of anger from the mild-mannered Hoffman. They said the police lab was analyzing a liquid—apparently homemade Mace—that was sprayed on the officers from squirt guns. Several of the officers had gone to the hospital to have their eyes washed out. It was one thing for P-9 to take on Hormel and engage in civil disobedience, a livid Hoffman said. It was another to assault his officers with rocks and chemicals. "I'm so irritated with P-9 saying they have rights to do this and do that." Hoffman fumed. "They do not have a right to assault my police officers." They declared the morning's fracas a "riot" and arrested seventeen people on felony charges. They had also issued summonses for Guyette and Rogers, who, they said, were seen giving orders from near the scene of the demonstration. They said they would ask the city council to cancel P-9's parade permit for the following day.

An hour later and four blocks away at the Austin Labor Center, Jim Guyette and a new attorney, Emily Bass of New York, weren't giving any ground on the rhetoric front. They entered a union hall press conference to a standing ovation from hundreds of P-9ers and demonstrators. "We feel we had a peaceful demonstration that was turned into a riot by the police," Guyette said. "We wonder how many people will support a company that would rather Mace its employees than negotiate with them." Guyette said Hormel and city officials had turned Austin into a police state. Asked about Goodnature's request to cancel the parade permit, Guyette said, "This guy has read too many comic books. If that city council thinks they can cancel our rally on a whim, then I think those people have had their heads in a can of Spam too long." In fact, the permit was upheld.

The next day's festivities began with an impromptu march to the Law Enforcement Center, where Friday's fifteen demonstrators were still in jail. Some three hundred P-9ers and visiting supporters marched around the block, chanting, "Free P-9! Let them go!" Back at the union hall, the offices were jammed with P-9 executives and their advisers planning the march and rally. Guyette, who was subject to arrest on felony charges, was nowhere to be seen. Dave Foster, the Steel Workers' grievance chairman from St. Paul, was in Winkels's office, ticking off names from a list of visiting union members: shipyard workers from Maine; electrical workers from Massachusetts; textile workers from Chicago; meat-packers from Nebraska; government employees from the Twin Cities; food workers from Michigan; cannery workers from California. Meanwhile, word swept the building that the Reverend Jesse Jackson had confirmed his plans to visit the next day. He'd been on Cable News Network the night before, saying he had spoken with Hormel executives and hoped he could find common ground in Austin.

The big march began just after lunch. Some three-thousand people marshaled along Fourth Avenue east of the union hall and in the parking lot behind Riverside Arena. The day remained chilly and gray, but once again the mood was festive. Participants in Friday's mayhem told their war stories; pamphleteers circulated a dozen leaflets and tabloids; union marshals unfurled banners; old pals from opposite coasts greeted each other in solidarity. The marchers headed west along Fourth Avenue, past the Labor Center and three more blocks to Main Street, down to Second Avenue, then east again to Riverside Arena. Mid-April is not a time of balmy sunshine in southern Minnesota, but the mood was upbeat, and Austin's streets echoed with strains of "Solidarity Forever."

The marchers took more than an hour to pour into the arena, filling most of the six thousand bleacher seats and folding chairs, pouring down the aisles and milling about literature tables at the back. When the cheering and chanting had quieted down, they heard speeches from Hollywood actor David Soul; Marsha Mickens, a bakery workers' union officer from Detroit; Bobbi Polzine, leader of a farmers' protest group from Minnesota; and other supporters, who assured them once again that theirs was the fight to turn labor's fortunes. Guyette slipped in quietly, surrounded by a phalanx of blue caps wearing their NO RETREAT, NO SURRENDER jackets. When he climbed the stage, the crowd roared. He scanned the sea of waving signs and raised fists and broke into a smile. "I'm sorry I couldn't be part of the parade," he began. "I understand our local police arrested seventeen people. Those people are leading the charge, and I know their sacrifice will not have been in vain." More cheering, hollering, and waving of signs across the big arena. "Somewhere we will find a fair judge," he continued. "Somewhere we will find a fair law enforcement system. And we will continue the fight against the Hormel Company."

On Sunday the Reverend Jesse Jackson arrived in Austin for a whirlwind tour that was part prayer meeting, part campaign swing. A motorcade escorted him into Austin, where he met with P-9's executive board. At the Hormel corporate office he met briefly with Nyberg. He gave a speech at the Labor Center and visited the jailed demonstrators, holding an informal prayer meeting in the jail and singing "We Shall Overcome." His day concluded with an impromptu rally at St. Edward's Church. He was gone again by afternoon, promising reporters and supporters his best shot at mediation. It was classic Jackson, inspiring hope, exuding confidence, building goodwill and optimism. Yet the visit created an unreal air—a potential presidential candidate kissing babies in the midst of a bitter labor dispute, a great black leader visiting an all-white town where racism still ran deep, the self-appointed Middle East mediator trying to restore peace in a town that had known nothing but harmony for fifty years. Who would have predicted a year earlier that Jesse Jackson, too, would get drawn into this strange drama? Who would have predicted that Communists would be handing out newspapers in the streets of Austin, that the son of a meat-packer would wind up sparring with Ted Koppel on *Nightline*, that three thousand people from across the nation would march down Main Street one blustery April afternoon bellowing "Solidarity Forever"?

CHAPTER

16

The strange melodrama returned to a more mundane stage the following Monday morning, when the UFCW convened its trusteeship hearing in downtown Minneapolis. But there was just one problem: No hotel in town was willing to accommodate what would likely turn into one of P-9's now-infamous demonstrations. So on Monday morning the Minneapolis Public Library, normally the province of businessmen, students, and a few vagrants, became host to a curious scene: dozens of blue-jacketed, blue-capped meat-packers climbing off charter buses, looking mad as hell, heading in procession for the library's second-floor meeting room. In its scramble to arrange a hearing site and inform the press, the UFCW had made it clear that it would not brook another P-9 demonstration. Seating would be limited to fifty-four—first come, first serve. When the P-9ers finally found their way upstairs and down a hallway to the meeting room, they discovered a long line of middle-aged men in neckties and suit jackets, many of them sporting the UFCW logo on lapel pins or breast-pocket patches. Two UFCW staffers were checking union cards at the door, and yes, the men waiting in line had first dibs on twenty or thirty of the available seats. Once again violence threatened. Once again the blue caps saw that they would have to play by rules stacked against them.

The closed-door hearing was conducted by Ray Wooster,

president of a big UFCW local in Houston, Texas, and a twenty-five-year veteran of the union and its predecessor, the Retail Clerks International Union. Joe Hansen played prosecutor, presenting evidence that Wynn had ordered an end to the strike and the boycott and that P-9 had violated the order. P-9's executive board broadly defended the actions of the rogue local. But Wooster confined the discussion to one narrow issue: Did P-9's officers defy the UFCW's order to end the strike and their Hormel boycott? Hansen presented evidence from Washington and from UFCW staffers who had been sent clandestinely to the Austin union hall. To Guyette, free on five-thousand-dollars bail from Austin, it seemed like a mockery. The witnesses testified repeatedly that P-9 was continuing its boycott. There in the room sat twenty P-9 members still wearing hats, pins, buttons, and bumper stickers that screamed "Boycott Hormel." But time and again Wooster frustrated Guyette in his efforts to introduce other evidence. Guyette brought up past rank-and-file votes, the origin of the strike, the UFCW's failure to support the strike or the campaign. For two days Hansen sparred with Guyette and the other executive board members, while the blue caps milled about the library and the ever-vigilant reporters cooled their heels, for once having something to read while they waited for a comment from Guyette or the others. When the hearing wrapped up on Wednesday, Wooster was off for Texas, promising a report to Wynn within three weeks.

Meanwhile, two lawyers new to P-9 were sitting in a borrowed law office four blocks from the library, chain-smoking cigarettes and researching case law on trusteeships. Margaret Winter and Emily Bass had just formed a law partnership in New York, where Winter had worked with the National Emergency Civil Liberties Committee and Bass had practiced with Rabinowitz, Boudin, a well-known civil liberties firm. Winter and Bass had gone to Austin in March to defend Rogers on the criminal syndicalism charge, a case they felt had important free speech implications. That case went well, and the law, like similar ones in many other states, was later declared unconstitutional. Now they believed they had another compelling constitutional case: Did workers have the right to decide when to strike and when to return to work, or could an international union order them back to work? Meanwhile, Winter's husband, Steve Wattenmaker, had quit his job at an oil refinery on the outskirts of St. Paul to work part time with Rogers on fund raising and public relations for P-9.

Wooster's report came out three weeks later, but once again P-9 beat the UFCW to the punch. On Monday, May 5, Winter and Bass filed a thirteen-million-dollar lawsuit in federal court in Washington, D.C., accusing the UFCW of undermining the strike and asking the court to block any UFCW takeover. On Wednesday, Wynn convened the UFCW's five-member executive committee to consider Wooster's report. They debated the issue for two hours. Jerry Menapace, a thirty-two-year veteran of the old Amalgamated Meatcutters union and now Wynn's second-in-command, urged that they wait a week or two and have another talk with Guyette and P-9's executive board. But others contended that the time for talk was over. By now, they said, the faster the UFCW moved, the better. With Wynn abstaining, the committee voted 4–0 to impose a trusteeship. Members quoted from Wooster's report: "There is a distinction between independence and arrogance. The stability and integrity of the organization we form for our benefit require some sense of discipline, a basic respect for the very rules which we ourselves have agreed to, and a fair means of enforcing them."

That afternoon the UFCW's enforcement machinery started humming. Foreman called Joe Hansen in Bloomington to tell him he had been appointed trustee. Another call went to Dubuque to draft Ken Kimbro, a young UFCW staff organizer who had been president and business agent of the local at FDL Foods. He would be an assistant trustee, with the thankless job of going to Austin and serving as Hansen's agent there. A third call went to Sioux Falls, South Dakota, to draft Jack Smith, a veteran of the Morrell packinghouse, to join Kimbro in Austin. The same afternoon Foreman conferred with the UFCW's outside attorneys to prepare a lawsuit asking the federal courts to enforce the trusteeship, throw out P-9's suit, and compel the meat-packers and their leaders to turn over their union hall to the troika of trustees. Foreman's staff alerted the UFCW's accounting department that he would want an audit of P-9's books to see if the local was solvent and to prevent accusations that the UFCW was stealing local funds. Al Zack conferred with Foreman and Lewie Anderson, then put the finishing touches on a press statement about the trusteeship, went home, and packed his bags for another trip to Minnesota.

The next morning Hansen called the Austin Labor Center and asked for Guyette. He was out, so Hansen asked for Lynn Huston. Lynn was out, so Hansen asked for Pete Winkels. Pete was gone, too. So Hansen spoke with Kathy Buck. Hansen told her that the executive board members would receive letters that day by courier and registered mail informing them that they were suspended and that he was in charge of P-9's affairs. Given the somewhat charged atmosphere in Austin, Hansen wanted to know whether the executive board members intended to comply. Buck said she would have to ask their lawyer. Hansen asked whether the executive board would turn over its keys to the Austin Labor Center. She said she would have to ask their lawyer. He asked if they would stop spending union funds and turn financial records over to him. She said she would have to ask their lawyer. That afternoon the UFCW filed suit in federal court in St. Paul seeking to force P-9 to comply with the trusteeship. The case was assigned to U.S. District Judge Edward Devitt, a retired judge who continued to hear cases and was familiar with the dispute through his handling of the NLRB's injunction against picket line violence by P-9.

Buck's terse reply to Hansen reflected the ugly mood that had developed at the Labor Center. Blue caps carrying baseball bats patrolled the sidewalk as if watching for a UFCW trustee. Others began removing file cabinets and boxes of documents from the building. Somebody wrapped a chain and padlock around the crash bars of the front doors. Guyette issued a statement that "Good union men and women will never allow union democracy to be put into trusteeship by Bill Wynn or anyone else." Asked if that meant a violent resistance, he said, "I don't believe our members are going to stand by and watch somebody else take over their union hall."

With P-9 and the international filing opposing lawsuits in courtrooms eleven hundred miles apart, it took three weeks of legal skirmishing to sort out the issues. In the third week of May 1986 U.S. District Judge Gerhard Gesell in Washington denied P-9's petition for a temporary restraining order to block the trusteeship. He scolded all the lawyers for piling up such litigation in a "judge-shopping" competition. A week later he sent the matter back to Judge Devitt in St. Paul.

On June 2 the parties appeared in Devitt's courtroom, an imposing high-ceilinged chamber paneled in dark wood. Guyette sat with Winter and Bass at one of the big polished tables; across the room Hansen sat with Harry Huge, a dapper trial specialist from Washington, and a handful of other UFCW attorneys. Bass went first, looking small and somewhat outgunned as she approached the high wooden lectern before Devitt. But she spoke with authority, reviewing the history of wage cuts, the rank and file's rebellion, the UFCW's long campaign to discredit Guyette and Rogers. Federal labor law, she said, does not permit an international union to impose a trusteeship to end a strike. Union members, she said, should have the right to choose when to start a strike and when to end one.

Huge, who looked imposing in a tailored navy blue suit, began haltingly. The issue was not about suppressing union democracy, he told Devitt. An international union is a voluntary federation of union locals, and they must observe certain rules to survive: central agreement on whom to strike and when, how to chart a bargaining strategy, how to recruit new members and protect current ones. A union local agrees to abide by an international's constitution and agrees that it will suffer the consequences if it breaks the rules. He finished after about twenty minutes and sat down.

Devitt began reading his order even as Huge was straightening the crease on his dark blue slacks. Devitt had a habit of deciding cases on the written record, but he liked to hear oral arguments to give the parties a final crack at the issues.

> The records in these cases reflect a sharp, long-time conflict between the International's President William Wynn and Vice-President Lewie Anderson, on the one hand, and P-9 President James Guyette and Corporate Campaign leader Ray Rogers, on the other. . . . But this hearing is not to receive evidence or arguments about the strike, on how it can be, or should have been, conducted. The basic issue here is a contract, not a labor dispute. The question is whether the International had authority under its constitution and federal labor law to appoint the trustee.

We conclude that since Local P-9 did not comply
with the International's directive to cease its strike
against Hormel or to cease its unsanctioned product boycott or to cease its roving picket line activities, the International acted within its authority in appointing the
trustee to manage P-9's affairs, and trustee Hansen is legally authorized to act as such.

Devitt threw out P-9's request to block the trusteeship, ordered its leaders to recognize Hansen as trustee, turn custody of
the union hall and P-9's assets over to him, and allow him "peace-
ably" to conduct the union's affairs as trustee.

Guyette, Bass, and Winter trailed out of the courthouse onto a
sunny St. Paul street, followed by a small parade of TV cameras
and scribbling reporters, granting a spontaneous interview in
clipped words and muted voices.

It was over.

The next day UFCW attorneys Robert Funk, Harry Huge, and
James Pfander drove to Austin to collect P-9's ledgers and bank
statements and pick up the Labor Center keys from Winter and Bass.
For all of the legal clout in Devitt's order, however, Ken Kimbro and
Jack Smith waited nearly another month before actually moving
into the Austin Labor Center. They were good choices for an
unenviable assignment. Kimbro was dapper, cocky, and well spoken. Smith was a rangy, broad-shouldered South Dakotan with a
handlebar mustache and the muscled hands of a meat-packer. For a
time in June they worked out of a storefront office down the street
from the Austin Labor Center. They had a few ugly visits from the
blue caps, but business went smoothly enough. Then the day before
what normally would have been a quiet three-day Fourth of July
weekend they drove over to the union hall to take charge. The front
doors were chained shut, so they entered through a side door near
the back of the building. Inside they found a shambles. Chairs and
wastebaskets were strewn about. File cabinets stood empty with
drawers hanging out. Wires hung from the walls where phones had
been torn out; Hansen had cut off service shortly after taking over as
trustee. The carpet was stained, and the off-white walls were
painted with obscenities.

Smith and Kimbro hadn't been surveying the mess for long

before they heard a pounding on the back door. It was a group of retirees, resentful of the trusteeship and demanding to know if they could hold their regular retirees' meeting in the hall that morning. Kimbro and Smith suspected a ruse but weren't sure what to say. They told the group that the building was in no condition for a meeting, but they said they would talk it over. While they were pondering their choices, they heard a pounding at the front doors. A crowd of blue caps had assembled and were demanding access to the building. Kimbro went to the glass doors and pointed at the chain; he didn't have a key. He motioned for the P-9ers to come around to the back. When he got there, he could hear them pounding on the metal door and trying to pull it open. He pressed the crash bar with his hand and opened the door a crack. Suddenly the door flew out and back against the building's wall. Kimbro went with it, his hand still gripping the bar, and he found himself face-to-face with a hundred angry Guyette supporters. "Who are you to take control of our union hall?" they demanded to know. The group crowded around him, pressing him back against the wide-open door. Somebody shouted, "Castrate the bastard," and another slammed his head back against the metal door. By this time Smith, six inches taller than Kimbro and a hundred pounds heavier, had reached the door. He glanced at the crowd, decided that conversation didn't look promising, and grabbed Kimbro by the shirt, hauling him back inside the building and slamming the door shut with him. "There are times," Kimbro later said, "when you know you would be a fool not to be scared. I was scared."

The pounding resumed at both doors, and Kimbro and Smith decided to call the police. One problem: no phone. A few anxious moments passed while the noise escalated outside and the two men considered their alternatives. Suddenly a middle-aged woman emerged from the office of the Oil, Chemical and Atomic Workers' union at the rear of the building. Its office was still open, and its phone still worked. A few minutes later an Austin squad car arrived at the hall, and by midmorning the crowd had dispersed.

Smith and Kimbro came back the next week, and the next, and gradually began to piece together a new local union operation. They discovered that P-9's finances were in as much disarray as the union hall. The local began 1985, the first full year of the campaign, with assets of more than $270,000. By the year's end, those had dwindled to less than $14,000. Among other expenses, the union spent $155,000 on administration, almost five times the previous year's total; more than $166,000 on professional fees, four times more than the year before; more than $44,000 on travel; and nearly $33,000 on education and publicity. Without $124,000 borrowed from a local bank, P-9 would have been down to its last $1,000 in cash.

The books got more confusing in 1986. Clearly P-9 was not strapped for money, even though union dues of nearly $7,000 a week had stopped when the strike started in the previous August. Instead, the union was getting regular infusions of cash, apparently from the United Support Group, but listed in the union's ledgers as simply "donation." The ledgers listed a "donation" of $5,000 on January 9, another for $4,000 the next day, another for $3,000 on January 14, and four more totaling $20,000 by January 31. The money continued to pour in: a total of $230,500 between January 9 and May 2, coming every few days in checks as big as $10,000 and $15,000. And apparently there was more money that was not accounted for. Dale Francis, one of the most ardent blue caps through early 1986, told the FBI later that year that he had routinely returned from fund-raising trips with thousands of dollars in cash, then turned it over to officers of P-9 or the Support Group without ever providing receipts or receiving them in return.

There also were questionable dealings in P-9's pension funds. According to a lawsuit filed later by the UFCW, P-9 borrowed thirty thousand dollars from a local bank in July 1985, pledging as collateral certificates of deposit in a pension fund set up for P-9 employees. P-9 apparently spent the money to fund the strike but repaid the loan by cashing a certificate from the pension fund, a step that the UFCW contended was a violation of federal law. A second certificate from the pension fund was later cashed, and some of the proceeds were used to finance P-9's activities. On a third occasion P-9 borrowed money from a local bank, pledged a pension plan certificate as collateral, and used part of the loan to pay off previous debts and part of the money to pay for strike activities. The UFCW sued Guyette and Buck, as financial secretary, for these activities and alleged that the loans violated federal guidelines separating pension funds from union operating accounts. The UFCW dropped the suit in 1988, saying Guyette and Buck had no money to pay a judgment. P-9's unorthodox handling of its finances indirectly had put its longtime financial secretary, Audrey Neumann, in the hospital in May 1985 with a stress-induced heart condition. Rogers and Guyette blamed her stress on Hormel and brought flowers to cheer her up. Neumann, disturbed by their handling of the finances, refused to let them in her room. She eventually retired shortly after the strike began. In February 1986, one of the three P-9 secretaries, Donna Nelson, resigned, complaining that she had been asked to take over most of the financial secretary's duties but hadn't been given a raise for three years or any of the seniority rights that P-9 itself was battling for.

The outflow of money also was remarkable. P-9 spent more than $10,000 on new wiring and an exhaust system for its basement kitchen after discovering that the new commercial-style kitchen equipment overwhelmed the building's electrical supply. Rogers had received $16,000 in 1986, bringing his total payments to about $160,000, by his own account. When the trusteeship went into effect, P-9 had $12,000 in cash on hand but had unpaid bills of more than $150,000.

But Kimbro and Smith had more to worry about than finances. True, the strike was over. The last picket signs were gone, and Hansen had written Hormel making an official return-to-work offer on behalf of P-9's members. That allowed the remaining strikers to qualify for unemployment benefits and obligated Hormel to hire from union ranks for future openings. But workers in the plant remained without a contract, in a state of limbo over who represented them and under what terms. Moreover, it was unclear how workers in the plant felt about a union. The 565 nonunion "scabs" clearly didn't hold much affection for trade unionism. The 460 P-9 members were still mostly loyal to the UFCW but were badly shaken by the experience of the last two years.

Bill Wynn ordered a team of thirty organizers into Austin, headed by Dwayne Carman, a veteran of dozens of organizing campaigns. By mid-July the Austin Labor Center was transformed. The walls were whitewashed, the basement kitchen and clothing shelf cleared out, the meeting rooms stripped clear of much of the furniture that had accumulated during the strike. In the president's office, where Guyette had hung a portrait of an Indian chief over the inscription, "To Give Dignity to a Man Is Above All Things," Kimbro taped up a picture of Bruce Springsteen. In a small office next door, where Rogers had presided over maps and charts and phone lists, there was nothing save for Carman and a telephone on a bare desk. Halls once jammed with volunteers in blue P-9 jackets now bustled with organizers in sweaters bearing the UFCW logo. Carman, who could count votes as well as any party ward heeler, estimated by mid-August that virtually all the returning P-9ers had signed cards for the UFCW and that two to three hundred of the new employees had done likewise.

Ray Rogers still kept his apartment in Austin, but by this time he was spending more and more time in New York trying to rebuild Corporate Campaign, Inc. He and Ed Allen were forced to lay off several of their staff in the lean months of early 1986, and they had put so much time into P-9's battle that they had virtually no other clients. They moved their computer, photocopier, and crates of financial guides to a cheaper office near Madison Square Garden and started drumming up new business. By that fall they had quietly put out feelers to a flight attendants' union at American Airlines and an environmental group.

Back in Austin, inside the packinghouse, plant manager Deryl Arnold and his supervisors were as eager as the UFCW to get things back to normal. The long, serpentine packaging lines were rushing along again; the killing floor and cutting room bustled with swinging knives and buzzing saws nearly as busily as before the strike. Yet Morrison and Bergstrom and the others who returned noticed something different about their supervisors. If the strike accomplished nothing else, it had alerted Hormel management to its mistakes during the first few years in the new plant. Arnold admitted publicly that the lines had run too fast, that Hormel had hired new workers too fast and explained too little. They were extraordinary confessions in the loyal, secretive world of corporate America.

Now the company was determined that supervisors would communicate with employees, that new workers would be well trained, that management would get its message across in regular employee meetings. Shortly after the plant reopening, Arnold had established a big brother system whereby returning P-9 members would train the new hirees on complicated jobs. Hormel also put a premium on safety, having been stung by Corporate Campaign's charges. Although it vigorously disputed the reasons, Hormel agreed with the strikers that the injury rate in Austin was too high. That spring Hormel made it known that any department to go thirty days without a lost-time injury would get a free white-tablecloth lunch, with Arnold and his underlings dishing it up. The program worked. Injury rates plummeted, and the P-9 veterans found themselves working reasonably peacefully side by side with nonunion replacements.

Hormel executives sought a degree of normality outside the plant as well, even though many were as bitter and as angry as the most ardent P-9ers. Sometime that summer Nyberg took the phone-answering machine off his phone at home as the hate calls began to taper off. He made a point of nodding and saying hello to P-9 members on the street. "We've got to live with each other in this community," Knowlton reminded his managers.

Things were far from normal for the eight hundred P-9ers who remained out of work, however, and the blue caps were not about to let anyone forget it. The big abandoned barn six miles north of town on Highway 218, which had become a sort of community wailing wall, now screamed "Scab City" in giant white hand-painted letters. Round blue stickers reading P-9 PROUD were replaced by red-and-white bumper stickers proclaiming SCAB CITY U.S.A., AUSTIN, MINN. Though they professed to sleep well at night because their consciences were clear, many of those who stayed out remained deeply bitter at Hormel, the international, and their own members who broke ranks. Some refused to go near the plant and, when they did, refused to look at it. The freeway exit at the north gate, the scene of so many predawn demonstrations, became one to boycott because it meant going near the plant. Most could drive down any street in town and point out which homes belonged to scabs and which ones were P-9ers. After all the strikers were placed on the rehiring list, however, many began to tone down their rhetoric, or vent it only privately, to protect their chances of getting recalled. They had been beaten badly, and they knew it, yet they clung to a hope and lived in fear of antagonizing a company that they really didn't like anyway.

Others became reclusive, moving out of town or finding new jobs in other towns where they might not be blackballed. They simply wanted to get on with their lives and leave the strike wounds behind. Either way, the bitter silence was a sharp departure from the days when Rogers made skillful, confident spokesmen out of people who had never been on TV in their lives.

The United Support Group, however, was not about to let up. Evicted from their basement headquarters in the Austin Labor Center, Vickie Guyette, Cindy Rud, and the others moved three blocks down the street to an old building once occupied by the Hormel employees' credit union. Its plate-glass windows were crammed with solidarity banners and a big lighted sign that often advertised MEETING TONIGHT; inside, it was much as the union hall had been: a constant flow of volunteers stuffing envelopes, chatting over coffee, eyeing the display of P-9 sweat shirts, jackets, and caps. Guyette, Winkels, Buck, Huston, and the others continued to meet with their loyalists almost every day.

On the evening of July 14 Carman held his first organizing meeting for workers in the plant. If he had any doubts, he learned that night that the blue caps were not about to leave the UFCW alone. A team of them turned up for the meeting, marching over from the Support Group office, hollering and cursing Carman and Kimbro, sneering at the new Hormel workers, and demanding to know why they weren't allowed into the "invitation only" meeting.

If the UFCW had taken their union away from them, the hardliners reasoned, they would form their own union. In July they applied to the NLRB as "Original Local P-9" and asked the board to conduct an election challenging the UFCW for the right to represent Hormel's employees in Austin. The board rejected their petition on the ground that their name was too confusing. So they chartered a new union: North American Meat Packers Union, or NAMPU. The charter membership roll read like a list of the most active P-9 volunteers: big Merrill Evans, who was always in the front line of any demonstration; Connie Dammen, a leading figure in the United Support Group; Pete Kennedy and Larry Gullickson, who were always around the union hall helping with phone calls and press releases; and Rod Huinker, Dick Shatek, and Dan Allen, among the most regular and most vocal Guyette supporters at rank-and-file meetings and on the picket line. For the record, Guyette, Winkels, Huston, Buck, and the other executive board members kept at arm's length from NAMPU. They had appealed Devitt's ruling on the trusteeship and didn't want to cloud their ability to regain control of P-9 by affiliating themselves with a competing union. But they could be found regularly at NAMPU's storefront office on Fourth Avenue.

NAMPU was partly the brainchild of Dave Twedell, the young Texas attorney whose father had been a UFCW regional officer and who was himself an alienated former UFCW officer. Twedell represented a UFCW local in Sherman, Texas, that had tried to bolt from the UFCW, and now he saw Austin as the most promising band of workers discontented with the union. With the Support Group's volunteers, NAMPU began distributing leaflets that launched an outright attack on the UFCW. One accused the UFCW of ordering P-9 to go on strike in August 1985; another blamed the UFCW for the firings of the 480 meat-packers in Ottumwa who had honored P-9's roving pickets. A third described a series of wage concessions among retail clerks and accused the UFCW of "leading the campaign to remove all clock-punchers from the middle class." It said: "In 1979 the Retail Clerks Association took over our union without even one clock-punching member having a chance to vote on this 'merger.' Since then, we have had nothing but trouble in the meatpacking industry." It went on to say: "North American Meat Packers Union gives you a chance to regain control of your union. We believe we must return to the one-plant/one-local philosophy that built our old union. Your plant's rank and file will elect officers that live in your town and answer only to you." NAMPU distributed the leaflets all over the Hormel chain—Iowa, Nebraska, Wisconsin—and at Oscar Mayer and FDL.

Four days after Kimbro and Smith moved into the labor center, NAMPU filed a petition asking the NLRB to conduct a decertification election in Austin and give Hormel workers a chance to switch from the UFCW to NAMPU or to go nonunion entirely. If NAMPU could somehow win a representation election at Austin, Twedell reasoned, it could launch new organizing drives at the rest of the Hormel plants when their contracts expired at the end of August. And the seeds of a new union would be sown.

Though Guyette was not officially a part of the NAMPU campaign, he didn't make any secret of his feelings toward the UFCW. He spent much of the summer preparing an appeal of Devitt's ruling on the trusteeship, conferring with lawyers, preparing for depositions, and appealing for money. His wife, Vickie, remained active in the Support Group. By now they were feeding their three children with the help of food stamps and living on the support checks that still trickled in from union halls around the country. Jim said that he almost lost his house that summer, but he gave no outward sign of being discouraged. He still gave occasional speeches in various cities, lambasting the UFCW and urging other union locals to fight on. Speaking with his frequent visitors, he insisted that P-9 would have won the strike and its demands if the UFCW had simply stepped aside. In a fund-raising letter for his lawsuit against the trusteeship, he accused the UFCW of spending "hundreds of thousands of dollars to destroy our local. They are trying to bury P-9's rank and file democracy and further undermine a struggle that has become a symbol of honest and militant trade unionism."

Pete Winkels divided his time between the Support Group office and NAMPU headquarters. He lacked Guyette's confidence that lawyers could ever overturn the trusteeship, and he began to ponder his future: Back to school? Back to the packinghouse if Hormel started hiring? He also pondered the recent past and spent a lot of time at home, as he put it, "staring at walls."

Meanwhile, Dave Larson and Joe Hansen had started the arduous negotiations toward a new contract for the Austin packinghouse. Shortly after Devitt's order granting the trusteeship in June, the two veteran negotiators began meeting at a Holiday Inn coffee shop in Burnsville, a Twin Cities suburb south of Hansen's office and north of Larson's. Both men were under considerable pressure. Hansen was caught in a squeeze between Washington and Austin, where the possibility loomed of a representation election. He was confident of Carman's organizing abilities, but it didn't help his bargaining position with Larson that a rival union was trying to take the Austin plant away from the UFCW. Every week that passed gave NAMPU another week to convince the meat-packers to dump the UFCW. Hansen wanted a contract that would avert a decertification vote. Lewie Anderson, however, was not about to settle cheaply just because the strike was over. He was wounded by the long series of attacks from P-9 and wanted to prove that the UFCW could drive a hard bargain. Hormel was still his hope to pull up wages in the meat-packing industry, and if it meant another strike—chain-wide this time— he was willing. He was all for keeping Austin without a contract until the other Hormel chain plants expired on September 1 and then threatening Hormel with a total shutdown.

For his part, Larson represented a company that had operated nearly a year without a union contract, and some of his management colleagues were beginning to like it. Nyberg argued that Hormel had been burned once by leaving employee communication to union leaders, and the company was not about to make the same mistake twice. Nyberg addressed weekly employee meetings to answer questions about the plant's status, and he wasn't shy about explaining the employees' right to dump the union. In addition, the company had lawyers in the plant every afternoon to explain labor law. The company would not look kindly on a demanding union.

Still, Larson and Hansen were seasoned adversaries and knew their terrain intimately. At their first actual negotiating meeting in June, Larson offered a token of reconciliation: a proposal to settle the union's outstanding grievances so that Hormel could distribute 1985 profit-sharing checks that were now several months overdue. Once the pleasantries ended, each man got right to the heart of the matter. Larson wanted to know Bill Wynn's bottom line: What would Hormel have to change in its implemented work rules to win a recommendation from the UFCW? Hansen said much the same thing he had said seven months earlier: an end to the two-tier wages; improvements in safety, seniority, and grievance procedures; common expiration dates with the rest of the Hormel chain. Hansen in turn asked for Hormel's tally of how many P-9 members were still on strike. How many had resigned or retired? How many had signed up to return to work? In other words, how big a job did he have negotiating jobs for the union members who had lost them? Of 1,422 P-9 members who had gone on strike, about 460 had returned to work. Another 200 or so had retired during the strike. Another 100 or so never returned company mail, and Larson assumed they had left town to find work. That left 600 to 700 P-9 members still in the Austin area and out of work.

Hansen and Larson negotiated about once a week at the Holiday Inn for the next three months, each time inching a little closer. Hormel was willing to move on seniority and safety language, but Larson was not about to promise any jobs. Hormel was getting all the production it wanted out of Austin, FDL, and the other plants, and it had learned the dangers of letting one plant grow too large. Hormel also was willing to move on wages, but wanted to stick with some kind of two-tier system to keep wages lower in the labor-intensive slaughter operation, which was a nagging money loser. Knowlton had hinted at the previous annual meeting that slaughtering in Austin might be shut down, and Larson reiterated that without a lower wage scale there Hormel would not keep killing its own hogs for long. Finally, Hormel was not about to give the UFCW common expiration dates for all the chain plants, but perhaps there could be a compromise of some kind. Hansen acknowledged Larson's concerns but warned that Anderson was not going to approve a soft contract.

At their last meeting in August, Larson gave Hansen a written list of the compromises Hormel was willing to make. It included seniority, two-tier wages, grievance procedures, and expiration dates. He told Hansen to bring it to Des Moines for the chain-wide talks and Hormel would see if it couldn't work it into the chain settlement.

Buoyed by a sense that Hansen and Larson were moving toward a settlement, Kimbro and Carman stepped up their efforts to fend off NAMPU. Now that the UFCW's Al Zack had control of *The Unionist,* P-9's membership newsletter, he used it to blast NAMPU's ties to the failed strike. In mid-July a revamped eight-page *Unionist* went out to P-9 members with a description of Hansen's efforts to win unemployment benefits for the remaining strikers, his success at resolving grievances and releasing profit-sharing checks to P-9 members, and the UFCW's efforts to rebuild the Hormel chain. The next issue featured a big cartoon captioned "The Winning Card" and showed a pair of hands holding three cards: one with the UFCW logo, one marked "No Union" with a growling bear, and one marked "NAMPU" with a dopey-looking boy in a copter beanie. It described NAMPU as:

"Resume strike. Resume picketing. Go-it-alone. Lots of publicity. Lots of failures." A third issue summarized an interim audit of P-9's finances and bore a cartoon of a man in a gas mask standing next to a dung heap labeled "Interim Audit Report" saying, "What smell?" The UFCW also filed a series of unfair-labor-practice charges against NAMPU and Hormel with the NLRB. UFCW attorneys alleged that Hormel was pressuring employees to vote nonunion and that NAMPU founders had been harassing Kimbro, Smith, and Hormel employees who tried to attend union meetings. An administrative law judge eventually threw out most of the charges, including one that NAMPU founders had harassed Kimbro and Smith the day they took charge of the union hall. But the charges served as a convenient delay tactic for Hansen. While unfair-labor-practice charges are pending, the NLRB typically refuses to conduct representation elections on the ground that one side might win as a result of activities later ruled illegal. Such an outcome was unlikely in this case, but it blocked NAMPU's election for several months and gave Hansen more time to negotiate a contract for the Austin workers.

On August 11 Hansen, Lewie Anderson, Dave Larson, and their respective teams gathered once again in Des Moines, Iowa, for a final sprint toward a contract settlement covering Austin and perhaps the rest of the chain. This time Anderson had a strong card in his pocket. Back in July, when he first broached issues in the chain contract with Larson, Hormel had been grudging on the wage issue. True, the company had a two-tier wage system in Austin, but its contracts at the other chain plants put Hormel wages just about at the top of the industry. Hormel was not about to step out any farther unless other packers also were raising wages. Anderson said to forget about it for now and resume talks in August. Meanwhile, he took off for Chicago, where he opened negotiations with Oscar Mayer, the only remaining old-line packer that still resembled Hormel in operations, wages, and profitability. Oscar Mayer also had a sort of chain, including three big packinghouses in Chicago, Madison, Wisconsin, and Davenport, Iowa. The labor contract for the Chicago plant had expired in March, leaving Oscar Mayer free to whipsaw that plant against the other two. But Anderson had a strategy: He refused to settle the contract in Chicago and left his members in the plant working without a contract and staging small protests until the contracts at Madison and Davenport expired in the summer. If Oscar Mayer fired them or locked them out, at least they could collect unemployment benefits. The strategy worked. When the contracts expired at Madison and Davenport, Anderson was in a position to put all three plants on strike. In the middle of August he negotiated a contract that would bring Oscar Mayer's wages back to $10.70 an hour by 1989, finally restoring the industry target wage rate.

Anderson took the Oscar Mayer contract back to Des Moines on August 20 and showed it to Larson. Hormel wouldn't be out front all alone on wages. Larson signed off.

On August 27 Hansen announced a tentative settlement that would finally bring the Austin dispute to an end: The two-tier wage system would be phased out; the grievance system would be improved; wages would go back to $10.70 an hour by 1988. But the settlement provided no guarantee that P-9's remaining strikers would ever get their jobs back. "Recall was the toughest issue," Hansen told a reporter that night. "They can't just create jobs."

Guyette and the NAMPU leaders reacted with scorn. They faulted Hansen for negotiating away the escrow payments that had compensated Hormel veterans for the loss of their incentive pay eight years earlier and noted that the contract put a two-year cap on the recall rights of strikers who were still out of work. The day that Anderson and Hansen presented the proposal to workers in Austin, NAMPU organizers circulated outside Riverside Arena, the same place they had demonstrated so boisterously just four months before, and urged Hormel's new workers to vote against the deal.

The UFCW scheduled ratification votes in the seven chain towns, and announced that Austin workers inside the plant and those still out on strike would be elegible to vote. On September 13 P-9's members approved the settlement, 1,060–440. Ratification of the contract blocked NAMPU's request for a representation election and, after an abortive effort to win representation rights at a packinghouse in Plainview, Texas, NAMPU quietly dissolved some months later.

It was over.

CHAPTER

17

It is 1989, and Pete Winkels and John Morrison haven't spoken face-to-face in three years. John was elected secretary-treasurer of Local 9 when the trusteeship ended in 1987. His desk sits a few feet from Pete's old office at the union hall. He can still rummage around in a desk drawer and find the programs from their weddings. Pete went back to Austin Community College to finish the degree he never completed in 1967. Asked about their falling-out, Pete says, "It just kind of eats at you."

Jim Guyette still speaks to other unions occasionally, still relishing the national platform that P-9's strike gave him. He and Vickie still live in Austin, where he spends a lot of time on schoolwork. He took some night classes in arbitration and history up in Minneapolis and thinks he might get back into the labor movement if he can find a union other than the UFCW. Two years after the UFCW removed him from office, he continued to convene regular meetings of the ousted executive board. He still says P-9 would have won if the UFCW hadn't interfered. It's a claim that the United Support Group, where Vickie remains active, continued to drive home in leaflets denouncing the big union more than a year after the strike ended.

John Anker replaced Guyette as union president after the trusteeship was lifted and immediately set himself apart from his predecessor by showing up at the union hall in a coat and tie. His hair and beard are grayer than his early forties would suggest. He and Morrison run the union's affairs on such a tight budget that they take phone calls and type letters themselves and make photocopies on the backs of used paper.

Lewie Anderson and Joe Hansen have moved on to new crises in the meatpacking industry, though their troubles in Austin didn't stop with the end of the trusteeship in 1987. In January 1988 Hormel made good on a threat to shut down the Austin plant's seldom-profitable slaughtering operations. The company found jobs for all three hundred slaughter workers on the plant's processing lines, but the shutdown seemed to foreclose the hopes of any former strikers waiting to be rehired. Then, in the spring of 1988, Hormel said it had built a wall right through the plant, dividing the processing lines from the abattoir, and that it planned to lease the slaughter facility to a new, nonunion subcontractor that could kill hogs in the same building and furnish Hormel with raw pork at wages competitive with other nonunion slaughtering firms. The UFCW challenged the step as a violation of Local 9's contract, and an arbitrator ruled that Hormel could not subcontract the work on site to a nonunion employer. Using the arbitrator's ruling as leverage, the union began negotiating with Hormel's subcontractor and by early 1989 had an agreement that the slaughterhouse would reopen with a union contract. It promised to bring back many of the former strikers who had lost their jobs, though at a wage two to three dollars below that of their counterparts on Hormel's processing lines.

All the while, strikers who lost their jobs continued to call Hansen's house regularly, wondering if he'd heard anything new, if there was a chance they would get back to work. For Hansen, who knows full well that the UFCW helped create the misery in their lives, they are the hardest calls of his life.

Anderson, in a surprise move, was fired as UFCW packinghouse director following an internal disagreement over future bargaining strategy. Nonetheless, he retained a broad measure of support among local leaders in the Midwest.

Dick Knowlton, Dave Larson, and Chuck Nyberg are doing their best to forget the events of 1985 and 1986, writing them off as a once-in-a-lifetime aberration. Like Guyette, they are in demand on the speaker circuit, a limelight they haven't gotten used to. During the dispute Knowlton turned down two offers to leave Hormel, both paying more than his $565,000 annual salary. Larson was at the Mayo Clinic in Rochester one day in early 1988 for a physical exam and a hearing test when he ran into his old nemesis Dick Schaefer. The retired business agent was there being treated for an impairment to his tear ducts. "You made me cry for my union so many times I ran out of tears," Schaefer kidded his old enemy. "You hollered at me so much I went deaf," Larson replied.

Deryl Arnold, plant manager during the strike, was promoted to a job with FDL Foods. He died of cancer in June 1988. Austin Mayor Tom Kough made an unsuccessful bid for the Minnesota Senate in the fall of 1986. The following January, at the Hormel annual meeting in Long Beach, California, he made a futile plea to Knowlton, his former classmate, to let former strikers return to work. A short time later he was fired for wearing a "Cram Your Spam" T-shirt in California while he and his wife, Carol, were trying to raise money to help out-of-work P-9 families. He was a victim of the new labor contract in Austin, which forbade employees from engaging in boycott activity. In mid-1987 he landed a job as maintenance man for a Minneapolis high-rise building, and Carol was hired to run the office. They moved into the building and took up residence in a thirteenth-floor apartment overlooking the Minneapolis skyline. They also get together once a month for potluck suppers with thirty former P-9 families who relocated in the Twin Cities. They make no secret of their bitterness toward Hormel and the UFCW. Both attend labor rallies wearing their blue P-9 jackets, which they keep decorated with union buttons. Tom said he considers himself and Knowlton "total enemies."

Council-member-at-Large Bob Dahlback took a run at Kough's job as mayor but never made it past the primary. His outspoken criticism of the corporate campaign made him a continual target for vandalism and threats shortly after he went back to work, but they gradually tapered off. He kept his job in the plant and his hand in civic affairs by getting named to a city riverfront development board. The other council member who went back, Gerald Henricks, thought his chances of getting reelected were nil. But he ran and won his council seat again in 1986. The following fall he stepped down from the council and quit his job at Hormel to test his new collegial skills as city manager in Kenyon, a small town fifty miles northeast of Austin. He had to commute because he was unable to sell his home. One day not long after he was hired, a group of former P-9ers showed up outside city hall in Kenyon to tell townspeople about their "scab" official.

Larry Maier moved to Huntsville, Alabama, during the summer of 1986 to take a job as administrator of another mental health clinic. At age forty-eight, he had never thought of leaving Minnesota and owned a trailer and some land up north to show for it. But the deeper he got involved in the dispute, the more he knew he wouldn't stay. After he left, he kept in touch with friends in Austin, who told him things were getting better. But the memories of a town torn apart gave him little desire to come back.

For Ray Rogers, the fight goes on as if little has changed. He moved back to his apartment in New York and launched another corporate campaign at the International Paper Company where 3,500 members of the United Paperworkers International Union were on strike or locked out at four paper mills in four states in a dispute over contract concessions.

Those who followed that campaign through 1987 and 1988 were struck by its parallels to the Hormel battle. Rogers organized demonstrations at the shareholders' meetings of International Paper's corporate allies, sent teams of strikers from Jay, Maine, and other IP mills across the country to tell their story in newsrooms and union halls, and developed a following among many of the same labor activists who had supported the fight against Hormel. But IP held fast at the four mills where United Paperworkers members were on strike or locked out and continued production at dozens of other mills and factories that weren't on strike. On October 9, 1988, top officers of the paperworkers' union called an end to the strike, saying the union's strike fund was virtually depleted and that workers must offer to go back to work if IP had any openings. Over the Fourth of July weekend in 1987 Rogers returned to Austin for a P-9 Support Group counterprotest of a town celebration of the fiftieth anniversary of Spam. Rogers walked the parade route, getting hugs from well-wishers and nasty looks from others proudly sporting blue and gold "Spam" shirts. "Ya bum, didn't you hear me? You ruined our town!" yelled one. Rogers's smiling response? "Thank you, sir, have a very good day."

There are hundreds more anonymous people who lost their jobs during the strike, and Larry Jensen has seen most of them. In the fall of 1986, after it became clear that former strikers who wanted to go back would be stranded on the recall list, Jensen became an outreach worker for a state-funded program to help them start their lives over. Operating out of a classroom at the Austin Area Vocational-Technical Institute, the dislocated-worker program anticipated perhaps 250 clients. By the end of 1987, 419 former strikers had come in asking for help. Three fourths received classroom training, ranging from a short course in computers or real estate to a two-year stay in a welding program. Even more received vocational counseling, steering them to aptitude tests and providing assistance on where and how to look for work. Nearly two hundred people were placed in jobs, and about thirty received money to help them relocate. About seventy people were phased out of the program when they didn't show up for a six-month status update. Others remained in training, either in the classroom or on the job.

But the workers' struggle to piece their lives together again cannot be tallied by statistics. Many strikers found themselves applying for work for the first time in twenty years, while others were writing résumés for the first time in their lives. Some were reluctant to reveal much personal information to a potential employer who, seeing their last job was at Hormel, would brand them troublemakers and find a way to hire around them. Jensen heard numerous stories about workers with unblemished records at the plant getting blackballed. He heard about family problems, divorces, and threats of suicide. Even for those who seemed to get on with their lives, pessimism ran so deep that even the news that Hormel had extended their recall rights from two years to perpetuity couldn't lift their spirits. "It's enough to make these people wonder what the hell they did," Jensen said one day in February 1988, seated behind a gray metal desk in the classroom, scanning a pile of newspapers for job openings.

Jensen gestured to another desk a few feet away, where two

middle-aged men were seated with their heads down, quietly filling out job applications. One of them was Ray Remington, a
stocky Austin High grad and third-generation Hormel worker
whose last job before the strike was snatching guts from hog carcasses. Remington had been loyal to Hormel: He missed three
days of work in eighteen years in the packinghouse and thought
nothing of driving a tractor through a snowstorm to punch in on
time. He was loyal to his union, too: He was one of the roving
pickets in Fremont who phoned in reports of how many people
refused to cross the line and hoped that a little pressure on
Hormel could help resolve the issues that separated the two
sides. He also was stung by the defections from P-9's ranks. He
said he felt like a soldier in a combat zone with a buddy who
turned and ran. Reflecting on the strike two years later, however,
he came to this conclusion: If the UFCW had been truly sincere,
it would have placed his union in trusteeship before Hormel
stopped hiring.

Next to him was Jim Krulish, who was among the first 124
people to sign up on Hormel's recall list after the UFCW lifted its
strike sanction. It was the second time he had to look for work
after losing what he had been led to believe was a job for life.
Hormel hired him in 1971, then laid him off in 1977. But he
climbed aboard again in 1983 during the new-plant hiring push.
He got involved in the corporate campaign, attended the First
Bank annual meeting, and did some bannering, but not nearly as
much as his wife. He supported the strike because he felt that
Hormel had adopted a new attitude in the new plant, one that
didn't consider workers' concerns. He went on the fall caravans
to the other plants. He envisioned a long walkout, at least
through Christmas. He knew the P-10ers were entitled to their
opinion but didn't like their divide-and-conquer tactics. When he
looked back on it later, he said, the mediator's proposal was the
one to take, but after that emotions hardened to the point where
it was fight, fight, fight all the way. When replacements were
pouring into the plant in late January 1986, he called the UFCW
office in Washington. "Don't cross," he was told. His sister did.
His mother, who had worked thirty-six years in the plant and had
had five operations on her hands, said he should, too. He stuck to
his principles instead. It took the death of their father to bring

Krulish and his sister together. They have agreed not to discuss the strike.

Jensen shook his head and recalled the strike's last wrenching months, the part that he still can't figure out. The people who obeyed the most fundamental principle of unionism—refusing to cross a sanctioned picket line—were the ones who got hurt the worst. Jensen remembered his son-in-law, whom he talked out of going back to work. He eventually landed a job with a cement-mixing company. "Did I do him justice or an injustice?" he asked. "I don't know."

His mind wandered back to people like Remington and Krulish, stranded in mid-life for sticking to their beliefs. "We were told that the company would not call anybody back to work unless they had an agreement ratified," he said with a tone of expectancy. "Now they have a ratified, signed agreement and eight hundred people on the recall list. And yet those two gentlemen haven't been called back to work. They're not rowdy, two-headed monsters. They're normal, hardworking midwestern people and right now, all they want to do is get on with their lives."

And understand what happened to them.

They aren't the only people trying to comprehend what happened in Austin. Since the strike's end several labor unions have held seminars on "The Lessons of P-9." Graduate students have put it under the microscope in management class. New York *Newsday*, the *Village Voice*, and *The Nation* have carried articles on its symbolic significance. Labor activists ask how P-9's defeat could have become a victory. M.B.A. students ask how Hormel management could have sweetened a bitter pill for employees without jeopardizing the enterprise. Society asks how a costly tragedy could have been prevented. A variety of partisan answers have emerged in the months following the strike, answers that we think cloud any understanding of it. We don't have short answers ourselves, but we'd like to address three of the most common.

Number one: Hormel was a greedy company on a gratuitous crusade to cut wages. Rogers and Guyette were fond of saying that Hormel was the industry's most profitable packer, and they raised a compelling question: Why does a profitable company need wage cuts? But it's well to remember that Hormel had been

376

operating under an income freeze, so to speak, of its own. Its profits had been flat or declining for three years when it first asked for wage cuts in 1983. In 1984 its profit of $29.5 million was actually lower than in 1979. For a company that routinely plowed profits back into plant and equipment it was not a healthy situation or an attractive one for investors. It is true that Hormel's profits jumped dramatically just after the strike began, from $29.5 million in fiscal 1984 to $38.6 million in 1985. But the reason for that was the same one cited by the UFCW in opposing P-9's strategy: Hormel was able to acquire another troubled packing firm—a low-wage competitor—that substantially increased Hormel's sales volume without a commensurate rise in its labor costs.

By our calculations, if Hormel's labor costs had remained where they were in 1984, the last fiscal year before the wage and benefit reductions, the company would have gone into the red by 1987, its first full fiscal year after the strike. It's impossible to say how much money Hormel would have lost because foreseeing red ink, it would probably have taken a variety of belt-tightening measures that we cannot calculate. But if we assume that Hormel couldn't significantly raise prices to consumers or significantly cut the price it paid for hogs—fair assumptions in the food business—it sooner or later would have faced the same squeeze on operating costs that all its competitors had faced and dealt with. Had P-9 triumphed in 1985 or 1986, it almost certainly would have been a Pyrrhic victory, one that forced Hormel into the same financial pinch that had led Wilson to slash wages in 1983. Either solution for Hormel would have been unpalatable to the union: financial distress, resulting in plant closings and layoffs, or subcontracting work—and eventually jobs—to low-wage or nonunion packers.

Perhaps more to the point, Hormel could skirt the moral debate about whether it needed wage cuts. It had specific contract language, negotiated in 1978, agreed to by the union, and affirmed by an arbitrator three times, giving it the legal right to cut wages. Expecting a company to forgo cost reductions for which it has an economic incentive and a legal right is simply naive. Rather than wait until crisis loomed, Hormel tried to have the fight up front. By offering workers a better deal than the contract called for—in the fall of 1984, the spring of 1985, and the winter of 1985—Hormel demonstrated it could pay its workers more than those employed by struggling companies. The fact that P-9 consistently turned down Hormel showed how much they differed philosophically on the need for cutbacks in the first place.

Number two: Jim Guyette was a demagogue who led his members over a cliff against their will. To be sure, Guyette was an extraordinary leader. He had courage; he had vision; he had the unfailing self-confidence that allows a leader to persevere in the face of adversity. He embodied an almost evangelical zeal, a commitment that reminded one union sympathizer in Austin of missionaries who drop their material lives to go work in the third word. Guyette has told us more than once that he never doubted his course, not even in the face of criticism by everyone from the governor of Minnesota to *The New York Times.*

He also displayed a persistent refusal to compromise, effectively converting bargaining issues to moral principles. Guyette always claimed that he was simply acting out the wishes of his rank and file, which, quite naturally, always wanted those principles upheld in their quest for a better contract. It's a claim we find a little disingenuous in light of his ability to organize petition drives within the membership, to quell similar efforts when they worked against him, to denounce contract proposals that a majority of his board had endorsed, to ensure that his supporters attended meetings and grabbed the floor, and to cast suspicion on the UFCW. The only time the P-9 board turned on him during the strike was when he was absent from a meeting, on the decision to pull back roving pickets from Fremont. There were several other instances when board members had their doubts, but they found Guyette was a persuasive arm twister who could take a 6–2 vote against him and turn it in his favor. His rank and file apparently found him persuasive, too. Only 350 people voted for him when he was elected president—barely 20 percent of the membership—but by the end of the strike more than twice as many stuck with his strategy and voted themselves out of their jobs. Add Rogers's ability to sustain the members' hopes in the face of adversity, and it's easy to see why they refused to quit.

And yet we don't believe the rank and file followed Guyette blindly. If anything, he was their creation. One out of five P-9ers was a knowledgeable veteran with twice Guyette's experience in the union. Another fifth were baby boomers, many of them college-educated and too smart to be buffaloed. The rest were newcomers, but not necessarily wild-eyed young people. Even if his election majority was slim, it demonstrated his ability to inspire a following at a time when the other candidates inspired apathy or worse. Once Guyette was elected, the rank and file had one opportunity after another to stop him if they didn't agree with him. These included three separate votes on an assessment to pay for Ray Rogers's campaign, the last occurring in the spring of 1985, when there was abundant evidence of Rogers's fallibilities for those in Austin who wanted to recognize it.

Morrison, Anker, and the other P-10ers offered several other opportunities for the membership to abandon Guyette. There was Anker's resolution directing the executive committee to negotiate for the chain offer in the spring of 1985. There was the campaign for executive board openings in December 1985. And there was a call to reconsider the mediator's proposal in January 1986. True, many of the opportunities were torpedoed early at rank-and-file meetings, where Guyette's supporters outorganized the P-10ers and demonstrated a remarkable ability to intimidate dissidents. But there were several paper ballots, and if the rank and file really was turning, they should have been able to stand up to the bullies in the blue cap crowd. The P-10ers never could muster more than about one fourth of the membership, and it wasn't just the vocal blue caps who spurned their efforts. Guyette and the executive board had the quiet support of a huge plurality of veterans and newcomers alike who resented Hormel and distrusted the UFCW. As for the fence-sitters, like those in any union, peer pressure probably was sufficient to persuade them that it was easier to bash the company than to argue for compromise. In reality, the louder the chorus of pleas became urging Guyette to back down, the more resolute the rank and file became in standing behind what he stood for.

As for P-9's last chance to settle—the mediator's proposal— we'll never know if the members misunderstood it; they refused to vote again after Arnold Zack issued his fact-finding report. Guyette, Huston, Rogers, and the others certainly did their best to shoot it down, and Zack was satisfied that they distorted the proposal. Clearly, several hundred of the members mistakenly thought they would get yet another offer. But if the rank and file were ever going to look for a way out, December 1985 was a good time. It was plain then that the corporate campaign was a failure and that Guyette had a habit—deliberate or accidental—of misinterpreting contracts. Yet they twice rejected the mediator's proposal by a solid three-to-two majority.

It's hard to imagine the entire dispute without Guyette at the helm of P-9. He campaigned on a promise of no concessions. He thought up the idea of hiring Ray Rogers. He led the drive to arbitrate the 1984 wage cuts rather than seek the chain compromise. He was a tireless worker and an articulate spokesman. In short, he channeled a stream of bitterness that ran deep in P-9. But even if he wasn't part of the picture, it's hard to imagine that bitterness simply dissipating and Hormel getting through the 1980's without a showdown sooner or later.

Number three: The meat-packers could have prevailed if the UFCW had stood behind them or even stood clear. When you sat in one of P-9's many rallies from March 1985 to April 1986, it was easy to believe that its campaign had massive support and the momentum to humble Hormel. Inside the thundering auditorium it was hard to understand why the UFCW and the AFL-CIO did not rally behind these brave union members. Outside, however, it was clear that trouble lay ahead.

On January 14, 1986, one day after Hormel reopened the packinghouse and the first day it handed out job applications, some two thousand people poured into the plant to apply for jobs at eight dollars an hour. We watched that parade from across the street. These were not, as Rogers suggested at the time, chartered buses packed with cardboard silhouettes or professional scabs. These were unemployed workers and hard-luck farmers from all over southern Minnesota and northern Iowa who seized the chance to earn what was then roughly the nation's median wage. One of the best-paying jobs in the rural Midwest was suddenly up for grabs. On that day the labor market vindicated Hormel's claim that its offer was competitive in light of events in the nation's economy.

Had the UFCW supported P-9 then—by sanctioning roving pickets—Hormel probably would have fired every worker who

honored the picket lines and hired replacements all over its operation. The damage to both sides would have been immense; but
Hormel almost certainly would have continued operating, and its
plants likely would have gone nonunion. By the time the rest of
the Hormel chain could legally have joined P-9's strike, in August
1986, the Austin plant was up and running at full capacity. In
other words, Hormel was in a perfect position to whipsaw Austin
against the other chain locals. That was not the fault of P-9's strategy or the UFCW's but of Hormel's immense clout back in 1978,
a position that allowed it to negotiate a no-strike clause for the
new plant that kept 40 percent of its production capacity out of
sync with the other plants.

Had the UFCW supported P-9's efforts to keep the Austin
plant closed—by interceding with Governor Perpich to stop the
National Guard—the union could have caused Perpich some un-
comfortable moments. But Perpich was faced with maintaining
safety and order after Austin authorities had lost control of the
streets, an obligation underlined by a court ruling against a previous governor in 1959. Moreover, he already had shown a
willingness to cross organized labor on legislative issues when
the stakes were high enough. And here the stakes were very high:
retaining a Fortune 500 company in a state often criticized for its
business climate. It's not realistic to think he would have let the
packinghouse remain closed for long when Hormel had proved it
could hire workers even though huge crowds were physically
trying to turn them away.

Had the UFCW supported P-9 earlier—by endorsing the corporate campaign against Hormel—perhaps there would have
been greater consumer pressure on Hormel and First Bank System. But why would the UFCW want to pressure the best-paying
company in the industry? So consumers would turn to Morrell,
which had cut wages more deeply? Or Wilson, which had tried to
abrogate its labor contracts completely? Or Armour, a former
union stronghold that went nonunion virtually overnight with
the sale of thirteen plants?

In short, to hope that the UFCW would rally behind P-9's
strategy is to ignore a long-standing philosophical rift that culmi-
nated in their crucial falling-out during the summer of 1984, long
before the feud reached crisis proportions. As a result, the UFCW

was in no position to ask workers at other Hormel plants to sacrifice their jobs for P-9 when P-9 was asking for more than those workers had negotiated without its help.

The tactical argument boiled down to two metaphors used by Lewie Anderson and Jim Guyette. Anderson said you have to rebuild a house from the foundation up, meaning the low-wage packing companies. Guyette replied that you can't fix the foundation if the roof leaks. Guyette's was a good metaphor for holding the line at the top, and it made a lot of people wonder why a profitable company couldn't pay higher wages than an unprofitable one. In fact, the strategy had worked for years for the UAW against the automakers and for the old Amalgamated Meatcutters against the packers: Strike the most profitable employer to set a pattern; then hold the other employers to the same pattern. But that was at a time when the pattern still existed, when there was rough parity among the major employers and even the least profitable could afford to match the labor contracts of the most profitable. Chrysler's near bankruptcy signaled the end of that pattern, not just in auto manufacturing, but in trucking, steel, airlines, and any number of other heavily unionized industries. When the Wilson bankruptcy broke the pattern in meat-packing, labor needed a new strategy. With the collapse of pattern bargaining, it was no longer possible to stage a fight at the top of the wage scale. To fight at the top ran two risks. First, you really could put your employer out of business because its competitors' costs were lower. Secondly, your employer could break a strike by hiring replacements or subcontracting work to lower-wage competitors.

In the final analysis, Hormel was not going to remain by itself at $10.69 an hour while all its competitors were cutting wages. And the economic evidence suggests that it could hire all the workers it wanted for $8 or $9 an hour.

In the absence of a potential for victory in the conventional sense, many of labor's partisans insisted that the UFCW should have supported P-9 because it was fighting the good fight. P-9 certainly demonstrated many of the qualities the labor movement desires. Its rank and file were intelligent, loyal, active, and emotionally engaged. It also galvanized a militant wing of the labor movement, and if its struggle accomplished anything, it may have been to nurture the horizontal labor movement growing within organized labor. If any dispute offered labor a chance to draw its line in the dirt and fight, the militants thought, this was it. But this kind of logic turns the members of P-9 into martyrs, a prospect few of them anticipated when the corporate campaign started and few embrace today.

This is not to say that the UFCW had to come down as hard as it did on P-9. In light of traditional solidarity among unionists, some of its news releases and leaflets were downright vicious— calling Rogers the Ayatollah of Austin or lampooning Guyette as a kid in a copter beanie. On the other hand, many international unions would have stepped in earlier. Tom Laney, the militant UAW leader in St. Paul who also feuded with his international leadership, found himself the target of a vigorous countercampaign when he ran for reelection in the spring of 1987 and lost. Lewie Anderson said long after the Austin strike that given the chance again, he would have moved to place P-9 in trusteeship in the fall of 1984, when the pesky local broke apart from the Hormel chain. But the structure of the UFCW's packinghouse division—predicated on dozens of far-flung, independent locals scattered across rural midwestern towns—made it hard for leaders like Anderson to keep tabs on the local politics in every affiliate. In addition, Anderson, who traveled eight months a year assisting locals, had his hands full with bigger crises at other packing companies in 1983, 1984, and 1985. Moreover, the UFCW was still reorganizing itself after the 1979 merger of the Retail Clerks and the Amalgamated Meat Cutters, and meat-packing was a small division in a shrinking industry.

In short, we find no clear villains in the strike and no easy lessons. Could Hormel have avoided a showdown? Not without rewriting several years of history in Austin and the meat-packing industry. Could the UFCW have salvaged a mutual victory? Not without mending a wound that took years to develop. Could the meat-packers have backed down from confrontation? Not without deposing a leader who was their own creation.

Dick Schaefer used to quote Jesse Prosten, Lewie Anderson's predecessor as national packinghouse director and a crusty mentor who taught Schaefer the fine points of collective bargaining.

"We were sleeping with the same whore," Prosten would say of a failed negotiating session. "But we were having different dreams."

For years Prosten, Anderson, Larson, and Schaefer always found a way to weave those dreams together. Suddenly Hormel and P-9 couldn't even describe their dreams to each other. The meat-packers assumed that because they were morally right, they would win. Hormel hoped that because they were tactically wrong, they would quit. Both were wrong.

The real puzzle is why the members of P-9 refused to back down in the face of evidence that they had badly underestimated Hormel's position and grotesquely overestimated their own. We think the answer to this puzzle lies in two sets of forces. One was peculiar to the history of Austin; the other was universal in America during the 1980's.

One day in August 1986 the familiar crowd of blue caps made one more pilgrimage to the federal courthouse in St. Paul. This time they were appealing Judge Devitt's ruling on the UFCW trusteeship, and they were as optimistic as ever. Now that they had gotten past Devitt to an appeals court panel, one said, they would finally get some justice. Reporters waiting with them simply looked at each other in bewilderment. Having lost before an outside arbitrator, the UFCW's internal tribunal, two Mower County judges, two regional offices of the National Labor Relations Board, two federal judges, two federal mediators, two state mediators, a Harvard professor, and the governor of Minnesota, P-9's loyalists were still convinced that they were just one fair hearing away from victory.

It wasn't the first time that friends and observers were struck by their naiveté. Guyette once told his friend Laney that if P-9 could just get a fair hearing before Wynn, he could expose the corruption of Anderson. Laney told him that if the UFCW was anything like the UAW, Wynn knew all about what Anderson was doing. P-9's leaders didn't grasp Minnesota politics any better than the politics of their own union. Dick Schaefer, P-9's business agent for thirteen years, said Guyette was the first P-9 president he could remember who wasn't a delegate to the Mower County convention of the Democratic-Farmer-Labor party. Likewise, a team of P-9 pamphleteers could engage AFL-CIO President Danny Gustafson in a shouting match at the federation's Minnesota convention in September 1985, then wonder why Gustafson didn't support them when Perpich called out the National Guard. At one of Paul Goldberg's many mediation sessions with P-9's executive board, Floyd Lenoch and Skinny Weis began describing the national ground swell rising behind them. Goldberg asked for their evidence. They cited all the checks pouring in from cities like Detroit, New York, and San Francisco. Goldberg told them that *any* appeal mentioning words like "progressive" or "fight back" could make the militants of these cities pull out their checkbooks.

How to explain this naiveté? The meat-packers in Austin certainly weren't the first midwesterners to hold a deep and abiding suspicion of the powerful institutions of the outside world. One needs only remember the Populist party of William Jennings Bryan to understand how militant yet reactionary the American Midwest has been. When the recession of 1982 and the subsequent farm crisis descended on the Midwest, volunteers at the Austin Labor Center weren't the only Americans who suspected that big corporations and banks were engaged in a conspiracy to expand profits at the expense of workers' standards of living. All manner of neopopulist and quasi-religious reformers attracted followings across the Farm Belt.

But the members of Local 9 had more to explain their conviction. Their union local had a long tradition of independence and strength, a tradition bolstered by the UPWA's democratic structure and Austin's geographic isolation from other industrial communities. Frank Schultz used to boast that he could keep UPWA brass out of Austin and negotiate contracts himself. In addition, they worked for a company whose corporate headquarters was not just in the same town but, until the 1960's, in the very same building. If Schultz could boast about keeping the international out of town, he could also claim that he got Local 9 as good a deal as any other union got, and usually a little better. Although long periods passed when Hormel wasn't hiring, those who got on the payroll came to regard the extraordinary Hormel compensation package as an entitlement, a benefit of living in Austin, and a gravy train that Hormel could protect through thick and thin. In the years that preceded the strike, there was a sense of ownership wrapped around a job in the Hormel plant. Not only the job but the high wages, the incentive pay, the extra "bracket" money for tough jobs, the medical insurance, the eye and dental care, the vacations, the pension, the company stock and profit-sharing checks every Thanksgiving. With a series of strong local presidents and business agents governing the good years from 1945 through the early 1970's, the rest of P-9's local elections became popularity contests in which local athletes or nice guys often won office.

The new-plant battle of the mid-1970's, far from confronting this sense of entitlement, simply planted a seed of bitterness that grew as the 1980's worsened economically. Hormel embarked on a competitive new era just as Jim Guyette's generation came to power in P-9, hoping to assert new leadership and address its old needs. Like so many other companies, Hormel was turning its workplace into a place of robots and computers just as it was hiring a generation that wanted autonomy and respect. For a company that had built its reputation on innovative labor relations techniques, Hormel handled the human side of the new-plant transition with surprising clumsiness. It was nearly two and a half years after the plant had officially opened before Hormel instituted an in-plant communication service to answer employee questions. But by that time the anticompany venom was loose in the packinghouse. The union was an amalgam of grizzled veterans hired in the paternalistic 1940's, baby boomers approaching twenty years of packinghouse service just as paternalism came to an abrupt halt, and a flood of newcomers hired into the new plant and a sea of bitterness. For the old workers, the new plant was a new world with callous foremen and industrial engineers holding stopwatches. The 850 new people who came on after it opened never got to know their employer's proud and storied past. Instead, they were shown once how to run bewildering equipment and given thirty days to do it right or lose their jobs. Hormel hired too many people too fast in its haste to work the kinks out of its first-of-the-world-to-see plant. But then it had always been enough to offer the best wages and benefits in Austin. Now workers seemed to want more than money.

In a ground-breaking book called *What Do Unions Do?* Richard Freeman and James Medoff of Harvard University suggest that one of the key functions a union serves is to give voice to workers who are otherwise almost powerless in an economy dominated by large employers. Far from being institutions of conflict, unions are often institutions of conciliation that give workers an alternative to going on strike or quitting their jobs. Anyone familiar with a healthy union knows that its leaders carry the members' complaints to management and carry management's concerns back to the workers. Management learns when the workers are restless; workers learn when management needs changes. Sometime after the election of Jim Guyette in late 1983, Hormel's managers stopped believing the officers elected to represent their employees, and the union leaders stopped believing the message they were getting from management. It was clear to Dick Knowlton and his executives that Hormel was going to have to compete harder. But for years they had relied on union leaders to communicate new messages to the rank and file, and they didn't realize that this time the message was not going over. Dick Schaefer tried to send messages back to management—warning Bob Gill to postpone the announcement of wage cuts until after P-9 had conducted executive board elections in 1983. But the executives at Hormel, confident that the new plant provided workers with a better place to work, gave little credence to the bitterness. The function of voice had broken down. One federal mediator has commented that the worst labor disputes seem to erupt between unions and employers with the best histories of harmony: They aren't used to adversity, and they don't know how to fight well. Geri Joseph, the former journalist and U.S. ambassador who served on the Hormel board, said the Hormel executives were stunned to learn that their employees hated them and even then seemed powerless to communicate with their own employees. Later, because the executives misread the depth of the bitterness, the company failed to tell its side of the story until the well was poisoned.

Once P-9 had started the corporate campaign, Hormel wasted no time taking advantage of the union's blunders. But in so doing, it only nurtured the bitterness growing since 1978. Much has been made of Hormel's legal help, Thomas Krukowski of Milwaukee. Hormel can't be faulted for seeking what it perceived to be a sharp, hardworking lawyer. Hormel executives insisted that Krukowski simply handled their grievances and unfair-labor-practice hearings and did not influence their bargaining strategy with P-9. But Hormel shouldn't have been surprised at the union's reaction. In a battle where symbols often scored more points than facts, Krukowski became another roadblock, a symbol of the new hard-ball Hormel and a rationale for hiring Ray Rogers.

As the campaign wore on, P-9 pulled back into its bunker, spurning offers of help and turning neutrals into enemies. Austin clergy and civic leaders, their mediation skills untested from years of leaving Hormel and P-9 alone, were spurned as corporate lackeys. Professional neutrals such as Paul Goldberg and Hank Bell, both of whom were former union members, were cast as manipulators who tried to trick P-9 into a settlement. Lewie Anderson became the archvillain and UFCW lawyers the agents of his deception. Certainly the UFCW was out of touch with both the P-9 rank and file and with Guyette. Anderson relied on bad local sources in 1983. Guyette was not a troublemaker who would go away. The members were not naifs who would come to their senses. By 1985 the UFCW's choices were unpleasant: Step in quickly to take over P-9—and risk a beating from the courts and the press—or wait for Hormel to crush the local.

P-9's false sense of victory was enhanced by the heady experience of constant attention from the news media. Asked for signs that the campaign was succeeding, Rogers typically rattled off a list of major newspapers and magazines that had published stories about P-9. Letters seeking support from other unions included a long list of newspapers that had published stories about P-9's fight. On the picket line in January Jim Retterath warned strikers, "If you swear, you won't get on national television." And it worked. In Austin strikers built a monument to ABC newsmen who died in a helicopter crash en route to cover the strike. Clearly, such coverage helped legitimize their cause. The memorial fails to mention that another pilot refused to fly the men in the foggy night and that a federal investigation found that they should not have been flying. Like so many other instances, the memorial suggests how P-9 displayed tunnel vision, taking a stand and presenting a compelling interpretation but overlooking facts that suggested a different reality.

For all these reasons, we would not argue that P-9 was a microcosm of labor in the 1980's. As Harvard economist Richard

Freeman pointed out, P-9 was the exception, not the rule, in labor relations during the 1980's. The nation's collective bargaining system responded with flexibility, not rigidity, to economic recession. Wages fell or were frozen in automaking, steel, mining, electrical machinery, rubber, trucking, airlines, textiles, chemicals, meat-packing, printing—virtually all the nation's major industries. Unions gave up old work rules and jurisdictional restraints. They paid a bigger share of their insurance premiums and started funding their own pensions. They bought stock in the companies that employed their members.

P-9's supporters liked to portray the Hormel strike as a pivotal battle for the nation's labor movement. "If not here, where? If not now, when?" became its final rallying cry. We disagree. The war over wage concessions will be decided by much bigger forces having to do with international competition, federal economic policy, and labor market conditions. The showdown at Hormel, for all its poetry, did not symbolize labor relations during the 1980's. It had too many peculiarities, from the hometown history of Hormel to the homegrown mystery of Guyette.

Why, then, did so many eyes turn to Austin? It was not a violent strike; not one shot was fired on the picket line, not one person was seriously hurt. Even the event that triggered national media attention—deployment of the National Guard—was prompted in part by a police report of a truck hit by gunshot that turned out to be false. It was not a big strike: fifteen hundred workers at one plant in an obscure industry far from the nation's population centers. It was not even a symbol; it was an aberration.

Yet perhaps that was its appeal. Here was a group of renegades who scorned the course of their colleagues, a union too proud to accept the indignity of industrial malaise. The men and women of P-9 were at once exotic and familiar. They slaughtered animals for a living; they swung razor-sharp knives; they worked in blood and danger; they lived a 1980's version of *The Jungle;* they did *real* work. Yet they were backyard neighbors out of a Norman Rockwell painting—friendly, polite, bright people who gave the impression that if they were mad about something, it must be right to be mad about it. Life had made them a promise, and all they asked was that the promise be kept.

In short, P-9 gave voice to a national anxiety: the demise of American superiority, powerlessness in the face of frightening powers, the end of life as *Leave It to Beaver.*

Lester Thurow, the MIT economist, has a phrase for America's dominance of the world economy after World War II: "effortless superiority." The biggest cars, the nicest homes, the best-fed children—all on forty hours a week and three or four weeks' vacation. Along with effortless superiority for the nation's economy went effortless generosity by the nation's employers. Of course, it wasn't effortless and it wasn't generosity any more than the labor of the nation's managers and workers was effortless in the years described by Thurow. But it did provide a long period of unparalleled prosperity and nearly unparalleled dominance, which allowed American corporations to grant ever-increasing wage and benefit packages to the nation's workers without seriously threatening their responsibility to shareholders. Jay Hormel might have been unusual, but postwar America was a place where you could be a paternalistic employer *and* a tough competitor because the United States dominated the world and enjoyed a period of steadily rising incomes.

Suddenly in the 1980's the generosity was gone—or if it remained, it certainly wasn't effortless. Recession crushed the social compact that had permitted both genteel collaboration and wasteful confrontation in American labor relations. Nowhere did the standard of living tumble so dramatically as in the small, gritty packinghouse towns of the Midwest—Waterloo, Iowa; Dakota City, Nebraska; Sioux Falls, South Dakota. With the nation facing a labor surplus and the labor movement in disarray, wages tumbled toward a floor defined only by the most desperate unemployed farmer or urban laborer. The cool arithmetic of the labor market seemed to sanction this assault on standards of living: If trade unions could no longer take labor out of competition, then wages would be set by supply and demand. But it confounded the moral logic of working-class Americans. "If my labor was worth ten dollars an hour yesterday," they asked, "why is it worth only eight dollars today? If society decided yesterday that I may own a house, a car, perhaps a fishing boat and a VCR, why is society repossessing them today?"

These were the questions asked by Jim Guyette, Kathy Buck,

Pete Winkels, and the people they led. There were answers, but they sounded so suspicious and implausible and cold that they had to be learned on the picket line and the unemployment line.

Some months after the strike ended, Winkels and Buck found themselves together in a humanities class at the Austin Community College. They were reading *Madame Bovary,* Gustave Flaubert's novel about a young woman with romantic ideas in nineteenth-century France. Their teacher told them the novel was a seminal feminist work, but Kathy found a deeper message. She thought Emma Bovary was a universal character, one who represented everyone's desire to realize his or her dreams in real life. Perhaps Emma carried it too far, Kathy thought, but that happens. She wondered if there wasn't an Emma Bovary walking around Austin, trying to make life live up to noble dreams.

There's a great deal about the Hormel strike that has to do with reality and dreams. It had to do with the American Dream: a small-town company that made good while remaining small-town; a bunch of hardworking people who built a prosperous community; a town that was profiled in *Fortune* and *Life* magazines during the 1950's. It also had to do with life in the 1980's: high unemployment, bankruptcies, fierce competition. Reality intruded on the dream, and the result was pain and chaos.

Floyd Lenoch saw it in other towns he visited in the Midwest, but he as much as anyone in Local 9 didn't want it to happen in Austin. The veteran union leader chafed at what he saw in Storm Lake, Iowa, where ramshackle trailer courts that housed low-paid nonunion IBP workers replaced the comfortable Victorian, rambler, and ranch-style houses that Hormel workers had long been able to afford in Austin. Unless the assault on workingmen and women was turned around, Lenoch told his friend Father Charles Collins in Austin, he feared the town would go the way of Storm Lake.

During the strike Lenoch and Collins became close friends, frequently getting together for lunch or afternoon coffee at a Mister Donut not far from St. Augustine's Church. Collins, who was assigned to the church in 1981, did not pretend to know the intricacies of meat-packing; but he fancied himself a friend of labor, and he knew a good man when he saw one. Lenoch went to mass every day and was a reliable usher on weekends. If there was a church dinner, Lenoch was in the kitchen doing the cooking. Every April he headed the Daffodil Day cancer fund raiser. In an effort to bring union and company officials closer together, he helped organize a prayer service and social hour, filling up the big church and producing one of the rare occasions when Guyette and Knowlton showed up at the same gathering.

As the strike wore on past its official conclusion, however, Lenoch began to get more emotional. Far from serving Hormel products in his house, he was actively spreading the union's boycott around the country, convinced that the union was winning the battle. The union had to make Hormel back down, he reasoned over coffee one afternoon in mid-January 1987, or a pattern would be set for other industries to follow. The boycott was the answer, and Lenoch reiterated his belief that all his trips around the country were turning up signs that P-9 was winning. Collins decided to challenge his friend.

"But, Floyd, their profits are so big and getting bigger," the priest said of Hormel.

Replied Lenoch: "They should be ashamed to make that much money and be cutting our wages."

The argument had gone full circle. Collins couldn't refute his friend. A justifiable comment, he thought, but it didn't address reality.

One month later, while making a plea with fifty other former strikers for support at the AFL-CIO executive council meeting in Florida, Lenoch was notified along with other former executive board members that Hormel planned to fire them for promoting the boycott. Later that week he returned to Austin and suffered a stroke. He died on Saturday, February 21, at St. Mary's Hospital in Rochester.

When Lenoch's casket was carried into St. Augustine's the following Tuesday morning, the church was once again filled, this time with row after row of blue P-9 jackets. Those in attendance called it one of the biggest funerals ever held in Austin. A heartbroken Collins delivered the homily, looking out over the crowd at what he later surmised was the proud union's last show of strength. They had come to say farewell to their friend, who many believed had been destroyed by the company where he so proudly went to work for thirty-eight years.

After the funeral a long procession of cars drove slowly out to nearby Calvary Cemetery, where a biting wind swirled new snow across the crusted ground. Accompanied by strumming guitars, the men and women in the blue jackets stood around the grave and sang "Solidarity Forever," the same refrain over and over, the last line ringing across the peaceful landscape. The death of a proud union man had become another solidarity rally, another poignant appeal to the emotion of P-9's cause. As Collins looked across the cemetery, he thought that perhaps reality was setting in, that the burial would symbolize the end of P-9's crusade. But the words on the backs of the jackets that circled the grave told him their dream would linger: "No Retreat, No Surrender."

INDEX

395